T0274066

DAILY
HOPE
DEVOTIONAL

RICK WARREN

DAILY HOPE

DEVOTIONAL

365 Days of Purpose, Peace, and Promise

A Tyndale nonfiction imprint

Visit Tyndale online at tyndale.com.

Visit Tyndale Momentum online at tyndalemomentum.com.

Visit Rick Warren at PastorRick.com.

Tyndale, Tyndale's quill logo, *Tyndale Momentum*, and the Tyndale Momentum logo are registered trademarks of Tyndale House Ministries. Tyndale Momentum is a nonfiction imprint of Tyndale House Publishers, Carol Stream, Illinois.

Daily Hope Devotional: 365 Days of Purpose, Peace, and Promise

Daily Hope devotions previously published at PastorRick.com/devotional. First printing by Tyndale House Publishers in 2024.

Cover photograph of abstract painting by Henrik Dønnestad on Unsplash.

Cover designed by Dean H. Renninger

Notes are located on page 381.

Scripture credits are located on page 383.

For information about special discounts for bulk purchases, please contact Tyndale House Publishers at csresponse@tyndale.com, or call 1-855-277-9400.

Library of Congress Cataloging-in-Publication Data

A catalog record for this book is available from the Library of Congress.

ISBN 979-8-4005-0112-8

Printed in the United States of America

30 29 28 27 26 25 24
7 6 5 4 3 2 1

Introduction

Hope Begins Here

Have you noticed how many people walk around with a smile, telling everyone they're "fine"? It can make you start to think that you're the only one who's tired and struggling. You wonder if you'll always feel stressed and worried and burned-out.

Wherever you find yourself today, Jesus has an incredible offer for you: *"If you are tired from carrying heavy burdens, come to me and I will give you rest"* (Matthew 11:28, CEV).

This is the opposite of what most people expect God will say to them. They think that if God wants them to come home to him, then he's going to make some demands along with it.

They think he'll say something like, "Come home to me, and I will give you rules. Come home to me, and I will give you restrictions. Come home to me, and I will give you religion. Come home to me, and I will give you rituals."

But God doesn't say any of those things. He says, *"Come to me, and I will give you* rest."

God is offering you true rest from your heavy burdens.

Do you find yourself in a constant state of fatigue and stress? That's because you're trying to live in your own strength. And God never meant for you to do that. Instead, God wants you to rely on and rest in his power.

Colossians 1:11 promises: *"God will strengthen you with his own great power so that you will not give up when troubles come"* (NCV). And the Bible says, *"He gives power to the tired and worn out, and strength to the weak. . . . They that wait upon the Lord shall renew their strength"* (Isaiah 40:29, TLB).

Notice what you need to do to access God's power. You need to *wait*—that's it. How often do you take time to stop and listen to God so you can be renewed and strengthened? That's what this devotional is designed to help you do. Each day you will connect with God and his Word for a few minutes. You can rest in his promises because God says he will *"keep in perfect peace all those who trust in him, whose thoughts turn often to the Lord!"* (Isaiah 26:3, TLB).

If you've been feeling down, anxious, hopeless, fatigued, or worried, turn to God. He's the source of all hope. He's the one who created you. He has been with you every moment of your life and knows everything about you—and he still loves you. Imagine starting each day anchored in hope. Your future is in his loving hands, and he is worthy of your complete trust.

If you're tired of waiting for things to change, wait on God instead. Come home to him today so you can find true rest and living hope.

Friend, I'm so excited to have you join me every day as we look to God and his Word to find real purpose, lasting peace, and faithful promises. But more than anything else, I pray you use this time to make knowing God your first priority and your daily passion.

Pastor Rick

Rick

JANUARY 1

What's at the Center of Your Life?

"Love the Lord your God with all your heart and with all your soul and with all your mind." This is the first and greatest commandment.

MATTHEW 22:37-38 (NIV)

God wants to be at the very center of your life. He doesn't want to be on the edge of your life, and he doesn't want to be just a segment of your life. The God of the universe—the God who made you and loves you—wants to be the hub of your heart and the axis of your existence.

Here's another way to look at it: God wants to have a love relationship with you.

The Bible says, *"'Love the Lord your God with all your heart and with all your soul and with all your mind.' This is the first and greatest commandment"* (Matthew 22:37-38, NIV).

The truth is, you're going to center your life around something. You may center it around your career, your family, or your hobbies. You may center it around making money or being popular.

But anything besides God at the center of your life is an idol. Exodus 20:3-4 says, *"You must not have any other god but me. You must not make for yourself an idol of any kind or an image of anything in the heavens or on the earth or in the sea"* (NLT).

How do you know when something other than God has taken center stage in your life? It's simple. When God's not at the center of your life, you start to worry and stress out; you get fearful. These are the warning lights that God is no longer the nucleus of your heart.

In contrast, how can you tell when your life is centered on God? You're at peace. You stop worrying. The Bible says, *"A sense of God's wholeness, everything coming together for good, will come and settle you down. It's wonderful what happens when Christ displaces worry at the center of your life"* (Philippians 4:7, MSG).

Ask yourself this: "What's going to be the center of my life for the rest of my life?"

It's the most important thing you will ever have to decide.

JANUARY 2

Embrace What God Is Doing

Do not cling to events of the past or dwell on what happened long ago. Watch for the new thing I am going to do. It is happening already—you can see it now!

ISAIAH 43:18-19 (GNT)

You can't go backward in life. You can only go forward. That means you have only two choices: You can long for the way things used to be and not change a single thing about today, or you can trust in God to do something new.

The Bible says, *"His mercies never come to an end; they are new every morning"* (Lamentations 3:22-23, ESV). God is a God of newness. He doesn't do the same old things all the time. To live the life he's planned for you, you need to cooperate with the new things he wants to do in your family, in your career, in your friendships, in his church, and in the world around you.

But people aren't always interested in the new things God is doing. Sometimes you'll daydream about the past and say, "I wish I lived during *that* era," or "I wish I could go back to *that* period of my life." But wishing for the past is like looking in the rearview mirror while driving and never looking out the windshield. If you keep that up, you're going to crash!

God says in Isaiah 43:18-19, *"Do not cling to events of the past or dwell on what happened long ago. Watch for the new thing I am going to do. It is happening already—you can see it now!"* (GNT). Before you can embrace the new things God is doing in your life and in the world, you have to be looking for them. If you're always looking backward, then you can't *"watch for the new thing"* God is doing.

Embrace means more than just agreeing with something or grudgingly accepting it. *Embrace* means to be content with it—or even love it! You don't embrace things you don't love. God wants you to welcome the new things he's doing.

How do you show God that you're focused on the new things he's bringing about? Instead of praying, "God, bless what I'm doing," you say, "God, help me to do what you're blessing." When that's your prayer, you'll be able to embrace the incredible things he is going to do next.

JANUARY 3

Focus on What Will Last Forever

Things that are seen don't last forever, but things that are not seen are eternal. That's why we keep our minds on the things that cannot be seen.

2 CORINTHIANS 4:18 (CEV)

Human beings can handle an enormous amount of frustration, delay, and pain as long as they have hope.

But when hope is gone, people give up.

Jesus offers the only hope that is eternal. And it is a hope that will never disappoint. But you need the right perspective to understand the hope found in Jesus.

That means you don't just look at what's going on right now. Instead of focusing on the temporary, focus on the eternal. For instance, pay more attention to God's Word than the news on your device.

Difficulties don't last. But hope in God lasts forever. The Bible says, *"These three things continue forever: faith, hope, and love. And the greatest of these is love"* (1 Corinthians 13:13, NCV).

There is a plaque engraved with Hebrew letters that hangs on the wall in my office. People ask me all the time what the letters mean. It simply says, "This too shall pass."

I like to look at the plaque when I'm going through a difficult time. It reminds me that no matter what my circumstances are, they are temporary. No problem comes to stay in your life. It will pass. Even if it is a lifelong chronic problem, you won't take it into eternity.

Paul reminds us of this in 2 Corinthians 4:18: *"Things that are seen don't last forever, but things that are not seen are eternal. That's why we keep our minds on the things that cannot be seen"* (CEV).

Your problems won't last forever. Uncertainty won't last forever.

But there are things in God's universe you can't see that *will* last forever. Faith, hope, and love will last forever. And if you trust in Jesus, you will be with God forever in eternity.

Put your hope in Jesus. *"Don't shuffle along, eyes to the ground, absorbed with the things right in front of you. Look up, and be alert to what is going on around Christ—that's where the action is. See things from his perspective"* (Colossians 3:2, MSG).

Your hope in Christ will become a hope fulfilled.

You're Already Chosen, Loved, and Accepted

Even before he made the world, God loved us and chose us in Christ to be holy and without fault in his eyes. God decided in advance to adopt us into his own family by bringing us to himself through Jesus Christ. This is what he wanted to do, and it gave him great pleasure.

EPHESIANS 1:4-5 (NLT)

Every person wants these three things more than anything else: to be loved, to be accepted, and to be chosen. Those longings are there, even if people aren't willing to admit them.

But there's good news: You don't have to look anymore for love and acceptance. You don't have to wonder if you matter. You're already chosen, loved, and accepted by Jesus Christ. You matter most to the Creator of the universe!

Everyone wants to be chosen—from your childhood days at recess to your adult workplaces and love life. Being chosen is key to establishing your self-worth.

The Bible says in Ephesians 1:4-5, *"Even before he made the world, God loved us and chose us in Christ to be holy and without fault in his eyes. God decided in advance to adopt us into his own family by bringing us to himself through Jesus Christ. This is what he wanted to do, and it gave him great pleasure"* (NLT). God created the entire universe because he wanted a family. The whole reason the universe exists is because God wanted children to love.

According to Ephesians 1, when did God choose you? God chose you before the world was made.

Before God chose to create the universe, he had already chosen you. Before God chose any tree, he chose you. Before God chose the oceans, he chose you. Before God chose every rock that exists, he chose you.

That's an amazing thought—even before he chose to create the sun and moon and stars, God knew you and chose to love you. That is the foundation of your identity.

Nobody wants to be chosen last. But you have never been last in God's thoughts. You have always been first on his mind. He chose you, he loves you, and he accepts you.

Knowing and believing these truths changes everything. When you are secure in your identity as God's child, you can rest in his love and acceptance.

JANUARY 5

Unchanging Truth for Changing Times

Give yourselves completely to God—every part of you—for you are back from death and you want to be tools in the hands of God, to be used for his good purposes.

ROMANS 6:13 (TLB)

A truly successful life is not measured by pleasure, popularity, possessions, power, or position. It's measured by your purpose. If you want to measure how successful your life has been, then you have to ask only one question: Did you fulfill the five purposes that God created you for?

Of course, you can't answer that question if you don't know what those purposes are. They are the same for everyone: First, God wants you to know him and love him. That's called worship. Second, he wants you to belong to his family. That's called fellowship. Third, God wants you to grow spiritually to be like Jesus. That's called discipleship. Fourth, he wants you to serve him by serving others. You may think you can't serve God because he's not here in person, but you can serve him by serving others. That's called ministry. Finally, God wants you to tell others the Good News of salvation through Jesus Christ. That's called evangelism.

God wants you to know him, to grow in him, to belong to him, to serve him, and to share him with others. If you miss these five purposes, then you don't have a clear, firm purpose in your life, and you'll miss the entire reason God created you. You'll just exist! You'll drift through life.

But God wants more for you. He created you for his five eternal purposes, and those purposes are never going to change. They give you an anchor in hard times, when everything else around you is changing.

Romans 6:13 says, *"Give yourselves completely to God—every part of you—for you are back from death and you want to be tools in the hands of God, to be used for his good purposes"* (TLB). No matter what you're going through right now, you need to reaffirm your commitment to God's five purposes for your life. When everything's changing, when you're confused, when you're in doubt, when you need direction—you always return to the basics. You get back to the truth.

God loves you. He created you for a purpose. And he will give you everything you need to fulfill your purpose as you follow him—even when it gets hard.

JANUARY 6

You're Still on God's Plan A

We know that God causes everything to work together for the good of those who love God and are called according to his purpose for them.
ROMANS 8:28 (NLT)

God does not have a plan B for your life.

No matter what has happened in your life, you're still on God's plan A. His original dream for your life is unchanged. It doesn't matter what other people have done to you or what poor decisions you've made. You can still fulfill God's dream for your life.

Even your mistakes are part of God's plan. This truth will set you free if you claim it. It will set you free from thinking, "I'm not worthy to dream, because I've messed up too much. And I certainly don't deserve to have a big dream." You don't have to believe those lies anymore. You serve a bigger God than that!

One of the most famous verses in the Bible says, *"We know that God causes everything to work together for the good of those who love God and are called according to his purpose for them"* (Romans 8:28, NLT).

Everything is in God's hands—the good, the bad, the evil, the poor decisions, the sins. He didn't cause all of it, but he is still in control of it all, so he can make it all work together for good.

The Bible doesn't say that everything *is* good—because it's not. There is a lot of sin and evil in the world. But God causes it all to work together *for* good, for those who love him and are called according to his purpose and his dream for their lives.

When you think God can't put back together the pieces of your life, remember that God can do anything. He is still working out his plan for your life. And if you haven't claimed it yet, he is still waiting to give you the dream he's prepared for you.

When you surrender your life to him, God will work to make all the pieces fit together so that your whole life serves his purposes on earth.

JANUARY 7

How to Focus on What's Important, Not Urgent

Make the most of every opportunity in these evil days.
EPHESIANS 5:16 (NLT)

It may feel like the 365 days you're given each year aren't enough time to do everything you want to do. In fact, you probably feel like there aren't enough minutes in *this* day to accomplish what you think you need to do!

But here's the good news: God doesn't expect you to do everything. He has given you just enough time to do everything he wants you to do—everything he planned and purposed for you to do.

That's why it's important for you to set goals. Goals help you focus your life. Paul modeled this when he said, *"I do not run without a goal. I fight like a boxer who is hitting something—not just the air"* (1 Corinthians 9:26, NCV).

Paul knew his purpose, and all his plans and goals were focused on it. You need to have that same kind of focus.

Too many of us focus our lives on unimportant causes. Trivial Pursuit isn't just a game; it's a description of our culture. Most of what's going on in our world today won't matter in a week—much less for eternity.

Many people can't tell the difference between "urgent" and "important." What seems urgent is almost never what is important. We put aside our time with family, our time with God, and our time with friends for the urgent matters that rarely matter for long.

Goals are how you focus and create the kind of life that chases the important rather than what feels urgent. Goals focus your energy and help bring health and balance to your life.

For example, if you make it your goal to get healthy in some specific way this year, then that decision will focus your energy on that task. Anytime you're tempted to eat junk food or skip a workout for extra sleep, your goal will help you stay on track. It will remind you of what's important.

The Bible says, *"Make the most of every opportunity in these evil days"* (Ephesians 5:16, NLT).

Make the most of your life by setting some goals. Don't waste another year on the urgent rather than the important.

JANUARY 8

A Little Faith Is All You Need

If you have faith as small as a mustard seed, you can say to this mountain, "Move from here to there," and it will move. Nothing will be impossible for you.

MATTHEW 17:20 (NIV)

Here's a surprising truth: You can have faith and doubt at the same time.

You can have faith in God and, at the same time, be nervous—or even terrified—about something he wants you to do. Courage is not the absence of fear. Courage is when you go ahead and do something—something you believe God has called you to do—in spite of your fear.

In Mark 9, a man brought his sick son to Jesus. Jesus told the father that he could heal the boy—if the father would believe. The man replied, *"I do believe; help me overcome my unbelief!"* (Mark 9:24, NIV). This man was filled with faith *and* doubt. He went to Jesus with his honest doubts, and Jesus did a miracle.

You don't need a lot of faith to be a great Christian—because it's not the size of your faith that makes the difference. What matters is where you put your faith. You just need a little faith in a big God.

Someone once asked me, "I want to be baptized and join the church, but don't you think I should have all my questions and doubts resolved first?" Of course not. I've been a Christian for more than fifty years, and there are still a lot of things I have questions about. You don't have to figure everything out in advance. You begin with the faith that you have.

Matthew 17:20 says, *"If you have faith as small as a mustard seed, you can say to this mountain, 'Move from here to there,' and it will move. Nothing will be impossible for you"* (NIV).

No matter how weak you think your faith is, it's enough to get you through. Why? Because God is able to accomplish far more in your life than you could ever imagine. It's not up to you anyway! God wants you to have faith. But he also wants you to trust him.

Every little step you take toward Christ moves you further away from doubt and discouragement. Take a step forward in faith today.

JANUARY 9

Choose Grace, Not Bitterness

See to it that no one falls short of the grace of God and that no bitter root grows up to cause trouble and defile many.

HEBREWS 12:15 (NIV)

If you're still holding on to resentment, then someone is controlling you.

Have you ever said, "You make me so mad"? That's an admission that the other person is controlling you. The only way to get this person out of your mind and heart is to heal the hurt with God's grace.

Hebrews 12:15 says, *"See to it that no one falls short of the grace of God and that no bitter root grows up to cause trouble and defile many"* (NIV).

Have you ever known a family where a bitter parent poisoned the whole family? Bitterness is contagious, and it can actually become generational. Someone needs to break the chain—and if bitterness has taken root in your family, that someone can be you.

Are your parents bitter because their parents were bitter because their parents were bitter? It's time to break the chain. And there's only one way to break it: with grace.

If you don't embrace God's grace, life will make you bitter. Why? Because there is sin in the world. We live on a broken planet. This is not heaven. Evil people get away with evil things all the time. Life is not fair.

Is forgiveness fair? Absolutely not. But forgiveness is not about fairness or about getting even. It's about grace.

You don't forgive a person because it's the fair thing to do. You forgive a person because it's the right thing to do. You don't want to hold on to the hurt and the hate.

Forgiveness is free, but it is not cheap. It cost Jesus his life. It cost God his Son.

As Jesus was dying on the cross, with his arms outstretched, he said, *"Father, forgive them, for they do not know what they are doing"* (Luke 23:34, NIV). It's like he was saying, "I love you, I love you, I love you." In effect, he said, "They don't deserve it. They don't even know what they're doing. But, Father, forgive them anyway."

Follow Jesus' example and offer forgiveness today. Heal your bitterness with his grace.

JANUARY 10

How to Be Stable in Ever-Changing Winds

Do not waver, for a person with divided loyalty is as unsettled as a wave of the sea that is blown and tossed by the wind.

JAMES 1:6 (NLT)

Have you ever made a tough choice but then started doubting yourself the moment you made the decision? You kept asking yourself if you did the right thing. Maybe you even agonized over it.

The Bible says when you do this, you're like a wave pushed around in a storm: *"But when you ask him, be sure that your faith is in God alone. Do not waver, for a person with divided loyalty is as unsettled as a wave of the sea that is blown and tossed by the wind. Such people should not expect to receive anything from the Lord. Their loyalty is divided between God and the world, and they are unstable in everything they do"* (James 1:6-8, NLT).

When you depend on your own wisdom, you get tossed around by your doubts. Instead, God wants you to ask him for guidance before you make a decision—and then trust him and his goodness once the decision is made.

Trusting God sets you free from second-guessing yourself. You won't be blown around, even if the winds keep changing and the future looks uncertain.

When you don't trust God in your decisions, James says your loyalty will be divided between God and the world. In some translations of James 1:8, this divided loyalty is rendered as "double-minded." This comes from a Greek word that means "two-souled." It means you're pulled in opposite directions, indecisive, and wavering back and forth.

James says you shouldn't expect God to give you his wisdom if you're constantly second-guessing yourself. That's because double-mindedness creates an unstable spiritual life. It affects your prayers and keeps you from receiving God's insight.

But here's the good news: God wants to give you wisdom! When you trust God in uncertain times—in all times—he will give you everything you need to make wise decisions.

JANUARY 11

It Pays to Be Patient

We count as blessed those who have persevered.

JAMES 5:11 (NIV)

God rewards patience. James 5:11 says, *"We count as blessed those who have persevered"* (NIV). In other words, it pays to be patient.

When you are patient, it builds your character, you avoid making mistakes, and you're more likely to reach your goals. When you're patient, you're going to be honored by others and have happier relationships. There are all kinds of blessings and benefits to patience.

The Bible promises, *"Let us not get tired of doing what is right, for after a while we will reap a harvest of blessing if we don't get discouraged and give up"* (Galatians 6:9, TLB).

There are blessings to be had when you're patient through seasons of difficulty, fatigue, and waiting—in your character, your circumstances, your family, and God's church. And they're not just rewards to enjoy right now. The Bible says there are going to be rewards in heaven too.

Jesus said in Matthew 5:11-12, *"Blessed are you when people insult you, persecute you and falsely say all kinds of evil against you because of me. Rejoice and be glad, because great is your reward in heaven"* (NIV). When someone hurts you, one of your strongest desires is to retaliate.

Whenever you're tempted to strike back, think first: Is this fight worth giving up your eternal reward? It's not. Choose patience instead.

As a leader, I get criticized a lot. People misjudge and question and doubt and second-guess me all the time. I've learned to not defend myself. I remain quiet because I've discovered that you're most like Jesus when you don't retaliate. You're most like Jesus when you refuse to fight back.

Even when he was accused and mistreated, Jesus chose to do what was right and not retaliate in the middle of a crisis. He chose to be patient. When you choose to be patient and let God handle things when someone hurts you, he sees it. And he will bless you.

Do You Have a Room in God's House?

After I go and prepare a place for you, I will come back and take you to myself, so that you will be where I am.

JOHN 14:3 (GNT)

The night before he went to the cross, Jesus was thinking about *you.*

He said, *"There are many rooms in my Father's house, and I am going to prepare a place for you. I would not tell you this if it were not so. And after I go and prepare a place for you, I will come back and take you to myself, so that you will be where I am"* (John 14:2-3, GNT).

The God who created the universe with a few words has been taking two thousand years to prepare an eternal home for you. It's going to be more than anything you could ever imagine!

In fact, the Bible says, *"No eye has seen, no ear has heard, and no mind has imagined the things that God has prepared for those who love him"* (1 Corinthians 2:9, GW).

We can't comprehend how wonderful heaven will be. It's a place of perfection, where we will joyfully be in God's presence. I want you to be there. Jesus wants you to be there. He gave his life so you could be there.

But going to heaven is not automatic. To get into God's family home, you need to become a part of God's family through faith in Jesus Christ.

You do that by admitting to God that you're a sinner and asking for his forgiveness. You tell him that you believe that Jesus Christ is his Son, that Jesus died for your sin, and that God raised him to life. You decide you're going to trust in Jesus for your salvation. You commit to following Jesus as Lord of your life, and you ask him to guide and direct you as you try to do his will and be obedient to him.

When you say and do those things, you show God that you want to be part of his family. And that means we will spend eternity together in God's home in heaven!

JANUARY 13

Know the Right Time to Take the Next Step

There is a right time and a right way to do everything, but we know so little!
ECCLESIASTES 8:6 (GNT)

In many aspects of life—from your business decisions to your closest relationships—timing can make all the difference. And, as a follower of Christ, it's critical for you to stay tuned in to God's timing.

Every great accomplishment involves timing. A successful catch in American football requires incredible timing between the quarterback and receiver. In business, good timing in the market—particularly decisions about hiring and expanding—can mean everything. If you sing, you know how important it is to keep time with the other musicians.

Many years ago, I wrote a book called *The Purpose Driven Church*. In the introduction, I compare leadership to surfing. No surfer says, "Let's go make some waves today." Surfers can't create waves in the ocean. Only God can do that. Surfers wait for the waves that God creates.

That means surfers spend a lot of time waiting. Sometimes they might see a wave and let it go, knowing it's not the right time. Then the surfer sees just the right wave, starts paddling faster and faster, catches the wave, rides the wave, and gets off the wave without wiping out.

Surfing looks easy, but it requires a lot of skill. The same is true in life. You have to develop the skill of timing. The Bible says in Ecclesiastes 8:6, *"There is a right time and a right way to do everything, but we know so little!"* (GNT).

There's a rhythm to life. Learning to do the right thing at the right time takes skill. Christians often call that skill "walking in the Spirit." The more you grow as a follower of Christ, the better you get at walking in step with the Holy Spirit.

If you want to know the right time and the right way to do something, then you need to ask for help from the Holy Spirit. Then you keep your eyes open for how he is moving.

You can live life trying to make your own waves. Or you can learn to see and catch the waves God is making all around you.

Let Go and Surrender to God

The battle is not yours, but God's.

2 CHRONICLES 20:15 (NLT)

Imagine you're sitting on a plane that's about to take off. As the plane goes down the runway, you start flapping your arms. As the speed picks up and the nose lifts in the air, you flap your arms faster and faster. Once in the air, the flight attendant approaches you and says, "What are you doing?"

And you say, "Oh, I was helping us get off the ground."

That's ridiculous, right? But that's basically what you do when you try to do things only God is equipped to do. Just like you don't need to hold up a plane, you don't need to hold up God.

Do you want to know why you're tired all the time? Why you're frustrated? Why you're worn out by life? One reason is you're trying to fight battles that belong to God—and you are not God.

"The battle is not yours, but God's" (2 Chronicles 20:15, NLT).

Most people lean toward independence. They see a problem and think, "I've got to figure this out. It's up to me!" But trying to take on God's role is exhausting because we were never meant to carry it in the first place.

Maybe you've been running in circles trying to solve problems in your marriage, your body, the economy, your school, the world. You're trying to solve them on your own power. You're trying to fight the battle alone, and you're tired.

When that happens to you and you finally give up and come back to God, you may think you've let him down.

But you haven't let God down because you were never holding him up. You don't have God in your hands; he's got *you* in *his* hands. You may think you've got God in your hands, but it's not God. It's an idol. If you're trusting in something you think you can control, then that thing is not God.

God is not disappointed in you because he's not expecting you to do what only he can do. You don't hold God up—he holds you up.

Let go and surrender to God. That's when he'll do his most powerful work in you.

JANUARY 15

How to Trust God in the Delays

See how farmers wait for their precious crops to grow. They wait patiently for fall and spring rains. You, too, must be patient. Don't give up hope. The Lord will soon be here.

JAMES 5:7-8 (GW)

Whatever problems you're facing, God is working behind the scenes. You just need to trust him and be patient.

But how do you build a faith that trusts God during the delays?

The Bible says, *"See how farmers wait for their precious crops to grow. They wait patiently for fall and spring rains. You, too, must be patient. Don't give up hope. The Lord will soon be here"* (James 5:7-8, GW).

Like a farmer, you need to wait expectantly. Farmers don't sit around thinking, "I wonder if this is going to grow." They *expect* their crops to grow. While they wait, they prepare for the harvest so that when it comes, they can reap the benefits.

You, too, can expect God to act and provide. Psalm 130:5 says, *"I wait expectantly, trusting God to help, for he has promised"* (TLB). And Isaiah 49:23 promises, *"No one who waits for my help will be disappointed"* (GNT).

What have you been waiting for God to do? Maybe you're waiting for him to transform your marriage, solve a financial problem, heal a hurt, or reach someone who is not a believer. Are you expecting with faithful certainty that God will answer your prayers, believing he will do what you've been waiting for? If you're not preparing yourself while you wait, then you're not really expecting anything to happen.

Quite often, when we think we're waiting on God, God is actually waiting on us. God may be waiting on you to mature spiritually so you'll be ready to handle the blessing he wants to give you.

To help you wait patiently on God, remember his goodness and grace. He is working in your life, even when you can't see what he's doing and even if you think his timing is too slow.

Slow down, be still, spend time in God's Word, and learn how to be more like Jesus. Then get busy doing the work that will prepare you for the harvest.

JANUARY 16

Just a Nibble of Sin Will Get You Hooked

Temptation comes from our own desires,
which entice us and drag us away.
JAMES 1:14 (NLT)

For my dad, a day without fishing was a wasted day. No matter what was going on, he managed to go fishing for at least thirty minutes every day. As I watched my dad catch fish after fish (while I caught nothing), I quickly learned a valuable lesson—fish don't bite bare hooks.

You can't just throw a line with a hook out in the water and expect to catch fish. You have to put bait on the hook! And a good fisherman knows that different fish like different kinds of bait.

Just like a fisherman knows how to bait different kinds of fish, Satan knows just how to bait you. He knows what gets your attention. He knows exactly where your weak spot is—that unmet emotional need or deep desire.

That's why you've got to think about what you're thinking about. The hook is sin, but the bait is whatever lie Satan knows you're vulnerable to: "If you do *this*, you'll feel better. If you do *this*, it will be rewarding. If you do *this*, everything will be okay."

Even when you know there's a hook beneath the bait, you may still keep nibbling. Why? Because you think you can keep biting without getting hooked. But the idea that you won't get hurt is another one of Satan's deceptions.

One of the most common lies is that, whenever you're tempted, something outside yourself has tempted you. But the real problem is not external. James 1:14 says, *"Temptation comes from our own desires, which entice us and drag us away"* (NLT).

Temptation starts with our inner desires—those vulnerable spots Satan uses for bait. Those desires lead to sinful actions, and those actions lead to death. What you *think* determines how you *feel*, and what you *feel* determines how you *act*.

Don't get in the habit of blaming your circumstances. When you're tempted, you may think you can't help it. You *can* help it! It starts by changing the way you think.

When you're tempted, stop and ask the question, "What lie am I believing?" Then replace it with God's truth. It will always lead to life.

JANUARY 17

Wherever You Go, God Is There

If I flew away beyond the east or lived in the farthest place in the west, you would be there to lead me, you would be there to help me.

PSALM 139:9-10 (GNT)

You are never ever alone because God is in every dimension at the same time.

God is in the past, he's in the present, and he's in the future. He's in heaven, and he's on earth. He's in the spirit world. He's in our world. He's in you, he's above you, he's around you—because he is multidimensional.

There are not a bunch of gods to cover every dimension. There is one God in the persons of Father, Son, and Holy Spirit. Because he is multidimensional, you are never alone.

"Where could I go to escape from you? Where could I get away from your presence? If I went up to heaven, you would be there; if I lay down in the world of the dead, you would be there. If I flew away beyond the east or lived in the farthest place in the west, you would be there to lead me, you would be there to help me" (Psalm 139:7-10, GNT).

It's no use trying to play hide-and-seek with God. He doesn't have to seek you out, because every place you try to hide, he's already there. This is God's omnipresence. He's everywhere! He's in all things. He is the beginning and the end. There is no place you've been, no place you are, and no place you're going to that God was not, is not, or will not be.

That should encourage you. No matter where you go, God will go with you, and he will already be there to meet you.

Because God is in every dimension of the world—and even the dimensions we don't know about—there is nothing we could bring to him from our past, present, or future that he is not already in complete control of. There is nothing that surprises him, nothing that could keep him from wanting to be close to you, and nothing that changes his love for you.

You cannot get away from God. He wants his presence to bring you comfort, peace, and joy. No matter where you are, God is near.

JANUARY 18

How Do You Respond to Grace?

God says he will accept and acquit us—declare us "not guilty"—if we trust Jesus Christ to take away our sins. And we all can be saved in this same way, by coming to Christ, no matter who we are or what we have been like.

ROMANS 3:22 (TLB)

Salvation is a free gift. You can have all your sins forgiven and get a free ticket to heaven. But, while salvation is free to you, it is also costly—because somebody had to pay for it. When Jesus went to the cross, he paid the price for your sins to be forgiven.

If there were any other way for you to go to heaven, don't you think God would have used it? If there were any other way for a holy God to let an imperfect person into a perfect place, don't you think God would have done it rather than sacrifice his own Son? Of course he would have.

Some people claim you can go to heaven by being a good person or by believing God exists. But if that's true, then why did Jesus have to die? He wouldn't have submitted himself to that kind of agony if it wasn't necessary.

The fact is, everyone is full of sin. There is no truly good person. The Bible says that every single one of us falls short of God's holiness. That's why you need a Savior!

The Bible says, *"God says he will accept and acquit us—declare us 'not guilty'—if we trust Jesus Christ to take away our sins. And we all can be saved in this same way, by coming to Christ, no matter who we are or what we have been like"* (Romans 3:22, TLB). You can come to Christ no matter who you are or what you've done. Isn't that the kindest thing that's ever been offered to you?

Coming to Christ starts by saying a simple prayer like this: "God, I confess that I have sinned and gone my own way. I believe that Jesus died on the cross and rose from the grave so I wouldn't have to pay for my sin and so I could live forever with you. Please forgive me for the ways that I've messed up and accept me into your family. I want to turn every part of my life over to you. Help me to follow and serve you faithfully. In Jesus' name, amen."

Turn from your sin today, and trust that Jesus has already paid for it by being your substitute on the cross. It is finished! That's how much Jesus loves you.

JANUARY 19

Plan for Tomorrow, but Live for Today

Don't worry about tomorrow, for tomorrow will bring its own worries. Today's trouble is enough for today.

MATTHEW 6:34 (NLT)

The good thing about the future is that it doesn't hit you all at once. If you had your entire life thrown at you at one time, you would be overwhelmed. So God gives it to you in bite-size, twenty-four-hour segments.

Since God gives you only one day at a time, that's how he expects you to approach your life. You only have to live it one day at a time.

Jesus taught, *"Don't worry about tomorrow, for tomorrow will bring its own worries. Today's trouble is enough for today"* (Matthew 6:34, NLT).

In other words, stop borrowing trouble. If there's something happening next week, don't mess up today by worrying about it.

Worry can't change the past. It can't control the future. Worry only makes you miserable today!

God gives you all the grace you need—but just enough for today, every day. He doesn't stockpile power for your next week or month. Jesus says to pray, *"Give us this day our daily bread"* (Matthew 6:11, ESV). He wants you to take life one day at a time.

When everything is uncertain and you don't know how to make wise decisions for the future, then just take care of today. God doesn't want you to worry about tomorrow. You can plan, pray, and trust God for the future. But put your energy into making today count.

One practical way to do that in today's world is to reduce your media intake. Focus instead on the things God loves and cares about, like your spiritual growth and caring for people in need. That's how you make the day count.

The Bible instructs, *"Don't brashly announce what you're going to do tomorrow; you don't know the first thing about tomorrow"* (Proverbs 27:1, MSG). When everything else in life seems unclear, this is about as clear as you can get!

Plan for tomorrow, but live for today. God will give you everything you need to be obedient in both.

JANUARY 20

How to Take an Inventory of Your Life

You have everything when you have Christ, and you are filled with God through your union with Christ. He is the highest Ruler, with authority over every other power.

COLOSSIANS 2:10 (TLB)

If you're ready to make a fresh start, then you need to take a personal inventory. That means you take stock of and evaluate what you've got to work with. When you do a personal inventory, ask yourself these three questions:

1. **What are my assets?** Look at your physical, educational, and financial assets—and remember your spiritual assets as a child of God. What has God given you to work with?

   Colossians 2:10 says, *"You have everything when you have Christ, and you are filled with God through your union with Christ. He is the highest Ruler, with authority over every other power"* (TLB).

2. **What have I learned?** Take time to write down lessons you've learned about life, yourself, God—whatever comes to mind. Galatians 3:4 says, *"Did all your experience mean nothing at all?"* (GNT). You won't waste your experiences if you learn from them.

   Especially pay attention to your painful experiences, because God never wastes a hurt. Don't have a pity party. Stop regretting and rehearsing your mistakes, and start learning from them.

   You can also review everything you've learned from good Bible teaching. The Bible says in 2 Timothy 3:14, *"You must remain faithful to the things you have been taught. You know they are true, for you know you can trust those who taught you"* (NLT).

3. **Who can help me with my fresh start?** Proverbs 15:22 says, *"Get all the advice you can, and you will succeed; without it you will fail"* (GNT).

   Pride often keeps people from reaching their dreams and goals. Instead of asking for advice, people insist on figuring things out themselves.

> The Bible says pride leads to destruction. It also says that God gives grace to the humble because they are teachable. You'll never have a fresh start if you act like you've already arrived. You need other people to speak truth, point out your blind spots, encourage you, and help you remember God's promises.

When you take a thorough, honest inventory of your life, you'll see how God has prepared you to make a fresh start.

As you ask yourself these questions, pray for God to lead your thoughts and reveal his wisdom to you. Say to him, "God, please show me how you've already provided for me—all the tools and experiences and people you've given me to make the most of my life. I want even my painful experiences to shape me into the person you want me to be. Help me to be humble and honest with myself and with you so that I can keep learning and become more like you. In Jesus' name, amen."

JANUARY 21

When It's Time to Clean House

We must get rid of everything that slows us down, especially sin that distracts us. We must run the race that lies ahead of us and never give up.

HEBREWS 12:1 (GW)

Real change requires cleaning house.

It can be difficult to find the motivation to get your physical house clean, and cleaning your spiritual house may seem like an even bigger task. But this is where you need to use your best energy—because God wants you to spend your life becoming more like him. And becoming more like him sometimes requires you to make difficult changes. The Bible says it like this: *"We must get rid of everything that slows us down, especially sin that distracts us. We must run the race that lies ahead of us and never give up"* (Hebrews 12:1, GW).

To decide what you need to clean in your spiritual house, you just have to figure out what needs to change in your life.

If you want a healthy body, then maybe you need to keep healthier food in your house or commit to regular exercise, even if you start small with fifteen minutes a day.

If you want a healthy mind, then you may need to unsubscribe to some publications or avoid watching certain TV platforms. You may need to delete some apps or put healthier boundaries around your screen time.

If you want a healthy schedule, then you need to decide what's most important to you. You can eliminate less-important activities—sometimes even good ones—and focus on what matters most to you.

If you want a clean heart, then you need to spend time in prayer, asking God what you need to confess and then repent of those things. This can be the most difficult step of spiritual cleaning. Through confession, you're recognizing and rooting out sins that cause unhealthy habits throughout your spiritual house.

The Bible says in Ephesians 4:22, *"Get rid of your old self, which made you live as you used to—the old self that was being destroyed by its deceitful desires"* (GNT). It's time to clean house—but it's not a onetime practice. Just like you have to regularly clean your physical home, you need to make a habit of asking the hard questions to identify what spiritual rooms need a good cleaning. Then, with God's blessing, you get to work.

How Often Should You Forgive?

Peter came to him and asked, "Lord, how often should I forgive someone who sins against me? Seven times?" "No, not seven times," Jesus replied, "but seventy times seven!"

MATTHEW 18:21-22 (NLT)

Forgiveness is rarely a onetime event. So how often do you have to keep releasing your right to get even?

Until you stop feeling the hurt—then you'll know you've forgiven that person.

Matthew 18:21-22 says, *"Peter came to him and asked, 'Lord, how often should I forgive someone who sins against me? Seven times?' 'No, not seven times,' Jesus replied, 'but seventy times seven!'"* (NLT).

Peter thought he was being pretty magnanimous. In Jewish law, you had to forgive a person three times, and after you'd forgiven them three times, that was it. You didn't have to forgive them anymore. So Peter is thinking, "The law says three times. How about if I double it, and add in one for good measure? Seven times? (God's going to be really impressed with this!)"

And Jesus says, "Wrong! You're not even close! How about seventy times seven!" He's saying you have to just keep on doing it. You just keep on forgiving until the pain stops. Every time you remember that hurt, make an intentional choice to say, "God, that person really hurt me, and it still hurts. But because I want to be filled with love and not resentment, I am choosing to give up my right to get even. I am choosing to bless those who hurt me. God, I pray you'll bless their life—not because they deserve it. They don't. I don't deserve your blessing either, God. But I pray that you'll show grace to them like you've shown to me."

It's not easy. In fact, I have no doubt that for some reading this, their marriage is about to self-destruct—not because of the hurt but because of the unforgiveness. It's not the hurt but the refusal to forgive that destroys a marriage.

You may say, "I don't feel like forgiving." Who does? Nobody ever *feels* like forgiving. You do it because it's the right thing to do, and you do it to get on with your life. These steps are not easy, but with God's power, you can do it.

JANUARY 23

You Need Vision Based on Faith, Not Fear

We should go up and take possession of the land, for we can certainly do it.

NUMBERS 13:30 (NIV)

Seeing life with eyes of fear causes you to bury your talents. When you look at the future with fear instead of faith, you end up underestimating the abilities God has given you.

When Moses sent spies to scope out the Promised Land, ten of the twelve came back and said, *"We can't attack those people; they are stronger than we are"* (Numbers 13:31, NIV). Even though God had promised to be with them, they responded in fear rather than faith. Only Joshua and Caleb believed God's promise that they could take possession of the land.

A vision based on fear rather than faith is going to limit you for your entire life. You're going to miss opportunities. You're going to waste the talent that God gave you. And you're going to set yourself up for defeat, because fear creates self-fulfilling prophecies.

The spies with fear-based vision saw themselves as inadequate. They said, *"The land we explored devours those living in it. All the people we saw there are of great size. . . . We seemed like grasshoppers in our own eyes, and we looked the same to them"* (Numbers 13:32-33, NIV).

There really were giants in the Promised Land! They caused some of the Israelites to see themselves as tiny bugs sure to get squashed. That's a defeating self-image. It didn't affect just the spies' confidence; it also caused them to project their fears on others. That's the problem with a fear-based vision: The way you see yourself and life will rub off on the people around you.

If the spies had looked at the Promised Land with faith instead of fear, they would have seen the same thing Joshua and Caleb did: a land flowing with milk and honey. Even when they looked at the giants, Joshua and Caleb saw their potential through God's eyes. They said, *"We should go up and take possession of the land, for we can certainly do it"* (Numbers 13:30, NIV).

Never underestimate what God can do through you when you obey him in faith. Whatever he has called you to do, you can certainly accomplish in his strength.

JANUARY 24

You Were Made for More

The smallness you feel comes from within you. Your lives aren't small, but you're living them in a small way. . . . Open up your lives. Live openly and expansively!
2 CORINTHIANS 6:12-13 (MSG)

A nationally known business leader once sent me a message that said, "In the eyes of everyone around me, I am a raving success. But inside, I feel insecure, insignificant, and small." He was talking about what is referred to as "imposter syndrome." People with imposter syndrome wonder, "If I'm so successful, then why do I feel like a fake? Why don't I feel more fulfilled? Why do I still feel like there's something missing in my life?"

If you're living for success, then there *is* something missing in your life. Success is not enough because it doesn't satisfy. You need to move beyond success to a higher level of living—from success to significance. You were made for more than money. You were made for meaning.

I know some of the wealthiest people in the world. Every one of them would tell you this: Money will make your life easier, but it will not give you meaning. Life without meaning and purpose is petty, pointless, and trivial. You were made for so much more! The Bible says it this way: *"The smallness you feel comes from within you. Your lives aren't small, but you're living them in a small way. . . . Open up your lives. Live openly and expansively!"* (2 Corinthians 6:12-13, MSG).

The truth is, your life is significant—so significant, in fact, that God cared enough about you to come to earth, live a perfect life, and then die for your sins. If you want to know how much you matter to God, just look at Jesus hanging on the cross. He'd rather die than live without you. He loves you so much it hurts.

Your life has eternal significance, but it's possible you are living it in an insignificant way. If you've given more thought to the things that will not last than you have to your relationship with Jesus, then it's time to refocus. As you give Jesus more of your time and attention, he'll fill your life with peace and power. Then he'll propel you into your purpose so that you can be part of his mission on earth.

You were made for this!

Trusting God Means Obeying Him Completely

Your job is not to decide whether this law is right or wrong, but to obey it.

JAMES 4:11 (TLB)

There are two important truths you need to understand about God's commands:

God's standard of right and wrong never changes. If something was wrong six thousand years ago, then it is still wrong today. Cultures change. Popular opinions change. But truth never ever changes. Truth is eternal.

God's perspective is bigger than yours. God sees what you can't see. It's humanly impossible to see back before time began or forward into eternity. And there's no way you can understand everything—seen and unseen—that is going on around you.

You need to trust God. "*Your job is not to decide whether this law is right or wrong, but to obey it*" (James 4:11, TLB).

The oldest temptation is the temptation to doubt God's Word. Satan is still using the same lie he did on Eve when he asked, "Did God *really* say not to eat that?" (see Genesis 3:1). He convinced her that her desires were more important than God's commands.

Faith is trusting God in the details and obeying completely, not just the portion you understand or the part you feel like doing. Proverbs 3:5 tells us, "*Trust GOD from the bottom of your heart; don't try to figure out everything on your own*" (MSG).

The story of Naaman in 2 Kings 5 illustrates the need for complete obedience. Naaman, the commander of the Syrian army, had leprosy. A messenger from the prophet Elisha told him to dip himself in the Jordan River seven times to be healed.

The instructions seemed ridiculous—and Naaman almost ignored them—but his servants convinced him to try. So Naaman immersed himself seven times in the river. And God healed him! Imagine if Naaman had gone home in anger or only gone under the water six times and then decided God was making him look like a fool. But Naaman trusted and obeyed God completely, and God healed him of his leprosy.

Imagine what God will do in your life when you fully obey him with your whole heart.

JANUARY 26

Don't Give In to Discouragement

Let us not get tired of doing what is right, for after a while we will reap a harvest of blessing if we don't get discouraged and give up.

GALATIANS 6:9 (TLB)

Sometimes doing the right thing makes you tired, because it's easier to do what's wrong than to do what's right. Have you ever noticed that?

It's easier to be undisciplined than disciplined. It's easier to lie than to tell the truth. It is easier to be selfish than to be unselfish. It's easier to be codependent than to confront someone in love.

To do what's right, we need self-control, wisdom, and willpower—and that's why we get tired. But God promises that if we keep doing what's right, even when we're tired, then we will experience God's blessing.

Galatians 6:9 says, *"Let us not get tired of doing what is right, for after a while we will reap a harvest of blessing if we don't get discouraged and give up"* (TLB).

When you plant a seed, you don't instantly get a plant. There is always a delay. You plant in one season, and you harvest in another.

In the same way, there may be a delay between when you do the right thing and when you see God's blessing. Why? Because God is not a vending machine, where you put in a good deed and instantly get a blessing back. You can't decide to start putting God first in your finances and giving generously to others and then expect all your problems to go away the very next day. That's not how God's promise works.

So what do you do before *"after a while"* comes? You keep on doing the right thing.

One of the great tests of faith is how you handle delay—when you're doing the right thing and you don't see the immediate reward.

God's promises can give you the courage and determination you need to keep going when life gets tough. Don't let discouragement overwhelm you; instead, remember what is waiting for you when you choose to do what's right.

Don't give up!

JANUARY 27

Knowing God Is What Matters Most

Everything else is worthless when compared with the infinite value of knowing Christ Jesus my Lord. For his sake I have discarded everything else, counting it all as garbage, so that I could gain Christ.

PHILIPPIANS 3:8 (NLT)

You can tell what's important to people by what they brag about. If your kids are most important to you, then you brag about your kids. If your job is the most important thing in your life, then you brag about your job. If traveling and having experiences are most important, then that's what you talk about. You brag about what you value most.

God says in Jeremiah 9:23-24, *"The wise should not boast of their wisdom, nor the strong of their strength, nor the rich of their wealth. If any want to boast, they should boast that they know and understand me"* (GNT).

Knowing God is what matters most. It's what life is all about! The God of the universe loves you and wants to have a relationship with you. And getting close to him will give you peace and perspective. John 6:63 says, *"The very words I have spoken to you are spirit and life"* (NLT).

Friendship is demonstrated through commitment to another person. Our friendship with God is best demonstrated and grown by spending time with him and reading his Word. But you're never going to become a friend of God by reading the Bible in your spare time. To become his friend, you have to make knowing him your number one priority—to the point that it's what you talk about and think about most. God wants you to want to spend time with him.

Paul said it like this: *"Everything else is worthless when compared with the infinite value of knowing Christ Jesus my Lord. For his sake I have discarded everything else, counting it all as garbage, so that I could gain Christ"* (Philippians 3:8, NLT).

Are you doing that? Are you seeking with all your heart to know Jesus more every day? You are as close to God as you choose to be. You're going to become a friend of God only when you decide you want to know him more than you want anything else.

Knowing and loving God is our greatest privilege. And being known and being loved by God is our greatest pleasure. It's what gives us life!

JANUARY 28

Make It about Jesus

Our message is not about ourselves. It is about Jesus Christ as the Lord. We are your servants for his sake.

2 CORINTHIANS 4:5 (GW)

It's not about you.

If you want God to use you, then you need to remember that life is not all about you. It's all about Jesus!

"It's not about you" is the exact opposite of everything you've been taught. Many cultures appeal to self-centeredness. Advertisements everywhere tell you, "You're number one! Do what's best for you! Think of yourself first!"

But you're not the center of the universe—God is. That's why you become frustrated and unfulfilled when you make every problem, opportunity, and criticism about yourself. And you eventually become bored, because life is so much more than living for yourself.

The Bible says, *"Our message is not about ourselves. It is about Jesus Christ as the Lord. We are your servants for his sake"* (2 Corinthians 4:5, GW).

Twice in this passage, the apostle Paul said it's all for Jesus. Everything Paul did was about Jesus and was for the sake of the gospel. In other words, learning to follow Jesus is about motivation.

There may be a hundred different things you could do with your life where God would say, "Because I made you and shaped you, any of those things would be fine with me."

God is far more interested in your motivation to do something than in your methodology. You could be using the right method and be very successful in life. But if you have the wrong motive—greed, competition, envy, or guilt—it won't count with God.

On the other hand, you could do everything wrong and fail in so many ways. But if you have the right motive—when you do it for Jesus—then God says, "That's good enough." God is more interested in your "why" than your "what."

The Bible says, "*Whatever you do, whether in word or deed, do it all in the name of the Lord Jesus*" (Colossians 3:17, NIV).

JANUARY 29

Habits of the Spiritually Fit

Let us go on instead to other things and become mature in our understanding, as strong Christians ought to be.

HEBREWS 6:1 (TLB)

Growing in faith is not an end in itself. As you grow in your faith, you become equipped for ministry. One mark of growing toward spiritual maturity is being able to share the gospel, the Good News about salvation through Jesus Christ, with others.

The Bible says, *"Let us go on instead to other things and become mature in our understanding, as strong Christians ought to be"* (Hebrews 6:1, TLB).

God doesn't want you to get stuck in perpetual immaturity and remain a spiritual baby. Instead, he wants you to become a lifelong learner and pass along what you've learned about him. He wants you to be a teacher! Hebrews 5:12 says, *"By now you should be teachers. Instead, you still need someone to teach you"* (GW).

Not everyone is called to be a full-time teacher. But, at different points in your life, God still has things he wants you to teach others. Sometimes you'll teach through one-on-one conversations with friends. Other times, you might share your experiences with people in your small group.

Great teachers are first great learners. What are some habits of lifelong learners? They regularly spend time in prayer and in God's Word. They read spiritual growth books and do Bible studies. They attend small groups and participate in classes that build their faith. In other words, they *"spend [their] time and energy in the exercise of keeping spiritually fit"* (1 Timothy 4:7, TLB).

Do you want to be spiritually fit so that you can effectively teach others about the hope you have in Jesus? Begin by asking yourself, "In which areas of my life do I need to grow the most?"

Maybe you need a better understanding of the Bible. Perhaps you need to learn to resist temptation. Or you might need to develop a more Christlike attitude or a love for biblical fellowship and community. Once you have a good goal in place, you can start building habits that lead to spiritual maturity.

JANUARY 30

Give God the Best of Your Time

Friendship with God is reserved for those who reverence him.
With them alone he shares the secrets of his promises.

PSALM 25:14 (TLB)

Friendship with God is like any other friendship—you have to make time for it. If you don't make time for your earthly friends, then they're not really your friends. If God is going to be your *best* friend, then you have to give him the best of your time.

The best of your time is not when you're in a hurry, when you're constantly distracted, or whatever is left at the end of your day. When you give God your best, you choose him first, over anything else you could give your time and attention. You schedule your time, and you keep your commitment.

The Bible says that if you want to know God, you have to be still (Psalm 46:10). And in today's frantic world, you can't be still without having a daily, consistent quiet time with God.

Psalm 25:14 says, *"Friendship with God is reserved for those who reverence him. With them alone he shares the secrets of his promises"* (TLB).

Many people don't know God. They haven't experienced his love or his power because they don't make time for him. Friendship with God is reserved for those who reverence him—in other words, those who slow down and spend time with him.

What would a friendship be if you never invested time in it? Friendships need attention. You will never know God intimately if your only commitment to him is going to church once a week.

You have to be still and just sit in awe of God. As you focus on him, he'll reveal himself through his Word and the Holy Spirit. As you study the Bible, you'll learn more about who he is, why you can trust him, and what he wants to do in the world through you. The more time you spend with him, the deeper your friendship will grow.

You've probably heard it said that your life is shaped by your friends. But God has shaped everything about you. Your friendship with him will be the most meaningful of your life when you make time to know him and love him more.

JANUARY 31

Peace That Endures

I am leaving you with a gift—peace of mind and heart! And the peace I give isn't fragile like the peace the world gives. So don't be troubled or afraid.

JOHN 14:27 (TLB)

When you make room for Jesus, he gives you one of the greatest gifts: *"I am leaving you with a gift—peace of mind and heart! And the peace I give isn't fragile like the peace the world gives. So don't be troubled or afraid"* (John 14:27, TLB).

The kind of peace the world gives is temporary. In the last three hundred years, hundreds of peace treaties have been signed—and almost none of them have been kept.

The peace that comes from the world is totally circumstantial. If you have a good job, then you're at peace. But if you lose your job, then you're not at peace anymore. If you've got money in the bank, then you're at peace. But when that money is gone, you're not at peace anymore.

Jesus gives you a different kind of peace. The Bible calls it peace that *"surpasses all understanding"* (Philippians 4:7, ESV).

What does that mean? It means you have peace when there's no obvious or visible reason why you should be at peace. Everything around you could be in chaos, but for some unexplainable reason, you are at peace. That is the peace that surpasses understanding—and it can only come from Jesus, the Prince of Peace.

Jesus wants to give you that kind of peace so you won't be troubled or afraid.

Whenever Jesus walks into a room, he fills that room with peace. Do you have rooms in your heart that are full of worry, disorder, anxiety, or fear? Those are the rooms you haven't invited Jesus into. Your worries reveal the areas you have not surrendered to God. That could include your finances, your dating life, your career, your parenting, your schedule, or your ministry. Whatever it is, you have to let it go. You have to give it over to Jesus.

Here's the only way you're going to have real peace: Give every part of your life to God to use for his purposes. Then you'll have peace that will stand up to all of life's pressures.

FEBRUARY 1

You're Qualified to Serve God

*Give yourselves completely to God—every part of you—
for you are back from death and you want to be tools in
the hands of God, to be used for his good purposes.*

ROMANS 6:13 (TLB)

There is no greater joy than to be used by God for a purpose bigger than yourself.

The purpose of life isn't to get an education, find a job, make money, and retire before you die. Your life is far more significant than your career. You were made for eternal purposes.

The Bible says, *"Give yourselves completely to God—every part of you—for you are back from death and you want to be tools in the hands of God, to be used for his good purposes"* (Romans 6:13, TLB).

The problem is, many people secretly fear that God could never use them. Some people feel *disqualified* because of their past sins and mistakes. Others feel *unqualified* because they don't think they have the right education, talents, or background.

Maybe you feel one of those two ways—disqualified or unqualified. But you only have to look at the life of the apostle Paul to know that God wants to use you in ways you can't even imagine.

Almost no one in history has been used by God more than Paul. He just about single-handedly spread Christianity all over the Roman Empire. He planted churches everywhere. He wrote about half of the New Testament. He lived with a purpose to please God.

But do you know what Paul was doing before he became a preacher, a pastor, and a church planter? He was an anti-Christian crusader. He was the exact opposite of someone you'd think God could use. Paul wrote, *"You know what I was like . . . how I violently persecuted God's church. I did my best to destroy it. . . . But even before I was born, God chose me and called me by his marvelous grace"* (Galatians 1:13, 15, NLT).

Your past does not determine your future. Your past is past! It doesn't disqualify you from being used by God. And the opportunities you've had or didn't have don't determine whether you're qualified for God's mission.

God chose you and called you, and he wants to use you today because of his marvelous grace.

FEBRUARY 2

You Don't Have to Live with Guilt Anymore

Then you will know the truth, and the truth will set you free.

JOHN 8:32 (NIV)

The burden of guilt can feel overwhelming—but it's one of the things Jesus promises to free you from! In John 8:32, he said, *"Then you will know the truth, and the truth will set you free"* (NIV).

You know what guilt feels like. Guilt robs you of happiness. It causes depression. It can make you physically sick. When David, a great king of Israel, had sinned, he felt the weight of guilt. He said to God, *"Restore unto me the joy of thy salvation"* (Psalm 51:12, KJV).

God has an answer to guilt: confession. The Bible says in 1 John 1:9, *"If we tell Him our sins, He is faithful and we can depend on Him to forgive us of our sins. He will make our lives clean from all sin"* (NLV).

You might have spent years working through a problem that really has a very simple solution: You just need a clear conscience. Jesus offers you that. He offers instantaneous forgiveness!

God promises, *"I will forgive their sins and I will no longer remember their wrongs"* (Jeremiah 31:34, GNT).

Satan wants to keep you weighted down under the burden of guilt. He wants to keep you bound up so you can't live in God's freedom. But that's not how God works.

Here's how God works: You ask for forgiveness. Then God forgives you. But then, he goes a step further and actually forgets what you've done wrong.

It's like God takes your sins and puts them in the deepest part of the ocean—and then he puts up a No Fishing sign. God won't pull up your sins again, and he doesn't want you to either. He wants you to be free.

Are you feeling the burden of guilt today? Remember that Jesus has come to set you free. When you confess your sins, he will forgive you and set you free from your guilt.

Then you can live in the true freedom of knowing your past is forgiven and you are no longer bound by it.

What You Can Count On in Uncertain Times

You, too, must be patient. Don't give up hope. The Lord will soon be here.
JAMES 5:8 (GW)

We're living in strange and uncertain times. But no matter what's going on in our communities and around the world, we can remain certain of this truth: God is in control.

The Bible gives this encouragement: *"Brothers and sisters, be patient until the Lord comes again. See how farmers wait for their precious crops to grow. They wait patiently for fall and spring rains. You, too, must be patient. Don't give up hope. The Lord will soon be here. Brothers and sisters, stop complaining about each other, or you will be condemned. Realize that the judge is standing at the door"* (James 5:7-9, GW).

Why does James remind us several times in this passage that the Lord is coming back? Because it's the ultimate proof that God is in control.

History is God's story. It's not circular; there is no circle of life. History is linear, and it's moving to a climax. God has a plan and a purpose. And one day Jesus is going to return.

Everything is on schedule. We don't know when he's coming back, but the Bible talks more about Jesus' second coming than about his first coming. Because of that, anticipation of the Second Coming should change our everyday lives. We should be living with great expectation!

Be patient. God's timing is perfect. He's never late, and he's always in control—even when your circumstances may seem out of control and what you're going through may be painful.

Jesus' promise is for you today: *"When everything is ready, I will come and get you, so that you will always be with me where I am"* (John 14:3, NLT).

There are few things that are certain in life. But you can say with absolute assurance that Jesus will come back one day. You can build your hope on this certainty. You will not be disappointed!

When you feel like you can't count on anything else, count on this: God's got this. And Jesus will come back one day soon to make all things right and new.

FEBRUARY 4

Do You See Others the Way Jesus Does?

When Jesus landed and saw a large crowd, he had compassion on them, because they were like sheep without a shepherd.

MARK 6:34 (NIV)

How do you know if you're looking at life from God's viewpoint? You start looking at other people differently.

This is a great test of your spiritual maturity—better than asking how much of the Bible you know, how often you go to church, or whether you serve, tithe, or pray.

Life is all about love and relationships. So if you want to gauge your spiritual maturity, think about how you see other people.

Consider this: God sees your spouse as valuable, acceptable, lovable, and forgivable. Is that the way you see your spouse?

How about the stranger at the grocery store? The person who cut you off in traffic? The person begging on the street? What do you see when you look at other people? Do you see them as irritations or burdens? Or do you see their inherent worth as God's creation?

What about the people you work with? Do you see them as enemies? Competition? Or do you see them the way God sees them, as those he wants to call his beloved sons and daughters?

All people matter to God. It doesn't matter who they are, what they've done, or even what they believe. Jesus loves them and died for them. God has a plan for every person, and he wants them to have a relationship with him.

The Bible says in Mark 6:34, *"When Jesus landed and saw a large crowd, he had compassion on them, because they were like sheep without a shepherd"* (NIV).

That's the way Jesus sees people. He doesn't pretend that they're perfect or always lovable. But he always looks through eyes of love and compassion. He chooses grace.

And that's the way you can grow to see people too. You can learn to have compassion for your own family as well as for your neighbors, your community, and the rest of the world.

Let your spiritual vision get stronger as you learn to see people the way Jesus does.

FEBRUARY 5

The Battle for Your Mind

I love to do God's will so far as my new nature is concerned; but there is something else deep within me . . . that is at war with my mind and wins the fight and makes me a slave to the sin that is still within me. In my mind I want to be God's willing servant, but instead I find myself still enslaved to sin.

ROMANS 7:22-23 (TLB)

There's a battle in your brain every second of your life—even right now! It could be between right and wrong, between easy and hard, or between healthy and unhealthy.

All your negative emotions, like stress, anxiety, loneliness, fear, and jealousy, are mental struggles. All your conflicts, both internal and external, start in your mind.

James 4:1 says, *"What causes fights and quarrels among you? Don't they come from your desires that battle within you?"* (NIV). The battle going on inside your mind between conflicting desires rages twenty-four hours a day, seven days a week, even when you are sleeping. This battle is constant and intense because your mind is your greatest asset. You *are* your thoughts, your will, your emotions, your soul. Without your brain, you're not *you.*

The Bible says in Romans 7:22-23, *"I love to do God's will so far as my new nature is concerned; but there is something else deep within me . . . that is at war with my mind and wins the fight and makes me a slave to the sin that is still within me. In my mind I want to be God's willing servant, but instead I find myself still enslaved to sin"* (TLB).

If you follow Jesus, then God's Spirit is in you; it's part of your new nature. So Satan can't control your mind, but he *can* make suggestions. In other words, he can put thoughts in your mind that get your attention—and that's a pretty big deal. Whatever gets your attention gets you. You have to decide whether to accept or reject Satan's suggestions.

There's a lot going on in your brain right now, and all of it will eventually show up in your attitude and your actions. Ask God to help you choose right over wrong, healthy over destructive, and his truth over Satan's lies. He is ready to give you the power you need through the Holy Spirit!

FEBRUARY 6

Obedience Should Come from Love

You are my friends if you do what I command.

JOHN 15:14 (NLT)

You can't say you love Jesus and then pursue a sinful lifestyle. You can't say you're a Christian and then keep living a self-centered life. You can't say you're a follower of Jesus and then pick and choose the verses you want to obey and ignore the ones you don't.

Jesus said in John 15:14, *"You are my friends if you do what I command"* (NLT).

Those who do not follow Jesus can't understand why his followers obey him. They think it's out of fear or guilt or obligation, and they don't want that for their lives. I wouldn't want that either!

So why do we *really* obey God? Because he loves us! He wants the best for us. He loves us like nobody else will ever love us.

We don't obey God out of fear or guilt or obligation. We obey God out of love—because he loved us first and saved us.

When I was in high school, certain people thought I couldn't do any of the fun things they were doing because I was a Christian.

I told them I could take all the drugs I wanted to, get as drunk as I wanted to, and go to all the parties I wanted to—but Jesus changed my *want to.*

I didn't want to do those things, because they are cheap, phony thrills that may look like freedom but never last. They only lead to despair, not dignity; they end in depression, not delight.

Obeying Jesus, on the other hand, leads to life. Jesus said, *"I have loved you even as the Father has loved me. . . . When you obey my commandments, you remain in my love, just as I obey my Father's commandments and remain in his love. I have told you these things so that you will be filled with my joy. Yes, your joy will overflow!"* (John 15:9-11, NLT).

God doesn't want you to obey him because you're afraid of him or scared of punishment. He wants you to obey him because of love. When you do, you'll find true joy and freedom.

FEBRUARY 7

Trust Jesus One Day at a Time

Don't worry about tomorrow, because tomorrow will have its own worries. Each day has enough trouble of its own.

MATTHEW 6:34 (NCV)

There are two days you should never worry about: yesterday and tomorrow.

Jesus said, *"Don't worry about tomorrow, because tomorrow will have its own worries. Each day has enough trouble of its own"* (Matthew 6:34, NCV).

You can't live in the past. You can't live in the future. You can only live today.

Why should you only live one day at a time? First, when you worry about tomorrow's problems, you miss the blessings of today. Second, you can't solve tomorrow's problems with today's power. When tomorrow arrives, God will give you the power, perspective, grace, and wisdom you need.

When I was a kid, I didn't worry about anything I *needed* in my life. Instead, I just went to my dad or mom and told them what I needed. I was never once concerned about how they were going to meet my needs because they took on that responsibility.

God wants you to be the same way with him.

Matthew 6:30 says, *"If God cares so wonderfully for flowers that are here today and gone tomorrow, won't he more surely care for you?"* (TLB).

When you worry, you assume responsibility that God never intended for you to have. You may be worrying today about a lot of things that are really God's responsibility. In fact, every time you worry, it's a warning that you're playing God and that you believe it all depends on you. You're acting like you don't have a heavenly Father who will feed you, lead you, and meet your needs.

The Bible does not say, "Give us this day our weekly bread." It says, *"Give us this day our daily bread"* (Matthew 6:11, ESV).

God wants you to depend on him one day at a time. He will provide *everything* you need—for today. Because he is a good God, you can trust that you will lack nothing.

It's okay to plan for tomorrow. But don't worry about it! Trust God for each day as it comes.

FEBRUARY 8

Trying to Overcome Temptation on Your Own?

Two people are better off than one, for they can help each other succeed. If one person falls, the other can reach out and help. But someone who falls alone is in real trouble.

ECCLESIASTES 4:9-10 (NLT)

Do you keep stumbling over the same temptation? Maybe it's related to jealousy, worry, lust, gossip, or gluttony. Whatever it is, you won't have victory over a persistent temptation if you try to overcome it by yourself.

The Bible says, *"Two people are better off than one, for they can help each other succeed. If one person falls, the other can reach out and help. But someone who falls alone is in real trouble"* (Ecclesiastes 4:9-10, NLT).

God made us to need each other, because he knows that we're better together. We're better when we serve together, when we worship together, when we grieve together, when we fellowship together—and when we fight temptation together.

Who's helping you fight temptation? Who's checking up on you? Who have you invited to help you grow spiritually? Who do you allow to ask you the tough questions? Who are *you* checking up on?

You don't have to tell everybody about the temptations you struggle with, but you do need to tell somebody. That person can support you and help you overcome your struggles.

When someone says, "I've never told this to anybody before . . . ," be quick to listen and pay attention, because it may mean they are taking the first step toward freedom. Remember this: Revealing your feeling is the beginning of healing. Talking about your temptations is the way you overcome them.

How serious are you about changing? Wouldn't you like to come out of this season of your life with a stronger faith, having overcome a persistent temptation? Why not reach out to a friend, who can hold you accountable?

There may be some bad habits in your life you're just not going to get over until you get support from a committed friend. Find that person, and then be that person for someone else.

FEBRUARY 9

Where God's Dream for You Starts

This means that anyone who belongs to Christ has become a new person. The old life is gone; a new life has begun!
2 CORINTHIANS 5:17 (NLT)

God has a big dream for your life. But before he can help you see that dream, he wants to change the way you see yourself—because the way you see yourself affects everything else in your life, including your dreams.

Too often you see yourself only as you've been told to see yourself. But the people who helped form your identity weren't always speaking the truth—and they didn't love you the way God loves you.

One of the ways God does his deepest work in you is by changing the way you see yourself.

That's what he did for Jacob. After Jacob wrestled with God, he got three things: a new identity, a blessing, and a daily reminder to depend on God and not himself.

God gave Jacob a new name, Israel, which means "prince of God," because God saw his potential. And God blessed Jacob with a dream greater than anything he could imagine: As part of God's covenant, Jacob's descendants would spread across the earth. But God also gave Jacob a limp so that he would stop his pattern of running away and instead learn to rest and trust in him.

Out of this experience, Jacob emerged weaker in his own strength but stronger in God's power and in his new identity. Only God can make the kind of radical change in a person that takes him from "deceiver and manipulator" (the meaning of Jacob's name) to "prince of God."

It doesn't matter what other people have said about you or how they've labeled you. No matter who you are or what you've done, God wants to give you a new identity. The Bible says in 2 Corinthians 5:17, *"This means that anyone who belongs to Christ has become a new person. The old life is gone; a new life has begun!"* (NLT).

God doesn't just want you to turn over a new leaf. He wants to give you a whole new life, with a dream and purpose beyond what you can imagine.

FEBRUARY 10

Don't Let Bitterness Wear You Down

A stone is heavy and sand is weighty, but the resentment caused by a fool is even heavier.

PROVERBS 27:3 (NLT)

Anytime you breathe bitterness, you suffocate your spirit.

That's because, when you have bitterness in your heart, you can't breathe spiritually. Bitterness chokes out your happiness and healthy emotions. And it also weighs you down, depresses you, and eventually strangles your spirit. Proverbs 27:3 says, *"A stone is heavy and sand is weighty, but the resentment caused by a fool is even heavier"* (NLT).

Choosing bitterness is like choosing to carry a huge weight with you everywhere you go, all the time. It's an unnecessary load, but you've made the choice to bear it.

Bitterness often develops because you hold on to what happened in the past, trying to hurt someone who hurt you. You think that if you stay mad, the other person will become miserable.

But bitterness is a worthless weapon. It doesn't hurt the other person. It only makes *you* miserable.

It's like drinking poison and hoping it kills the person who hurt you. But that person is out there somewhere, maybe living their best life. They're not even thinking about you—and they certainly aren't aware that you're thinking about them! They've already moved on.

That's what you need to do too. You need to move on, because it's a waste of your time to keep trying to use bitterness as a weapon. That bitterness will only hurt you.

You may have been hurt by someone a long time ago, and I'm sorry you had to experience that pain. But here's the good news: They can't hurt you anymore! The only way they can continue to hurt you is if you choose to hold on to the hurt. The Bible says in Job 18:4, *"You are only hurting yourself with your anger"* (GNT).

You don't have to hurt anymore. Let go of your hurt. Surrender it to God. When you do, you'll breathe in the fresh, sweet air of freedom and be able to move forward with purpose.

FEBRUARY 11

You'll Find God's Light in God's Word

For anyone out there who doesn't know where you're going, anyone groping in the dark, here's what: Trust in GOD. Lean *on your God!*

ISAIAH 50:10 (MSG)

On dark days, you need the light of Jesus. When you can't see the way forward, when you're confused or undecided, when you don't know what's best, when you can't figure out what to do next, you need his light.

When you're bewildered, well-meaning people will tell you, "Trust yourself. Just follow your instincts!" But anybody who's tried that knows, at best, you're right only about 50 percent of the time. Your perspective is limited. Your light is weak. It's like using one of those tiny penlights that fit on a key chain—they don't really illuminate anything. And as a result of relying only on yourself, you've probably had difficulty making good decisions.

Instead, here's what the Bible says to do: *"For anyone out there who doesn't know where you're going, anyone groping in the dark, here's what: Trust in* GOD. Lean *on your God!"* (Isaiah 50:10, MSG). Don't count on your own light. Trust the light of the Lord.

If you want to have God's perspective and viewpoint on your problems, then you need to get to know God through the Bible. You need to read and study and saturate your mind and heart with it, because God's will is always found in his Word.

I'm always amazed at how many people are waiting around for God to give them a sign instead of just reading the directions that he's already given them. If you want to stay on the right path, then you have to study the Bible.

God promises to guide you if you'll let him. He says, *"I'll take the hand of those who don't know the way, who can't see where they're going. I'll be a personal guide to them, directing them through unknown country. I'll be right there to show them what roads to take, make sure they don't fall into the ditch. These are the things I'll be doing for them—sticking with them, not leaving them for a minute"* (Isaiah 42:16, MSG).

Let God be your personal guide, starting right now. You'll never have to stumble around in the dark if you let the light of his Word light up your life.

FEBRUARY 12

Pray with Confidence

This is the confidence we have in approaching God: that if we ask anything according to his will, he hears us.

1 JOHN 5:14 (NIV)

Why doesn't God heal everyone who asks him for healing?

When you pray and ask for God's healing, you can trust that he'll hear and answer you. But he may not answer in the way you hope, because he won't give you something against his will. God always wants what's best for you—and the best thing may be to use an illness in ways you did not expect.

Sometimes God uses an illness to get your attention and redirect you. He may have to lay you flat on your back in order to get you to look up to him. Proverbs 20:30 says, *"Sometimes it takes a painful experience to make us change our ways"* (GNT).

Sometimes God allows an illness to be a testimony to others. Paul said, *"Now I want you to know, brothers and sisters, that what has happened to me has actually served to advance the gospel"* (Philippians 1:12, NIV). Paul was sick and in prison when he wrote that, testifying to how God used his circumstances to spread the Good News.

The greatest witness you will ever have is your example of trusting God in the midst of pain. When you respond to pressure and pain in a way that points people back to God, it brings glory to him.

Sometimes God allows an illness to take a person into eternity. Hebrews 9:27 says, *"Everyone must die once, and after that be judged by God"* (GNT). If you could be healed of every sickness just by having enough faith, then if you had enough faith, you might never die. That certainly isn't God's will.

When you are sick, you can pray and ask God in confidence for healing. Why should you have confidence? *"This is the confidence we have in approaching God: that if we ask anything according to his will, he hears us"* (1 John 5:14, NIV).

When you pray in God's will, he always hears you. His answer may not come through the method or in the timing you want. But his answer and the way he is using your pain is always for his good purpose.

FEBRUARY 13

Who Should You Trust?

For the word of the LORD holds true, and
we can trust everything he does.
PSALM 33:4 (NLT)

One of the great questions of life is this: Who are you going to trust?

The way you answer that question will determine whether you're happy or miserable, whether you succeed or fail, whether you make something of your life or waste your life.

To determine who you should trust, ask yourself questions like these: Who always has your best interest in mind? Who will help you make important decisions? Who wants to see you succeed?

Should you trust popular opinion? That may not be a good idea since it constantly changes. Should you trust celebrity trendsetters? Trends change, and fads fade. Should you make critical decisions based on what you read on social media? Just because it's online doesn't mean it's reliable.

What about trusting yourself? The truth is, your emotions can lie to you. The Bible says, *"The heart is deceitful above all things, and desperately wicked: who can know it?"* (Jeremiah 17:9, KJV).

If you're going to entrust your life to someone, you better choose someone who has your best interest at heart, knows everything, is perfect, and will never lie to you. That kind of limits your options to God.

No one else will *always* tell you the truth. Even someone who loves you and wants the best for you may filter the truth and try to make it sound nice. But what you need to hear is the truth—because the truth sets you free.

Even though the truth will set you free, it may make you miserable at first; that's why people often avoid the truth. You don't want to hear that most of your problems were brought on by your poor decisions or that your own ego causes much of the stress in your life—but it's true.

Psalm 33:4 says, *"For the word of the LORD holds true, and we can trust everything he does"* (NLT). Each day voices all around you are trying to get you to trust them. But there's only one trustworthy voice that will always have your best in mind. Trust God for your present and your future. He will never let you down.

FEBRUARY 14

God's Love for You Lasts Forever

The LORD is good; his love is eternal and his faithfulness lasts forever.
PSALM 100:5 (GNT)

Nobody loves you like God loves you.

In fact, God says, *"I have loved you . . . with an everlasting love. With unfailing love I have drawn you to myself"* (Jeremiah 31:3, NLT). No matter how much people love each other, that love always fails in some way. For example, I love my wife dearly, but I fail her sometimes. I've failed my kids, despite how much I love them. I love the people at Saddleback Church, but I failed them at different points.

But God has an everlasting and unfailing love. The Bible says God's love even draws you to him! You need to understand two aspects of God's love:

First, God's love is unconditional. God's love doesn't say, "I love you *if*. . ." That's conditional. Conditional love says things like "I love you if you love me. I love you if you please me. I love you if you change in *this* way. I love you unless you *do* change." That's not real love. What happens when someone loses their good looks? What happens when you find someone else more interesting? Does your love just stop? That kind of love is conditional.

But God's love for you says, "I love you—period. I love you even though you don't always love me, you're not always faithful, and you don't always do the right thing." God's love is unconditional.

Second, God's love is consistent. It's not fickle. It's not unpredictable. Maybe you grew up with inconsistent parents. Inconsistent parents create insecure kids. A man once said to me, "I never knew if my dad was going to slug me or hug me. He was unpredictable." That's inconsistent love.

But with God, you'll never have to ask, "Will God love me today?" His love is consistent and eternal. Psalm 100:5 says, *"The LORD is good; his love is eternal and his faithfulness lasts forever"* (GNT).

You'll never find another love like God's love for you. It will last forever—no matter what.

FEBRUARY 15

Move Quickly to Do Good and Accept Salvation

Do not withhold good from those who deserve it when it's in your power to help them.

PROVERBS 3:27 (NLT)

There are many times when you should move quickly in response to God's Spirit, like obeying when God tells you to do something or asking for forgiveness.

Here are two more times when you should move quickly.

First, move quickly when you have the opportunity to do good. The Bible says it over and over: When you see a chance to do something good for someone else, do it immediately.

God puts people with needs in your life over and over again—you just have to be on the lookout for them. Their needs might be physical. Some could be emotional, like the need for kindness or encouragement.

Proverbs 3:27 says, *"Do not withhold good from those who deserve it when it's in your power to help them"* (NLT). For example, if you see someone who is experiencing homelessness, don't say, "I've got to help the homeless one of these days." Instead, do something to help right then.

The Bible says in Ecclesiastes 11:4, *"If you wait for perfect conditions, you will never get anything done"* (TLB). There's never a perfect time to do anything. Plus, you're not even guaranteed tomorrow. In John 9:4, Jesus says, *"All of us must quickly carry out the tasks assigned us by the one who sent me, for there is little time left before the night falls and all work comes to an end"* (TLB).

Second, move quickly when God offers salvation. This is the most important time not to delay! God has offered you salvation, and today is the day to accept it.

Not to decide is to decide. When you say, "Not yet," you're saying, "No" to Christ. The Bible says in 2 Corinthians 6:2, *"Right now God is ready to welcome you. Today he is ready to save you"* (TLB).

How do you accept salvation? You turn away from yourself and toward God. You trust Christ to come into your life, forgive your sins, and make you who he wants you to be.

Salvation is the best gift you'll ever be offered. Be quick to accept it today.

FEBRUARY 16

A Good Time to Slow Down

It's smart to be patient.
PROVERBS 14:29 (CEV)

Sometimes God wants you to move quickly, but sometimes he wants you to slow down. As Proverbs 14:29 says, *"It's smart to be patient"* (CEV).

When should you slow down?

First, you should always move slowly when you don't have all the facts. Our culture worships impulsiveness and spontaneity. It tells you that spur-of-the-moment, gut decisions are the right ones. But the Bible says, *"What a shame—yes, how stupid!—to decide before knowing the facts!"* (Proverbs 18:13, TLB).

You've probably heard repeatedly that you should "follow your heart." But the Bible says, *"The heart is the most deceitful thing there is and desperately wicked"* (Jeremiah 17:9, TLB). Feelings often lead you in the wrong direction. You need to rely on truth outside of yourself. So, when you don't yet have all the facts, slow down. Don't rely on your gut, your heart, or your feelings. Take the time to look for objective truth, which comes only from God.

Second, move slowly when you're hurt, angry, or depressed. When you're upset, it's often easier to react and retaliate rather than to act wisely.

James 1:19 says, *"Everyone should be quick to listen, slow to speak and slow to become angry"* (NIV). Do you see the rhythm in that verse? It says quick, slow, slow. If you're quick to listen and slow to speak, you'll automatically be slow to become angry. But if you're slow to listen and quick to speak, you'll most likely be quick to become angry.

Proverbs 15:28 says, *"The heart of the godly thinks carefully before speaking"* (NLT). In other words, godly people put their minds in gear before their mouths. Sometimes you're going to feel angry, hurt, or depressed. That's just part of life. But the next time that happens, slow down. Proverbs 14:29 says, *"Patient people have great understanding, but people with quick tempers show their foolishness"* (NCV).

Avoid making quick decisions driven by emotions or when you don't have all the facts. Instead of just "following your heart," take the time to slow down and make a careful decision.

It's smart to be patient!

How to Fight Temptation Step-by-Step

I have made up my mind to obey your laws forever, no matter what.

PSALM 119:112 (CEV)

When people feel ineffective or defeated in life, it's often because they don't know how to fight the battle going on in their minds. They don't realize that temptation involves a process; it's not an isolated act. And even though it's a process, that process can happen quickly in just four steps.

Step one is desire. God gave you the desire to drink, sleep, eat, and have sex, and there is nothing wrong with those desires. But temptation turns a natural desire into a runaway desire. It becomes more important than other things, and it's all you can think about.

Step two is doubt—about God, his Word, and his love. Doubt happens anytime you're wondering, "Well, I know the Bible says *this*, but did God really mean *this* applies to sex [or food or whatever]?" You start to doubt if you can trust God and his Word.

Step three is deception. You start believing a lie. Satan knows your weaknesses. He knows what will get your attention and move you from desire to doubt to deception.

Step four is disobedience and defeat. This is when your temptation becomes a sin. What got your attention turns into attraction, and attraction becomes an attitude, and the attitude becomes an action. Temptation is not a sin—action is.

The Bible explains it this way: "*Temptation comes from our own desires, which entice us and drag us away. These desires give birth to sinful actions. And when sin is allowed to grow, it gives birth to death*" (James 1:14-15, NLT).

You're free to choose what you think about in life. But you are not free from the consequences of your choices. That's why the best time to win the battle of your mind is before it starts. Psalm 119:112 explains it this way: "*I have made up my mind to obey your laws forever, no matter what*" (CEV).

Have you made up your mind to obey God's Word, no matter what? Resolve today to recognize temptation and turn away from it before it goes a step further.

FEBRUARY 18

Rejoicing When It Doesn't Make Sense

Dear brothers and sisters, when troubles of any kind come your way, consider it an opportunity for great joy.

JAMES 1:2 (NLT)

No matter what challenges and difficulties you face, you can trust God to see you through them.

That's why you can rejoice when you face all kinds of trouble: *"Dear brothers and sisters, when troubles of any kind come your way, consider it an opportunity for great joy"* (James 1:2, NLT).

It's easy to misunderstand this verse. God is not saying you should seek out difficulty, deny reality, or "fake it till you make it." You don't have to be happy about your circumstances.

You don't need to rejoice *for* trouble. But you can still rejoice *during* trouble because of what you know is true.

What is true? God sees and cares about everything you're going through. You're never alone; God is always with you. And he will give you strength if you trust him.

One of the greatest comforts when you're going through troubles is God's promise in Romans 8:28: *"We know that in everything God works for the good of those who love him"* (NCV).

God has promised to bring good out of bad for you—in *everything*. That's not a promise for everybody. It's a promise for believers, those who follow Jesus and are committed to living according to his plan and purpose.

When you're in a tough time, you can choose joy as you rely on God's goodness. Joy is based on what you know is true, and it's based on faith that God will fulfill his promise to work things out for good, according to his purpose. Because joy is not based on circumstances, you are able to make the choice to rejoice, no matter what your situation is.

In Psalm 34:1, King David said, *"I will praise the LORD at all times; his praise is always on my lips"* (NCV). Even now, you can thank God. Praise God. And rejoice in God—not just in good times.

At all times.

FEBRUARY 19

Let Your Trials Make You More like Jesus

For you know that when your faith is tested, your endurance has a chance to grow. So let it grow, for when your endurance is fully developed, you will be perfect and complete, needing nothing.

JAMES 1:3-4 (NLT)

Jesus is coming back! When he does, he will make all things right. And if you are his follower, then you will spend eternity with him.

That's how the story ends—but what do you do in the meantime? In life you will undoubtedly face stress and troubles. But God wants you to use those trials to develop endurance and become more like Christ.

The Bible says, *"For you know that when your faith is tested, your endurance has a chance to grow. So let it grow, for when your endurance is fully developed, you will be perfect and complete, needing nothing"* (James 1:3-4, NLT).

Does becoming like Christ—*"perfect and complete, needing nothing"*—sound impossible? The Bible says God can do that work in you: *"May God himself, the God who makes everything holy and whole, make you holy and whole"* (1 Thessalonians 5:23, MSG).

Are you whole, or are you fragmented? Are you put together or falling apart? If you're feeling fragmented right now, that's okay. You're not supposed to have it all together. You can't be perfect while you're here on earth.

What you can do is work toward being spiritually fit in preparation for the coming of Jesus Christ.

It's important to stay physically fit and take care of your mental health. But don't neglect your spiritual fitness. You don't have to be the strongest, fastest, or healthiest when it comes to being spiritually fit. You just need to keep working on it and let the troubles you face help you grow in faith.

If you're out of work, suffering through an illness, or feeling the weight of prejudice, turn to God's Word and his promises. When it feels like you're falling apart, remember that God is working to make you more like him. And he can use even the most difficult circumstances in your life to do it.

FEBRUARY 20

God Can Use Your Weaknesses for Good

Now I am glad to boast about how weak I am; I am glad to be a living demonstration of Christ's power.
2 CORINTHIANS 12:9 (TLB)

God is strong where we are weak, and he can bring good even out of our weakest places.

Here are four ways God uses your weaknesses for good:

Your weaknesses prevent arrogance. Realizing you're not perfect makes you humble. And being humble makes you more like Jesus. The apostle Paul had a *"thorn in the flesh"* that kept him from becoming arrogant. He asked God to take it away: *"Three times I pleaded with the Lord to take it away from me. But he said to me, 'My grace is sufficient for you'"* (2 Corinthians 12:8-9, NIV). God's grace is enough for you too.

Your weaknesses help you value others. The Bible says, *"Some parts of the body that seem weakest and least important are actually the most necessary"* (1 Corinthians 12:22, NLT). As you learn to depend on people who have what you lack, your weaknesses help you learn to live in biblical community.

Your weaknesses make you more dependent on God. If you had no weaknesses, then you'd live self-sufficiently, as if you didn't need God. Paul said, *"Now I am glad to boast about how weak I am; I am glad to be a living demonstration of Christ's power. . . . For when I am weak, then I am strong—the less I have, the more I depend on him"* (2 Corinthians 12:9-10, TLB).

Your weaknesses give you a ministry. God uses your strengths *and* weaknesses in ministry. He *"comforts us in all our troubles, so that we can comfort those in any trouble with the comfort we ourselves receive from God"* (2 Corinthians 1:4, NIV). When you've worked through a problem or learned to live with a weakness, you can help others in similar circumstances.

Perhaps you've been like Paul, begging God to take away a weakness. But today may be the time to start trusting God instead to use that weakness to make you more like Jesus.

FEBRUARY 21

God's Speed Is Always Just Right

Ponder the path of your feet; then all your ways will be sure.
PROVERBS 4:26 (ESV)

When you're making any major decision, God wants you to slow down.

The book of Proverbs has a lot to say about this. Proverbs 21:29 says, *"Wicked people bluff their way, but God's people think before they take a step"* (CEV).

And Proverbs 4:26 says, *"Ponder the path of your feet; then all your ways will be sure"* (ESV). What does *ponder* mean? It means to think about, meditate on, or carefully consider. You can't ponder quickly.

When do you need to ponder your path? When you're making big decisions—maybe about a career move, ministry change, marriage partner, or major purchase.

Proverbs 22:3 says, *"Sensible people will see trouble coming and avoid it, but an unthinking person will walk right into it and regret it later"* (GNT). The number one place "unthinking" decisions happen is in your spending. That's why so many people are in debt.

The solution? *"Plan carefully and you will have plenty; if you act too quickly, you will never have enough"* (Proverbs 21:5, GNT).

You also need to move slowly when you're waiting for a seed you've planted to grow.

The Bible talks a lot about sowing and reaping. When you plant a seed, you harvest a crop.

This happens in every area of your life. If you plant kindness, you reap kindness. If you plant gossip, you reap gossip. If you plant generosity, you reap generosity. Whatever you sow, you will reap.

But there is always a delay between planting and harvest. You don't put a seed in the ground and the next day have an apple tree.

Maybe you feel like you've spent a long time waiting for the harvest. Here's a promise for you: *"At the time I have decided, my words will come true. You can trust what I say about the future. It may take a long time, but keep on waiting—it will happen!"* (Habakkuk 2:3, CEV).

Know that you can trust God's timing. Sometimes God wants you to go fast and sometimes he says to go slow, but his speed is always just right.

FEBRUARY 22

Faith, Not Feelings, Pleases God

Naked I came from my mother's womb, and naked I will depart. The LORD gave and the LORD has taken away; may the name of the LORD be praised.

JOB 1:21 (NIV)

When you are a new Christian, God will often give you emotions that assure you he's there and he cares. But as you grow in faith, God will wean you of any dependency on your emotions to believe he is present and at work in your life.

God's omnipresence and the manifestation of his presence are two different things. One is a fact; the other is often a feeling. God is always present, even when you are unaware of him, and his presence is too profound to be measured by mere emotion.

Yes, he wants you to sense his presence, but he's more concerned that you trust him than feel him. Faith, not feelings, pleases God.

Situations that will stretch your faith the most will be those times when life falls apart and God seems nowhere to be found. This happened to Job. On a single day, he lost everything—his family, his business, his health, and everything he owned. And, most discouraging, God said nothing to Job for thirty-seven chapters of the Bible!

How do you praise God when you don't understand what's happening in your life and God is silent? How do you stay connected in a crisis without communication? How do you keep your eyes on Jesus when they're full of tears?

You do what Job did: *"Then he fell to the ground in worship and said: 'Naked I came from my mother's womb, and naked I will depart. The LORD gave and the LORD has taken away; may the name of the LORD be praised'"* (Job 1:20-21, NIV).

You tell God exactly how you feel and pour out your heart to him. You unload every emotion you're feeling. Job did this when he said, *"I can't be quiet! I am angry and bitter. I have to speak"* (Job 7:11, GNT).

God can handle your doubt, anger, fear, grief, confusion, and questions. Feelings in themselves do not prove God's presence. But God is pleased when you express your feelings to him, believing that he hears and cares.

FEBRUARY 23

Three Steps to Reveal Your Blind Spots

Point out anything in me that offends you, and
lead me along the path of everlasting life.
PSALM 139:24 (NLT)

Our natural tendency is to lie to ourselves. We believe our feelings, though our feelings aren't always accurate. We believe our thoughts, though our thoughts aren't always the truth.

This is because we all have blind spots, which are attitudes or weaknesses we cannot see or refuse to see, even though they cause conflict with others.

So how can you see beyond your self-deceptions to the truth? Here are three simple steps to get started.

First, ask God for clarity. Say to him, *"Point out anything in me that offends you, and lead me along the path of everlasting life"* (Psalm 139:24, NLT). The Bible says the heart is deceitful, so ask God to remind you of what is true about him and about you. Ask him to help you trust him.

After you've asked God for clarity, ask some trusted Christian friends or family for help. God puts people in your life to help you, because they see your blind spots, just like you can see theirs. Proverbs 12:15 says, *"Fools think their own way is right, but the wise listen to others"* (NLT). If you think you can work on yourself by yourself, that in itself is a blind spot.

Then, ask Jesus to change you. Jesus said, *"I am . . . the truth"* (John 14:6, NIV). And the Bible says *"the truth will set you free"* (John 8:32, NIV). The closer you are to Jesus, the less vulnerable you'll be to self-deception as you walk in the light of God's truth. Why? Because God's truth helps you see yourself and others as you really are.

Jesus said in John 9:39, *"I have come into the world to give sight to those who are spiritually blind and to show those who think they see that they are blind"* (TLB). Jesus came to earth to help you see your blind spots and to help you get your sight so you can see yourself as you really are.

God can deliver you from your hidden faults, blind spots, and self-deceptions. Ask him for clarity, ask some trusted Christian friends or family for help, and then ask Jesus to change you.

The truth will set you free!

FEBRUARY 24

Unity Is Our Greatest Witness to the World

I have given them the glory that you gave me, that they may be one as we are one—I in them and you in me—so that they may be brought to complete unity. Then the world will know that you sent me and have loved them even as you have loved me.

JOHN 17:22-23 (NIV)

Our unity as God's family, the church, is our greatest witness to unbelievers.

That's why Jesus' last prayer before he went to the cross was that the church would live in unity: *"The goal is for all of them to become one heart and mind—just as you, Father, are in me and I in you, so they might be one heart and mind with us. Then the world might believe that you, in fact, sent me"* (John 17:21, MSG).

Did you notice that Jesus tied the unity of his followers with people coming to Christ? He said that others would believe in him when they saw Christians loving each other and living in unity. This is Jesus' vision and goal for anybody who claims him as their Savior.

The next verses of Jesus' prayer say that God gives us his glory so that we will be unified and others will see the gospel: *"I have given them the glory that you gave me, that they may be one as we are one—I in them and you in me—so that they may be brought to complete unity. Then the world will know that you sent me and have loved them even as you have loved me"* (John 17:22-23, NIV).

The purpose of God's presence in your life is to make you more loving—not harsher or more opinionated or more stubborn, but more loving. Jesus said, *"This is my commandment: Love each other in the same way I have loved you"* (John 15:12, NLT).

Do you want God's glory in your life? Do you want God's power in your life? Do you want to feel God's presence in your life? Jesus says he gives his glory—his power—to those who lay aside secondary differences with other Christians. He wants you to put the needs of others above your preferences so that you can live in unity with other believers. Paul shared that same message with some of the first Christians: *"Be completely humble and gentle; be patient, bearing with one another in love. Make every effort to keep the unity of the Spirit through the bond of peace"* (Ephesians 4:2-3, NIV).

More than ever, people need to see that unity is possible, and it is found in the church. It is our responsibility to lay down our pride and preferences so we can focus on God's purpose.

If you want God to use you in this way, then pray to him today, "Father, you have given your church a great mission in the world, and I want to be part of it. I confess my pride and selfishness that have kept me from considering the needs of others before my own. Please develop in me the character of Jesus so that I will choose to let go of my preferences and needs for the sake of unity in the church. Help me to see people as you do so I will treat them with compassion and grace. Only you can change our hearts, and I want my life to display that. I pray this in Jesus' name, amen."

Our love for one another will show the world we belong to Jesus and will be a testimony of the power of Christ to transform lives.

FEBRUARY 25

Fulfilling God's Mission Will Take a Step of Faith

Without faith it is impossible to please God, because anyone who comes to him must believe that he exists and that he rewards those who earnestly seek him.

HEBREWS 11:6 (NIV)

When God gave Jonah his mission to go to Nineveh, it required a huge step of faith—a step so big that Jonah initially ran from it.

Nineveh was the biggest, most important city in the world. It was the capital of Assyria, the strongest empire of the day. Nineveh was known for its beauty—wide boulevards, parks, canals, great architecture, palaces, and temples.

But the Assyrians were also known to be cruel and wicked. They destroyed nearly everything in their path!

For Jonah to preach to them required incredible faith. Assyria had captured, dominated, and enslaved the Jews over and over again. They hated Israel, and Israel hated them. They were mortal, political, religious, and racial enemies.

God wanted to save the Assyrians, so he sent Jonah to preach repentance in Nineveh. But instead of obeying God, Jonah ran in the other direction. He refused to take the step of faith necessary to start his mission, let alone complete it.

Jonah eventually fulfilled his mission and learned that God is with us at every step of our mission, guiding and providing for us. Jesus promised this when he gave us the Great Commission: *"Therefore go and make disciples of all nations, baptizing them in the name of the Father and of the Son and of the Holy Spirit, and teaching them to obey everything I have commanded you. And surely I am with you always, to the very end of the age"* (Matthew 28:19-20, NIV).

Like Jonah's mission, your God-given mission will test your faith. It may challenge your comfort zones, your prejudices, or your politics.

The Bible says, "*Without faith it is impossible to please God, because anyone who comes to him must believe that he exists and that he rewards those who earnestly seek him"* (Hebrews 11:6, NIV).

God will help you accomplish his mission on earth. Just take a step forward in faith!

FEBRUARY 26

You Can't Run from God

Jonah immediately tried to run away from the LORD by going to Tarshish.
JONAH 1:3 (GW)

God gives every one of us a unique mission—and he lets us choose whether or not we fulfill that mission.

Jonah's mission from God was to warn the people of Nineveh that judgment was coming. But *"Jonah immediately tried to run away from the LORD by going to Tarshish"* (Jonah 1:3, GW).

Jonah faced consequences for his decision, the same kind of consequences you may encounter if you run away from God's mission for your life.

The Bible says that when Jonah boarded a ship to get away from his mission, God sent a powerful storm to push the boat back (Jonah 1:4).

Why did God do that? One reason is because he loved Jonah and wanted him to make a good decision that would give him a life of purpose and fulfillment. God sends opposition our way to encourage us to make better decisions.

Jonah's disobedience also threatened the lives of everyone on the boat to Tarshish. When you run away from God, the consequences don't just affect you. Innocent people, including those you care about, can get hurt. Maybe it's your spouse, your kids, your grandkids, or your friends. Sometimes it's people you don't even know. Your disobedience hurts other people too.

Jonah shows that when you run from God, your life starts a downward trajectory. Your disobedience will cost you financially, physically, and relationally.

Nineveh was 550 miles away from where Jonah lived in Israel, but he tried running to Tarshish, which was 2,500 miles away in the opposite direction. He took what he thought was the easy way, because it would be better for him. That's part of the problem: He was only thinking of himself! He didn't want to be part of Nineveh's redemption, because he didn't think they deserved it.

The truth is, you can't run from God. He's everywhere, and he knows everything. But he doesn't make you follow him, because he wants you to *choose* to love him and follow him.

Don't try to run from God, who made you, saved you, loves you, and is working for your good. Following him and fulfilling your mission will always be the right choice.

FEBRUARY 27

God Works Miracles When You Embrace Your Mission

The sailors were awestruck by the LORD's great power, and they offered him a sacrifice and vowed to serve him.

JONAH 1:16 (NLT)

When you embrace God's mission for your life, miracles happen.

You can see this in the life of Jonah. God told him to warn the people of Nineveh, but Jonah didn't want to do it. So he boarded a ship heading far away from where God wanted him to be.

To get Jonah back on mission, God sent a violent storm. *"'Throw me into the sea,' Jonah said, 'and it will become calm again. I know that this terrible storm is all my fault'"* (Jonah 1:12, NLT).

When Jonah was finally ready to obey God, three miracles happened. These same miracles will happen as you embrace God's mission for *your* life.

Life calms down. God ended the storm the moment Jonah was tossed into the sea. And the water went from crashing waves to complete calm.

When you accept God's mission, he'll calm the storm he sent to get your attention. Your outward circumstances may not change immediately, but you'll find a sense of peace where there had been a storm; you'll find rest where you once were panicked.

Unbelievers will believe. The unbelievers on board the ship were astounded that God stopped the storm when they threw Jonah overboard: *"The sailors were awestruck by the LORD's great power, and they offered him a sacrifice and vowed to serve him"* (Jonah 1:16, NLT). Because a follower of God went the right way, unbelievers believed.

You probably have a friend or relative who isn't a Christian. When you choose to follow God with all your heart, they may be more willing to put their trust in Jesus.

God shows you mercy. The Bible says in Jonah 1:17, *"The LORD sent a big fish to swallow Jonah"* (GW). That doesn't sound like mercy, but it was. Jonah was tossed overboard in a storm—but he lived because God sent a big fish to swallow him up.

Some people think that if they return to God and embrace his mission, he'll punish them for all the time they wasted. That's just not true! He wants you to fulfill your mission, so he will welcome you back with open arms.

God can take whatever you give to him and turn it into something miraculous.

FEBRUARY 28

When You Feel Hopeless, Pray Passionately

I cried out to the L*ORD in my great trouble, and he answered me.*
I called to you from the land of the dead, and L*ORD, you heard me!*

JONAH 2:2 (NLT)

When you pray, do you only tell God what you think he wants to hear? Or do you have a pattern you tend to follow without really thinking about it? Maybe you start with a simple, "Hi, God. How's it going?" Then you move forward with a predictable prayer that sounds a whole lot like the last time you prayed.

But God isn't looking for a trite, memorized, mechanical prayer that you don't really mean. He gets bored with prayers like that. Instead, God wants you to pray with sincerity and passion.

Jonah can teach us a lot about how to pray passionately. As he dropped down into the ocean and was swallowed by a large fish, he said, *"I cried out to the LORD in my great trouble, and he answered me. I called to you from the land of the dead, and LORD, you heard me!"* (Jonah 2:2, NLT).

As a parent, I always knew when my children said something they didn't mean. God does too. I can't imagine Jonah praying mechanically from inside of the fish, "Now I lay me down to sleep." Jonah didn't pray that way. Instead, he *"cried out to the LORD."* His prayer probably sounded something like, "God! I need help right now!"

God answers sincere prayers, including frantic, emotional ones that we pray in the middle of a crisis. He wants you to pray what's on your heart. God even wants to hear your complaints. In the Bible, that's called *lamenting*; it's another word for complaining. He is interested in every detail of your life—even when you're not happy.

Many of the psalms are laments, or prayers of complaint to God. There's even a book of the Bible called Lamentations, and it's full of the prophet Jeremiah's complaints. God cares about your pain. He wants to hear what's on your heart. He would rather listen to your complaints than to a polite prayer you don't really mean.

If you find yourself in a desperate situation right now (if not, then you will at some point), skip the rote prayer. Share your heart with God.

He wants to hear it.

MARCH 1

Don't Let the Fear of Failure Hold You Back

God did not give us a spirit that makes us afraid
but a spirit of power and love and self-control.
2 TIMOTHY 1:7 (NCV)

Just three months after Kay and I got married, I had a total physical and mental breakdown and ended up in the hospital. I was filled with the fear of failure, and I thought my life was over—though I was just twenty-one years old. The psychiatrist at the hospital told me that I needed to take some time off.

So we went to my parents' home in northern California, where I continued to feel like a total failure. I thought I couldn't handle anything. Everything made me upset and nervous.

Then one night I had a dream that felt evil. I woke up in a cold sweat. As I was lying there in bed, breathing fast, I heard the phone ring. My mom picked it up. The guy on the phone said, "Is this the house where Rick Warren is? Could I talk to him?"

When I picked up the phone, the man said, "Rick, you don't know me. We've never met. How I got this number doesn't really matter. But I live in San Diego, and God told me to call you and give you this verse: *'God did not give us a spirit that makes us afraid but a spirit of power and love and self-control'* [2 Timothy 1:7, NCV]. And, Rick, you have a right in Jesus Christ to a sound mind." And then he hung up.

You don't think God uses people in that way? Well, he does. It could have been an angel, but it didn't have to be. Maybe God just said to a man, "Call that guy." And, in obedience, he did.

I held on to that verse during that year of depression when I thought I was such a failure, even though my life had barely even started. But God wasn't done with me, and he's done many things in my life since then.

God is not done with you either. It doesn't matter what you've been through. I'm sorry for all the pain you may have experienced, but you cannot let fear hold you back. Push yourself to trust God in everything you do. Then live in faith and love.

MARCH 2

God Grows Your Faith through Prayer

Ask and it will be given to you; seek and you will find;
knock and the door will be opened to you.
MATTHEW 7:7 (NIV)

God is *able* and *eager* to meet our needs! But sometimes we forget how committed God is to helping us. Then we stop asking for his help and start depending on ourselves.

Perhaps you only ask God for the "big stuff," not the "small stuff." Guess what? Everything is small to God. None of your requests are big in God's eyes. He has every hair on your head numbered, and he knows how many fell out in the sink this morning.

You're not bothering God with your requests; he's the one who set up the system of prayer. That's why the New Testament tells you more than twenty times to ask for whatever you need in prayer. Matthew 7:7 says, *"Ask and it will be given to you; seek and you will find; knock and the door will be opened to you"* (NIV).

Sometimes, instead of asking God for something, you just worry about it. But if it's big enough to worry about, it's big enough to pray about. Worry won't solve anything, but prayer will.

God grows your faith and your trust the same way a parent teaches a child to trust. The Bible says, *"If you . . . know how to give good gifts to your children, how much more will your heavenly Father give . . . to those who ask him"* (Luke 11:13, NLT).

Here's how it works between a parent and child. First, the child recognizes an unmet need. Second, the child expresses that need. Third, the parent meets that need.

God uses this same cycle to teach you how to trust him. You have an unmet need. You express that unmet need to God. He meets that need, and you learn to trust him more. If you're not expressing your needs to God, how can you grow in trust? When you ask God, he will always prove his goodness.

Go ahead—try it today. Take your needs to God in prayer. Then watch for the ways he answers your prayers and meets your needs. You'll learn to trust that God is reliable and that you can count on him, no matter what.

MARCH 3

Be Who God Created You to Be

We don't try to trick anyone or distort the word of God.
2 CORINTHIANS 4:2 (NLT)

Nothing is more discouraging than trying to be something you're not.

Maybe you maintain a facade because you're afraid that other people will find out who you are or that God might not love you. But when you live this way, you miss out on God's best for your life.

God didn't make you to be a fake or a phony. If you want God's blessing on your life, then you have to stop living for the approval of other people and start being who God made you to be. When you get to heaven, he isn't going to ask, "Why weren't you more like your sister or the popular kid or your successful friend?" He's going to hold you accountable for how you fulfilled his purposes for *your* life.

The world doesn't need two of you or anybody else. But the world *does* need you to do the work God has for you on earth. He shaped you and gifted you in a unique way, and we're all missing out if you decide to be anyone but yourself.

Paul said in 2 Corinthians 4:2, *"We don't try to trick anyone or distort the word of God"* (NLT). In other words, we're not putting on a disguise or a mask. We're not pretending we're something we're not. And we teach the truth of God's Word plainly, reflecting who we really are as followers of Christ.

Nothing is more discouraging than trying to please everybody. I've been on the cover of *Newsweek* magazine twice, once as the hero and once as a zero. That's just life! Even God can't please everyone. When somebody's praying for a snow day, somebody else is praying for blue skies.

If you're always trying to be something you're not, then you'll be stressed, afraid of being found out, and prone to discouragement.

To defeat discouragement, be authentic. You don't have to be perfect for God to bless you—just be who he made you to be.

MARCH 4

Are You Telling Yourself the Truth?

Those who are dominated by the sinful nature think about sinful things, but those who are controlled by the Holy Spirit think about things that please the Spirit.

ROMANS 8:5 (NLT)

Have you ever felt like you are a hostage to your thoughts? Maybe you can't get a certain thought out of your mind. Or you know something is not good for you, but you do it anyway.

Romans 7:23 says, *"I see a different law at work in my body—a law that fights against the law which my mind approves of. It makes me a prisoner to the law of sin which is at work in my body"* (GNT). There's a battle in your mind, and if you're not actively fighting against your old nature, then you're losing the battle.

Your old nature—who you were before Jesus changed your life—is not your friend. It is the source of all your self-defeating habits.

Do you want to break those habits and have more control over the way you think? Then you need to remember this truth: You don't have to believe everything you think.

Your mind lies to you all the time. Just because you think or feel something doesn't make it true. Part of spiritual growth is learning to know the difference between thoughts that are true and those that are not.

One of the most important disciplines you can learn is how to challenge your own thoughts. Ask yourself, "Is what I'm thinking really true?"

No matter how much you grow spiritually, your old, sinful nature will keep trying to take control of your thoughts. You have to learn to question your thoughts throughout your day—and throughout your life!

When you start thinking things like "Life will never get better" or "I'm worthless," ask yourself if those things are really true. Then replace those thoughts with truth from God's Word.

As Romans 8:5 says, *"Those who are dominated by the sinful nature think about sinful things, but those who are controlled by the Holy Spirit think about things that please the Spirit"* (NLT).

MARCH 5

A Powerful Prayer for When You Feel Powerless

We are helpless in the face of this large army that is attacking us. We do not know what to do, but we look to you for help.

2 CHRONICLES 20:12 (GNT)

Breakthrough prayers are different from other prayers.

You likely often pray and ask God for his help, strength, or wisdom. When you say, "God, I need your help," that means you still think you can accomplish something with God's help. And there's nothing wrong with those prayers!

But in a breakthrough prayer, you say, "God, I can't possibly do this. It's beyond my ability. I need you to do it!" It's the prayer you pray when you feel powerless.

In the face of insurmountable odds, King Jehoshaphat turned his focus to God and said, *"We are helpless in the face of this large army that is attacking us. We do not know what to do, but we look to you for help"* (2 Chronicles 20:12, GNT).

You should do the same thing when you're praying for a breakthrough in your life. First, you tell God exactly how you feel. Do you feel powerless, like you've been battling something constantly without any change? Tell God about it! Tell him it feels hopeless and admit your weakness. You don't have to be powerful or know everything if you're connected to God—because he's all-powerful and all-knowing. You don't have to be in every place if you're connected to God—because he is everywhere.

What should you do when you're in a situation that you cannot control, change, or manage? You should wait, trusting in all the things you know to be true about God. Sometimes faith means doing nothing. You just stand still, you wait, and you trust. If you try to do something about it, it puts control back in your court.

Here's what faith looked like for King Jehoshaphat's people: *"All the men of Judah, with their wives and children and little ones, stood there before the LORD"* (2 Chronicles 20:13, NIV). By simply standing before God, they were showing that what they were facing was too big for them. They were at the end of their rope, but they kept hanging on because they trusted God to provide.

When you're in need of a breakthrough, follow their example. Wait, watch, and trust.

MARCH 6

God's Trying to Talk to You

Do not be afraid! Don't be discouraged by this mighty army, for the battle is not yours, but God's.

2 CHRONICLES 20:15 (NLT)

Prayer is a conversation, not a monologue. When you pray, don't do all the talking! You can't build a friendship with God if you don't let him talk to you.

How do you let God talk to you? Through the Bible. Much of what God wants to say to you is already in his Word. People are always looking for some sign, thinking, "I wish God would tell me what he wants me to do. I wish he would write it in the sky." God is not going to write his will in the sky, because he's already written it in a book.

Stop looking for a sign and start looking at Scripture. Stop looking for a vision and start looking for a verse. God's will is in God's Word. The more you read the Bible, the more you're going to know what to do.

King Jehoshaphat was facing three enemy armies that teamed up and advanced against him and the people of Judah. They knew that, in their own power, they would be defeated. So they prayed for help. This is what God said to them through one of his people: *"'Do not be afraid! Don't be discouraged by this mighty army, for the battle is not yours, but God's. . . . You will not even need to fight. Take your positions; then stand still and watch the LORD's victory. He is with you, O people of Judah and Jerusalem. Do not be afraid or discouraged. Go out against them tomorrow, for the LORD is with you!' Then King Jehoshaphat bowed low with his face to the ground. And all the people of Judah and Jerusalem did the same, worshiping the LORD"* (2 Chronicles 20:15, 17-18, NLT).

Imagine an entire nation bowing down, with their faces to the ground, and worshiping God because he told them he would take care of it. Jehoshaphat and the people believed what God promised them, and it caused them to worship, not worry. When you believe what God has promised you, he will take care of it for you too.

God has so many amazing promises for you. But you'll never know about them until you open the Bible and start reading.

MARCH 7

You Can't Talk People Out of Their Pain

Then they sat on the ground with him for seven days and nights. No one said a word to Job, for they saw that his suffering was too great for words.

JOB 2:13 (NLT)

If you're in a hurry, then you can't be a great listener. Great conversations require an investment of time.

Job was a wealthy man who'd lost virtually everything, including his money, health, and even his children. *"When three of Job's friends heard of the tragedy he had suffered, they got together and traveled from their homes to comfort and console him. . . . Then they sat on the ground with him for seven days and nights. No one said a word to Job, for they saw that his suffering was too great for words"* (Job 2:11, 13, NLT).

Job's friends offered the ministry of presence. When you're ministering to someone in pain, you must remember: The deeper their pain, the fewer words you use. If somebody's having a bad hair day, then you can talk about it for thirty minutes. But if that person has a major crisis, talking about it for a long time usually won't help.

You may not know how to help someone in crisis. So maybe you typically just stay away because you're afraid of saying the wrong thing.

The truth is that you don't need to say anything to a friend who's hurting. Just show up and be present! You can't talk people out of their pain, because some pain is beyond words. When it's the right time, both you and your friend will be able to say something.

This kind of investment takes time. Job's friends sat on the ground with him for seven days and nights. Do you have anyone in your life who would sit silently with you for seven days? That takes a very mature person and a true friend.

To be the kind of friend who gives people the love, attention, and presence they need in their pain, you have to be willing to invest your time.

MARCH 8

Look Past Their Words to Their Feelings

Sympathize with each other. Love each other as brothers and sisters. Be tenderhearted, and keep a humble attitude.

1 PETER 3:8 (NLT)

What people *say* in a conversation is not nearly as important as what they *feel.* Many times, someone says one thing while feeling another.

If you want to be a great listener, then you need to look past people's words, even when what they're saying is offensive. Hurt people hurt people, and words are an effective weapon.

When people lash out or get defensive, it's often because they're afraid, insecure, or frustrated. Once you recognize those feelings in others, it's much easier to listen to what they're really trying to say.

Words don't always give you the whole picture. Instead, you need to listen for the pain—the experiences that cloud every interaction a person has—and understand that sometimes it has nothing to do with you.

In other words, learning to listen in love means looking past the things people are saying to what they might be feeling. The Bible says it this way: "*Sympathize with each other. Love each other as brothers and sisters. Be tenderhearted, and keep a humble attitude*" (1 Peter 3:8, NLT).

When you're humble, you're open to new ideas. You're willing to consider someone else's feelings and needs above your own. When you're tenderhearted, you choose compassion over a comeback. When you're loving and sympathetic, you don't bite back. If people get angry with you, you look past their anger and ask, "What are they afraid of? What are they anxious about? What has hurt them? What do they need me to understand?"

You won't always know people well enough to figure out exactly what's pressing on their nerves or going on with their emotions. But you can give them the benefit of the doubt. You can choose to act with humility and kindness over needing to have the last word. You can give people grace instead of getting even.

Even when faced with harsh words, a great listener always chooses love.

MARCH 9

Are You Doing What You're Hearing?

Be doers of the word, and not hearers only, deceiving yourselves.
JAMES 1:22 (ESV)

God wants you to focus on *doing* what he tells you to do, not just on *hearing* what he tells you to do. He calls you to be an active follower of Jesus, not a passive listener. As James 1:22 says, *"Be doers of the word, and not hearers only, deceiving yourselves"* (ESV).

The truth is, you can listen to sermons and study the Bible for decades. But if you never do anything about what you've heard and learned, then you're not growing more like Christ.

The Bible says, *"All Scripture is given by inspiration of God, and is profitable for doctrine, for reproof, for correction, for instruction in righteousness, that the man of God may be complete"* (2 Timothy 3:16-17, NKJV).

That verse points to four things about God's Word. The Bible shows you the path to walk on; that's doctrine. It shows you where you got off the path; that's reproof. It shows you how to get back on the path; that's correction. And it shows you how to stay on the path; that's instruction in righteousness. God's Word is practical, real-world truth.

The problem is that most of us know a lot more than we put into practice. You say you believe in forgiveness, but do you forgive people who've hurt you? You say you believe in waiting on God, but are you patient?

God doesn't want you to just take notes and say you believe things about his Word. He wants you to be a *doer* of his Word.

Jesus said in Matthew 28:20, *"Teach them to do everything I have commanded you"* (GW). He didn't say, "Teach them to know everything I commanded you," or "Teach them to think about everything I commanded you." He said, "Teach them to *do*."

Don't fool yourself into thinking that hearing God's Word also means you're applying God's Word. Make plans to do something about what you hear so that you can grow into the person God created you to be.

MARCH 10

You Can't Lose What Jesus Has Secured

My sheep hear my voice, and I know them, and they follow me. I give them eternal life, and they will never perish, and no one will snatch them out of my hand.

JOHN 10:27-28 (ESV)

You cannot lose your salvation. Just as Jesus saves you from your sins, he also guarantees that your salvation is secure.

Jesus promised in John 10:27-28, *"My sheep hear my voice, and I know them, and they follow me. I give them eternal life, and they will never perish, and no one will snatch them out of my hand"* (ESV).

There are evil forces in the world that want to lure God's children away. Like any loving father, God doesn't want to lose any of his children—and he won't. You are secure in God's promise of salvation.

One of the biggest lies Satan whispers is that, if you commit your life to Christ, you won't be able to keep that commitment. And it leads some people to think, "There are so many temptations in my life, I doubt that I can keep myself saved."

But you don't have to work to keep yourself saved. Once you accept Jesus as Lord and Savior of your life, no one can take your salvation away from you, no matter what.

Nothing you do will ever make God love you less, and nothing you do will ever make God love you more than he loves you right now. Jesus' dying on the cross shows you just how much God loves you.

You can lose a lot of things in life. You may lose your family, your job, your health, or your mind. But the one thing you can never lose is your salvation. Jesus guarantees you have eternal security. You can faithfully trust he will take you to heaven to live with God forever one day.

The apostle Paul said of Jesus, *"I know the one in whom I trust, and I am sure that he is able to guard what I have entrusted to him until the day of his return"* (2 Timothy 1:12, NLT).

MARCH 11

Jesus Is Praying for You

My prayer is not for the world, but for those you have given me, because they belong to you. All who are mine belong to you, and you have given them to me, so they bring me glory.

JOHN 17:9-10 (NLT)

Did you know that Jesus constantly prays for you? The Bible says repeatedly that Jesus is praying for you all the time.

"Wait a minute," you might be thinking. "Isn't Jesus God? How can he pray to himself?"

But think about it: You talk to yourself all the time! That's because you are made in God's image. Jesus *is* God; he's part of the Trinity—Father, Son, and Holy Spirit. And he is talking to himself about you all the time. You are precious to him. You are the object of his affection. Of course he thinks and talks about you!

Even before Jesus died on the cross, he was praying for you. John 17:9-10 says, *"My prayer is not for the world, but for those you have given me, because they belong to you. All who are mine belong to you, and you have given them to me, so they bring me glory"* (NLT).

God is constantly hearing Jesus say, "Help her, Lord. Help him, Lord. Help that family, Lord. Help that relationship, Lord." This is called interceding, and it means to advocate on behalf of someone.

Jesus has been interceding for you every moment of your life. He can do that because he's God. He doesn't get confused or overwhelmed. Your circumstances aren't too much for him. He is your Advocate who sits at the right hand of the Father in heaven *"and is also interceding for us"* (Romans 8:34, NIV). Every time you sin, Jesus leans over and reminds the Father that he already paid for that one; it's covered.

Because Jesus is interceding for you, you can pray a simple prayer anytime, even if you don't know what else to pray. Just say, "Jesus, thank you for praying for me right now—because I'm really struggling."

And you can find comfort in knowing that Jesus is always thinking of you and praying for you.

MARCH 12

When You Do What You Know Is Wrong

Whoever walks in integrity walks securely,
but whoever takes crooked paths will be found out.
PROVERBS 10:9 (NIV)

When making decisions, you need the integrity test. Why?

The Bible says, *"Whoever walks in integrity walks securely, but whoever takes crooked paths will be found out"* (Proverbs 10:9, NIV). If you don't walk with integrity, your wrongs will be discovered.

You pass the integrity test when your public life and your private life match. It's when the desires of your heart match the way you live your life. You ask yourself, "Would I want everyone to know about this decision I'm making?" The truth is, when it comes to integrity, even if you can fool everyone else, you can't fool yourself. You often violate your own conscience.

Sometimes we know we're about to do the wrong thing. We know we shouldn't do it, but we think we might as well go ahead and do it anyway. We convince ourselves it's not a big deal because we know God is a forgiving God.

Do you think you can do something that God says is wrong and not have consequences in your life? That's the very reason God *doesn't* want you to make that decision. It's not to keep you from having fun but rather to keep you from the negative consequences that he knows come with every bad decision. He knows they will leave scars in your life, and he wants something better for you because he loves you.

That doesn't mean, of course, that God doesn't forgive us for the wrong things we do. He is a forgiving and gracious God.

It just means that forgiveness won't free you from the pain and the consequences that often come from bad decisions. You can be forgiven and still have regrets. You can be forgiven and still face pain. You can be forgiven and still have a broken relationship.

God created you, and he knows what's necessary for you to live a full and purposeful life. When you apply the integrity test to your decisions, it reveals you are trusting in God's Word to show you the right way and to guide your steps.

MARCH 13

Is That Really the Best Use of Your Life?

Be very careful how you live. Do not live like those who are not wise. Live wisely. I mean that you should use every chance you have for doing good, because these are evil times. So do not be foolish with your lives. But learn what the Lord wants you to do.

EPHESIANS 5:15-17 (ICB)

If you want to make an impact with your life, then you've got to get control of your time. Your time is your life. When you don't learn to manage your time, you limit the legacy of your life.

Ephesians 5:15-17 says, *"Be very careful how you live. Do not live like those who are not wise. Live wisely. I mean that you should use every chance you have for doing good, because these are evil times. So do not be foolish with your lives. But learn what the Lord wants you to do"* (ICB).

We all have the same amount of time every week. It's what you do with it that counts! If you're always wasting your time, then you're wasting your life, because your time *is* your life. Before you do something, stop and ask, "Is this the best use of my time? Is this the best use of my life?" You don't have time for everything. The good news is that God doesn't expect you to do everything. There are only a few things worth doing in the first place.

Effective people figure out what's essential in life and what's trivial, and they spend more time doing the essential things and less time doing the trivial things. You can't eliminate all that's trivial in your life, but you can reduce it.

This sounds easy, but it's often difficult to choose between what's best for your life and what's easiest for your life—especially when you're tired. When you're tired, you don't want to do the best thing. You want to do what's easy. That's why you need to get adequate rest. If you don't, you won't have the mental, emotional, and physical strength to say, "I'm going to do the right thing instead of the easiest thing."

Don't waste your life. Don't settle for second best. You were not created to just coast. God made you for a mission. So start spending your time doing what is best and helps you accomplish God's purpose for your life.

MARCH 14

Learn to Relax in Your Limitations

We have this treasure from God, but we are like clay jars that hold the treasure. This shows that the great power is from God, not from us.
2 CORINTHIANS 4:7 (NCV)

You'll always get discouraged when you try to be a superhero and do more than is humanly possible. You need a more realistic view of yourself: You can't fix everybody's problems. You can't be in more than one place at a time. You can't do everything you want to do. And you can't spend money you don't have.

You need to learn to relax in your limitations. Anytime you live outside the limitations of your life, you're going to get discouraged. It's easier to fill your schedule than it is to *fulfill* your schedule. It's always easier to get in than it is to get out. It's easier to make a promise than to keep a promise. It's always easier to get into debt than it is to get out of debt.

Often the first signs of living an overextended life show up in your body. Why? Because our bodies are like clay jars. We crack easily, so we need to know our limits. The apostle Paul said in 2 Corinthians 4:7, *"We have this treasure from God, but we are like clay jars that hold the treasure. This shows that the great power is from God, not from us"* (NCV). In other words, you need to recognize the warning signs when you're overextended and realize you're just the vessel and God is the power.

It's amazing to think that God often puts his greatest gifts in the weakest people, giving us the opportunity to point back to him and say, "That's got to be God. That could have only happened through God's power."

Throughout history, God has used flawed instruments to put his glory on display. Nothing would get done if God only used perfect people—because there aren't any!

Though you may think it's best to hide your weaknesses, God wants to use them in your life. But first, you've got to recognize and respect your limitations. Then you trust in God's power, not your own, to accomplish his purpose for you.

MARCH 15

Commit to Jesus and His Family

The human body has many parts, but the many parts make up one whole body. So it is with the body of Christ.

1 CORINTHIANS 12:12 (NLT)

God never meant for you to go through life on your own. He wants you to be part of his family—the church. In fact, the church has been God's plan from the very beginning.

Some people think of the church as a building, an institution, or an event you attend. The church isn't any of those things. It's a family you belong to. The Bible says, *"His unchanging plan has always been to adopt us into his own family by sending Jesus Christ to die for us. And he did this because he wanted to!"* (Ephesians 1:5, TLB).

When you're part of the church, two things are true of you: You're committed to Jesus, and you're committed to the people in your church family. The Bible says in 2 Corinthians 8:5, *"First they gave themselves to the Lord; and then, by God's will they gave themselves to us as well"* (GNT).

You give yourself to the Lord, and then you give yourself to a group of people in God's family. The first choice makes you a Christian. The second choice connects you with other believers. I'm not the church. You're not the church. But together, we are the church—the body of Christ.

What does it mean to be part of the body of Christ? The Bible says, *"The human body has many parts, but the many parts make up one whole body. So it is with the body of Christ"* (1 Corinthians 12:12, NLT). To understand how the church operates, look at the way God designed your body. Your hand, nose, spleen, and liver are all parts of your body. They all have separate functions, but together they make up one physical body—just like God's church makes up one spiritual body.

That's why you are such a necessary part of your church family. You can't say, "My part—my talents and abilities—isn't needed." There are no unnecessary parts. We are all dependent on each other, and each of us has a different role to play.

God's intention from the beginning of time is that we live our lives together in his family. If you want to fulfill your purpose in life, you have to do it in the context of community with God's family. Your church needs you, and you need your church.

MARCH 16

What Real Success Looks Like

Be very careful, then, how you live—not as unwise but as wise, making the most of every opportunity, because the days are evil. Therefore do not be foolish, but understand what the Lord's will is.

EPHESIANS 5:15-17 (NIV)

People who spend their lives serving God experience real success.

Hezekiah lived that way. The Bible says he *"remained faithful to the LORD in everything, and he carefully obeyed all the commands the LORD had given. . . . So the LORD was with him, and Hezekiah was successful in everything he did"* (2 Kings 18:6-7, NLT). Hezekiah was successful in everything he did. Few people are ever that successful, but Hezekiah was because he always did what God wanted him to do. He knew his purpose, and he obeyed God.

But one day Hezekiah became ill, and God told him he was going to die. The Bible says, *"When Hezekiah heard this, he turned his face to the wall and prayed to the LORD, 'Remember, O LORD, how I have always been faithful to you and have served you single-mindedly, always doing what pleases you.' Then he broke down and wept bitterly"* (Isaiah 38:2-3, NLT).

Imagine saying to God, "God, I'd like a few more years here on earth, because I've served you faithfully." That's exactly what Hezekiah did—and God agreed with him and said, *"I have heard your prayer and seen your tears. I will add fifteen years to your life"* (Isaiah 38:5, NLT).

God gave Hezekiah fifteen more years of life because he had made the most of the previous years. He was a good steward of all that God had given him. He had not wasted his life.

Being a good steward of what God gives you doesn't necessarily mean you'll have a longer life—but it does mean you'll have a truly successful life. Because, in God's eyes, good stewardship *is* success. Ephesians 5:15-17 says, *"Be very careful, then, how you live—not as unwise but as wise, making the most of every opportunity, because the days are evil. Therefore do not be foolish, but understand what the Lord's will is"* (NIV).

Maybe you haven't always lived your life the way God intended. Just tell God that you want to start using your life for the purposes he created you for. It's never too late to start!

MARCH 17

The Reason You Are Fully Capable

I can do everything through Christ, who gives me strength.
PHILIPPIANS 4:13 (NLT)

God says you are competent and fully capable of becoming exactly who he made you to be.

In fact, every believer in Christ is a priest! The Bible says, *"You are royal priests. . . . As a result, you can show others the goodness of God, for he called you out of the darkness into his wonderful light"* (1 Peter 2:9, NLT).

What are you supposed to do as a priest? God says, *"I am sending you . . . to open their eyes, so they may turn from darkness to light and from the power of Satan to God. Then they will receive forgiveness for their sins and be given a place among God's people, who are set apart by faith in me"* (Acts 26:17-18, NLT).

I developed the PEACE Plan because of this truth that every believer is a priest. The PEACE Plan wasn't created for pastors only. It was created for every believer around the world to serve in the following ways: Promote reconciliation and plant churches, Equip ethical leaders, Assist the poor, Care for the sick, and Educate the next generation. In doing this, the church shows love to people affected by spiritual darkness, corruption, poverty, disease and sickness, and illiteracy.

Because Christ lives in you, you are fully capable of doing these things—but not based on your own power. Philippians 4:13 says, *"I can do everything through Christ, who gives me strength"* (NLT). And 2 Corinthians 3:5 says, *"Not that we are competent in ourselves to claim anything for ourselves, but our competence comes from God"* (NIV). You can't do everything in your own strength. But you can do everything God has called you to do with his power.

Yet many people live with a gnawing sense of insecurity. They don't feel capable, often because they still believe negative things people said to them years ago. But those things weren't true then, and they aren't true now.

Here's what is true about you: If you are a Christian, then you are God's child, you have his Spirit inside you, you're a priest, and you can do everything through Christ. In him, you are fully capable.

MARCH 18

Five Reasons to Serve God

Whatever you did for one of the least of these brothers and sisters of mine, you did for me.

MATTHEW 25:40 (NIV)

How do you serve God? By serving others.

Jesus said, *"Whatever you did for one of the least of these brothers and sisters of mine, you did for me"* (Matthew 25:40, NIV). When you do something that makes someone else's life better in some way, you're serving God.

Here are five things the Bible says about serving God:

Serving is one of your life's purposes. Mark 8:35 says, *"Only those who throw away their lives for my sake and for the sake of the Good News will ever know what it means to really live"* (TLB). Until you learn how to serve, you're not really living—you're just existing.

Serving makes you more like Jesus. *"Even the Son of Man came not to be served but to serve others and to give his life as a ransom for many"* (Matthew 20:28, NLT). If you don't learn how to serve others, then you will never grow to spiritual maturity.

Serving is the highest use of your time. The Bible says, *"Always give yourselves fully to the work of the Lord"* (1 Corinthians 15:58, NIV). If you want to make an impact and leave a legacy, then serve God by serving others. Your service to the Lord is never wasted.

Serving is the secret to greatness. Matthew 20:26 says, *"If you want to be great, you must be the servant of all the others"* (CEV). True greatness comes from servanthood, not from living for yourself. The greatest leaders are those who serve the most.

Serving will be rewarded in heaven. Jesus said in Colossians 3:24, *"You will receive an inheritance from the Lord as a reward. It is the Lord Christ you are serving"* (NIV). Your real boss, Jesus, will reward you one day for everything you've done for him. That's a guarantee!

If your enthusiasm for serving God could use a boost, then remember how God wants you to serve—not out of guilt, duty, or pressure but out of gratitude for what he's done for you. Gratitude is the best motivation to serve.

MARCH 19

Imagination Takes Courage

If any of you lacks wisdom, you should ask God, who gives generously to all without finding fault, and it will be given to you. But when you ask, you must believe and not doubt, because the one who doubts is like a wave of the sea, blown and tossed by the wind. That person should not expect to receive anything from the Lord.

JAMES 1:5-7 (NIV)

When you were a kid, you had a great imagination. But the older you get, the more your imagination grows rusty. You stop imagining the way things *could* be, and you just start living the way they are. You get stuck in the status quo. Your doubt becomes the enemy of imagination.

Doubt and fear neutralize what God wants to do in your life. It takes courage to imagine, but most people don't use their imaginations, because they're afraid of failure. If you're not afraid, then you don't need courage. Courage is when you're scared to death and you say, "I'm going to do it anyway." You acknowledge the insecurity you're feeling and that you can't do it in your own power—and then you go for it, trusting in God's faithfulness.

During my many years of ministry, every great thing my teams and I accomplished scared me to death. But I wasn't about to let fear dominate my life. So I moved forward, despite my trembling.

You may wonder, "Should I wait until all my doubts are gone?" No! You need to move against your fears and go after God's plans for you. James 1:5-7 says, *"If any of you lacks wisdom, you should ask God, who gives generously to all without finding fault, and it will be given to you. But when you ask, you must believe and not doubt, because the one who doubts is like a wave of the sea, blown and tossed by the wind. That person should not expect to receive anything from the Lord"* (NIV).

Your imagination is either going to be ruled by fear or by faith. It's your choice. If you let fear govern your imagination, then you'll be stressed out and miserable all the time. When you allow fear to control your imagination, you live a miserable life.

Instead, decide that you're going to let faith, not fear, lead the way. Trust God. Then move forward and allow your imagination to be filled with all kinds of possibilities—because all things are possible with God.

MARCH 20

Why Showing Love at Work Matters

The quality of each person's work will be seen when the Day of Christ exposes it. For on that Day fire will reveal everyone's work; the fire will test it and show its real quality.

1 CORINTHIANS 3:13 (GNT)

God wants to use your job to make you more like Jesus. But learning Christlike qualities such as responsibility, character, and love is never easy. To learn those things, you have to respond to people the way Jesus would—and that can be particularly difficult at work.

So why should you make such an effort to become like Jesus in your job?

First, because God is going to evaluate your work one day. The Bible says, *"The quality of each person's work will be seen when the Day of Christ exposes it. For on that Day fire will reveal everyone's work; the fire will test it and show its real quality"* (1 Corinthians 3:13, GNT).

Everything you've done in your career eventually will be seen—because Christ is going to inspect it on the Day of Judgment. On that day, everyone's work will be tested by fire to show the character and quality of what each person has done.

So much of your work may be done without anyone seeing or watching—but God knows. He is watching, and you will give him an account for your work, no matter how menial it seems. You don't have to always get it right. And you certainly don't have to be the best. But you do have to work as if you're doing it for Christ—because you really are.

Second, you should try to become more like Jesus in your work because God is going to give eternal rewards for whatever is done in love. Hebrews 6:10 says, *"God is fair. He won't forget what you've done or the love you've shown for him"* (GW). You need to remember that verse every Monday morning. God is not going to forget how hard you work, how you give your best, and how you show love in his name.

Your work matters to God. One of your purposes in life is to become like Christ. And your job could be one of the most important ways God teaches you to be responsible, to develop character, and to love others. And it could be one of the most significant ways he uses you to bring others to him.

MARCH 21

To Really Change, You Must Know the Truth

Use the truth to make them holy. Your words are truth.

JOHN 17:17 (GW)

If you want to be transformed, you can't be conformed.

The Bible says in 1 Corinthians 3:18-19, *"Don't fool yourself. Don't think that you can be wise merely by being relevant. . . . What the world calls smart, God calls stupid"* (MSG).

If you want God to transform your life, then you have to choose not to conform to what society and culture say you should be or do. But you can't make this life change in your own power.

Changing your life starts by changing the way you think, and that's not something you can do by yourself. Ephesians 4:23 says, *"Let the Spirit renew your thoughts and attitudes"* (NLT).

How does the Holy Spirit do that? Real change requires learning the truth. You may already know these famous words of Jesus: *"You will know the truth, and the truth will set you free"* (John 8:32, NLT).

But did you know that the night before Jesus went to the cross, he prayed, *"Use the truth to make them holy. Your words are truth"* (John 17:17, GW). God uses the truth of his Word, the Bible, to make you complete.

The secret to personal change is not willpower. It's not about making resolutions. The secret to personal change in the hard areas of your life is knowing and applying the truth—which you'll find in God's Word.

If you spend time reading the Bible, soaking your mind with the truth, you'll discover this promise: *"Then we will no longer be like children, forever changing our minds about what we believe because someone has told us something different or . . . made the lie sound like the truth. Instead, we will lovingly follow the truth at all times . . . and so become more and more in every way like Christ who is the Head of his body, the Church"* (Ephesians 4:14-16, TLB).

The more you get to know Jesus, the more truth you'll know. And you'll find yourself moving past the lies you've been believing. You'll grow, change, and transform more into the likeness of Christ. And you'll realize that the truth really does set you free.

MARCH 22

The Cross Makes Prayer Possible

Since he did not spare even his own Son but gave him up for us all, won't he also give us everything else?
ROMANS 8:32 (NLT)

In fairy tales, everyone is willing to die for the king and protect the king at all costs. There is only one story in the world where the King dies for his people. It's called the gospel.

Christianity is marked by a unique storyline, different from every other religion in the world. God says you've sinned and deserve punishment—but that's not the end of the story. This story ends in hope! The Bible says in Romans 6:23, *"For the wages of sin is death, but the gift of God is eternal life in Christ Jesus our Lord"* (NIV).

Because God is just, somebody must pay for your sin. But because he is a good God and he loves you, he made a plan to save you. He came to earth as the Son of God, Jesus Christ, and died for your sins. This is the ultimate expression of love: the King dying for his people, the Shepherd dying for his sheep.

What God did for you at the cross made a way for you to be restored to God. It gives forgiveness for the past, purpose for today, and hope for the future. And it makes prayer possible. *"Since he did not spare even his own Son but gave him up for us all, won't he also give us everything else?"* (Romans 8:32, NLT).

When Jesus Christ died for you on the cross, he solved your biggest problem. Any other problem you have in your life is small to him! If he loved you enough to die for you, don't you think he loves you enough to help you with your bills and your health and your relationships?

Nothing is too big for God. But also, nothing you care about is too small to talk to him about. You can bring everything to God in prayer. He loves you enough to die for you. That means you can be sure he loves you enough to hear and care about your prayers.

The cross makes it possible for you to talk to the Creator of the universe. What will you bring to him in prayer today?

MARCH 23

How Do You Forgive?

What we mean is that God was in Christ, offering peace and forgiveness to the people of this world. And he has given us the work of sharing his message about peace.

2 CORINTHIANS 5:19 (CEV)

In January 1956, five American missionaries headed deep into Ecuador's rainforest. They were visiting the Huaorani tribe, which anthropologists said was earth's most vicious, violent society. Not long after setting up camp near the tribe's settlement, the missionaries were speared to death. The brutal murders of these men, who included Nate Saint and Jim Elliot, made news around the world.

A couple of years later, Elisabeth and Valerie Elliot, wife and daughter of Jim, and Rachel Saint, sister of Nate, moved into the Huaorani village to minister and show love and forgiveness. Eventually the tribe's leader and other men who participated in the missionary murders became Christians. The forgiveness Elisabeth Elliot, Valerie Elliot, and Rachel Saint modeled only makes sense when you have been forgiven by God. So, once you've experienced God's forgiveness, how do you forgive? You do the four things these women did:

Relinquish your right to get even. Romans 12:19 says, *"Don't try to get even. Let God take revenge"* (CEV). Leave it up to God. He'll take care of it, and he'll do a much better job than you ever could.

Respond to evil with good. How can you tell when you've completely forgiven someone? You can actually pray for God to bless the person who hurt you. The Bible says, *"Do good to those who hate you, bless those who curse you, pray for those who mistreat you"* (Luke 6:27-28, NIV).

Repeat these steps as long as necessary. Peter asked Jesus in Matthew 18:21, *"How many times should I forgive someone who does something wrong to me? Is seven times enough?"* (CEV). Jesus replied, *"Not just 7 times, but 77 times!"* (Matthew 18:22, CEV). Sometimes forgiveness has to be continual.

Rescue others with the Good News of God's forgiveness. The Bible says in 2 Corinthians 5:19-20, *"God was in Christ, offering peace and forgiveness to the people of this world. . . . We speak for Christ and sincerely ask you to make peace with God"* (CEV).

Because you've been forgiven by God, he expects you to forgive other people. You don't have to minimize the hurt they've caused—but you also don't have to wait for them to be sorry. When Jesus forgave on the cross, no one had asked for it; he just offered it: *"Father, forgive them, for they do not know what they are doing"* (Luke 23:34, NIV). Whatever your hurt is, Jesus will help you work through it and give you the grace to forgive those who've hurt you.

Forgiveness is rarely the easy choice! It doesn't just take willpower to forgive someone who's hurt you. It takes God's power in you. It requires you to pray, "God, I know you want me to forgive this person. Please give me the strength to do that! I need you to help me surrender my pride and pray for this person so I can see them like you do. Please use me not just to show forgiveness but also to show them that you have forgiven them and want them in your family. In Jesus' name, amen."

Whatever your hurt is, Jesus will help you work through it and give you the grace you need to forgive those who have hurt you.

MARCH 24

Your Biggest Problem, and What to Do about It

It is your evil that has separated you from your God. Your sins cause him to turn away from you, so he does not hear you.
ISAIAH 59:2 (NCV)

Today, most cultures don't think sin is ugly. In fact, many people think sin is fun!

Think about consuming media. TV shows, social media memes, and movies use sin for humor. This is Satan's strategy: to get you to laugh at the same things that put Jesus on the cross. Satan disguises sin to make it look attractive. Rarely in media do you see sin's consequences. If you want to know how ugly sin really is, look at the cross. Jesus' suffering shows how much it takes to pay for your sins. The cross shows the damage sin does.

Sin has all sorts of consequences in your life! Here are three of them.

Sin alienates you from God. Why? Because God is holy, and you are not. Isaiah 59:2 says, *"It is your evil that has separated you from your God. Your sins cause him to turn away from you, so he does not hear you"* (NCV). Sin always leaves estrangement in its wake, even between you and God.

Sin creates significant stress in your life. One of the greatest sources of stress is unrecognized and unresolved guilt. King David said, *"My guilt has overwhelmed me like a burden too heavy to bear"* (Psalm 38:4, NIV). Holding on to sin takes an emotional toll. Breaking God's laws leads to worry, fear, guilt, and insecurity.

Sin condemns you. When you violate God's laws, there's always a penalty—in both self-condemnation and judgment from a righteous God. Psalm 7:11 says, *"God is a righteous judge and always condemns the wicked"* (GNT).

You may think your biggest problem is a relationship conflict, a health issue, or trouble finding a job. But the reality is, your biggest problem is that you're at war with God. That's why you're so frustrated! That's why you don't sleep well. That's why you're stressed out. You weren't made to live out of harmony with your Creator, who loves you. He made you, and he sent his Son to die for you. He wants you to be in harmony with him.

Repent of your sin today—and every day—so that you can be at peace with God.

MARCH 25

Lasting Love Extends Grace

Always be humble and gentle. Be patient with each other, making allowance for each other's faults because of your love.
EPHESIANS 4:2 (NLT)

No relationship will survive without grace. You've got to cut people some slack! You've got to let things go.

The Bible says, *"Love patiently accepts all things"* (1 Corinthians 13:7, NCV). In the original Greek, the basic meaning of the word translated *"patiently accepts"* is to "cover with a roof." Would you buy a house without a roof? Of course not. You'd have no protection from wind and rain. A roof covers and protects your home.

In the same way, biblical love covers a relationship and lets some things slide. It doesn't hold people accountable for every little mistake they make. You need a roof on your relationship because people are damaged pretty easily, and we need the kind of love that extends grace.

Why is grace essential to relationships?

Because we are all sinners. If you're married, you married a sinner—and your spouse did too! Two imperfect spouses will never make a perfect marriage. And it's the same way in friendships. No friendship is perfect—because no friend is perfect. Two imperfect people will never create a perfect relationship.

The Bible says in Romans 3:10, *"There is no one who always does what is right, not even one"* (NCV). Nobody gets it right 100 percent of the time. It's rarely just one person's fault. We all make mistakes, and there's always responsibility on both sides. The saying goes, "It takes two to tango." It also takes two to disagree!

That's why the Bible says we have to learn to extend grace to each other. Forgiveness is a two-way street. We cannot receive what we're unwilling to give to other people.

You build strong relationships by treating other people the way God treats you. Romans 15:7 says, *"Accept each other just as Christ has accepted you"* (NLT). Accepting others may include listening to a friend without judging or giving space to a tired, grumpy family member.

When you accept others as they are, looking past their faults for the sake of love, that's extending grace.

MARCH 26

Is Christianity Worth It?

What profit is there if you gain the whole world—and lose eternal life? What can be compared with the value of eternal life?
MATTHEW 16:26 (TLB)

The apostle Paul said, *"If our hope in Christ is good for this life only and no more, then we [Christians] deserve more pity than anyone else in all the world"* (1 Corinthians 15:19, GNT).

Why did Paul say this? For one thing, it isn't easy to live for Christ in a world that doesn't like Christ.

So here's one of the most important questions you can ever answer: "Is Christianity worth it?" Everything in life has a price tag. Anytime you say yes to something, you're saying no to something else. Is the prize worth the price of following Christ?

Jesus asked, *"What profit is there if you gain the whole world—and lose eternal life? What can be compared with the value of eternal life?"* (Matthew 16:26, TLB). *The Message* paraphrase of the same verse asks it like this: *"What kind of deal is it to get everything you want but lose yourself? What could you ever trade your soul for?"*

People trade their souls for a lot of things—for money, fame, self-centeredness, sex, and materialism, just to name a few. But your soul is worth so much more.

Paul realized this. As he was sharing his testimony, he said, *"I once thought these things were valuable, but now I consider them worthless because of what Christ has done. Yes, everything else is worthless when compared with the infinite value of knowing Christ Jesus my Lord. For his sake I have discarded everything else, counting it all as garbage, so that I could gain Christ"* (Philippians 3:7-8, NLT). Paul realized that nothing—no status, no amount of money, no pleasure—is worth more than Jesus.

We need a new definition of success. Real, meaningful success isn't based on what you have, your appearance, or feeling good. Real success comes from living your life by God's values. And it comes with the ultimate reward of enjoying eternity in heaven.

Reflecting on the sacrifices required to tell unreached people about Jesus, the martyred missionary Jim Elliot said, "He is no fool who gives what he cannot keep to gain that which he cannot lose."

MARCH 27

How to See the Purpose in Your Pain

[Jesus] did not give up because of the cross! On the contrary, because of the joy that was waiting for him, he thought nothing of the disgrace of dying on the cross, and he is now seated at the right side of God's throne.

HEBREWS 12:2 (GNT)

If you're very far into adulthood, you've probably learned that you can handle more pain than you ever thought. In fact, it probably took going through difficult times for you to realize just how much you could handle.

Human beings can stand an enormous amount of pain if they can see a purpose in the pain and a reward past the pain. That's exactly what Jesus did when he went to the cross. He was in excruciating pain, but he looked past the pain to the reward in heaven. He had an eternal perspective.

Jesus wasn't just looking at the here and now. If he was, his future would have looked bleak, and he would have despaired. But Jesus looked past the pain to the reward in heaven. He valued that eternal reward far more than any temporary relief on earth.

When you're in pain and just looking at the here and now, you can get discouraged and depressed. Sometimes you may feel like giving up. The only way you're going to make it through the toughest times in life is to look past the pain to the reward in heaven.

Hebrews 12:2 says, *"[Jesus] did not give up because of the cross! On the contrary, because of the joy that was waiting for him, he thought nothing of the disgrace of dying on the cross, and he is now seated at the right side of God's throne"* (GNT).

Jesus endured the shameful pain on the cross because he knew of the joy that would be his afterward. The greatest joy for Jesus—and us—is the hope of an eternity in heaven, where we will be in God's presence forever.

When you get the mind of Christ, you begin to think the way Jesus does—about your past, your present, your future, God, life, death, sin, salvation, your friends, and your confidence. You realize there's more to life than just the here and now, and that gives you the strength to endure.

MARCH 28

It Is Finished

After this, Jesus knew that everything had been done.
So that the Scripture would come true, he said, "I am
thirsty." . . . When Jesus tasted the vinegar, he said,
"It is finished." Then he bowed his head and died.

JOHN 19:28, 30 (NCV)

During his earthly ministry, Jesus repeatedly said that he came to do the work God gave him to do.

And the Bible says this about when he was dying on the cross: *"After this, Jesus knew that everything had been done. So that the Scripture would come true, he said, 'I am thirsty.' . . . When Jesus tasted the vinegar, he said, 'It is finished.' Then he bowed his head and died"* (John 19:28, 30, NCV). When Jesus said, *"It is finished,"* it was a shout of victory. The phrase is a single word in the original Greek: *tetelestai*. It was a common word in ancient Greek society, with many meanings, and Jesus embodied each of them:

- It was used by servants and employees who returned to their master with news they had finished the task. Jesus had finished the task God had given him.
- It was a legal word judges used to announce that a prisoner had completely served his prison time. Jesus made sure that justice had been served for our sin.
- It was a word used in accounting to indicate a debt had been paid in full. Jesus completely paid our sin debt.
- Artists used the word when painting a picture to denote their final stroke. Jesus' sacrifice finished God's great masterpiece, making it possible for us to be redeemed from our sin.
- Priests used the word when they offered a sacrifice to God to declare, "The sacrifice has been made." Jesus' death on the cross was the sacrifice for our sin.

That one single word—*tetelestai*—separates Christianity from every other religion. All other religions are about what you need to do to be right with God. Christianity is about what God has already done on your behalf.

Jesus said, *"It is finished."* You don't need to do anything to have access to God. He's done everything!

MARCH 29

God Is a Caring Father

As bad as you are, you know how to give good things to your children. How much more, then, will your Father in heaven give good things to those who ask him!
MATTHEW 7:11 (GNT)

Every person needs an answer to one question: "Does anyone care about me?" God's emphatic answer is "Yes!"

In Mark 4, the disciples asked this very question. They were in a boat out on the lake when a storm came up suddenly. As the wind blew harder, they began to sink. Through it all, Jesus was asleep. The disciples woke him up with an important question: *"Teacher, don't you care that we are drowning!"* (Mark 4:38, NCV).

That's the ultimate question people want to know about God. We want to know if he really cares about what is happening to us.

There are many examples in the Bible of God's love and care for us. Jesus showed his love and care for the disciples when they woke him up in the storm. He spoke to the wind and waves and calmed the storm immediately.

God's answer to you is the same: He cares about you. God cares about all the different aspects of your life. He cares about your family, your job, your health—every single detail! If you are a parent, you understand this. You care about every part of your child's life. Their well-being matters to you. Nothing they can do changes that.

Jesus reminds us that the love a parent has for their kids gives us a glimpse of God's love: *"As bad as you are, you know how to give good things to your children. How much more, then, will your Father in heaven give good things to those who ask him!"* (Matthew 7:11, GNT). God is the ultimate loving Father. When you get to know God better, you'll understand more about his love for you—and you won't doubt that he cares about your life.

People who believe all their problems exist because they don't love God enough actually have a different problem: They don't recognize how much *God* loves *them.*

Our love for God is a natural response to how much we believe God cares about us. You can't help but love God once you realize how much he loves you. *"We love because God first loved us"* (1 John 4:19, GNT).

MARCH 30

With the Mind of Christ, You'll Never Feel Alone

I am not really alone, because the Father is with me.

JOHN 16:32 (GNT)

It can seem daunting to *"think the same way that Christ Jesus thought"* (Philippians 2:5, CEV). But part of having the mind of Christ just means always being aware that God is with you.

Even Jesus did this. No matter how busy he was, he stayed in tune with the Father. Jesus said, *"I am not really alone, because the Father is with me"* (John 16:32, GNT).

This is why the greatest antidote to loneliness is thinking like Jesus. When you have the mind of Christ, you're able to say, like Jesus, "I'm not alone, because I know the Father is always with me."

When you feel alone, it's often the result of not living with the mind of Christ and not being aware of God's constant care. One way to stay mindful of God's care is through prayer. Jesus made prayer a daily habit: *"Jesus would often go to some place where he could be alone and pray"* (Luke 5:16, CEV).

Notice this verse says that Jesus *often* slipped away so he could pray. Jesus' prayer life was continual. He made it the priority of his life to be in his Father's presence.

Do you stop and pray throughout the day? If Jesus felt the need to slip away often to pray, then think about how much more we need it!

When you don't take the time to talk with God, you miss his gifts. It's not God's will for you to be too busy for him. In fact, you'll get more done in every area of your life if you take the time to stop and pray. That's because, when you take time to let God's Spirit remind you what your purpose is, you're better able to focus your mind and heart on what matters most.

Jesus knew who he was and what his purpose was. He was always aware of God's presence. When you learn to think like Jesus, you'll have those things, too, and you'll always be aware that God is with you.

MARCH 31

God Can Restore You after You Sin

If you return to me, I will restore you so you can continue to serve me.
JEREMIAH 15:19 (NLT)

When you become a believer in Christ, you are born again into God's family, and you cannot be unborn. Although sin can damage your fellowship with God, it can't take away your relationship. You're always only one step away from returning.

So what should you do when you sin? Return! Come back to Christ. It's that simple. God says, *"No matter how deep the stain of your sins, I can take it out and make you as clean as freshly fallen snow"* (Isaiah 1:18, TLB).

On the night Jesus was arrested, his disciple Peter denied three times that he knew or followed Jesus. If ever there were a sin you'd think was unforgivable, it would be that! But Jesus knew Peter would deny him, and he knew Peter would come back to him. In fact, before it even happened, Jesus said to Peter, *"I have pleaded in prayer for you that your faith should not completely fail. So when you have repented and turned to me again, strengthen and build up the faith of your brothers"* (Luke 22:32, TLB).

Jesus knew Peter's ministry would be more effective after his denial than it was before. And sure enough, it was. Peter wrote two books of the Bible: 1 Peter and 2 Peter. Then he shared his memoirs with the author of the Gospel of Mark.

You may think God has forgotten you. He hasn't. The Good Shepherd leaves the ninety-nine sheep to go after the one. He knows how you've turned away. Maybe it happened in one giant step, or perhaps it was a series of tiny steps.

Whatever it was, you need to pray what David prayed when he returned to God after committing adultery. He said, *"Restore to me the joy of your salvation"* (Psalm 51:12, NLT). David did not have to pray, "God, restore to me my salvation," because he hadn't lost his salvation. He had lost the joy.

Have you lost your joy too? Why not come home to Christ today?

APRIL 1

Jesus Sees, Cares, and Intervenes in Your Struggle

No, I will not abandon you as orphans—I will come to you.

JOHN 14:18 (NLT)

Sometimes you find yourself in situations you don't want and don't like. In fact, on some days you may feel like the storms of life threaten to drown you. So how do you keep from being blown over by life's devastating winds? One way is to remind yourself how much Jesus cares. In fact, Jesus sees your struggle, cares about your struggle—and does something about it.

You can see this pattern of Jesus seeing, caring, and doing in the story of Jesus walking on water: *"Later that night, the boat was in the middle of the lake, and he was alone on land. He saw the disciples straining at the oars, because the wind was against them. Shortly before dawn he went out to them, walking on the lake"* (Mark 6:47-48, NIV).

The disciples had four things going against them: It was dark, they were in the middle of a lake, they were alone, and *"the wind was against them."*

How did Jesus respond? He didn't just stand on the shoreline and tell them what to do. Instead, he walked out to them—on the water—in their moment of desperation. He said, *"Take courage! It is I. Don't be afraid"* (Mark 6:50, NIV). Then Jesus climbed into the boat and the wind calmed down.

That's what Jesus does in your moment of desperation. He cares enough to walk out to where you are—wherever you are—and intervene.

Friends, that's the gospel. God came to earth, became one of us, and died on the cross for our sins. He didn't just shout instructions from heaven. He came to us and said, "I'll solve the problem that you can't solve."

I don't know what you're going through right now. But I will tell you this: You may feel abandoned, but you're not. God sees you, cares for you, and is with you—even in the darkest hour of the stormiest night.

John 14:18 says, *"No, I will not abandon you as orphans—I will come to you"* (NLT).

No matter what problems you're up against, remind yourself that Jesus cares, and let him come to you today.

APRIL 2

Keep Your Prayers Simple

And when you pray, do not keep on babbling like pagans,
for they think they will be heard because of their many words.
. . . Your Father knows what you need before you ask him.
MATTHEW 6:7-8 (NIV)

Longer prayers are not necessarily stronger prayers.

You may be tempted to go on and on when you talk to God in prayer, as if talking more will get more of his attention. But God is listening. And he is much more interested in humble and authentic prayers than a long-winded sermon of a prayer. Just get to the point!

Jesus had a lot to say in the Sermon on the Mount about praying simply and not trying to sound super spiritual: *"And when you pray, do not be like the hypocrites, for they love to pray standing in the synagogues and on the street corners to be seen by others. Truly I tell you, they have received their reward in full. But when you pray, go into your room, close the door and pray to your Father, who is unseen. Then your Father, who sees what is done in secret, will reward you. And when you pray, do not keep on babbling like pagans, for they think they will be heard because of their many words. Do not be like them, for your Father knows what you need before you ask him"* (Matthew 6:5-8, NIV).

You don't have to convince God of what you need. He already knows! Just come to him as simply, honestly, and humbly as you can, and talk about what you need.

Don't use prayer to show off. I'm sure you've seen people who do. But that doesn't mean they get any credit for that kind of prayer. God doesn't want to hear prayers that are meant to get the attention of others. Instead, be sincere. Don't spout off clichés. Don't add in fillers because you're afraid your prayers are too short.

Prayer is an ongoing conversation. You don't have to neatly wrap up every one. You can just pick up where you left off at a later time and keep the conversation open. You can talk to God like you would to a loved one or a good friend.

Adding extra words to your prayer doesn't make it any stronger. Keep it simple, expressing yourself with a sincere heart and sure faith.

APRIL 3

Your Temptation Emergency Plan

Call on me when you are in trouble, and I will rescue you.

PSALM 50:15 (NLT)

Sometimes you're going to need an "emergency plan" for temptation.

When you get in a situation where you're tempted and you don't know what to do, you need to cry out to God.

If you're facing a temptation and you start to panic because you feel the adrenaline rushing through your body, then you won't have time for a long conversation with God. Instead, you can just do what I call a "microwave prayer," and it's one word: *Help!* You tell God, "This is not where I want to be right now, and I'm about to step across the line. I need your help right now."

Of course he knows what's going on. So when all you can do is cry out for help, God will hear your prayer, and he will intervene.

You can know he will help you because the Bible says, *"Call on me when you are in trouble, and I will rescue you"* (Psalm 50:15, NLT).

Cry out to God. When you do, he helps you because he's sympathetic to your situation. The Bible says, *"This High Priest of ours understands our weaknesses, for he faced all of the same testings we do, yet he did not sin"* (Hebrews 4:15, NLT).

Did Jesus ever struggle with anger? Yes. Did Jesus ever wrestle with loneliness? Yes. Did Jesus ever deal with sex and sexuality? Yes. Was he ever tempted by fatigue and discouragement? Yes. How? Because even though he's God, he was God in a fully human body. Jesus became a man and experienced everything we would so that he could intercede for us before God.

Jesus faced the same temptations we do, so we can expect him to help us when we cry out to him. And we don't have to feel shame because his grace sustains us: *"So let us come boldly to the throne of our gracious God. There we will receive his mercy, and we will find grace to help us when we need it most"* (Hebrews 4:16, NLT).

That is a great comfort—and it is the power to change. Just tell God you need his help!

APRIL 4

Settle Your Salvation Today

I assure you, today you will be with me in paradise.
LUKE 23:43 (NLT)

When the criminal hanging next to Jesus on the cross asked Jesus to remember him, Jesus replied, *"I assure you, today you will be with me in paradise"* (Luke 23:43, NLT). With his response, Jesus gave four characteristics of salvation that you can trust and believe in.

First, salvation is immediate. Jesus said, *"Today."* When you die, you either go straight into the presence of God or you go straight into separation from God. And salvation is immediate too. The moment you ask Jesus Christ to save you, it's done.

Second, salvation is certain. He said, *"Today you will."* He didn't say, "You might" or "I hope." His answer wasn't, "Let me think about it."

Jesus said, *"You will."* When you accept Christ, you can be certain of your salvation.

Third, salvation is a relationship. Jesus said, *"You will be with me."* Salvation is not a religion. It's not rules or regulations or rituals. It's a relationship. That relationship doesn't begin when you get to heaven. It begins here on earth. Jesus Christ wants to be your best friend; he wants to talk with you all the time. God made you for a relationship with him!

Fourth, salvation leads to a real place. Jesus said, *"Today you will be with me in paradise."* Heaven is a real place, and it's forever.

Two criminals were crucified with Jesus, one on either side. Jesus gave them the choice of salvation, and he gives you the same choice. He won't force you to love him. He's not going to force you to trust him or accept heaven. One of the two criminals rejected Jesus. The other turned to him in faith. You have the same choice.

Romans 10:13 says, *"Everyone who calls on the name of the Lord will be saved"* (NIV). Do you believe these truths about salvation? Are you ready to call on the name of the Lord? The Bible says, *"This is the hour to receive God's favor; today is the day to be saved!"* (2 Corinthians 6:2, GNT).

Choose to settle the issue of your eternal destiny today. Trust Jesus' promise of salvation.

APRIL 5

Somebody Has to Pay for Sin

Your eyes are too pure to look on evil; you cannot tolerate wrongdoing.
HABAKKUK 1:13 (NIV)

In Greek and Roman mythology, all the gods—like Zeus, Mars, and Apollo—have human frailties. They get angry. They lust. They're impatient. They zap people with lightning bolts. They are inconsistent and unreliable.

But the real God, the God who created the universe, is 100 percent pure, just, and unpolluted. He's never done anything wrong, impure, or imperfect. He's holy. Habakkuk 1:13 says, *"Your eyes are too pure to look on evil; you cannot tolerate wrongdoing"* (NIV).

Because God is perfect, you can trust him. But his perfection also means that he cannot stand to be around sin. So, at the cross, God took every sin of the world and poured it all on his perfect Son, Jesus Christ, who volunteered to pay for it.

God sent Jesus to be your substitution. If Jesus hadn't been your substitute on the cross, then you would've had to pay for your own sins. But Jesus satisfied the law. He did what justice demands.

But it wasn't easy for Jesus. In fact, it was torture. You know how guilty you feel over one sin? How would you like to carry the guilt of every sin—from the sins done in secret to the public, horrific ones? That would be mental, physical, emotional, and spiritual torture.

On the cross, Jesus cried out, *"My God, my God, why have you forsaken me?"* (Matthew 27:46, NIV). He was experiencing physical agony—and the torment of being separated from his Father.

A holy God could not stand even to look at his Son, full of the sins of the world. God looked away because he is perfect. Can you imagine what this cost Jesus?

But he was willing to go through that pain because he wanted you to have a way to be in fellowship with a holy God.

Somebody had to take the punishment, and Jesus did it for you. Jesus became your substitute so that, when God looks at you, he doesn't see your sin. He sees the righteousness of Jesus Christ.

And because of that, you can experience both eternal life and a full and purposeful life here on earth.

APRIL 6

What It Means to Have Holy Spirit Power

The power of the life-giving Spirit—and this power is mine through Christ Jesus—has freed me from the vicious circle of sin and death.

ROMANS 8:2 (TLB)

None of us are immune to persistent sins. Some people struggle with anger, while others wrestle with worry or gossip or lust.

How do you break free from persistent sin?

You understand what Jesus has done for you. On the cross, Jesus paid for the penalty of your sins so you don't have to pay for it. All of your sins—even the ones you haven't committed yet—have been paid for on the cross.

Jesus not only paid for your sin, but he also paid to break the *power* of sin in your life. Now you have a power you didn't have before—the power to say no to sin. It's more than willpower. It's Holy Spirit power!

The Bible says in Romans 8:2, *"The power of the life-giving Spirit—and this power is mine through Christ Jesus—has freed me from the vicious circle of sin and death"* (TLB).

If you're a Christian, you know Jesus died to pay for your sin. That's the Good News. And if that was all there was, that would still be the best news in the world. But when he died on the cross, Jesus also took your old sin nature and gave you a new nature, one that no longer has to live in persistent sin. The Bible teaches, *"We know that our old sinful selves were crucified with Christ so that sin might lose its power in our lives. We are no longer slaves to sin"* (Romans 6:6, NLT).

Sin no longer has any power in your life. A dead person can't be tempted! That old nature can't be tempted, and since it died with Christ, you can be confident that you also share in his new life.

Willpower will never be enough to break the power of sin in your life. But thanks to Jesus, you have more than enough power in the Holy Spirit to resist temptation and break *"the vicious circle of sin and death."*

APRIL 7

You Will Find Joy Again

He will give a crown of beauty for ashes, a joyous blessing instead of mourning, festive praise instead of despair.
ISAIAH 61:3 (NLT)

God promises that, for all who mourn, *"he will give a crown of beauty for ashes, a joyous blessing instead of mourning, festive praise instead of despair"* (Isaiah 61:3, NLT).

The greatest example of how God transforms grief into joy is the resurrection of Jesus Christ. After he was crucified, Jesus' disciples went through two days of the deepest fear, pain, and grief anyone could ever experience. Though Jesus had promised his disciples he would come back to life, their grief kept them from grasping the reality of that happening.

But once the disciples saw Jesus resurrected, they understood that sin and death had been defeated. They were released from their fears and anxieties—and in that release, they found joy again.

Your grief is important, and God does not want you to get over it. In fact, he wants to walk with you *through* it. He wants you to remember that he's with you and that your pain will not always cut so deep. As you hold on to God's promises while grieving, you, too, will find release from your fear and anxiety, and you will find joy again.

How can that happen? By relying on God's power—the same power that resurrected Jesus! It can change your ashes into beauty, your grief into joy, and your despair into praise. Your grief will change you. But, by God's grace, it will not cripple you.

In a time of grief, reach out for the one thing that is absolutely certain: the forgiveness and hope found only in Jesus.

That's how we get God's power—*"by placing our faith in Jesus Christ. And this is true for everyone who believes, no matter who we are. For everyone has sinned; we all fall short of God's glorious standard. Yet God, in his grace, freely makes us right in his sight. He did this through Christ Jesus when he freed us from the penalty for our sins"* (Romans 3:22-24, NLT).

APRIL 8

On Your Best Days and Worst Days, God Is with You

When you go through rivers of difficulty, you will not drown! When you walk through the fire of oppression, you will not be burned up—the flames will not consume you.

ISAIAH 43:2 (TLB)

Life is filled with unexpected circumstances. And some of them make you feel like the roof just caved in.

What do you do when your world collapses? When the dreaded phone call comes? When the divorce papers arrive? When you file for bankruptcy?

The first question many people ask is, "Who cares about me?"

It's a question the disciples likely asked soon after Jesus was crucified. One evening they met together behind locked doors because they were afraid of the Jewish leaders who had sent Jesus to the cross. They felt like they were alone. And because of that, they expected the worst.

But then this happened: *"Jesus came and stood among them and said, 'Peace be with you!' After he said this, he showed them his hands and side. The disciples were overjoyed when they saw the Lord"* (John 20:19-20, NIV).

The change was immediate. The presence of Christ turned their panic into praise, their fear into good cheer.

The Bible says, *"The LORD is near to those who are discouraged; he saves those who have lost all hope"* (Psalm 34:18, GNT).

During every moment of your life, from the very best to the very worst, God is with you. He cares for you when you feel hopeless. You will never walk through tough times alone.

He tells you, *"When you go through deep waters and great trouble, I will be with you. When you go through rivers of difficulty, you will not drown! When you walk through the fire of oppression, you will not be burned up—the flames will not consume you"* (Isaiah 43:2, TLB).

Are you hurting today? Are you asking, "Who cares about me?" Are you afraid that no one does?

You can rest easy today knowing that God cares. He is with you now. He has been with you all along. You are not alone!

APRIL 9

Think about What You Think About

Fools will believe anything, but the wise think about what they do.
PROVERBS 14:15 (NCV)

Every behavior is based on a belief.

If you act scared, it's because you believe you're in a scary situation. If you act resentful, it's because you believe you've been devalued, so you want to defend yourself. If you're acting prideful, you may believe you're not good enough, so you try to compensate by being boastful.

If there is a behavior in your life you don't like or know is wrong, then go to the source and change the thought behind it. God said in Haggai 1:5, *"Carefully consider your ways!"* (GW).

Ask yourself: Why do I act *that* way with this person? Why do I act *this* way at work or school or with certain neighbors? What thought triggered that response? What assumption is behind that action? What belief is beneath that behavior?

Maybe you've been in this kind of conflict before: It starts off simple enough—but before you know it, something in the argument triggers your emotions, and you go from zero to 100 in emotional intensity in two seconds. Then you're out of control, upset, nervous, or fearful. You may start sweating, or your voice may rise. Maybe tears start coming down your cheeks.

Something in that moment tapped into an unspoken belief. You may believe the other person is going to leave you. You may believe you haven't been heard. You may believe your idea isn't being validated and you're not being treated with respect. A belief you hold has triggered an emotional response.

If you're ever in a situation like that, you need to examine the beliefs behind your behavior.

The Bible says in Proverbs 14:15, *"Fools will believe anything, but the wise think about what they do"* (NCV).

To grow in any area of life, examine what's going on in your mind. Start thinking about what you're thinking about so your thoughts can lead to healthy, purposeful action.

APRIL 10

You Need God's Help to Change

As the Spirit of the Lord works within us, we become more and more like him.
2 CORINTHIANS 3:18 (TLB)

Do you need a reset in your life? It won't happen with just human ability. Only God can produce that kind of transformation.

Think of it like this: Someone could make a law that says, "No more prejudice. No more racism. No more bigotry." But no law will turn a bigot into a lover. Only God has the power to do that—because it requires an internal change, and only God can produce lasting transformation in our hearts.

In the same way, you can tell yourself that you're ready to change, that you want to change, that you can change, and that you will change. But nothing will ever happen—nothing that lasts or has eternal significance—without the help of the Holy Spirit. The Bible says in Zechariah 4:6, *"'You will not succeed by your own strength or by your own power, but by my Spirit,' says the LORD All-Powerful"* (NCV).

Just like you can't transform yourself into a tiger, you can't transform yourself to be like Christ. You can't change your life on your own power. Willpower is not enough.

You didn't collect your hurts, habits, and hang-ups overnight, and you're not going to eliminate them overnight either. It's going to take time. In fact, it's going to take the rest of your life! It's a slow process. And on your own, you won't have enough patience and endurance to finish strong.

But there's good news. The Bible promises, *"As the Spirit of the Lord works within us, we become more and more like him"* (2 Corinthians 3:18, TLB).

Change is a lifelong process that requires the Holy Spirit's power. As the Spirit works within you, God transforms you into who you were created to be and makes you more and more like him.

When God wants to make a mushroom, he takes six hours. When he wants a mature oak tree, he takes sixty years. Do you want to be a mushroom or an oak tree?

God wants you to grow into an emotionally mature, spiritually strong, happy, and healthy woman or man of God. It won't happen quickly. But it will happen with the Holy Spirit's help.

APRIL 11

Jesus Chose to Suffer for You

God demonstrates his own love for us in this:
While we were still sinners, Christ died for us.
ROMANS 5:8 (NIV)

Few people are willing to suffer for someone else. But Jesus was. In fact, he didn't suffer for just one person; he chose to suffer for all the people in the world!

John 19 describes some of Jesus' suffering: *"After this, Jesus knew that everything had been done. So that the Scripture would come true, he said, 'I am thirsty.' There was a jar full of vinegar there, so the soldiers soaked a sponge in it, put the sponge on a branch of a hyssop plant, and lifted it to Jesus' mouth"* (verses 28-29, NCV).

Jesus was in agony on the cross—and he was thirsty. He was suffering not just from pain but also from great thirst.

Jesus didn't deserve to suffer for everyone's sin. We each deserve to suffer for our own sins. But Jesus was willing to suffer and thirst for you so that you could go to heaven.

Jesus did nothing wrong. He committed no crimes. He didn't hurt anyone. He lived a perfect life. So why did they kill him?

Jesus died for the redemption of others. He was thirsty on the cross for *your* benefit.

"God demonstrates his own love for us in this: While we were still sinners, Christ died for us" (Romans 5:8, NIV).

Jesus' love for you is so great, so deep, and so wide that he was willing to take your sin as his own and cover it with his righteousness. Your sin cost him his life. *He considers you worth it!*

He suffered so you don't have to. He went through hell on the cross so you don't have to go through hell for eternity. He covered you and protected you from the punishment and pain of being separated from God forever.

Jesus willingly died so you could have eternal life. He chose to suffer to buy your redemption.

You never have to wonder how much God loves you. He's already shown you on the cross!

APRIL 12

Believe God's Word Before You Open God's Word

So get rid of all the filth and evil in your lives, and humbly accept the word God has planted in your hearts, for it has the power to save your souls.

JAMES 1:21 (NLT)

You may not always understand what the Bible says. But to anchor your life on the solid foundation of God's Word, you need to humbly accept whatever God tells you.

James 1:21 says, *"So get rid of all the filth and evil in your lives, and humbly accept the word God has planted in your hearts, for it has the power to save your souls"* (NLT).

The word translated *accept* is a hospitality term. It means to receive like a stranger.

You are to receive God's Word fully into your life. That means before you even open your Bible, you tell God that you accept whatever he tells you. You agree to believe his Word, whether or not you understand it. You trust him.

But in order to accept God's Word, you first have to take care of the *"filth and evil"* stuff in your life. You clean it out! Now, this doesn't mean you need to clean up your life before you can come to God. Instead, it means sin can block you from *hearing* God. You can't hear him when you've got something else filling your mind and heart.

You've got to make space for the truth. Then, believing and applying God's truth will change you and make you more like Jesus.

In the Bible, God often compares our accepting his Word to gardening. He wants us to accept the seeds he is planting in our hearts and minds. But before the seeding and the feeding comes the weeding. Before you meet with God, you have to take out the emotional and spiritual garbage in your life.

How do you do that? You confess and turn away from your sins. You admit to God what you've done that goes against his Word. You ask him for forgiveness and thank him in advance for how he is working in your life.

When you confess and accept and trust God's Word, he can produce understanding of the truth and the fruit of obedience in your life.

APRIL 13

This Is the News You Need

The LORD *will work out his plans for my life—*
for your faithful love, O LORD, *endures forever.*
PSALM 138:8 (NLT)

It's hard to watch or read the news today without getting concerned. The world isn't necessarily in any worse shape than it's ever been. We just know a lot more about it! We have constant access to what's going on in every corner of the world—and not much of what's being reported is encouraging. That leads to stress, anxiety, worry, and fear.

We need to stop freaking out! The news report will tell you what's happening (or at least people's opinions of what's happening). But it won't tell you the best news: God has a master plan. It started before the foundation of the earth, but it was revealed when Jesus Christ came to earth.

All through the Old Testament, God is hinting at his plan. But the people of the Old Testament didn't know the plan like we do. They were looking forward to what God promised. We're looking back because God's big plan has already been revealed. And what's that plan?

"God has now revealed to us his mysterious will regarding Christ—which is to fulfill his own good plan. And this is the plan: At the right time he will bring everything together under the authority of Christ—everything in heaven and on earth" (Ephesians 1:9-10, NLT).

That's why God sent Jesus to earth—to save you from sin so that you could know God and be part of his family forever. And that's why it's the best news ever! When you believe in Jesus Christ as your Savior, he gives you power over death *and* the power you need to pursue righteousness. He gives you purpose as you seek him and choose his plan for your life.

Psalm 138:8 says, *"The* LORD *will work out his plans for my life—for your faithful love, O* LORD, *endures forever"* (NLT).

This is the news the world needs to hear: When you seek God, you'll never be disappointed. As you let him guide you and trust in his plan for your life, you'll discover the joy and peace that come from following God's way—the best way.

God Can Provide through Any Faucet

But remember the LORD your God, for it is he who gives you the ability to produce wealth, and so confirms his covenant, which he swore to your ancestors, as it is today.

DEUTERONOMY 8:18 (NIV)

The Bible teaches that God is the source of our finances. He is the one who provides for our needs.

Deuteronomy 8:18 says, *"But remember the LORD your God, for it is he who gives you the ability to produce wealth, and so confirms his covenant, which he swore to your ancestors, as it is today"* (NIV).

So what does that mean for your everyday life?

It means that instead of looking to your employer for financial security, you look to God. It means that instead of looking to your savings account for financial security, you look to God. Instead of looking to your investments or assets, you look to God. It means that you don't depend on anyone or anything other than God to provide for your needs.

Let me illustrate it this way: When you turn on the water at your kitchen sink, you know the water doesn't actually come from the faucet. The water comes *through* the faucet. The water comes from a reservoir or a well, and the way you happen to receive it is through the faucet.

In the same way, the income that God wants to give you may come through a job or an investment or through something or someone else.

But the source is always God.

You don't need to worry about which faucet God uses to supply your needs. In a sense he says, "If I turn off one faucet, I can just as easily turn on another. If you lose one job, I can give you another. Your job isn't your source. Your bank account isn't your source. I am your source."

Maybe you feel like your faucet has run dry. But because you know God's supply will never run dry, you can trust that he has already chosen another way to provide for you.

Worry reveals the places where we aren't trusting God. Ask him to help you identify those areas where you struggle to trust him. Pray for more faith to trust that he will supply everything you need to do his will.

Then, look for the "faucets" he uses to meet your needs.

APRIL 15

God Uses Time to Help You Grow

At the right time I will hear your prayers.
On the day of salvation I will help you.
ISAIAH 49:8 (NCV)

At the right time, God can do anything instantly. In Isaiah 60:22, God says, *"I am the LORD, and when it is time, I will make these things happen quickly"* (NCV).

This is hard for us to accept, because God's waiting room is sometimes the most difficult place in life. When we're in God's waiting room, we're often in a hurry for something to happen—but God isn't. Maybe you're in a hurry to graduate or get married or close a big deal. Or you're waiting for test results or for information to make an important decision. You're watching the time get shorter and shorter, and you think, "God, there isn't a whole lot of time left! This either has to happen now, or it's not going to happen at all."

But God isn't subject to time. Because he created time, he operates outside of it. That's why the Bible says in Psalm 90:4 that a thousand years to God *"are like one day; they are like yesterday, already gone, like a short hour in the night"* (GNT).

God is using time to test your faith and build your character. While you're working on your goal, God is working on you. And God's much more interested in *you* than in what you're trying to accomplish, because you're not taking your accomplishments to heaven. You're only taking your character.

A lot of times we think we're waiting on God for something to happen, like a prayer to be answered. God wants you to know that you're not waiting on him. He's waiting on you. He's preparing you. He's testing your faith and trying to mature you, because the blessing he wants to give you is so much bigger than you can handle right now.

Delays can be part of God's design, to teach you to trust him and to grow your character.

Isaiah 49:8 says, *"At the right time I will hear your prayers. On the day of salvation I will help you"* (NCV). Not "might"—God *will* hear and answer and help when the time is right.

APRIL 16

Use Your Words to Build Others Up

Do not let any unwholesome talk come out of your mouths, but only what is helpful for building others up according to their needs, that it may benefit those who listen.
EPHESIANS 4:29 (NIV)

Sometimes our words are like a sledgehammer. We swing away without thinking, and then we're surprised to find ourselves in a pile of relational rubble. When you use your words to tear people down, your relationships are going to suffer.

When it comes to your mouth, think of it as a power tool. It has the power to tear something down—but it also has the power to build something.

God wants you to use your words to build others up. Ephesians 4:29 says, *"Do not let any unwholesome talk come out of your mouths, but only what is helpful for building others up according to their needs, that it may benefit those who listen"* (NIV).

One reason we're not effective with our words is we don't realize that our mouths and words are impactful, God-given tools. You may remember something someone said to you carelessly in grade school. That's how powerful words are! Just as you have to be cautious with power tools, you have to learn to use your words with care.

How can you use your words more carefully?

Stop excusing. Stop saying, "I didn't really mean to say that" or "That's just how I am before my first cup of coffee." You can choose the right words at any time, no matter how you feel.

Talk less. We often get in trouble because we just don't know when to stop talking. If you use your mouth as a precision tool, then you don't have to keep hammering away.

Listen more. When you take the time to listen, you can better understand someone's needs and why they may be choosing to use sledgehammer words themselves.

Start building. When you meet someone, let your first thought be, "How can I use a word of encouragement to build them up?" or "What can I say to make a difference in their life?"

Ask God to help you use your words wisely by starting each morning with this prayer: *"May these words of my mouth and this meditation of my heart be pleasing in your sight, LORD, my Rock and my Redeemer"* (Psalm 19:14, NIV).

APRIL 17

Your Gifts Are Not Just for Your Own Good

I always thank my God for you and for the gracious gifts he has given you, now that you belong to Christ Jesus. . . . Now you have every spiritual gift you need as you eagerly wait for the return of our Lord Jesus Christ.

1 CORINTHIANS 1:4, 7 (NLT)

When God thought you up, he created you with different gifts, talents, abilities, and skills. There are certain ways you think and things you do that you're just naturally good at.

Those gifts and abilities are how God shaped you. But he didn't make you uniquely just for your own benefit. Though your gifts are for your own good, they also are for the benefit of everyone else. And that means other people's gifts are for your benefit too.

One of my gifts is teaching. I've put that gift to work for many years now to benefit other people. In the same way, your gifts can benefit the people in your life.

Think right now of some specific things you're really good at doing. Why do you think God made you good at those things? It's because he wants you to use those gifts for other people! In the time you have left on earth, you should use your gifts to reach others for Jesus—to be an ambassador of love in the world. In fact, if you're not using your unique gifts the way God intended, then you're really just wasting them.

God didn't give you gifts just to use them for yourself. James 4:17 says, *"Remember, it is sin to know what you ought to do and then not do it"* (NLT).

If you're not sure how God wants you to serve, then think about this: What are you good at doing? Who can benefit from it? The answers to those questions will tell you where the world needs your help and who you need to serve. God has given you everything you need to serve well. The apostle Paul said it like this to the Christians in Corinth: *"I always thank my God for you and for the gracious gifts he has given you, now that you belong to Christ Jesus. . . . Now you have every spiritual gift you need as you eagerly wait for the return of our Lord Jesus Christ"* (1 Corinthians 1:4, 7, NLT).

Don't waste your God-given abilities. Use your gifts to serve God by serving others.

APRIL 18

Focus on Living for an Audience of One

No one can serve two masters.

LUKE 16:13 (NIV)

When you're always worried about what other people think of you, you can't be what God wants you to be. You'll be too busy pleasing other people to live your purpose. But when you learn to think like Jesus, you won't worry about pleasing everyone—because Jesus had the right focus. He was only concerned with pleasing his Father.

God says in Matthew 3:17, *"This is my Son, whom I love; with him I am well pleased"* (NIV). Jesus was obviously doing it right.

Jesus was never manipulated by crowds or by the approval or disapproval of anybody else. He lived for an audience of one: *"I try to please the One who sent me"* (John 5:30, NCV). When you have the mind of Christ, your focus aligns with his.

Wouldn't it simplify your life to live for an audience of one? If God likes what you're doing, then you know you're doing the right thing.

The truth is, even God can't please everybody! When someone is praying for their team to do well, someone else wants the opposing team to win. You can't please everybody.

When you're always looking for validation from other people, it means you don't really understand who you are or what God made you to do. You don't believe he has a plan and purpose for your life. You don't believe he is always with you.

Luke 16:13 says, *"No one can serve two masters"* (NIV).

You have to decide whose approval you're going to seek—other people's approval or God's approval. Are you going to live for what other people think or what God thinks?

Jesus never let someone else's approval or a fear of rejection control him. He wasn't out to win a popularity contest, and he didn't need other people's opinions to validate himself.

When you have the mind of Christ, you will be so secure in your identity, your purpose, and God's presence in your life that you won't need to look to other people for approval.

APRIL 19

Grieve Your Failure

Immediately a rooster crowed, and Peter remembered the words Jesus had spoken, "Before the rooster crows, you will deny me three times." And he went outside and wept bitterly.

MATTHEW 26:74-75 (CSB)

When you experience failure, sometimes it feels like you'll never recover. But whether you've experienced failure in finances, marriage, career, or something else, you *can* recover.

Recovery starts with grieving your failure. Don't minimize it or pretend it didn't happen. Don't rush to try to feel better. Instead, take the time to feel the pain.

This highlights an important life principle: To get past it, you've got to go through it. That's true in so many areas of life, but it's particularly true with failure.

Grief is the way to go through the failure. When you fail, you often just want to forget it and quickly move on. But that's a mistake. Grief is the way you learn failure's lessons.

Peter, one of Jesus' disciples, experienced the grief of failure. In a time of crisis, he denied that he knew Jesus, and that failure led to deep sorrow. The Bible says, *"Immediately a rooster crowed, and Peter remembered the words Jesus had spoken, 'Before the rooster crows, you will deny me three times.' And he went outside and wept bitterly"* (Matthew 26:74-75, CSB).

Imagine how disappointed Peter must have felt. He had walked alongside Jesus, watching him offer mercy and forgiveness over and over again. Yet the first time his commitment to Jesus was tested, he denied him three times in a row. Instead of ignoring his failure, Peter did the right thing: He was humble and regretful. He owned up to his failure and grieved—and that's the key to healing.

Many people want to take shortcuts when they fail. They want to bypass the affair and pretend it didn't shatter their marriage, so they jump into another relationship. Or they pretend it was someone else's fault the business failed and start another one the next day. They simply never learn the lesson.

But there is no shortcut to grieving and recovering from failure. The greater the failure in your life, the more time it's going to take to heal.

Let God work in your heart. You can't force healing. Recovery is an act of God's mercy, and it will come in time.

APRIL 20

Jesus Saves You from the Fear of Death

The Son also became flesh and blood. For only as a human being could he die, and only by dying could he break the power of the devil, who had the power of death. Only in this way could he set free all who have lived their lives as slaves to the fear of dying.

HEBREWS 2:14-15 (NLT)

Death is a universal fear. Nobody is exempt from it!

But did you know Jesus saved you from that fear? That's right—Jesus didn't just save you from your sin. He also saved you from the power and fear of death. *"The Son also became flesh and blood. For only as a human being could he die, and only by dying could he break the power of the devil, who had the power of death. Only in this way could he set free all who have lived their lives as slaves to the fear of dying"* (Hebrews 2:14-15, NLT).

As Jesus died on the cross, he shouted, *"It is finished!"* Translated as the Greek word *"Tetelestai!"* in the Gospel of John, it was his battle cry. *Tetelestai* is the shout of a victorious conqueror who says, "I have defeated death. I have proven to you that you don't have to be afraid of death—because I'm going to come back to life. I am the Resurrection, and you can be resurrected by believing in me. Death is not the end. You don't have to fear it anymore!"

Because Jesus died on the cross in my place, I am not afraid. Death does not have power over me. I know death is just a transfer, and I know where I'm going when I die. It can be the same for you too—when you trust Jesus as your Savior.

Romans 5:17 says, *"For the sin of this one man, Adam, caused death to rule over many. But even greater is God's wonderful grace and his gift of righteousness, for all who receive it will live in triumph over sin and death through this one man, Jesus Christ"* (NLT).

When you become a Christian, you die to sin and are raised to new life, confident that one day you'll live with Jesus forever. It's the best thing that could ever happen to you.

Do you have that confidence in Jesus already? Now you can live your life helping other people have that same assurance. As you talk about death and life in Jesus, your story can make other people want to trust Jesus as their Savior too.

APRIL 21

God Shows His Love When He Says No

All the ways of the L*ORD* *are loving and faithful.*

PSALM 25:10 (NIV)

When God says no to one of your prayers, you always want to keep this in mind: Everything God does is for your good, and he does it because he loves you. The Bible says, *"All the ways of the* L*ORD* *are loving and faithful"* (Psalm 25:10, NIV).

It's not important that you understand why God says no. The important thing is to remember that no matter how God answers your prayer, his motivation is always love.

Satan wants you to doubt God's love, so he'll whisper lies to you: "God doesn't love you. He doesn't care about you; otherwise, he'd give you everything you want!" But Satan is a liar, and he's *never* motivated by love for you.

And the truth is, God loves you too much to give you everything you ask for. It may be that what you want will have severe consequences you are unable to see right now, but God can. Or that what you ask for will undermine your ability to complete your life mission.

So when God says no, you've got three options: You can resist it, resent it, or relax in it.

You can fight God and angrily respond, "Okay, God, if you don't play the game my way, I'm going to take matters into my own hands." When you do that, you're refusing to trust that God has a bigger perspective and a greater plan.

You can turn your back on God in resentment and rebellion. Some people live their entire lives in bitterness and misery because they will not accept the truth that God only does what is good in our lives.

Or you can trust that God loves you and relax in his goodness. When you believe that God always has your best interest at heart, you can look with new eyes at the things he does that don't make sense.

You may not understand God's answer to your prayer. You don't have to. You can say, "Even in this, God's love still remains."

APRIL 22

Stop Passing Judgment

Speak and act as those who are going to be judged by the law that gives freedom, because judgment without mercy will be shown to anyone who has not been merciful. Mercy triumphs over judgment.

JAMES 2:12-13 (NIV)

As followers of Jesus, we want to honor God and do what he wants us to do.

But how do you do that when God's Kingdom is at odds with the ways of the world? How do you respond when your values are different from the values that surround you?

Too many Christians respond by judging other people. But God did not give us a right standing with him so that we could use it to look down on others. When you've been shown grace, you should extend grace to others.

James tells us that God desires mercy over judgment and that he expects his followers to be merciful. James 2:12-13 says, *"Speak and act as those who are going to be judged by the law that gives freedom, because judgment without mercy will be shown to anyone who has not been merciful. Mercy triumphs over judgment"* (NIV).

How can you avoid being judgmental? You can explain how disobeying God will lead to negative consequences but do it without passing judgment. In other words, tell the truth with gentleness.

You're judgmental when you hold the truth over people's heads in order to make yourself feel superior. Christians should tell the truth to help people, not to harm them or put them down. You can disagree with someone without being disagreeable. Even if you are right about something, being rude about it puts you in the wrong.

Being judgmental means that you expect an unbeliever to act like a believer. And that doesn't make sense! The Bible says people can't act the way God wants them to act until they invite Jesus into their lives and accept his power to change their ways.

You will be able to stop passing judgment on others when you remember that everyone is accountable to God. That means they *aren't* accountable to you. You can be faithful to God by letting some things go.

"Do not judge others, and God will not judge you; do not condemn others, and God will not condemn you; forgive others, and God will forgive you" (Luke 6:37, GNT).

Are You Fasting or Feasting on God's Word?

How sweet your words taste to me; they are sweeter than honey.
PSALM 119:103 (NLT)

After my wife, Kay, and I got engaged, we did something unusual: We moved to opposite sides of the world. She moved to Birmingham, Alabama, to work in an inner-city church, and I moved to Nagasaki, Japan, to plant a church. We were separated for most of our engagement.

In those days, we didn't have cell phones. It cost fifteen dollars a minute to call Japan, and we were dirt poor. So we had only one alternative: writing letters. We each wrote a letter every day, and receiving hers was the highlight of my day. The moment a love letter arrived, I would tear it open and read it. Then I would reread it and try to read between the lines. I'd underline and memorize portions of it. I was trying to gather every drop of love this woman had for me.

What if you read the Bible—God's love letter to you—that same way?

If you're not poring over the Bible, trying to glean every bit of wisdom from it, then you are not fully tasting the banquet that God has prepared for you. Psalm 119:103 says, *"How sweet your words taste to me; they are sweeter than honey"* (NLT).

The Bible is full of nourishment; it has spiritual food that will keep you healthy.

Are you fasting or are you feasting on the Word of God? Keep in mind that going to church once a week and hearing a sermon is not a feast. If you only ate one meal a week, you wouldn't grow or be healthy.

Jesus said, *"Man shall not live by bread alone, but by every word that comes from the mouth of God"* (Matthew 4:4, ESV).

You can truly taste the sweetness of God's Word when you are feeding on it every day—reading it, studying it, and meditating on it—and letting it saturate your heart and mind.

APRIL 24

How to Stop the Worry Habit

Therefore I tell you, do not worry about your life, what you will eat or drink; or about your body, what you will wear. Is not life more than food, and the body more than clothes?

MATTHEW 6:25 (NIV)

God is the source of everything you need to live. He is the Good Shepherd who feeds you, leads you, and meets your needs. You don't have to look anywhere else. You don't have to look to Wall Street. You don't have to look to the government. You don't have to look to your spouse, your retirement account, or your job.

If you're going to put your security in something, you need to put it in something that can never be taken from you. You can lose your health. You can lose your job. You can lose your good looks. You can lose your family. You can lose your life. You can lose your mind. You can even lose your way.

But God is never lost. And there is nothing you need that God can't supply. Philippians 4:19 says, *"God will supply every need of yours according to his riches in glory in Christ Jesus"* (ESV).

So why do people worry so much? Worry may be the most common sin on the planet. It is the direct result of forgetting that God is good all the time. When you forget God's goodness, you panic instead of pray; you worry instead of worship.

The Bible says, *"Therefore I tell you, do not worry about your life, what you will eat or drink; or about your body, what you will wear. Is not life more than food, and the body more than clothes?"* (Matthew 6:25, NIV).

Clearly, God doesn't want you to be anxious about anything. Yet it's hard to stop the worry habit. It's part of human nature!

So how do you stop worrying? First, recognize that worry keeps you from the goodness of God. Next, decide that you don't want worry to get the best of you. Then, take your concerns to God in prayer instead of worrying about them.

Remember: The best way to stop worrying is to start praying.

APRIL 25

Choose Faith over Fear

By faith he left Egypt, not fearing the king's anger; he persevered because he saw him who is invisible.

HEBREWS 11:27 (NIV)

Moses chose to live by faith rather than by fear. It was an intentional choice he made about how to live his life.

You face the same choice. Will you choose to live by faith or by fear?

The Bible says in Hebrews 11:27, *"By faith he left Egypt, not fearing the king's anger; he persevered because he saw him who is invisible"* (NIV).

Moses confronted the most powerful man in the world and basically said, "Those slaves who are building your pyramids? I'm taking them, and we're all leaving. You're not going to have slave labor anymore. Let my people go."

Moses had every reason to be afraid. He stood against the most powerful man on the planet. In those days, Pharaoh was considered a god, and whatever Pharaoh said was the law.

But Moses was not afraid because he reported to a higher authority than Pharaoh.

How can you have that kind of faith? The closer you get to God, the more you'll be filled with faith. The further away you get from God, the more you'll be filled with fear.

I cannot overemphasize the importance of living by faith for the rest of your life. The Bible says, *"Whatever is not of faith is sin"* (Romans 14:23, TLV).

How many times did you sin this week? A lot? So did I. Anything I did in doubt instead of faith was a sin.

The Bible also says, *"Without faith it is impossible to please God"* (Hebrews 11:6, NIV). How many times did you please God this week?

Do you want change in your life? Stop complaining and start believing. God is not moved by complaints. God is moved by faith: *"According to your faith let it be done to you"* (Matthew 9:29, NIV). Your faith has a big impact on what God does in your life.

Here's the key: What matters is not the size of your faith but the size of our God. A little faith in a big God gets big results!

APRIL 26

Knowing Who You Are Lowers Your Stress

See what great love the Father has lavished on us, that we should be called children of God! And that is what we are!

1 JOHN 3:1 (NIV)

We are living in stressful times. More than ever, we need to learn resilience so we can do what God has called us to do. That's why the first step to being resilient is to remember how much God loves you. That's the antidote to stress!

Part of fulfilling our purpose is becoming more like Jesus. And Jesus had no doubt in his mind that God the Father loved him. He talked about it over and over in verses like John 10:17, which says, *"The Father loves me"* (NLT).

Knowing and remembering that God has unconditional, extravagant, continuous, and never-ending love for you, just like he did for Jesus, is the foundation of a resilient life. As Paul said, *"I am convinced that neither death nor life, . . . nor anything else in all creation, will be able to separate us from the love of God that is in Christ Jesus our Lord"* (Romans 8:38-39, NIV). We can be resilient, knowing that we can never be separated from God's love.

You may be thinking, "Well, of course God loves Jesus. He's his Son." But did you know Jesus says the same thing about his love for you as God's daughter or son? In John 15:9-10, Jesus said, *"As the Father has loved me, so have I loved you. Now remain in my love. If you keep my commands, you will remain in my love"* (NIV).

Understanding how much God loves you is the basis of your personal security. If you're not convinced that God loves you at all times—unconditionally and completely—then you're going to be easy prey for the disapproval of other people. You're going to be a people pleaser. But when you understand and accept how God feels about you as his child, then you can face difficult times with confidence and less stress.

When you need to be reminded of how much God loves you, just look to his Word. *"See what great love the Father has lavished on us, that we should be called children of God! And that is what we are!"* (1 John 3:1, NIV).

Humility Builds Relationships

Be humble and give more honor to others than to yourselves.
PHILIPPIANS 2:3 (NCV)

Pride destroys relationships. It shows up in a lot of different forms, like criticism, competition, stubbornness, and superficiality.

The problem with pride is that it's self-deceiving. When you have too much pride, you don't see it in your life—but everyone else does! Proverbs 16:18 says, *"Pride leads to destruction; a proud attitude brings ruin"* (NCV). The same verse in *The Message* paraphrase says, *"First pride, then the crash—the bigger the ego, the harder the fall."*

While pride destroys relationships, humility serves as its antidote, building relationships instead. Philippians 2:3 tells you how to combat pride by choosing humility: *"Be humble and give more honor to others than to yourselves"* (NCV). The Bible also says in 1 Peter 3:8, *"Everyone must live in harmony, be sympathetic, love each other, have compassion, and be humble"* (GW).

How do you grow in humility? You let Jesus Christ begin to control your thoughts, heart, attitude, and reactions. You take full advantage of the Holy Spirit in you. You ask him to help you change the way you think so you can change the way you feel so you can change the way you act—with humility, compassion, and grace.

The basic law of relationships is this: You tend to become like the people you spend time with. If you spend time with grumpy people, you get grumpier. If you spend time with happy people, you get happier.

If you want to become a new, humbler person, then you need to spend time with Jesus Christ, because he is humble. By building a relationship with him through prayer and reading his Word, you'll get to know him and become more like him. *"You must have the same attitude that Christ Jesus had. Though he was God, he did not think of equality with God as something to cling to"* (Philippians 2:5-6, NLT).

Jesus is the ultimate example of humility. He left heaven to give his life for you on the cross—from the highest position to the lowest—and he did it because of love. When you spend time with him, you learn how to show the kind of love that doesn't just build relationships but transforms them.

APRIL 28

Is That Really the Best Option?

Anyone who lets himself be distracted from the work I plan for him is not fit for the Kingdom of God.

LUKE 9:62 (TLB)

The older I get, the more I realize how important it is to be selective. There will always be a lot of options and opportunities. The key to effectiveness is being selective.

The Bible says in 1 Corinthians 10:23, *"Someone may say, 'I'm allowed to do anything,' but not everything is helpful. I'm allowed to do anything, but not everything encourages growth"* (GW).

In other words, some things aren't necessarily wrong—they're just unnecessary. Once you figure this out, you'll be able to better withstand the hard times in life. You'll be resilient!

When you know where you're headed and you focus in that direction, then you're less likely to be distracted by less important things. You'll set priorities that have an eternal focus. You'll realize what matters most in life, and you'll choose not just good things but the most important things.

Jesus was a master of concentration. He lived a selective life, allowing him to give his life for God's Kingdom and do what pleased his Father.

Luke 9:51 says, *"As the time drew near for his return to heaven, [Jesus] moved steadily onward toward Jerusalem with an iron will"* (TLB).

He modeled an iron will and fulfilled his purpose—even though he knew it would lead to his death. His focus helped him endure the pain and stress and persecution. Paul was the same way. He said, "This one thing I do," not "these forty things I dabble in." He did one thing with his life—the most important thing.

You have incredible potential to be used by God, but the barrier is often that you haven't settled what's most important. If you think you don't have time to serve God, then you're not focused. If you have to do something else before you follow Jesus, then you are not focused.

The Bible is clear: *"Anyone who lets himself be distracted from the work I plan for him is not fit for the Kingdom of God"* (Luke 9:62, TLB).

One day you're going to stand before God. How will you answer him when he asks what you did with what you were given?

APRIL 29

Building Unity in Your Church

So then, we must always aim at those things that bring peace and that help strengthen one another.
ROMANS 14:19 (GNT)

Do you want to become an agent of harmony and unity in your church? Then focus on what you have in common with other Christians, rather than your differences.

What are the things you have in common with your brothers and sisters in God's family? Ephesians 4:4-6 says that Christians share seven things: *"There is one body and one Spirit, just as you were called to one hope when you were called; one Lord, one faith, one baptism; one God and Father of all, who is over all and through all and in all"* (NIV).

We're one body. Jesus doesn't have multiple bodies. He just has the church!

We have one Spirit. We were all given the same Holy Spirit at salvation.

We share one hope. We share the hope of the second coming of Jesus, who was resurrected, went back to heaven, and promised to return.

We have one Lord. We have unity with all believers through our relationship with Jesus.

We have one faith. Our faith is contained in one book, the Bible.

We have one baptism. We don't have to be rebaptized every time we sin.

We have one God. We don't worship multiple gods. We worship the one, true God who knows all things, sees all things, and is with us at all times.

As members of God's family, we also share the same salvation, the same forgiveness, the same grace, the same mercy, and the same future. These factors are far more important than your economic status, your gender or race, your shape or size, your background, your sins, your good deeds, or anything else.

Even while you focus on those seven significant things in Ephesians, don't forget that God didn't just give you things in common with the other people in your church. He also created differences: *"Just as there are many parts to our bodies, so it is with Christ's body. We are all parts of it, and it takes every one of us to make it complete, for we each have different work to do. So we belong to each other, and each needs all the others"* (Romans 12:4-5, TLB).

As you think about all the unique ways God has gifted and shaped you and the people around you, take a moment to say to him, "Thank you, Father, for your creativity, which is displayed in everyone in your family. I pray that I would be someone who celebrates diversity in the church and who also remembers what we have in common because of the gospel. Help us to use all of our different gifts to serve and love others well. In Jesus' name, amen."

God chose to give people different personalities and equipped each person with different gifts. You can unite around the foundation of the gospel, while you also value and learn from all the ways God made you unique.

Don't just get along with the people in your church. Work toward true harmony and unity as you remember the hope you share.

APRIL 30

Is Your Soul Weary? Come to Jesus

Come to me and I will give you rest.
MATTHEW 11:28 (CEV)

When Jesus says, *"Come to me and I will give you rest"* (Matthew 11:28, CEV), what kind of rest is he talking about?

Jesus offers a rest for your soul that's much deeper than physical rest—because he knows that the problem you need help with right now is probably not overworked muscles.

When you come to Jesus in your emptiness, what you probably have is an overloaded mind, soul, and spirit. You need rest not just from physical work but from tension, stress, anxiety, hurry, and worry. You need the kind of rest that can't come from taking a good nap or going on vacation.

Most people have a way to unwind when they're physically tired that's different from how they unwind when they're emotionally and spiritually exhausted. Maybe when you're tired, you watch a movie or spend time on your phone. Maybe you have to lie down, or maybe you need to go for a walk. Maybe you choose to spend time with friends, or maybe it's better to be alone.

Those can all be good things—but none of them can restore your soul.

Only God can restore your soul. That's why, when you have soul emptiness, soul depression, or soul overload, Jesus wants you to come to him.

Isaiah 40:29 says, *"He gives power to the tired and worn out, and strength to the weak"* (TLB).

When you're empty inside, culture says you need to do more. You need to make more money, get more things, do more things, travel more places. Go, go, go. More, more, more. But that's probably the very reason you're empty!

Jesus wants you to do the opposite: Don't go. Come to him—and come just as you are.

Your soul will never find rest in anything the world has to offer. That's because your soul was not created to be filled by anything in this world.

You were made for God, and you only find real rest when you bring your weary soul to him.

MAY 1

How to Satisfy Your Spiritual Thirst

Anyone who drinks this water will soon become thirsty again. But those who drink the water I give will never be thirsty again. It becomes a fresh, bubbling spring within them, giving them eternal life.

JOHN 4:13-14 (NLT)

Do you feel unsatisfied with your life? Are you ready to live a fulfilled, meaningful life? It's time to start looking for satisfaction in Jesus alone.

If you're like most people, you're always looking around, trying to find something to make your life happy and significant. You think, "If I could just wear *this* kind of clothes, then I'd be cool. If I could just have plastic surgery and get *this* fixed, then life would be grand. If I could just get *this* job, I'd be satisfied."

The pursuit of those things leaves you exhausted because they will never really satisfy you. The Bible says, *"My people have done two evils: They have turned away from me, the spring of living water. And they have dug their own wells, which are broken wells that cannot hold water"* (Jeremiah 2:13, NCV).

Not only have you rejected God and not looked to him to meet all your needs and satisfy your life, but you're also trying to meet your needs on your own. The wells you've dug—things like a lucrative career, good looks, or the perfect house—aren't going to hold water.

In John 4:13-14, Jesus said, *"Anyone who drinks this water will soon become thirsty again. But those who drink the water I give will never be thirsty again. It becomes a fresh, bubbling spring within them, giving them eternal life"* (NLT).

Sin is addictive. It only makes you thirstier! If you don't believe that, ask anybody who's looked at pornography—once is not enough. If you are addicted to prescription medication, one pill is never enough. If you have a problem with anger, you're not going to lash out just once. Sin creates greater thirst for satisfaction.

That's how it is with every pursuit outside of Jesus. It will only leave you thirstier than you were before!

But Jesus offers living water that will permanently satisfy your thirst.

If you feel unsatisfied with your life, you're spiritually thirsty. And the only one who can quench that thirst is Jesus.

MAY 2

How to Withstand Destructive Forces

We won't be tossed and blown about by every wind of new teaching. We will not be influenced when people try to trick us with lies so clever they sound like the truth.

EPHESIANS 4:14 (NLT)

One of the most powerful forces of nature is wind. That's why the Bible uses wind as a metaphor for so many things. There are winds of testing, trouble, conflict, and temptation. But God makes it possible to withstand each one.

Ephesians 6:13 says, *"Take up the whole armor of God, that you may be able to withstand in the evil day, and having done all, to stand firm"* (ESV). The word *withstand* means "to remain undamaged by a destructive force." One of the best ways to remain undamaged by the winds of life is to stay connected to your spiritual family.

God never meant for you to withstand difficult days by yourself. One of the first things God said was, *"It isn't good for man to be alone"* (Genesis 2:18, TLB). You need a spiritual family—a church—for support when hard winds blow in.

Look at this passage from Ephesians: *"Now these are the gifts Christ gave to the church: the apostles, the prophets, the evangelists, and the pastors and teachers. Their responsibility is to equip God's people to do his work and build up the church, the body of Christ. . . . Then we will no longer be immature like children. We won't be tossed and blown about by every wind of new teaching. We will not be influenced when people try to trick us with lies so clever they sound like the truth"* (Ephesians 4:11-12, 14, NLT).

God's church is his tool for building up his people. And it's the job of *"the apostles, the prophets, the evangelists, and the pastors and teachers"* to keep the church from being blown away by false ideas and *"every wind of new teaching."*

People's beliefs can easily shift. But truth never changes. If it was true two thousand years ago, it will also be true two thousand years from today. Isaiah 40:8 says, *"The grass withers, the flower fades, but the word of our God will stand forever"* (ESV).

There are many shifting winds in our culture today that are simply wrong. They're deceptions, lies, and half-truths. Don't get *"tossed and blown about."* Stay connected to your church family instead.

MAY 3

There's Purpose to Your Work Problems

We can rejoice, too, when we run into problems and trials, for we know that they are good for us—they help us learn to be patient. And patience develops strength of character.

ROMANS 5:3-4 (TLB)

Have you ever had a problem at work? Of course you have. Everyone—no matter where they work or who they work with—has had some kind of trouble at some point in their job.

The Bible tells you what to do with that kind of trouble: *"We can rejoice, too, when we run into problems and trials, for we know that they are good for us—they help us learn to be patient. And patience develops strength of character"* (Romans 5:3-4, TLB).

God is far more interested in your character than he is in your comfort. He's working to perfect you, not to pamper you. His goal in your life and in your work is not to make you comfortable; his goal is to help you grow up. And he uses problems in your life to grow your character.

When you have a problem at work, don't ask God why you're having that problem. Instead, ask God, "What do you want me to learn from this? What are you trying to teach me? What's my blind spot? What character issue needs to be worked on?" And remember this simple truth: While you're working on your job, God is working on you.

Sometimes work problems come in the form of temptation—but God can use even temptations for your good! Many believers say they don't like working with unbelievers because those unbelievers bring more temptations. But that's just not true. You'll be tempted with believers just as much as with unbelievers. And it's not a sin to be tempted; it's just a sin to give in to temptation. The Bible says Jesus was tempted in every way, just like you are, and yet he never sinned.

You're going to be tempted the rest of your life, no matter where you work. But God can use those temptations for good. He can use them to build character. Every time you're tempted, you get to make a choice. You can choose to resist temptation, or you can choose to act on it.

Every time you give in, temptation harms you. Every time you choose to do good, temptation becomes a stepping stone for growth.

MAY 4

You Can Be Sure about Getting into Heaven

Those who hear my words and believe in him who sent me have eternal life. They will not be judged.

JOHN 5:24 (GNT)

Jesus' death and resurrection release you from judgment.

Maybe you've imagined a Day of Judgment that goes something like this:

You're standing outside the gates of heaven in a really long line. You're slowly moving forward, one step at a time. As you get closer, you start to sweat and wonder, "Am I going to get in? Am I going to make it? Is God going to use a giant TV screen to show every foolish or wrong thing I've ever done? Will my every sin be exposed?"

I have good news for you, promised by Jesus Christ himself: *"Those who believe in the Son are not judged"* (John 3:18, GNT).

Or, as he said later in the book of John: *"Those who hear my words and believe in him who sent me have eternal life. They will not be judged"* (John 5:24, GNT).

Is that good news? Oh, yeah!

I have a friend named Buddy who said that when he was a little kid, his Sunday school teacher taught him that God was sitting in heaven, writing down every bad thing that Buddy ever did. She actually made the class sing a song every week that went, "My Lord is writing all the time. Writing, writing, writing all the time." Buddy said, "It scared me. I just thought, 'I'm never going to make it to heaven. My list is getting longer and longer.'"

Is that the way God treats you when you come to him and put your faith in Christ? No! In fact, God is erasing, erasing, erasing all the time. Forgiving, forgiving, forgiving all the time. He's sitting in heaven, hitting the Delete button.

Why? Because the Bible says, *"God is love"* (1 John 4:8, NIV) and love *"keeps no record of wrongs"* (1 Corinthians 13:5, NIV). If you put your trust in the love of Jesus Christ, your sins are wiped out.

You can count on God to keep his promise: *"There is no condemnation for those who belong to Christ Jesus"* (Romans 8:1, NLT).

MAY 5

Your Creator Has Creative Solutions

When I tried to understand all this, it troubled me deeply
till I entered the sanctuary of God; then I understood.

PSALM 73:16-17 (NIV)

Gordian knot is a term used to describe a problem that seems unsolvable. It's based on a myth that anyone who could unravel a complex, tightly twisted knot made by Gordius, King Midas' father, would become ruler of all of Asia. Legend says that Alexander the Great simply sliced the knot in half with his sword (and went on to conquer much of Asia).

Do you have some Gordian knots in your life, problems that you just can't figure out? You may not know how to fix your relationship, your finances, or your chronic health problem. Your problems are complex, and you've had them so long. You wonder, "Am I ever going to get a solution to this?"

What do you do when you have a problem you can't figure out? You praise God.

When you praise him, God will give you answers you would never come up with on your own. David said in Psalm 73:16-17, *"When I tried to understand all this, it troubled me deeply till I entered the sanctuary of God; then I understood"* (NIV).

The sanctuary of God is a metaphor for coming into God's presence with praise. It wasn't until David started worshiping, praising, and thanking God that he got the answer he needed.

The best way to get new and creative ideas is to worship and praise God. Nobody is more creative than God. The more in tune you are with the Creator of the universe, the more creative you will be.

The Bible instructs, *"Enter his gates with a song of thanksgiving. Come into his courtyards with a song of praise"* (Psalm 100:4, GW). The doorway to creativity is praise and thanksgiving.

You're going to have problems in life. And the problems that seem the biggest and most unsolvable need creative solutions.

If you need solutions, then come into God's presence and praise him, even before you have a solution. The Creator will give you creative ideas.

MAY 6

Facing the Facts with Faith

Abraham was almost a hundred years old, much past the age for having children, and Sarah could not have children. Abraham thought about all this, but his faith in God did not become weak.

ROMANS 4:19 (NCV)

Sometimes people mistakenly believe that faith means ignoring the facts. But nothing could be further from the truth!

Abraham understood this: *"Abraham was almost a hundred years old, much past the age for having children, and Sarah could not have children. Abraham thought about all this, but his faith in God did not become weak"* (Romans 4:19, NCV).

Abraham was ninety-nine years old; his wife was eighty-nine. It was physically impossible for them to have children. But Abraham didn't deny the facts. He faced them with faith.

Faith isn't stubborn foolishness; it doesn't ignore reality. It doesn't live in denial, pretend there isn't a problem, or cling to the past. Faith faces the facts in your life without being discouraged by them.

If you have cancer, you can't deny the diagnosis, but you can defy the verdict. Instead of denying reality, you do all you can to beat it.

Some people teach that Christians should deny their problems and smile their way through life. But that's not the way of Jesus.

You may need to do some legitimate grieving for an unexpected diagnosis or a broken dream. But you don't need to have a pity party. Instead, tell God, "It didn't turn out like I wanted, but I know you have a better plan for my life." That's what faith looks like.

Faith believes God isn't through with your life. Faith knows God has good things in store for you!

When she was young, author and Holocaust survivor Corrie ten Boom was engaged to be married. But the man unexpectedly broke up with her and married a friend. She was devastated and never married. But Corrie ten Boom didn't pull herself into a shell. She redirected her love. She became one of the most loving Christian leaders of the twentieth century, influencing millions of people. She was able to do that because she refused to deny the facts. Even as she faced challenges, she trusted God and his plan for her life and loved others through her faith.

You can do the same.

MAY 7

What Will You Do Today That Requires Faith?

Let us not become weary in doing good, for at the proper time we will reap a harvest if we do not give up.
GALATIANS 6:9 (NIV)

Failure is never final. You're never a failure until you quit, and it's always too soon to quit!

You don't determine a person's greatness by their talent, their wealth, or their education. You determine a person's greatness by what it takes to discourage them.

The Bible says in Galatians 6:9, *"Let us not become weary in doing good, for at the proper time we will reap a harvest if we do not give up"* (NIV).

Do you know how many times I wanted to resign when I was senior pastor at Saddleback Church? Just every Monday morning when I would think, "God, surely somebody could have done a better job than I did yesterday. This thing is too big for any one person."

And it's as if God said, "Just keep on keeping on." I may not be real bright sometimes, but I don't know how to quit; I don't know how to give up.

God works in your life according to your faith. The Bible says, *"Without faith it is impossible to please God"* (Hebrews 11:6, NIV) and *"Whatsoever is not of faith is sin"* (Romans 14:23, KJV) and *"According to your faith let it be done to you"* (Matthew 9:29, NIV).

You need to ask every day when you get up, "God, what can I do today that will require faith?" That's an important question—because living each day by faith pleases God.

You don't have control over many things—like who your parents were, when you were born, your nationality, your race, or your talents. But you do have complete control over how much you choose to believe God. He uses people who expect him to act, who never give up, who take risks in faith, and who go after the dream he's given them.

Do you want to be the kind of person God uses to accomplish his purpose? Don't let anything discourage you from following his dream!

MAY 8

The Importance of Being You

It's healthy to be content, but envy can eat you up.

PROVERBS 14:30 (CEV)

To live an abundant life overflowing with God's goodness, the first thing you need to do is start being grateful and stop complaining. The second thing you need to do is start being content and stop comparing.

God made you to be you. He doesn't want you to be anybody else! When you compare yourself to others, you get envious and resentful; you might even start copying them.

But God has never made a clone. God only makes originals. Even identical twins are different in thousands of ways.

The truth is, comparing gets you in trouble. When you compare your looks, grades, spouse, career, or kids, it causes two problems.

One, you get full of discouragement because you can always find someone who is better looking, makes more money, or has more talent. And two, you get full of pride. Why? Because you can always find someone who's *not* doing as good a job as you.

The Bible says, *"It is better to be content with what little you have. Otherwise, you will always be struggling for more, and that is like chasing the wind"* (Ecclesiastes 4:6, NCV).

Because of social media, it's easier than ever to compare yourself to others. When you see posts every day that shout, "Look at me! Look what I can do! Look what I've got!" it can draw you into a state of envy and discontent. It can even cause you to try to impress others with your posts. But the thing is, you don't need to impress anyone. A key to living a life overflowing with joy is to simply be yourself, content with who God made you to be.

Are you tired of feeling overwhelmed? Do you want to be spiritually and emotionally healthy? The Bible says, *"It's healthy to be content, but envy can eat you up"* (Proverbs 14:30, CEV).

Contentment comes when you enjoy what you have rather than waiting for something else to make you happy. Stop comparing yourself to other people, and start being content with what God has given you—and then watch your joy overflow!

MAY 9

With God's Presence, You Have What It Takes

The LORD says, "Do not cling to events of the past or dwell on what happened long ago. Watch for the new thing I am going to do. It is happening already—you can see it now!"
ISAIAH 43:18-19 (GNT)

When people stop following God's vision for their lives, they're usually thinking one of two things: "I don't have what it takes" or "I have failed in the past."

If you want a fresh start in pursuing God's vision, then stop making those excuses and believe these two truths:

You *do* have what it takes. Have you ever said, "I don't have what it takes to go after my dream"? In the Bible, Moses and Jeremiah and a lot of other people tried to use this excuse on God when he had an assignment for them. But my favorite example of "I don't have what it takes" is Gideon. God told Gideon he wanted to use him to free the Israelites. Gideon responded, *"'But Lord . . . how can I rescue Israel? My clan is the weakest in the whole tribe of Manasseh, and I am the least in my entire family!' The LORD said to him, 'I will be with you'"* (Judges 6:15-16, NLT).

When you think you don't have what it takes, you need to remember that you're not doing it by yourself. If God is with you, then you can rely on his power, his presence, his promises, and his protection. You don't have to worry about anything!

Your past is past. Everyone has failed. You are a product of your past, but you don't have to be a prisoner of your past. You may have been shaped by what happened to you and the things you've done, but you are not a victim unless you choose to be. God is far more interested in your future than your past. Isaiah 43:18-19 says, *"The LORD says, 'Do not cling to events of the past or dwell on what happened long ago. Watch for the new thing I am going to do. It is happening already—you can see it now!'"* (GNT).

The biggest barrier to your success may be your own excuses. God wants you to let go of your feelings of inadequacy and your past. Then you can move into the future he's prepared for you.

MAY 10

God's Multiplication System

No one who has sacrificed home, spouse, brothers and sisters, parents, children—whatever—will lose out. It will all come back multiplied many times over in your lifetime.

LUKE 18:29-30 (MSG)

Whatever you give God, he multiplies.

If you give him your time, he multiplies it. If you give him your money, he multiplies it. If you give him your talent, he multiplies it. If you give him your energy, he multiplies it.

Farmers know that the seed must be given away—planted in the ground—for it to serve a purpose. If you keep seed in a sack, it doesn't do any good. But when you plant it, it multiplies. When you plant one corn seed, you get a stalk with hundreds of corn kernels. In the same way, God multiplies whatever you give him.

"Remember this—a farmer who plants only a few seeds will get a small crop. But the one who plants generously will get a generous crop. . . . 'For God loves a person who gives cheerfully'" (2 Corinthians 9:6-7, NLT).

One of the great lessons my wife, Kay, and I have learned is that you cannot outgive God. Whenever we obeyed God's leading to give sacrificially, he replenished what we gave him in greater ways than ever before.

I'm not saying that if you give away all of your money, God is going to somehow make you rich. But God receives what you joyfully give him and increases your joy and satisfaction in him—and that is the real gift. He promises that you will have everything you need to live fully, even if that doesn't look like what the world calls riches.

God wants you to give your resources cheerfully and in faith. Faith is different from bargaining. Bargaining is when you say, "God, help me close this deal, and I'll give you part of it." That's not how it works! Faith is sacrificing in advance and trusting God with what you'll get in return.

Jesus promised, *"You won't regret it. No one who has sacrificed home, spouse, brothers and sisters, parents, children—whatever—will lose out. It will all come back multiplied many times over in your lifetime. And then the bonus of eternal life!"* (Luke 18:29-30, MSG).

What a promise! You will never regret giving God your first and best.

Five Things You Won't Find in Heaven

Can you understand the mysteries surrounding God All-Powerful? They are higher than the heavens and deeper than the grave. So what can you do when you know so little, and these mysteries outreach the earth and the ocean?

JOB 11:7-9 (CEV)

When I was a little boy, we traveled to Disneyland for a family vacation. My dad tried to explain to me what it was going to be like. But there was no way for me to understand just how amazing it was until I walked into the park for the first time.

The Bible says in Job 11:7-9, *"Can you understand the mysteries surrounding God All-Powerful? They are higher than the heavens and deeper than the grave. So what can you do when you know so little, and these mysteries outreach the earth and the ocean?"* (CEV). Heaven is a mystery we won't fully understand until we arrive there. But the Bible does tell us five things that will *not* be in heaven:

There will be no sickness. The Bible says this about our bodies: *"When buried, it is ugly and weak; when raised, it will be beautiful and strong"* (1 Corinthians 15:43, GNT). There won't be any sickness because you'll get a new, perfect body.

There will be no sadness. God *"will wipe every tear from their eyes"* (Revelation 21:4, NIV). In heaven, there will be no more rejection, loneliness, grief, or heartache.

There will be no suffering. The Bible says, *"Never again will they hunger or thirst; neither sun nor any scorching heat will burn them"* (Revelation 7:16, GNT). Every need will be satisfied in heaven.

There will be no sin. *"God . . . will bring you with great joy into his glorious presence without a single fault"* (Jude 1:24, NLT). Jesus Christ died on the cross and paid for all your sin so that when you see him face-to-face, your character will instantly reflect his.

There will be no death. *"There will be no more death or sorrow or crying or pain"* (Revelation 21:4, NLT). Heaven is glorious in many ways, but the best thing is that you'll be in God's presence—*forever.*

One day in heaven, everything will be clear and make sense. You'll be able to say, "So *that's* why God allowed that in my life!" Until then, God wants you to trust him.

MAY 12

Two Ways to Set Goals in Uncertain Times

We should make plans—counting on God to direct us.
PROVERBS 16:9 (TLB)

God is not moved by your complaints, regrets, or wishes. But he is moved by your faith.

Matthew 9:29 says, *"According to your faith let it be done to you"* (NIV).

You know you're acting in faith when you attempt to do something that you couldn't do in your own power—something that requires you to rely on God.

Goal setting is an act of faith.

When you set a goal, it's like saying, "God, with your help, I'm expecting to accomplish *this* specific task by *this* specific date." That kind of goal is a statement of faith, and God honors faith.

If you've found it difficult to set goals during uncertain times, especially because circumstances keep changing so quickly, then try doing these two things:

First, you can do scenario goal setting. This means that you set up multiple goals and plans, depending on which scenario unfolds. For example, "I will do *this* by *this* date if *this* happens. On the other hand, I will do *that* by *that* date if *that* happens."

Scenario goal setting is a legitimate way to plan for the future as you trust God during uncertain times. Proverbs 16:9 says, *"We should make plans—counting on God to direct us"* (TLB).

Second, you can focus on character goals rather than activity goals. In other words, you can set goals for what you want to *be* instead of what you want to *do*. How do you want to be different this time next year? How do you want to be more like Christ? What character trait do you want to work on?

No matter how out of control the world feels, you can always make the choice to change and grow to become the person God wants you to be.

It's time to get to work! Stop wondering what "could be," and start moving in faith. The Bible says, *"Without faith it is impossible to please God"* (Hebrews 11:6, NIV). When you act in faith, God will honor your goals and help you reach the greatest goal: bringing glory to him.

MAY 13

Spirit-Led Thinking Leads to Life

If your thinking is controlled by your sinful self, there is spiritual death. But if your thinking is controlled by the Spirit, there is life and peace.
ROMANS 8:6 (ERV)

Making changes in any area of your life requires that you change the way you think. That's because your brain is where God's Spirit works in you.

We often use the metaphor of our heart being the place where God works. For example, we say, "I invited Jesus into my heart." But your heart is really just a symbol for your brain. Your brain is where you think—so it's in your mind where God begins the transformation process. It's where God resets your life.

The Bible says in Ephesians 4:23-24, *"Let the Spirit change your way of thinking and make you into a new person"* (CEV).

You were created to be like God. But that doesn't happen instantly. To grow into someone who's more like Jesus, you have to go through a lot of change—including a lot of resets—in your life. And those changes that help you become a new person in Christ start with changing the way you think.

How does this work? When Satan suggests an idea in your mind, that's called temptation. When God suggests an idea in your mind, that's called inspiration.

Whether you accept or reject a temptation or an inspiration is up to you. Are you going to let the Spirit change your way of thinking? In fact, at each moment of your life, you're choosing which ideas you're going to hold on to and which ones you're going to reject.

As you make those choices, you're deciding what ideas are going to control your life. Romans 8:6 says, *"If your thinking is controlled by your sinful self, there is spiritual death. But if your thinking is controlled by the Spirit, there is life and peace"* (ERV).

God wants you to live a full, meaningful, purposeful life. He wants you to grow in faith and spiritual maturity.

But it's your choice at each moment of every day. Will you choose the way that leads to life?

MAY 14

How to Defeat Discouragement

It is God himself, in his mercy, who has given us this wonderful work of telling his Good News to others, and so we never give up.

2 CORINTHIANS 4:1 (TLB)

God loves you.

It's a truth you may have heard all your life.

But there is a difference in intellectually knowing God loves you and really sensing and believing in his love. When you don't really believe God loves you, you get discouraged. Why? Because if you don't believe God loves you, then it becomes more difficult to detect his ever-present grace and mercy in your life.

The best way to defeat discouragement is to remember how much God loves you and to stay focused on that truth. And the best way to be reminded of God's love is to read his Word, the Bible. You'll be able to focus better on God and feel closer to him when you pick up your Bible every day.

The Bible says, *"It is God himself, in his mercy, who has given us this wonderful work of telling his Good News to others, and so we never give up"* (2 Corinthians 4:1, TLB).

What is mercy? Mercy is when God gives you what you need, not what you deserve. Mercy is when God knows every mistake you have made and will make, and he still gives you every good thing in your life. God's mercy is what keeps you going when you start to feel hopeless or worn down or discouraged. Remembering the ways God has been good to you will help you sense his love for you.

A lot of people who have been Christians for a long time don't sense God's love because they think God only speaks to them with a critical voice. But if the voice you're listening to is always negative, then it's not God's.

God made you to love you. The number one purpose of your life is not for you to do good. It's not even for you to love God back.

The number one purpose of your life is to let God love you. You believe it, and you accept his grace. Then you'll experience even more mercy and grace! When you live securely in God's mercy, grace, and love, you'll have the confidence and hope to pursue the good things he's planned for you.

MAY 15

Three Things to Focus on Instead of Yourself

Let heaven fill your thoughts; don't spend your time worrying about things down here.
COLOSSIANS 3:2 (TLB)

True freedom comes when you focus your mind on God's truth. But there are so many things to distract you throughout your day. How do you focus your mind on the right things so you can experience freedom?

Here are three things that will make a big difference in managing your mind:

First, think about Jesus. Hebrews 12:3 says, *"Think about Jesus' example. He held on while wicked people were doing evil things to him. So do not get tired and stop trying"* (NCV). What gives you the power to keep going? You think about Jesus. You stay in God's Word. Keep your mind on who the Bible says he is and the example he's given you for how to live a life that pleases God.

Second, think about others. *"Let us think about each other and help each other to show love and do good deeds"* (Hebrews 10:24, NCV). Most everyone in the world thinks about themselves first. That means anyone who thinks more about others than they do themselves is going to shine.

When you choose to think about the needs of others and how you can help them, you'll find it harder to let your problems get you down. Choosing to focus on others gives you a new perspective on your own circumstances and concerns.

Third, think about eternity. The Bible says in Colossians 3:2, *"Let heaven fill your thoughts; don't spend your time worrying about things down here"* (TLB). Whatever you're worried about today may seem like a big deal. But it is probably not going to matter in five years, much less in eternity. The things you're struggling with are not minimized when you think about spending forever with Jesus in heaven. But you view everything rightly when you view it in light of eternity.

Whatever situation you're facing today, stop and think about what you're thinking about. Then choose to focus on Jesus, other people, and your home in eternity. It will take the focus off of yourself, which is how God intended for you to live. And it will transform your life!

MAY 16

How Can You Help?

Each one of us needs to look after the good of the people around us, asking ourselves, "How can I help?"
ROMANS 15:2 (MSG)

If you're driving and get a flat tire, and the president of the United States drives by, nobody expects him to stop and help you. He's too important to deal with your problems.

But that's not Kingdom values—that's worldly values. Jesus said that if you want to be great, you must be the servant of all. The more you give of yourself and serve other people, the greater you are in God's Kingdom.

A few years back, my wife had four major speaking engagements within a short period of time. She got home from one trip and was totally wiped out. But she went immediately to the kitchen and started cooking a meal for neighbors who were going through a major struggle. She didn't think she was too important. She put her exhaustion aside so she could help others. She has done this over and over again—because she wants to be like Jesus. She wants to serve.

What does it mean to love like Jesus? *"Each one of us needs to look after the good of the people around us, asking ourselves, 'How can I help?'"* (Romans 15:2, MSG).

In fact, one way to serve *like* Jesus is by serving others as if you're serving Jesus himself. Look for how Jesus may be in your life disguised as a hurting person. He may be refilling his coffee at the office on Monday morning. He may be at the soccer game. He may be behind you in the grocery store line. He may be the most unlovable person you know who is carrying a deep hurt. If you want to serve Jesus, then start by showing up for the hurting people around you.

Romans 12:13 says, *"When God's children are in need, you be the one to help them out. And get into the habit of inviting guests home for dinner or, if they need lodging, for the night"* (TLB). Many people in your church, neighborhood, and even family are single parents working to put food on the table, widows who are lonely in their empty houses, or students who are overwhelmed.

What are ways you can love them like Jesus loves them?

MAY 17

When You Start to Doubt, Choose to Believe

Be bold and strong! Banish fear and doubt! For remember, the Lord your God is with you wherever you go.

JOSHUA 1:9 (TLB)

Doubt is a great enemy of God's dream for your life. Doubt limits your potential, causes procrastination, and makes you miss God's best.

The Bible says, *"Anyone who doubts is like a wave in the sea, blown up and down by the wind. . . . They should not think they will receive anything from the Lord"* (James 1:6, 8, NCV).

Before God can use you in any significant way, you have to deal with your doubt.

Joshua was a great leader who led the Israelites into the Promised Land. But he also had a problem with doubt. Even though God chose him to play an important role in Israel's story, he struggled with self-confidence—and for good reason.

First of all, he was Moses' successor. And the Bible says in Deuteronomy that Moses was the greatest man who ever lived! I'd have some self-doubt, too, if I had to follow a reputation like that. God also gave Joshua some big assignments, like leading the Israelites into a land inhabited by seven bigger, stronger enemy nations.

To let God use him, Joshua had to let go of his doubt. So the night before the Israelites began their campaign to take over the Promised Land, God gave Joshua a pep talk. He said, *"Be bold and strong! Banish fear and doubt! For remember, the Lord your God is with you wherever you go"* (Joshua 1:9, TLB). God told Joshua to dump his doubts—and he wants you to do that too.

Doubt is a choice. Whenever you're doubting God, your abilities, or other people, you are *choosing* to believe your doubts and doubt your beliefs. Instead, you need to doubt your doubts and believe your beliefs. Believe that God is with you, he will help you, and he wants to work in your life.

Joshua believed God's promises to be with the Israelites and help them. He believed God when he said Joshua would be a great leader. He wanted to fulfill God's mission for him. So whatever doubts he had, Joshua chose to believe in God's promises and faithfulness.

Don't trust your doubts. Believe your beliefs!

MAY 18

Tell God Exactly How You Feel

I can't be quiet! I am angry and bitter. I have to speak.

JOB 7:11 (GNT)

God can handle your emotions. After all, he gave them to you!

He can handle your anger, doubt, fear, questions, grief, and even your complaints. So tell God exactly how you feel. That's what Job did.

Job was brutally honest with God: *"I can't be quiet! I am angry and bitter. I have to speak"* (Job 7:11, GNT).

Then he continued to unload his feelings: *"Why do you keep me under guard? Do you think I am a sea monster? I lie down and try to rest; I look for relief from my pain. But you—you terrify me with dreams; you send me visions and nightmares until I would rather be strangled than live in this miserable body. I give up; I am tired of living. Leave me alone. My life makes no sense. Why are people so important to you? Why pay attention to what they do? You inspect them every morning and test them every minute. Won't you look away long enough for me to swallow my spit? Are you harmed by my sin, you jailer?"* (Job 7:12-20, GNT).

If you were God, how would you react to that? Zap Job with a thunderbolt?

But that's not what God did—because God understood Job. God understands you too. When you say, "God, I don't like this!" God's not going to be surprised. He created your emotions; he gave you the capacity to get angry and express your feelings.

In hard times, don't "grin and bear it." Instead, honestly tell God your struggle with him. Lamentations 2:19 says, *"Cry out in the night. . . . Pour out your heart like water in prayer to the Lord"* (NCV).

Job questioned God's actions, but he never stopped trusting him. The Bible says, *"Job stood up, tore his robe in grief, and shaved his head. Then he fell to the ground and worshiped"* (Job 1:20, GW). Did you know that trusting God with your feelings is an act of worship?

So go ahead—unload all your feelings on the God who created those feelings in the first place. He understands your hurt and wants you to trust him with your emotions.

MAY 19

The Battle against Evil Is Already Won

Do not be overcome by evil, but overcome evil with good.

ROMANS 12:21 (NIV)

When you're faced with evil, don't return it. Overcome it.

This is the opposite of human nature. When somebody hurts us, we want to hurt them back, right? When somebody hits us, we want to hit them back. When somebody slanders us, we want to slander them.

But God says that isn't the way to win the battle against evil. Romans 12:21 says, *"Do not be overcome by evil, but overcome evil with good"* (NIV). That is God's way of winning the battle.

Jesus Christ came to earth to show that you don't destroy evil by retaliating; you destroy it by overcoming it with good.

The Bible says, *"The Son of God came to destroy the works of the devil"* (1 John 3:8, NLT). Jesus came to obliterate evil. He came to wipe it out. Evil is going to end one day. It is not going to exist forever. One day God is going to close the books. He's going to settle the score. He's going to end history and take his family into eternity with him.

If you want to be on the winning side, you'd better get on God's side because evil is going to lose. Evil wins a few battles here and there, but the final outcome of the war has been predetermined.

Good and evil are not equal in force or competition. It may feel like evil is stronger and that evil is winning. But love is far stronger than evil. Kindness is far stronger than evil. Good is much greater than evil. Good will win the day a hundred times over evil.

In the end, God and his followers will win. Good will triumph over evil because God is love, and his love will last forever.

Jesus said, *"I will build my church, and all the powers of hell will not conquer it"* (Matthew 16:18, NLT).

You can use goodness to fight against evil with the confidence that God has already won the war. Evil is going to lose. Victory is assured!

MAY 20

When God Doesn't Immediately Answer

I wait expectantly, trusting God to help, for he has promised.
PSALM 130:5 (TLB)

God wants you to wait patiently for him to answer your prayer, but he also wants you to wait expectantly. Have faith. Trust God to hear and to answer. When you wait expectantly, you show God that you believe his promises. You believe he's going to keep his word.

Daniel Boone, the famous frontiersman, was once asked whether he'd ever gotten lost in the wilderness. He said, "I can't say as ever I was lost, but I was bewildered once for three days."

Some of you may feel bewildered right now. You're bewildered about your marriage: "I'm praying for it to get better, but it's not happening." You're bewildered about your career: "Do I go up, down, or change jobs?" You're bewildered about relationships. You may feel powerless and hopeless, like you can't do anything to change your situation on your own.

Don't be discouraged! Don't give up! Turn to prayer. I've asked God for many requests in my life that have never been answered. I can think of one prayer that I have prayed almost every day for twenty-four years, and it hasn't been answered. I don't know why God hasn't chosen to answer that prayer, and I don't understand it. But I have decided this: Whether or not God ever answers that prayer, I am going to die believing his promises. Because God is a good God, and he knows what's best, even when I don't understand it.

When God doesn't answer your prayers, you need to remember a couple of important truths: First, God is in control, and you're not. He knows what you need better than you do. There is no mountain too tall that he can't move, no problem too big that he can't solve, and no sorrow too deep he cannot soothe. God is in control, and he has a plan.

The second thing you need to remember is that whether or not you ever receive your answer, God will honor your patience—if not in this world, then in eternity.

"I wait expectantly, trusting God to help, for he has promised" (Psalm 130:5, TLB).

MAY 21

Build Your Life on Things That Last Forever

For we fix our attention, not on things that are seen, but on things that are unseen. What can be seen lasts only for a time, but what cannot be seen lasts forever.
2 CORINTHIANS 4:18 (GNT)

What's going to last forever? That's an important question to ask if you're trying to decide what you're going to build your life's values on—because you need to invest your life in the things that will last the longest.

Here's the truth: Most people rarely evaluate their values or question their perceptions until they have a crisis. It's when you're in deep pain that you begin to examine what you're basing your life on. You may realize you've been living your life to feel good, look good, or accumulate wealth or power. The crisis helps you realize instinctively that there has to be more to life.

But there's no reason to wait for a crisis to evaluate your values. Instead, stop today to consider what you should value. Start by asking yourself that critical question: "What's going to last?"

The world seems to value the here and now. The message is that tomorrow doesn't matter. Next year doesn't matter. A thousand years from today doesn't matter. Eternity and heaven don't matter. Live for today.

But the Bible says something different: *"The world and its desires pass away, but whoever does the will of God lives forever"* (1 John 2:17, NIV). Living only for the here and now is incredibly shortsighted. Temptation is a great example of that. Temptation isn't just a battle between good and bad or what's best and what's not best. Temptation is always a battle between now and later, between the long-term and the short-term: "Will I do what God says and enjoy the benefits later, or will I do what I want and enjoy the benefits now?"

The Bible teaches us to *"fix our attention, not on things that are seen, but on things that are unseen. What can be seen lasts only for a time, but what cannot be seen lasts forever"* (2 Corinthians 4:18, GNT).

Whether you're in a crisis or not, take some time to evaluate what you're basing your life on. Choose to build your life on God's truth. It will last forever and never let you down.

MAY 22

Five Things You Must Learn in Your Family

He makes the whole body fit together perfectly. As each part does its own special work, it helps the other parts grow, so that the whole body is healthy and growing and full of love.

EPHESIANS 4:16 (NLT)

Strong families encourage growth by creating an atmosphere of lifelong learning. They help each other develop. They encourage the discovery of each person's spiritual gifts and abilities. They allow each other to learn new things and develop new interests.

But you don't necessarily need a biological or adoptive family to help you grow. Your church family can—and should—be a force for growth in your life.

The Bible explains it like this: *"He makes the whole body fit together perfectly. As each part does its own special work, it helps the other parts grow, so that the whole body is healthy and growing and full of love"* (Ephesians 4:16, NLT).

There are some things that you're never going to learn if you don't learn them in relationship with others. You can't learn them at school or work. You can only learn them with other people. You need community.

In fact, most of your problems as an adult come from the fact that you didn't learn certain things correctly as a child. Here are five things you must learn in your family—biological or otherwise:

1. **You learn what to do with feelings.** In a healthy family, you learn how to identify, own up to, and express your feelings. Strong families let everyone be honest and let kids express their emotions too.

2. **You learn how to handle conflict.** Kids need to see their parents working problems out in front of them and dealing with disagreements in a healthy way.

3. **You learn how to handle loss.** You don't want your kids to win all the time. If they do, they'll find it devastating when they face inevitable losses as adults in the real world. They need to learn that failure won't destroy them, that a loss isn't the end of life.

4. **You learn which values matter most.** It's important to teach kids the three basic temptations of life so they are not swayed by what the world values. Those temptations have to do with how you feel, what you do, and what you get in life—in other words, sex, salary, and status.
5. **You learn good habits.** Habits determine your character. Families should help each other grow so that everyone's character is more like that of Jesus Christ.

If you want to grow spiritually and help others within God's family grow, then you can start with this prayer: "Father, I know you gave me your family, the church, for a reason. I'm not meant to go through life on my own! You want me to be more like Jesus, and the best place to learn how to do that is in community with my church family. Please show me the opportunities you've already given me to do that, and give me wisdom and grace as I help build the kind of community, at my church and in my home, that helps people grow in these five areas. In Jesus' name, amen."

Start to make changes today so that your family is a safe place for everyone to learn and grow.

Love Is a Choice

If I have a faith that can move mountains,
but do not have love, I am nothing.
1 CORINTHIANS 13:2 (NIV)

Love is not a feeling. Love is a choice. Love is an action. Even when you don't feel like it, you can choose to show love anyway.

I once talked with a young mother who felt overwhelmed and battled depression. She felt like all she did was nag her kids and scold them incessantly. When she looked at herself, she saw a failure. In her despair, she cried out to the Lord.

As she spent more time reading the Bible, this one truth in 1 Corinthians 13:2 leaped out at her: *"If I don't have love, I am nothing"* (GW). So she wrote out these words and placed the notes all over her house—on her refrigerator door, on the dashboard of her car, at the top of her calendar.

"I realized the single most important thing I could do was love my family," she said. "So I began to live my life by love. I began to run my home on love. It was as transforming as when I accepted Christ into my life. It brought the happiness back into my life and my home."

What made the difference for this young mom? She made a choice. It wasn't always the easy choice, but it changed the whole dynamic of her home and the way she saw herself as a mother and as God's child.

Acting in love when you don't feel like it is actually a greater expression of love than when you *do* feel like it. Love is getting up in the middle of the night to help a sick kid after you've already had a long day and gone to bed late. Love is being patient with your spouse when they're irritable. Love is giving a person what they need, not what they deserve.

It's easier to act your way into a feeling than feel your way into an action. If you act lovingly, eventually the feelings will follow. That's important to remember when you are trying to love people who seem unlovable.

When you love despite your feelings, that's called loving by faith. And it doesn't just change the other person. It changes you, too, and makes you more like Jesus.

MAY 24

The Cross Frees You to Forgive

We know that our old life died with Christ on the cross so that our sinful selves would have no power over us.
ROMANS 6:6 (NCV)

On the cross, Jesus broke the power of sin. Romans 6:6 says, *"We know that our old life died with Christ on the cross so that our sinful selves would have no power over us"* (NCV). This is great news, especially because our natural inclination is to hurt others when they hurt us. If someone says something bad about you, you want to say something bad about them. We tend to hold on to hurts and struggle to forgive.

But you can break that bondage to bitterness, guilt, resentment, and worry. You can avoid becoming a slave to the past and hurtful memories. You can choose to forgive.

What hurt are you hanging on to? Here's an important question about that hurt: How badly do you want to be healed of it? Do you want to let it go? Maybe you've gone over it a thousand times in your mind—what your parents, siblings, or spouse did. Every time you think about it, it still hurts.

The cross has the power to free you from grudges, grief, and resentment. There's nothing outside of the cross that will empower you to let go of the emotions that are weighing you down. On the cross, Jesus broke the power of sin, death, and bondage in your life.

I want you to think of the person you need to forgive—the person whose offense planted a seed of bitterness in you—and pray this prayer right now:

"Father, only you understand how much I've been hurt by this person. I don't want to carry the pain for another second or become bitter. I need your grace and the power of the cross to release my hurt and to forgive.

"I need to experience your forgiveness. You know all the ways I've hurt others, and I'm sorry for my sins. Jesus, thank you for dying for me. I accept your grace and forgiveness, and I need it daily.

"Today I'm turning to you, and I'm choosing to forgive like you forgave me. Every time the memory returns, I'll forgive that person again until the pain is gone. Heal my heart with your grace. In Jesus' name, amen."

MAY 25

When Hope Starts Fading, Start Praying

From inside the fish Jonah prayed to the LORD his God.

JONAH 2:1 (NIV)

Have you ever felt swallowed up by life? Maybe you were surrounded by depression, conflict, worry, or guilt—and you started to feel hopeless.

I hope you're not feeling that way right now, but at some point, you will. We all will! You might lose a loved one, a job, or your health.

When you're faced with a hopeless situation, think about what Jonah did.

Jonah received a mission from God, but he chose to run away from it. So God stopped him by sending a great fish to swallow him up. And as Jonah sat in that great fish, he finally looked up to God.

In fact, the entire second chapter of Jonah is about him praying while he sinks into the ocean and gets swallowed by a giant fish: *"From inside the fish Jonah prayed to the LORD his God"* (Jonah 2:1, NIV).

It's a lesson for us when we're feeling overwhelmed, when we're feeling swallowed by life's problems. That's the time we need to look up to God in prayer.

There are problems in life so difficult that they can only be overcome through prayer. In Mark 9, some of Jesus' followers had been trying to drive a demon out of someone, but they couldn't. They asked Jesus why.

Jesus responded, *"This kind can come out only by prayer"* (Mark 9:29, NIV).

Some problems are so deeply rooted that only *persistent* prayer will solve them. That means you don't just pray about them one time and then expect God to answer. If you only care about something enough to pray about it once, then you don't really care about it. If you truly want to see something happen in your life, then you will pray about it over and over.

Never give up! God wants to build your faith through your persistent prayer. If you're feeling hopeless today, look up to God and keep praying, knowing that he hears you and will answer in his time.

MAY 26

Two Ways to Be a Kinder Person

There is no fear in love, but perfect love casts out fear.

1 JOHN 4:18 (ESV)

The parable of the Good Samaritan in Luke 10 teaches profound lessons about kindness, like being aware of the needs around you and sympathizing with others.

One of the most important lessons the Good Samaritan teaches is that, if you want to become a kinder person, then you must be willing to do two things:

You must be willing to be interrupted. Kindness doesn't happen on *your* schedule. It happens on *others'* schedule. That's why they need kindness. When you see someone in need, you've got to drop everything and stop. Love is often inconvenient, and kindness takes time.

Think of the excuses the Good Samaritan could have given to the wounded man on the side of the road. He could have said, "I've got my own problems to think about" or "I've got important business to care for. Besides, it's probably a lost cause." Anytime you want an excuse for being unkind, the devil will be right there to give you one.

God intentionally puts hurting people in your path so that you will learn kindness. When you encounter those opportunities, will you seize the moment?

You must be willing to take risks. Your own fears can keep you from being kind. Just imagine the legitimate fears the Good Samaritan could have had.

He could have said, "What if it's a trap?" or "What if he rejects my help?" Today, we might say, "What if he sues me?" or "What if I can't really help him? I'm not trained in first aid." One big fear we often have is that getting involved in someone else's pain reminds us of our own brokenness. We're afraid to deal with others' pain because then ours might bubble out.

But we'll never learn how to truly show kindness until we move past our fears and extend God's love to people who are hurting. The Bible says, *"There is no fear in love, but perfect love casts out fear"* (1 John 4:18, ESV).

God's love helps us heal from our hurt and move past our fears so that we can show love and kindness to others.

MAY 27

Seize Every Opportunity to Show Kindness

Never walk away from someone who deserves help; your hand is God's *hand for that person.*

PROVERBS 3:27 (MSG)

When you read the story of the Good Samaritan in the Bible, it's important that you notice *all* the specific ways the Samaritan showed kindness. First, he opened his eyes to see the need around him. Next, he listened to the injured man's pain and sympathized with him.

Then, the Good Samaritan seized the moment: *"Going over to him, the Samaritan soothed his wounds with olive oil and wine and bandaged them"* (Luke 10:34, NLT). He didn't wait or procrastinate. He did what he could at the very moment he saw the need.

Love is something you *do*. Love doesn't just say, "I'm sorry for this guy. Isn't it a shame? Isn't that too bad?" Love seizes the opportunity.

The Good Samaritan did several things in that moment. Some translations say that he *"stooped down."* He didn't pretend he was superior, and he didn't talk down to him. He got on the man's level.

Next, he used what he had. He dressed the man's wounds with wine and oil. Why? That's what he had on his donkey. The wine worked because it contained alcohol; it was an antiseptic. The oil worked because it would be soothing to the man's wounds. Then the Good Samaritan dressed the man with bandages. Where did he get the bandages? He didn't have a first aid kit. And the hurt man had been stripped naked, so he didn't have any clothes. The bandages were the Samaritan's own clothes.

The Good Samaritan did what he could with what he had at that particular moment. Proverbs 3:27 says, *"Never walk away from someone who deserves help; your hand is* God's *hand for that person"* (MSG).

The world is full of wounded people. Do you ever wonder how many people you walk by every day who are wounded? Maybe they're not wounded physically, but they're wounded emotionally. They're wounded spiritually. They're wounded financially. And they need your love. They need your kindness.

Don't wait for better conditions or until it's more convenient. Don't put off what you know you should do for someone today. God will be with you as you seize the moment.

MAY 28

Why You Do What You Don't Want to Do

You will know the truth, and the truth will set you free.

JOHN 8:32 (NIV)

Have you ever wondered why you do what you don't want to do? Ever wondered why it's so hard to do the things that you know are the right things to do?

Because of our sinful nature, we often make the wrong choice. You can probably relate to the apostle Paul when he said, *"I don't really understand myself, for I want to do what is right, but I don't do it. Instead, I do what I hate. . . . So I am not the one doing wrong; it is sin living in me that does it. And I know that nothing good lives in me, that is, in my sinful nature. I want to do what is right, but I can't"* (Romans 7:15, 17-18, NLT).

Even after you become a follower of Jesus, there's this tension inside of you. You have your good nature that God gave you, but you also have your old sinful nature that is pulling at you.

But there is a way out! Jesus promised in John 8:32, *"You will know the truth, and the truth will set you free"* (NIV).

The secret to personal change is not willpower or something you do or say. It's not a pill, resolution, or vow you make.

The secret to personal change is something you *know*.

You know the truth. When you change the way you think, it changes the way you feel. And when you change the way you feel, it changes the way you act.

Behind every self-defeating act is a lie you believe. It may be a lie about yourself, your past or future, God, or others.

Why do you do something that you know is bad for you? Because you think there's some kind of payoff. That's the lie! You can only change and fulfill God's purpose for your life if you start with God's truth. If you want to change the way you live, you need to start in your mind. You need to know and believe God's truth.

When you know the truth, the truth will set you free.

MAY 29

Mercy Could Be Your Greatest Witness

Be merciful, just as your Father is merciful.
LUKE 6:36 (NIV)

In an increasingly unkind world, your greatest Christian witness could be showing people mercy.

Have you noticed how unmerciful and unforgiving our world is? It seems the highest form of humor is the put-down. Even comedians get paid for their sarcastic and cynical jabs at others.

But when people see you showing mercy, especially considering how rude and mean society has become, they'll say, "That's what I expect a Christian to be like—like Jesus."

Jesus said in Luke 6:36, *"Be merciful, just as your Father is merciful"* (NIV). How do you do that? Here are two ways you can be more merciful.

Look and listen for people's needs. Mercy always begins with awareness. If you're not aware, then you don't care. The Bible says, *"Look out for one another's interests, not just for your own"* (Philippians 2:4, GNT).

You don't struggle to be merciful because you're a bad person. It's because you're too busy! When you're moving from event to event and task to task, it's hard to pay attention to the people around you. Start looking up and around more. There are always opportunities to show mercy, if you'll just be more aware of what people are feeling and going through.

Don't be offended by the sins of others. You can't say, "Go clean up your life, and then I will accept you." Mercy is unconditional. If you're going to show mercy to people, you can't be offended by them. You can't minister to people if you're looking down on them.

Jesus wasn't offended by people's sins. In fact, he hung out with the worst kinds of sinners. That doesn't mean Jesus approved of everything they did. God doesn't approve of everything you do either, but he accepts you completely.

Showing mercy doesn't mean you say everything someone does is okay. But you can still show mercy.

You can do for others what Christ has done for you. *"Above all, love each other deeply, because love covers over a multitude of sins"* (1 Peter 4:8, NIV).

MAY 30

Three Ways Jesus Responds to Your Failure

The steadfast love of the Lord *never ceases; his mercies never come to an end; they are new every morning; great is your faithfulness.*
LAMENTATIONS 3:22-23 (ESV)

Failure can be isolating. When you're in the middle of a failure, you often feel ashamed and just want to be alone. But Jesus is with you always, even in your greatest failure.

To help you through your failures, Jesus does three things:

Jesus prays for you. Even before Peter failed by denying Jesus three times, Jesus told him, *"I have prayed for you, that your faith will not fail"* (Luke 22:32, NASB).

At this very moment, Jesus is praying for you. *"He is able, once and forever, to save those who come to God through him. He lives forever to intercede with God on their behalf"* (Hebrews 7:25, NLT).

Jesus believes in you. In fact, he expects you to heal and recover. That's why he told Peter before his big failure, *"When you have repented and turned to me again . . ."* (Luke 22:32, TLB). Jesus knew Peter would sin and fail—and eventually come back to him.

We all fail. But no matter how many times you fail, God will always believe in you.

Jesus shows you mercy. When you're down, Jesus doesn't add to your guilt. Instead, he saves you.

Just weeks after Peter denied Jesus, the disciples went fishing. Though they fished all night, they caught nothing. At dawn, Jesus told them where to throw their nets. *"So they did, and they couldn't haul in the net because there were so many fish in it"* (John 21:6, NLT). When Peter followed Jesus' instructions, he caught more fish than he could handle. Jesus can do more in five minutes of your life than you can do in fifty years of planning.

Here's more good news: God's mercy toward you is not dependent on your performance. Lamentations 3:22-23 says, *"The steadfast love of the* Lord *never ceases; his mercies never come to an end; they are new every morning; great is your faithfulness"* (ESV).

You may give up on God, but he's never going to give up on you. Jesus is praying for you, he believes in you, and he will always show you mercy. No matter what you do, God is faithful.

MAY 31

Three Things to Remember When You're Opposed

God blesses those who are persecuted for doing right, for the Kingdom of Heaven is theirs. God blesses you when people mock you and persecute you and lie about you and say all sorts of evil things against you because you are my followers. Be happy about it! Be very glad! For a great reward awaits you in heaven.

MATTHEW 5:10-12 (NLT)

When you feel pressured by the world because you love Jesus and other people don't, you need to remember three things:

1. **Opposition can make you more like Jesus.** Jesus said in John 15:18-19, *"If the world hates you, remember that it hated me first. The world would love you as one of its own if you belonged to it, but you are no longer part of the world"* (NLT).

   If you're going to grow up and be like Jesus Christ, you're going to have to go through the things Jesus went through, including loneliness, discouragement, stress, and temptation. Why would God spare you when he didn't spare his own Son from those things?

2. **Opposition will deepen your faith.** Your faith is like a muscle. A muscle grows by being stretched, strained, and tested. You're never going to grow a muscle if no weight is ever pulling in the opposite direction.

   If you don't have opposition in your life, your faith is not growing. The strongest believers in the world are those who are having their faith tested the most. The Bible says in 1 Peter 1:7, *"[Your faith] is being tested as fire tests and purifies gold—though your faith is far more precious than mere gold"* (NLT).

3. **Opposition will give you eternal rewards.** Matthew 5:10 says, *"God blesses those who are persecuted for doing right, for the Kingdom of Heaven is theirs"* (NLT).

   God's going to bless anybody who's persecuted for living for him. But notice that you don't get rewarded for being rude or obnoxious. If you're persecuted for living a self-righteous life, you're not a martyr. You're just a troublemaker. You don't get rewarded for that.

   You get rewarded for being like Jesus. When you share your faith, share it with gentleness and respect, and you'll be rewarded for it one day in heaven.

JUNE 1

How to Move from Overwhelmed to Overflowing

I am the vine, and you are the branches. If you stay joined to me, and I stay joined to you, then you will produce lots of fruit. But you cannot do anything without me.

JOHN 15:5 (CEV)

It's better to rest in God's goodness than to be overwhelmed with work and worry. But it's also easier said than done. It can be hard to take the steps that lead to rest and the abundant life God has for you.

These four daily habits will help you move from overwhelmed to overflowing.

1. **Stay connected to Jesus.** *"If you stay joined to me, and I stay joined to you, then you will produce lots of fruit"* (John 15:5, CEV). If you try to live on your own power, you're going to be overwhelmed. But when you plug in to God's power, you can fulfill your purpose and enjoy God's goodness.

2. **Replace complaining with gratefulness.** *"Do everything without complaining and arguing"* (Philippians 2:14, NLT). While complaining is unhealthy, studies have shown that gratitude is the healthiest emotion. It produces brain chemicals that boost happiness and lower stress.

3. **Stop being stingy, and start being generous.** *"Bring the full amount of your tithes. . . . Put me to the test and you will see that I will . . . pour out on you in abundance all kinds of good things"* (Malachi 3:10, GNT). God wired a universal law into the world: The more you give away, the more you get. God did that because he wants you to become more like him—and he is a giver.

4. **Stop comparing, and start being content.** *"It is better to be content with what little you have. Otherwise, you will always be struggling for more, and that is like chasing the wind"* (Ecclesiastes 4:6, NCV). Contentment doesn't mean you don't have goals, dreams, or plans. It simply means you don't need *more* to be happy. By nature, people are discontent. But by God's grace, you can rest contentedly in his goodness. When you grasp that most things are simply gracious gifts from God, your life will go from overwhelming to overflowing with God's abundance.

JUNE 2

God Wants You to Rest

He makes me lie down in green pastures,
he leads me beside quiet waters.
PSALM 23:2 (NIV)

Are you always in a hurry? Is your to-do list unrealistically long? Has more than one person told you to slow down? Do you feel guilty when you relax? Do you have to get sick to take time off?

The pace of modern society pushes us to keep going and going and going. Many people work even on their day off. And those who go to a church service often head home afterward only to dive right back into work (whether it's housework, schoolwork, or paid work), trying to do all the stuff they didn't accomplish during the regular workweek.

No wonder we're exhausted! Most of us are maxed out. But that's not the way of the Good Shepherd.

Psalm 23:2 says, *"He makes me lie down in green pastures, he leads me beside quiet waters"* (NIV).

God makes you lie down in green pastures—that's rest. And he leads you beside quiet waters—that's refreshment.

God, in his goodness, created rest, and he considers it as important as work. A loving shepherd makes sure his sheep get enough rest to stay healthy. It's the same with God, your Good Shepherd. If you won't lie down, God will make you lie down. Sometimes the only way God can get you to look up is to lay you flat on your back. He will do that because he cares about your physical, emotional, and spiritual health.

Isn't it amazing how much better things look after a good night's sleep? The difference between being stressed and being blessed is often rest.

A lot of your worry, hurry, scurry, and restlessness come from not understanding the goodness of God in your life. When you understand what God has done for you and wants to do for you in the future, you can relax, let go, and learn to rest.

You can live in the goodness of God.

JUNE 3

Four Steps to Help You Stop Worrying

Give all your worries and cares to God, for he cares about you.
1 PETER 5:7 (NLT)

It takes more than willpower to stop worrying—but you already know that because you've already tried. You've thought, "I shouldn't worry about this," yet it stays on your mind.

Here are four steps to help you stop worrying:

1. **Get to know God.** Jesus said in Matthew 6:32, *"People who don't know God and the way he works fuss over these things"* (MSG). Without a relationship with God, you have reason to worry. But as a believer, you have a heavenly Father who has promised to take care of you. You are God's child, and children get special privileges. When you worry, you're acting like you don't have a loving Father who is with you and for you.

2. **Put God first in every area of your life.** Matthew 6:31-33 says, *"Don't worry at all about having enough food and clothing. . . . Your heavenly Father already knows perfectly well that you need them, and he will give them to you if you give him first place in your life"* (TLB). Anytime you take God out of the center of your life and put anything else there, you're going to worry.

3. **Live one day at a time.** The Bible says, *"Don't worry about tomorrow, because tomorrow will have its own worries. Each day has enough trouble of its own"* (Matthew 6:34, NCV). If you're worrying about tomorrow, the future seems overwhelming and you can't enjoy today. God promises to give you grace and strength when you need it. Right now, you only need enough power for today.

4. **Trust God to care.** *"Give all your worries and cares to God, for he cares about you"* (1 Peter 5:7, NLT). How do you do that? One way is to memorize God's promises in the Bible. They're like an insurance policy for believers. When you know something's covered, you don't worry about it anymore. You can also pray. If you prayed as much as you worried, you'd have a lot less to worry about.

What's the result of taking these four steps? *"You will experience God's peace, which is far more wonderful than the human mind can understand"* (Philippians 4:7, TLB).

JUNE 4

The Characteristics of a Pure Heart

God blesses those whose hearts are pure, for they will see God.
MATTHEW 5:8 (NLT)

Our culture is obsessed with appearance. We celebrate the beautiful, the brightest, and the best. But God's priorities are different. While the world around you applauds beauty, wealth, power, and popularity, God cares most about your heart.

In his most famous sermon, the Sermon on the Mount, Jesus said, *"God blesses those whose hearts are pure, for they will see God"* (Matthew 5:8, NLT).

What does it mean to have a pure heart? The word we use today for that is *integrity*. Having integrity doesn't mean that you're blameless or never make mistakes. It means that you have a heart that is turned toward God. And God says that's the kind of heart he blesses!

David had a heart like that. Though David made huge mistakes, God said about him, *"David . . . is a man after my own heart"* (Acts 13:22, TLB).

Do you want to be a person of integrity—someone after God's own heart? One of the words that defines integrity is *wholeness*. When you have integrity, you are whole.

Think of your life like a pie. Some people's pies are divided up into slices. One slice is career, while another is church, another is family, and so on. But when you have integrity, your life isn't divided up; it's one whole, consistent pie. No matter where you are or who you're with—at church, at work, or at home alone—you're the same person. You're consistent. You're whole. You have integrity.

And what's the result of being a person of integrity? You are blessed by God for all of eternity. As the master said to his faithful worker in Matthew 25:21, *"You are a good and loyal servant. Because you were loyal with small things, I will let you care for much greater things"* (NCV).

We tend to think that God's blessings come from the big moments of life, when everybody is watching. But it's the small moments that reveal real integrity. Every small word of encouragement you give this week will be rewarded in eternity. Every small act of kindness will be rewarded in eternity. Every time you reject a temptation, you will be rewarded in eternity.

Integrity is powerful. It makes a difference not just now but for eternity!

JUNE 5

God Is Working for Your Good

Surely your goodness and unfailing love
will pursue me all the days of my life.
PSALM 23:6 (NLT)

Even in the middle of your hurts, habits, and hang-ups, God is watching over you.

King David said to God in Psalm 23:6, *"Surely your goodness and unfailing love will pursue me all the days of my life"* (NLT).

When David said, *"Surely your goodness . . . will pursue me,"* he wasn't saying, "Surely only good things are going to happen to me." David knew as well as anyone that bad things happen to good people. He had been abused and treated unfairly and was still a man who followed God's heart. But he also sinned terribly against people who had done no wrong to him.

David's point was that no matter how bad, evil, or difficult something seems—and no matter how much we mess things up—God will work it out for good. His goodness is pursuing us, no matter which way we turn.

It's one of God's great promises that he gave believers: *"And we know that in all things God works for the good of those who love him, who have been called according to his purpose"* (Romans 8:28, NIV).

In everything that happens to us, God is working for our good—if we love God and are following his plans. This verse does not say all things are good. But if you're a believer, all things are working together for God's plan and purposes, which are always good.

That means there is no difficulty, dilemma, defeat, or disaster in the life of a believer that God can't ultimately turn toward his purpose.

When you believe that, it changes how you view everything in your life—your relationships with God and other people, your past, your future, and whatever you are facing today. As you trust in God's good work in your life, you will be able to face even your toughest challenges with confidence.

JUNE 6

Focus on Pleasing God, Not People

Our purpose is to please God, not people. He alone examines the motives of our hearts.

1 THESSALONIANS 2:4 (NLT)

God made you to be *you*. He didn't make you to be what your parents, spouse, boss, or friends want you to be.

God wants you to be exactly who he created you to be. That means you have to refuse to be defined by others.

Hebrews 11:24 says, *"By faith Moses, when he had grown up, refused to be known as the son of Pharaoh's daughter"* (NIV). Moses had an identity crisis. He was born a Hebrew slave but raised as Egyptian royalty, the grandson of Pharaoh. When he grew up, he had two choices: He could pretend to be Pharaoh's grandson for the rest of his life and live with luxury, fame, and power.

Or he could admit who he really was: a Hebrew. If he did, his family would kick him out to live with slaves for the rest of his life. He would be disgraced and humiliated and live a life of pain and drudgery.

Which would you choose?

Most people today are living lies—trying to be people they're not. But Moses refused to live a lie because he was a man of integrity. Against all kinds of peer pressure, he insisted on being who God made him to be.

Who are you letting determine your identity?

Some people's parents died years ago, but they're still trying to live up to their expectations. Some people are hanging on to what their ex-husband or ex-wife said, trying to prove that person wrong. Some people are striving to keep up with what the culture says they should be. But the Bible says this: *"Our purpose is to please God, not people. He alone examines the motives of our hearts"* (1 Thessalonians 2:4, NLT).

Choose to be who God made you to be. Simply say, "I resolve to no longer let other people press me into their mold. I'm going to do what God wants me to do and fulfill the plan he has for my life—not somebody else's plan for my life."

That is true success in life. God wants you to be exactly who he created you to be—nothing more.

JUNE 7

Look at Others the Way God Looks at You

I came so that my sheep will have life and so that they will have everything they need. I am the good shepherd. The good shepherd gives his life for the sheep.

JOHN 10:10-11 (GW)

What's in our hearts often determines what we feel when we look at people. When we see a crowd, we can get irritated or impatient. But when Jesus saw a crowd, *"he had compassion for them, because they were harassed and helpless, like sheep without a shepherd"* (Matthew 9:36, ESV).

That's how God looks at you: with compassion. He doesn't put you down. He lifts you up! No matter how angry, hurt, or betrayed you feel, Jesus will always respond with compassion. He knows how helpless we are without him, *"like sheep without a shepherd."*

Sheep are defenseless on their own. They don't have claws, they don't run fast, and their teeth aren't very sharp. They need the protection of a shepherd.

Throughout the Bible, sheep are a symbol of God's people. John 10:10-11 says, *"I came so that my sheep will have life and so that they will have everything they need. I am the good shepherd. The good shepherd gives his life for the sheep"* (GW).

This kind of compassion comes only from Jesus, our Good Shepherd. And it's different from sympathy and empathy. Sympathy says, "I'm sorry you're hurt," and it stops there. Empathy is a deeper commitment that says, "I hurt with you." But compassion says, "I'll do anything it takes to stop your hurt."

In essence, that's what Jesus did through his life, death, and resurrection. He did whatever it took to stop your hurt, even dying on the cross and having nails pounded through his hands and feet. Compassion does whatever it takes. Jesus said the reason he came was *"not to be served but to serve others and to give his life as a ransom for many"* (Mark 10:45, NLT). Notice the two words *serve* and *give*. They define what it means to follow Jesus.

Do you look at hurting and helpless people the way Jesus does? Are you full of love and compassion, willing to do whatever you can to stop their pain?

The Bible repeatedly tells us that when Jesus looked at people in pain, he was moved with compassion. God wants you to look at others the same way.

JUNE 8

God Is Good, Even When You're in Pain

"My thoughts are nothing like your thoughts," says the LORD.
"And my ways are far beyond anything you could imagine. For just as the heavens are higher than the earth, so my ways are higher than your ways and my thoughts higher than your thoughts."

ISAIAH 55:8-9 (NLT)

There probably have been many times that you've prayed for something and God didn't answer the way you wanted, or you felt like he didn't answer at all.

Does that mean prayer doesn't work? No—because you've seen it work too many times. Does it mean that God isn't good? No, because God's character does not change. He is always good. Does it mean that you should give up on prayer? No! God is not a vending machine, and prayer is not a painkiller. He has not guaranteed us a pain-free life.

When you're in pain and you pray but don't see the answers, don't give up. Your job is to keep praying and keep trusting God, because you know that everything he does and allows in your life, he will use for good.

If a doctor cuts you open during surgery, then that's going to cause some pain. But if that surgery saves your life, then you wouldn't say the doctor was bad. You would recognize that the painful work saved your life. When God doesn't immediately end your pain, he is saying to you in that moment, "This pain may feel like too much. But my grace is sufficient for you."

I've had a lot of pain in my life. And, in fact, almost everything I've learned in life, I've learned through pain. That's because God is more interested in making us people of character than he is in making us comfortable. If you never experienced any pain or trouble, then you would never grow to spiritual maturity. You would never learn to trust God's wisdom and his plan for your life. *"'My thoughts are nothing like your thoughts,' says the* LORD. *'And my ways are far beyond anything you could imagine. For just as the heavens are higher than the earth, so my ways are higher than your ways and my thoughts higher than your thoughts'"* (Isaiah 55:8-9, NLT).

God wants good for your life, even more than you do. As you trust him in your pain, he will answer every prayer with his greatest gifts: his presence, his power, and his promises.

JUNE 9

How to Live a Life of Significance

Jabez was more honorable than his brothers. . . . Jabez cried out to the God of Israel, "Oh, that you would bless me and enlarge my territory! Let your hand be with me, and keep me from harm so that I will be free from pain." And God granted his request.

1 CHRONICLES 4:9-10 (NIV)

You may feel ordinary, but God made you to live a life of significance.

The Bible is filled with ordinary people who lived extraordinary lives because they believed God made them for a purpose and intended for them to successfully fulfill their mission.

One example is an ordinary man named Jabez. The Bible says that he lived a life that was anything but average. Here are some secrets to his success:

1. **He had great ambition.** While many people are content with being average, Jabez wanted God to do something significant through him. He didn't want to live half-heartedly; he wanted a full and meaningful life.

   Jabez was ambitious and motivated by the right things. How do we know Jabez's motives were genuine and not selfish? Because we read, *"And God granted his request."* God will never honor an unworthy request.

   Many people drift through life without goals, a master plan, or overall purpose. As a result, they never go anywhere. If you want to live above average, dream big! You're not meant to go through life wondering, "What am I doing? Where am I going?" God wants you to have a great ambition—fueled by the desire to serve him.

2. **He had a growing faith.** Jabez had a deep trust and belief in God. There's no mention of him having any special ability, talent, wealth, or education. He was just a common man with an uncommon faith.

   More important than ability and talent is faith—believing God will work through you.

How do you break out of mediocrity? Like Jabez, you get a great ambition and a growing faith—and depend on God to do the impossible. William Carey, often called the father of modern missions, summed it up this way: "Expect great things from God, and attempt great things for God."

JUNE 10

How to Recognize God's Voice

Heaven and earth will pass away,
but my words will never pass away.
LUKE 21:33 (NIV)

Sometimes it's hard to recognize God's voice. When an idea comes into your mind, you wonder if it's an instruction from God, a deception from Satan, or just something you want to do. But it's important to know how to discern God's voice because it can have eternal consequences.

A lot of evil gets blamed on God when people say, "God told me to do it!" The Bible says in 1 John 4:1, *"Don't always believe everything you hear just because someone says it is a message from God: test it first to see if it really is"* (TLB).

God will never contradict his Word. So you can ask yourself: "Does the idea in my mind right now agree with the Bible?"

God doesn't say one thing and then change his mind and say something else. If he said it, it's true—and it will always be true.

God is consistent. He isn't moody. He doesn't change his mind. He will never tell you to violate a principle that he's already given in his Word, the Bible.

So, when you're wondering whether you're hearing God's voice, the first question you need to ask is, "Does this thought line up with what God has already said?" If what you're thinking contradicts something that God has already said in the Bible, then you know it's wrong.

Jesus said in Luke 21:33, *"Heaven and earth will pass away, but my words will never pass away"* (NIV). God's Word is eternal because truth never changes. If something was true five thousand years ago, it was true a thousand years ago, it is true today, and it will be true five thousand years from today.

People might say, "God said it, I believe it, that settles it." No! God said it, and that settles it—whether you believe it or not!

God won't contradict himself. So, when you're trying to recognize his voice, the best starting place is to ask yourself, "Is this idea in harmony with the Word of God?"

JUNE 11

Let Go, and Trust That God Is in Control

Let go of your concerns! Then you will know that I am God. I rule the nations. I rule the earth.

PSALM 46:10 (GW)

Every day you need to decide who's going to be in control of your life—you or God.

That choice is a battle because there are things in life you want to control. You want to make your own rules. But relief from stress always starts with letting God be God. It always starts with saying, "God, I'm giving up control, because only you can control the things that are out of control in my life."

One reason you're stressed is because you're trying to take charge of things that only God can control. You can't control your spouse, kids, job, future, or past. When you try to play God, it puts you in opposition to God. Not only are you going to lose that conflict, you're also going to be tired—and stressed. Let go of control and trust that he is in control. Psalm 46:10 says, *"Let go of your concerns! Then you will know that I am God. I rule the nations. I rule the earth"* (GW).

When people face out-of-control situations and feel stressed, they usually go to one of two extremes. For some, the more out of control their life gets, the harder they try to control it. Others do the opposite: They give up and have a pity party. Neither of those reactions to stress work. Instead of being a victim or hypercontrolling, pray a prayer of surrender.

Millions of people pray the Serenity Prayer, which is based on the Lord's Prayer, but most haven't read the last eight lines of the prayer: "Living one day at a time, enjoying one moment at a time; accepting hardship as a pathway to peace; taking, as Jesus did, this sinful world as it is, not as I would have it; trusting that You will make all things right if I surrender to Your will; so that I may be reasonably happy in this life and supremely happy with You forever in the next. Amen."

That's where the power is! Power comes when you surrender to God anything you've been trying to control. And that will lead you to living a life of serenity.

JUNE 12

When You Need Wisdom and Power, Turn to God

True wisdom and real power belong to God; from him we learn how to live, and also what to live for.

JOB 12:13 (MSG)

The Bible tells the story of Job, a man who loved and served God. But he lost almost everything—his wealth, health, and children—in the span of one day.

Job's story shows us how to worship even when we're wounded. Even in the worst times, we can worship God by invoking his wisdom and strength.

Soon after Job had lost it all, he was on the ground in agony, grieving his losses and suffering physically from illness.

Three of Job's friends showed up and eventually started giving advice. A lot of it wasn't very helpful, but one friend, Eliphaz, told him, *"If I were you, I would call on God and bring my problem before him"* (Job 5:8, NCV).

Eliphaz was telling Job to invoke God's help. What does it mean to "invoke"? It means to appeal to someone greater than yourself for a special act, power, or privilege. That was good advice. When you're confused, angry, doubting, or wounded, don't turn away from God. Instead, turn *toward* him because he's the only one who has the power to really comfort you.

Once when Jesus was talking to a crowd, he told the people what changes they would have to make in their lives in order to follow him. But they didn't want any demands on their lives, so they started walking away.

Jesus turned to his disciples and asked, *"Do you also want to leave?"* (John 6:67, CEB). One of the men, Peter, said, *"Lord, where would we go? You have the words of eternal life"* (John 6:68, CEB).

If you turn away from God in pain, where will you go? No one else can help you like he can. So instead of turning away from him, invoke his strength and wisdom.

The Bible says, *"True wisdom and real power belong to God; from him we learn how to live, and also what to live for"* (Job 12:13, MSG). Following Jesus doesn't exempt you from life's problems. But it does mean God's wisdom and strength are available to you. Turn to him, and he'll show you what to do and give you the power to do it.

JUNE 13

There Is Power in Thanking God in Advance

The king appointed singers to walk ahead of the army, singing to the LORD *and praising him for his holy splendor. This is what they sang: "Give thanks to the* LORD*; his faithful love endures forever!"*

2 CHRONICLES 20:21 (NLT)

Prayer and praise are verbalized faith.

When you say, "God, thank you for taking care of my financial problems. Thank you for taking care of my pain. Thank you for working out this conflict," that's thanking him in advance for delivering you out of a difficult situation.

The story of King Jehoshaphat perfectly illustrates the power of thanking God in advance— *before* you get the answer to your prayer. When faced with an attack by three enemy armies, Jehoshaphat had an unusual battle strategy: *"The king appointed singers to walk ahead of the army, singing to the* LORD *and praising him for his holy splendor. This is what they sang: 'Give thanks to the* LORD*; his faithful love endures forever!'"* (2 Chronicles 20:21, NLT).

Would you agree this is an unusual way to organize an army? Imagine what the opposing armies thought when they saw the Israeli army led by a bunch of harpists and trumpeters.

I'm sure the choir wondered what was going on too. But Jehoshaphat had reminded them that the battle belonged to God, and if they believed in him, they would succeed. That's why they were able to thank God in advance for their upcoming victory and then *show* him that they believed by putting the choir before the army.

The way you show God that you have faith is by thanking him in advance for the answers to your prayers.

What happened when the choir thanked God in advance through their singing? *"At the very moment they began to sing and give praise, the* LORD *caused the armies of Ammon, Moab, and Mount Seir to start fighting among themselves"* (2 Chronicles 20:22, NLT). Jehoshaphat's army didn't lift a finger (except to play their instruments). How did they win the battle? They thanked God in advance. They believed he would take care of them and save them from their enemies. They showed faith in their battle formation. And then they watched as God delivered them.

Remember, because you can trust God to bring you through a difficult situation, you can praise him in advance for his deliverance.

JUNE 14

Why Change Doesn't Happen Instantly

People with their minds set on you, you keep completely whole, steady on their feet, because they keep at it and don't quit.
ISAIAH 26:3 (MSG)

God wants to change you—and your life—for the better. You may want change to happen fast. But God is not in a hurry because he's interested in growing your character, and that doesn't happen quickly.

A man once told me, "Rick, I feel like my life is flooded with problems and I'm about to drown in the flood." The first verse that came to my mind was about Noah and the flood: *"The floodwaters gradually receded from the earth. After 150 days . . . the boat came to rest"* (Genesis 8:3-4, NLT). The flood didn't disappear instantly, and I knew this man's problems wouldn't either. Lasting change takes time.

The truth is, growth happens little by little over your lifetime. Growth doesn't happen in a single step or a single leap. It doesn't even come from a single decision. It happens through incremental change. It happens through sanctification—the process by which God grows you up.

The apostle Paul said, *"I am certain that God, who began the good work within you, will continue his work until it is finally finished on the day when Christ Jesus returns"* (Philippians 1:6, NLT).

God's good work within you starts with a conscious commitment, that moment you say, "Okay, I'm in. I don't want to be stuck in a good life; I want the better life. I want all God has for me. I want the rest of my life to be the best of my life."

Isaiah 26:3-4 talks about that commitment: *"People with their minds set on you, you keep completely whole, steady on their feet, because they keep at it and don't quit. Depend on GOD and keep at it because in the LORD GOD you have a sure thing"* (Isaiah 26:3-4, MSG).

Do you want to be whole and steady? Set your mind on God, and *"keep at it and don't quit."*

When you understand that God *"will continue his work until it is finally finished on the day when Christ Jesus returns,"* you'll be much more patient in the long process of moving from a good life to the better life.

JUNE 15

Follow the Gentle Ways of Jesus

Take my yoke upon you. Let me teach you, because I am humble and gentle at heart, and you will find rest for your souls.
MATTHEW 11:29 (NLT)

Everyone wants to know the antidote to anxiety because we all experience it. We live in stressful times, and rest for our bodies and souls often seems elusive.

But it's not a secret: Jesus wants you to worry less and trust him more. He said in Matthew 11:29, *"Take my yoke upon you. Let me teach you, because I am humble and gentle at heart, and you will find rest for your souls"* (NLT).

After you come to Jesus and let him share your load, he wants you to learn from him. Why? Because Jesus is never in a hurry. He sets a pace that comes from a gentle and humble heart that is meant to bring life, not weariness. Jesus modeled for us how to live with peace and purpose, and following his example is how we refill our spiritual and emotional tanks. Watch how he lived, and do it the way he did.

But learning how to live like Jesus is a process. You don't learn it overnight because you didn't develop your overloaded lifestyle overnight. Learning takes time.

What will you learn from Jesus? You'll learn how to be gentle and humble. But how is that going to help you? Gentleness and humility don't seem like the natural cure for being stressed out and tired. Maybe you would expect him to say, "Learn from me, and I'll teach you how to have endurance and stamina."

Jesus wants you to learn to be gentle and humble because aggression and arrogance are two of the biggest causes of stress and emptiness.

Aggression is when we don't want to wait for anything and get overcommitted. It's the opposite of gentleness. Arrogance is when we try to control everything. Our ego is responsible for more stress and arrogance in our lives than we realize.

That's why the antidotes to the two biggest causes of stress in your life are gentleness and humility. You learn them by reminding yourself every day that you are not God and you are not anybody's savior.

Spend time with Jesus, and you'll see how gentleness and humility lead to rest.

JUNE 16

Grow in the Light of God's Word

I am the light of the world. If you follow me, you won't have to walk in darkness, because you will have the light that leads to life.

JOHN 8:12 (NLT)

As a vegetable gardener, I can tell you that the more hours of light you have, the bigger your crops will grow. For more than thirty years, I've used a special light bulb for gardening called a grow light. It emits a certain kind of light that causes plants and trees to grow. You use it in areas where there isn't enough light for plants to survive. I planted young redwood trees on the shady side of my house and used the grow lights on them until they got tall enough to get sunlight on their own. Today those trees are about forty feet tall.

Light is the key to life. Every plant grows by photosynthesis, which is dependent upon light. Humans depend on light to see and for our body's systems to function normally. No light, no power. No light, no growth. You can't live without light.

What's true of light in the physical realm is also true in the spiritual realm. On your dark days, when the sun is hidden and you can't see the light, you need the light of Jesus to change you for the better.

There are two ways that you change: when you see the light and when you feel the heat. One of those ways is far less painful than the other. If you would just change when you see the light, then you wouldn't have to change when you feel the heat.

Do you want to know what your grow light is? It's God's Word. Studying God's Word will help you grow in your knowledge of God and love for him. Ephesians 1:16-17 says, *"I pray for you constantly, asking God . . . to give you spiritual wisdom and insight so that you might grow"* (NLT). When you know God's Word, his light will flood your heart and give you wisdom and a new perspective. Then you'll understand the wonderful future God has promised you.

In the Bible, light and life go hand in hand: *"You are the giver of life. Your light lets us enjoy life"* (Psalm 36:9, NCV).

Life is meant to be enjoyed, not merely endured. The key is to live in God's light.

JUNE 17

Do You Really Need Everything You've Got?

Sell your possessions and give to those in need. This will store up treasure for you in heaven! And the purses of heaven never get old or develop holes. Your treasure will be safe; no thief can steal it and no moth can destroy it.

LUKE 12:33 (NLT)

Did you know there's a bank in heaven?

There is! In his Gospel, Luke talked about storing up treasure in heaven. As a Christian, you should make the greatest investments of your time, talents, and resources in this heavenly bank.

Everything you have is because of God's generosity. You would have nothing if it weren't for God. You wouldn't even exist! *"Every generous act of giving and every perfect gift is from above and comes down from the Father who made the heavenly lights"* (James 1:17, ISV). God's generosity with you should make you generous with other people. You should use what you've been given to help others.

Whatever you use to help other people and point them to Jesus Christ will be stored in your bank in heaven. You're making an investment in eternity when you use your resources for the most important thing: helping people have a relationship with God.

One day a very wealthy man came to Jesus and asked him how to prepare for eternity in heaven. This man had far more money than he needed or could even enjoy. He wanted to know how he could have eternal life.

Jesus gave this man some investment advice: *"Sell your possessions and give to those in need. This will store up treasure for you in heaven! And the purses of heaven never get old or develop holes. Your treasure will be safe; no thief can steal it and no moth can destroy it"* (Luke 12:33, NLT). In other words, liquidate some of your assets here on earth and send them on ahead to heaven, where your treasure will last forever.

What about you? Do you really need everything you've got? Or is Jesus speaking to you through these verses—telling you to give some of what you have to help people who have a lot less?

When you're generous, it changes your perspective on what you actually need. And, more importantly, every time you choose generosity, you're storing up treasure in heaven.

JUNE 18

Four Ways to Pray Effectively

Please remember what you told your servant Moses: "If you are unfaithful to me, I will scatter you among the nations. But if you return to me and obey my commands and live by them . . . I will bring you back to the place I have chosen for my name to be honored."

NEHEMIAH 1:8-9 (NLT)

You may know *what* you want to pray for—but sometimes it can be hard to know *how* to pray. Nehemiah was living in exile in Persia when he heard that the walls of Jerusalem had been torn down. Nehemiah mourned over this news, and his prayer teaches us four ways to pray effectively:

1. **Base your request on God's character.** Nehemiah called God *"the great and awesome God who keeps his covenant"* (Nehemiah 1:5, NLT). Pray like you *know* God will answer you: "I'm expecting you to answer this prayer because of who you are. You are faithful, great, loving, and wonderful! You can handle this problem, God!"

2. **Confess the sins of which you're aware.** Nehemiah confessed his sins: *"I confess that we have sinned against you. Yes, even my own family and I have sinned! We have sinned terribly by not obeying the commands, decrees, and regulations that you gave us"* (Nehemiah 1:6-7, NLT). It wasn't Nehemiah's fault that Israel went into captivity; in fact, he was most likely born in captivity. Yet he included himself in the national sins. He said, "I've been a part of the problem."

3. **Claim the promises of God.** Nehemiah prayed, saying, *"Please remember what you told your servant Moses"* (Nehemiah 1:8, NLT). Can you imagine saying *"remember"* to God? Nehemiah reminded God of a promise made to the nation of Israel. In effect, Nehemiah prayed, "God, you warned through Moses that if we were unfaithful, we would lose the land of Israel. But you also promised that if we'd repent, you'd give it back to us." Does God have to be reminded? No. Does he forget what he's promised? No. Then why do we claim God's promises? Because it helps *us* remember what God has promised.

4. **Be specific in what you ask for.** If you want specific answers to prayer, make specific requests. If your prayers consist of general requests, how will you know if they're answered?

What do you need to pray to God about today? Use Nehemiah's example to shape your prayer and add the specifics of your situation as you say, "God, I know you care about this, and I know it's not too big for you. I'm sorry for my part in causing this problem. You have promised not to leave me in my confusion and fear, and I'm trusting in that as I face this with your help. Please help me in this specific way: ______________________________."

When you're not sure how to pray, follow Nehemiah's example. And then trust that God hears and watch expectingly as he answers.

JUNE 19

Run to God with Your Pain

We were really crushed and overwhelmed, and feared we would never live through it. We . . . saw how powerless we were to help ourselves; but that was good, for then we put everything into the hands of God, who alone could save us.

2 CORINTHIANS 1:8-9 (TLB)

Whenever you experience something painful in your life, you have a choice: You can run *from* God, or you can run *to* God.

Running from God never made sense to me. How are you going to get any comfort when you're running from the greatest source of comfort? I've spent more time alone with God in the years since my youngest son died than in all the previous years. In the grief of that loss, what kept me going through all my painful days was worshiping God and being close to him.

If you'll choose to run *to* God, you can use your pain to draw closer to him in worship. How do you do that? You don't tell him what you think you ought to say. Instead, you tell him exactly how you feel. You tell him you don't like the pain. This is called lament. The Bible is full of people crying out to God in lament. That includes one-third of the psalms.

Even complaining to God is an act of worship. You can worship in all the phases of grief. You can express your shock, unload your sorrow, share your struggle, and surrender. You can ask God to use the pain for good in your life.

In 2 Corinthians 1:8-9, Paul said, *"We were really crushed and overwhelmed, and feared we would never live through it. We . . . saw how powerless we were to help ourselves; but that was good, for then we put everything into the hands of God, who alone could save us"* (TLB).

I've heard thousands of stories of people who came to know Jesus out of their pain, whose lives were completely transformed in the process of worshiping while grieving. And I can say to them, like Paul said in 2 Corinthians 7:9, *"I am glad . . . not because it hurt you but because the pain turned you to God"* (TLB).

When you're in pain, it's not a time to run away from God. It's a chance for you to draw close to God, trust him more, worship him more, and—ultimately—know and love him more.

JUNE 20

The Key to Reaching Your Goals

Two can accomplish more than twice as much as one, for the results can be much better. If one falls, the other pulls him up; but if a man falls when he is alone, he's in trouble. . . . And one standing alone can be attacked and defeated, but two can stand back-to-back and conquer; three is even better, for a triple-braided cord is not easily broken.

ECCLESIASTES 4:9-10, 12 (TLB)

God never meant for you to go through life isolated, trying to do everything by yourself. Success happens when you work alongside others.

One reason Nehemiah succeeded in rebuilding Jerusalem is because he broke the work down into manageable tasks among many different people. In Nehemiah 3, eighteen teams helped to make repairs, and you see the phrase *"next to him"* or *"next to them"* twenty-one times.

Nehemiah wanted the people to understand something. He gave them a pep talk that went something like this: "If you get tired and discouraged, just look to your left and look to your right, and you'll see people working next to you. You'll realize you're not alone. You're part of a team." He helped people feel part of something bigger than themselves. He did this by creating a spirit of teamwork among the people.

The New Testament uses the phrase *"one another"* fifty-eight times. The Bible says we're to love one another, help one another, serve one another, bear one another's burdens, and so on. This is how you develop a team spirit.

Why is a team spirit essential to reaching your goals? The Bible says, *"Two can accomplish more than twice as much as one, for the results can be much better. If one falls, the other pulls him up; but if a man falls when he is alone, he's in trouble. . . . And one standing alone can be attacked and defeated, but two can stand back-to-back and conquer; three is even better, for a triple-braided cord is not easily broken"* (Ecclesiastes 4:9-10, 12, TLB).

The apostle Paul understood this principle of developing a team spirit. He never did any of his ministry alone. He always took a team with him. The same is true with Jesus. His entire ministry was done with a group of twelve people. In fact, the first thing Jesus did in his ministry was build a small group.

Maybe you're struggling to accomplish your goal because you've been going at it alone. Remember, you were never meant to live without community. The work God has for you will always be accomplished in partnership with others.

JUNE 21

Before God Speaks, Decide to Say Yes

The seeds that fell in good soil stand for those who hear the message and retain it in a good and obedient heart, and they persist until they bear fruit.

LUKE 8:15 (GNT)

God speaks to people who decide they're going to do what he tells them to do, even before he tells them.

This kind of person says things like, "God, if you want me to move, I'll move. If you want me to get married, I'll get married. If you want me to leave this job, I'll leave this job. Before you even tell me, my answer is yes. Whatever you want me to do, I will do it."

Luke 8:15 says, *"The seeds that fell in good soil stand for those who hear the message and retain it in a good and obedient heart, and they persist until they bear fruit"* (GNT). I used to study this parable of Jesus and think it was talking about four kinds of people: those who are resistant, those who are shallow, those who are busy, and those who are good.

But this parable represents four attitudes. You can have all four attitudes on the same day! One moment you think, "God, I don't want to hear you, because I know what you're going to say." And the next moment you say, "Lord, tell me quickly." Then you hear it and think it's good, but you don't do anything about it. Maybe the fruit starts to appear in your life, but then you get busy with your job or school or your kids, and the weeds grow up. Other times you say, "God, do whatever you want. I'm open to you."

God wants you to have an attitude of obedience so you can bear fruit—the biblical term for being successful. God wants you to be fruitful in your business, your family, your friendships, your relationship with him, your relationships with others, and your health.

What's the best and quickest way to bear fruit? By taking what God told you and sharing it with someone else. Another version of Luke 8:15 says, *"They listen to God's words and cling to them and steadily spread them to others who also soon believe"* (TLB).

When God tells you something, accept it with an obedient heart and then share it with someone else!

JUNE 22

Three Things That Keep You from Hearing God

The seed that fell among thorns stands for those who hear, but as they go on their way they are choked by life's worries, riches and pleasures, and they do not mature.

LUKE 8:14 (NIV)

You can't hear God if your mind is crowded with other thoughts or concerns—particularly worries, plans, and activities. If you're always looking at your phone or watching TV, it's difficult to hear God when he calls. To hear God, you have to eliminate distractions.

Jesus said in Luke 8:7, *"Some other seeds fell where thornbushes grew up and choked the plants"* (CEV). In this story Jesus tells, seeds are planted and begin to grow—but the seeds are in weed-infested soil. So as the plants grow, the weeds grow up around them. The weeds choke out the life of the plants, and they never bear fruit.

Here's what Jesus said is the meaning of Luke 8:7: *"The seed that fell among thorns stands for those who hear, but as they go on their way they are choked by life's worries, riches and pleasures, and they do not mature"* (Luke 8:14, NIV).

Three things can choke spiritual growth and keep you from hearing God:

Worry. Worries are weeds. When you're preoccupied with the problems and pressures of daily living, it's harder to hear God.

Riches. Are you so busy making a living that you don't make a life? Working to pay bills for things you don't need, to get out of unnecessary debt, or to make more money than you actually need can stunt your spiritual growth.

Pleasure. There's nothing wrong with pleasure, but be careful that you don't become so busy pursuing fun that you miss God and his plans for your life.

Do you know what's always true of weeds? You don't have to cultivate them. They grow automatically. In fact, weeds are a sign of neglect. If you see weeds in your yard or garden, it means you're not tending it. It's the same with your spiritual life. The weeds in your spiritual life show that you're neglecting time with God.

Spend time each day tending to your spiritual garden. Pluck out the weeds as soon as they appear so they don't take over the good work God wants to do in you.

JUNE 23

Four Things to Remember When God Changes Your Plans

My thoughts are not like your thoughts. Your ways are not like my ways.
ISAIAH 55:8 (NCV)

Sometimes when our plans and God's plans don't match, we keep pushing back, trying to go our own way—but then things get worse.

Just ask Jonah. He learned the hard way how to respond when God's plans and his plans didn't line up. God told Jonah to warn the people of Nineveh that they needed to repent. But Jonah ran from God's plan and ended up in the belly of a big fish. God rescued him, and Jonah went to Nineveh. But when the people of Nineveh repented and God didn't punish them, Jonah was disappointed. He didn't want the Assyrians to receive grace because they were enemies of the Israelites.

So God gave Jonah an object lesson. God caused a plant to grow large enough to give Jonah shade. Then God sent a worm to attack the plant and kill it. The next day, as the sun beat down, Jonah let God know he was frustrated!

God reminded Jonah of four truths to remember when God's plans differ from ours.

God can see things you can't. He can see the past, present, and future all at the same time. He created time, so he is not subject to time.

God is good to you, even when you're cranky. Even when you're running from God, like Jonah, God still cares about your comfort and loves you.

God is in control of every detail of your life. God has a purpose in everything. He uses both the big and small things to direct your life.

God wants you to focus on what will last. Most of what worries you won't be around tomorrow. He wants you to focus on growing more like him and telling others about him.

When your plans don't turn out the way you want, God is still working in his wisdom for good. Isaiah 55:8 reminds us, *"My thoughts are not like your thoughts. Your ways are not like my ways"* (NCV).

Ask God to help you see his hand in your broken plans, and trust his goodness as he shows you the way forward.

JUNE 24

Whose Opinion Matters Most?

Blessed are you when people insult you, persecute you and falsely say all kinds of evil against you because of me. Rejoice and be glad, because great is your reward in heaven.

MATTHEW 5:11-12 (NIV)

When people criticize you for living a life that is pleasing to God, remember: You have a great reward waiting for you in heaven.

The Bible says, *"Blessed are you when people insult you, persecute you and falsely say all kinds of evil against you because of me. Rejoice and be glad, because great is your reward in heaven"* (Matthew 5:11-12, NIV).

Focusing on eternity is the antidote to insult and ridicule. Why? Because the opinions of others won't last. Their disapproval won't last. Yes, you can listen to their opinions, but don't overvalue what they say.

The only thing that *will* last is God's church. Only God's family will be in heaven forever. That's why you don't want to waste your life worrying about what people say about you. Instead, God wants you to spend your days doing the things that please him—using the gifts, talents, and abilities he's given you to worship him and make an eternal difference with your life.

If God likes what you're doing, then you know you're doing the right thing. Imagine how simplified your life would be if you lived for an audience of one!

But so often you care too much about what people think, and you put yourself at the mercy of their judgments. If someone thinks you're a loser, then you must be a loser. If someone thinks you're odd, then you must be odd. I don't want to live that way—do you?

The truth is, you won't be in heaven one minute when you'll say, "Why did I worry so much about what other people thought about me?"

As the apostle Paul said, *"What I want is God's approval! Am I trying to be popular with people? If I were still trying to do so, I would not be a servant of Christ"* (Galatians 1:10, GNT).

Today, instead of living for the approval of people, live for the joy of heaven. And know that your reward in heaven will be great when your only concern on earth is to please God.

JUNE 25

Keep Your Strengths in Perspective

If you think you are standing strong, be careful not to fall.
1 CORINTHIANS 10:12 (NLT)

Failure is part of life. No matter who you are or what your story is, you're going to experience failure at some point. It's part of living as an imperfect person in an imperfect world.

The night Jesus was arrested, before he went to the cross, his friend Peter failed him in a significant way. Peter denied Jesus—not just once but *three* times.

During the Last Supper, Jesus told his disciples he was going to be arrested, die, and three days later come back to life. Jesus said to the disciples, *"Tonight all of you will desert me"* (Matthew 26:31, NLT). Yet Peter kept insisting he would never deny Jesus. In fact, Peter said it *three* times!

Peter overestimated his strength—and it eventually led to his failure.

Overestimating our strengths is still a common cause of failure today. We think we're stronger than we are. We believe we can handle temptation, even though we have plenty of evidence that proves that is not true.

When we overestimate our strengths, there are dire consequences: Businesses fail, battles are lost, and marriages crumble. When we lose the right perspective on our abilities, we make unwise decisions. It's easy to think, "That could never happen to me." But 1 Corinthians 10:12 says, *"If you think you are standing strong, be careful not to fall"* (NLT).

No one is exempt. Given the right situation, you and I are capable of any sin.

When you don't pay attention to your strengths, they become weaknesses. In other words, an unguarded strength becomes a double weakness. Why? Because you have a sense of pride about it.

Peter's biggest failure, denying Christ, happened right after the Last Supper, a very intimate and powerful experience. The next area you stumble in may be right on the heels of a major victory in your life.

Resist the temptation to overestimate your strengths. Instead, remember you are a sinful human who needs God's grace. Keep your strengths in perspective so they don't become your source of failure.

JUNE 26

God Won't Let Go of Your Hand

My sheep listen to my voice; I know them, and they follow me. I give them eternal life, and they will never die, and no one can steal them out of my hand.

JOHN 10:27-28 (NCV)

You can't save yourself—but you don't have to! All you need to do is put your hand in God's hand and say, "God, I surrender my life to you—all the good and bad parts. I'm accepting your gift of salvation." When you do that, you can relax in your salvation.

Someday you might want to let go of God's hand and say, "I don't even know what I believe." But God won't ever let go of your hand—he loves you too much. Jesus said, *"My sheep listen to my voice; I know them, and they follow me. I give them eternal life, and they will never die, and no one can steal them out of my hand. My Father gave my sheep to me. He is greater than all, and no person can steal my sheep out of my Father's hand"* (John 10:27-29, NCV).

The *"eternal life"* God gives you begins the moment you put your hand in his, and you can't ever lose it. Why? Because your salvation is not based on having more good works to outweigh your bad works. It's based on the merits of Jesus Christ.

If you could get to heaven simply by being a nice person, then Jesus dying on the cross was a total waste of suffering, sorrow, and pain. If there was any other way for you to get into heaven except by Jesus, God would have chosen it. But there wasn't.

Jesus *"came to seek and to save the lost"* (Luke 19:10, NIV), which means the world is lost. Not everyone is going to heaven. If they automatically were, then Jesus didn't need to come to earth, live a perfect life, and carry *"our sins in his body to the cross, so that we might die to sin and live for righteousness"* (1 Peter 2:24, GNT).

When you put your life in God's hands, he promises he'll hold on to you forever. If you truly trust in Christ, then nothing can steal your salvation from you—not Satan, sickness, or society. You're in the hands of the Good Shepherd.

JUNE 27

When You Pray, Focus on God First

Jehoshaphat was frightened and prayed to the LORD *for guidance.*

2 CHRONICLES 20:3 (GNT)

In a crisis, it's natural to ask God for help. He wants you to pour out your heart to him—but don't start your prayer by telling God what you need. Start by focusing on him.

When three enemy nations decided to team up against King Jehoshaphat and Israel, the king knew there was no way he could overcome those odds, and so he prayed God-focused prayers. Here's how you can pray like Jehoshaphat:

First, remind yourself of God's greatness. Jehoshaphat prayed, *"O LORD God of our ancestors, you rule in heaven over all the nations of the world"* (2 Chronicles 20:6, GNT). When you're praying for something you can't control, don't focus on the problem. Focus on God's greatness. The bigger God gets in your mind, the smaller the problem becomes.

Next, remind yourself of God's unlimited power. In the midst of his problems, the king took time to praise God: *"You are powerful and mighty, and no one can oppose you"* (2 Chronicles 20:7, GNT). When you realize that God has all the power in the world, you can trust him. As you pray, think of all the ways God has helped you, people around you, and people in the Bible.

Then, remind God of his promises. Jehoshaphat reminded God of his promise to Israel that the land would be theirs forever: *"When your people Israel moved into this land, you drove out the people who were living here and gave the land to the descendants of Abraham, your friend, to be theirs forever"* (2 Chronicles 20:7, GNT). The Bible is filled with promises God has made to you too—thousands of them! When your kids remind you of the promises you've made to them, it can be frustrating. But God loves to have his Word quoted back to him.

Finally, ask God for a breakthrough. Jehoshaphat said of the attacking forces, *"Punish them, for we are helpless in the face of this large army that is attacking us. We do not know what to do, but we look to you for help"* (2 Chronicles 20:12, GNT).

Don't just ask God to bless your life. Focus on *him*, and then tell him the specific thing you need for your breakthrough. When you do, you'll see him provide as you pray like Jehoshaphat.

JUNE 28

Don't Be Afraid to Take Risks

All glory to God, who is able, through his mighty power at work within us, to accomplish infinitely more than we might ask or think.

EPHESIANS 3:20 (NLT)

What does it mean to have bold faith? It means taking risks. The Bible says, *"Without faith it is impossible to please God"* (Hebrews 11:6, NIV).

You see an example of taking risks in the parable of the talents. In Matthew 25, Jesus tells the story of a man who went away for a while and gave his servants some *"talents"*—a large amount of money. He gave one person one talent, another person two talents, and another person five talents.

The five-talent person invested his money and doubled it. The two-talent person invested it and got two more talents. When the master came back and saw what they had done, he said to them, *"Well done, good and faithful servant!"* (Matthew 25:21, 23, NIV).

But the person who was given one talent became afraid, so he hid his talent in the ground. When the master saw this, he said, *"You wicked, lazy servant! . . . You should have put my money on deposit with the bankers, so that when I returned I would have received it back with interest"* (Matthew 25:26-27, NIV).

The lesson Jesus was teaching is this: God wants you to take risks in faith. If you make the most of what he's given you, then you're going to be given even more. But if you're scared and take no risks, then you're actually being unfaithful—*you're not acting in faith*—with what God's given you.

I remember when Saddleback Church was buying our 120-acre campus in Orange County, California. People in the community began to ask, "Who do those people think they are, buying that much land in Orange County?"

When I heard them, I thought, "Wrong question." The right question is: "Who do we think God is?" Then we let the size of our God determine the size of our goal. Ephesians 3:20 says, *"All glory to God, who is able, through his mighty power at work within us, to accomplish infinitely more than we might ask or think"* (NLT).

So go ahead, take big risks and have bold faith. Because God says to you, "I can take your biggest dream—and top it!"

JUNE 29

Sin Grows from the Seeds of Selfishness

There will be more and more evil in the world, so most people will stop showing their love for each other.

MATTHEW 24:12 (NCV)

Someone once asked Jesus, "What's the most important command in Scripture?" His reply could be summed up like this: "There are two of them: Love God with all your heart, soul, mind, and strength, and love your neighbor as yourself" (see Matthew 22:36-40).

If those are God's two most important commands, then their opposite—not loving God and not loving your neighbor—is sin. Sin is always unloving.

Matthew 24:12 says, *"There will be more and more evil in the world, so most people will stop showing their love for each other"* (NCV). Have you noticed that today? People in general have become more critical, less civil, and ruder than ever. Why? Because as sin increases, love decreases.

Sin is unhelpful, unhealthy, unfair, unwise, untruthful—and it is always selfish.

We often tell ourselves we're doing something for the benefit of others when we're really doing it for our own benefit. The Bible says, *"Wherever there is jealousy and selfish ambition, there you will find disorder and evil of every kind"* (James 3:16, NLT). At the root of every sin is self-centeredness.

Why are you here on earth? God did not make you to live for yourself. You were made for something far bigger than that.

You were made by God and for God, and until you understand and believe that, life's never going to make sense. God didn't create you so you could center your life on yourself and push other people to the side. You were made to know God, enjoy him, have a friendship with him, serve him, and center your life on him.

Whatever you build your life around is your god, whether it's your boat or your business or a sport or another person.

God wants you to center your life on him, but sin will always put the focus back on you. So choose love, because where love is abundant, selfishness will not grow.

JUNE 30

God's Purpose Requires His Vision

Where there is no vision, the people perish.
PROVERBS 29:18 (KJV)

Why is vision so important in your life? Because *"where there is no vision, the people perish"* (Proverbs 29:18, KJV).

You cannot live the full life God has called you to without vision! Here are three reasons why it's essential to have a clear vision of God's purpose for your life.

Without God's vision, there is indecision. James 1:8 says, *"A person who has doubts is thinking about two different things at the same time and can't make up his mind about anything"* (GW).

Without God's vision for your future, you drift and wander through life. You don't have goals, purpose, or meaning. When you just let life happen to you, you're not really living!

Without God's vision, there is division. If you don't understand God's vision for your life, how can you expect others to support you in your purpose? In fact, the lack of vision makes you vulnerable to others steering you toward what they think or assume your purpose is.

Only God can tell you your purpose, because he created you specifically and uniquely to live it out. Proverbs 28:2 says, *"When the country is in chaos, everybody has a plan to fix it—but it takes a leader of real understanding to straighten things out"* (MSG).

Without God's vision, there is collision. For many people, life is just a series of relational confrontations, financial crashes, and personal crises. It's like a bumper car ride, where you just keep getting hit from all sides.

The Bible warns of the consequences of not following God's vision for your life: *"Some have refused to let their faith guide their conscience and their faith has been destroyed like a wrecked ship"* (1 Timothy 1:19, GW).

Getting God's vision for your life requires prayer, careful thought, and a continual effort to hear God's voice. It's the result of seeing things clearly, with eyes of faith rather than eyes of fear. When your faith guides your conscience, you'll gain a clearer understanding of how to move forward with purpose.

JULY 1

Where Do You Need a Reset?

Look closely at yourselves. Test yourselves
to see if you are living in the faith.
2 CORINTHIANS 13:5 (NCV)

You can ask God anytime for a fresh start in your life. But be specific. Don't just say, "God, I want you to change me." Tell God exactly what you have in mind!

Nothing becomes transformative until it becomes specific.

You cannot solve any problem until you first identify it as a problem—and that means you have to admit there are problems in your life. The more specific you are about what you want God to change in your life, the sooner it's likely to happen.

The Bible says it like this: *"Look closely at yourselves. Test yourselves to see if you are living in the faith"* (2 Corinthians 13:5, NCV).

Where do you need a reset? What would you like God to change in your life to give you a fresh start?

How about in your connection to God? If there has ever been a time in your life when you felt closer to God than you do right now, then you need a reset.

How about in your body? Do you need help making healthier choices or navigating a chronic illness? You can ask God for that!

Do you need a reset in your priorities? Have you started spending all your time doing things you know are not important? You need a reset in your schedule.

What about a relationship? Do you need to reset a stagnant or deteriorating relationship? You can ask God to help with that.

How about in your career? If you're out of work right now or if your job is keeping you from pursuing Christ, then you need a reset.

Do you need a reset in your thought life? If you're having thoughts that you know are wrong, that you can't control, or that worry you, then you need God to help you reset your thoughts and give you new ones.

Maybe you need a reset in your habits, your parenting, your schedule, your finances, or even your dream.

Whatever needs a reset in your life, just ask God for it—and be specific!

JULY 2

Four Ways the Bible Helps You Reset Your Life

All Scripture is inspired by God and is useful to teach us what is true and to make us realize what is wrong in our lives. It corrects us when we are wrong and teaches us to do what is right. God uses it to prepare and equip his people to do every good work.

2 TIMOTHY 3:16-17 (NLT)

Jesus said in John 17:17, *"Sanctify them by the truth; your word is truth"* (NIV).

What does *sanctify* mean? It simply means to grow up and to be made more like Christ—to get a reset. After you choose to follow Jesus, you're not the same person. You're different. You're being sanctified.

How are you sanctified? By God's truth. The more you incorporate God's Word into your life, the more you're going to be transformed and made new. With the help of the Holy Spirit, you will be able to reset the areas of your life where you want to experience change.

Making a change will always require you to know God's Word. It's the manual for resetting your life!

When you decide that you don't like the way you're living and the decisions you've made are just not working, then go to God's Word. It's going to help you in four very practical ways: The Bible shows you the path to walk on. It shows you where you got off the path. It shows you how to get back on the path. And it shows you how to *stay* on the path.

The apostle Paul outlines the four ways in 2 Timothy 3:16-17: *"All Scripture is inspired by God and is useful to teach us what is true and to make us realize what is wrong in our lives. It corrects us when we are wrong and teaches us to do what is right. God uses it to prepare and equip his people to do every good work"* (NLT).

In his Word, God has given you everything you need to make changes and then stay on the right path. This is why a daily quiet time of Bible study and prayer is important. When you're not in God's Word, you're not learning and facing the truth on a daily basis.

The Bible is like a mirror, reflecting the good, the bad, and those areas that need a reset. Let God show you the truth he offers in his Word so you can make changes that will lead to a life of purpose and joy.

JULY 3

The Power of Appreciation

I never stop giving thanks for you as I mention you in my prayers.
EPHESIANS 1:16 (ISV)

There is no complicated secret to working well with others. You just have to learn to appreciate them!

How do you appreciate them? It's simple. First, you practice recognizing someone's value and contribution. Then you make a habit of telling them, "Thank you."

Nehemiah demonstrates four practical ways to show appreciation for others:

Recognize individuals by name. When you thank the people in your life who are making a difference, don't just say, "You all are doing a great job. Thanks!" Get specific, like Nehemiah did. He singled out more than forty individuals and groups for special appreciation and called each one by name.

Recognize specific work. People feel appreciated when you point out the details of their work. Simply telling them they did a good job isn't enough. It's better to say, "I'm proud of you for doing *this* specific thing." Nehemiah recognized the detailed work of the people. He said, *"The Old City Gate was repaired by Joiada son of Paseah and Meshullam son of Besodeiah. They laid the beams, set up its doors, and installed its bolts and bars"* (Nehemiah 3:6, NLT). The Bible shows that details matter!

Recognize great attitude. It's hard not to notice great attitudes in a world filled with bad attitudes. In Nehemiah 3:20, Nehemiah singles out one man for his great attitude: *"Baruch . . . zealously repaired an additional section"* (NLT). When you call attention to the passion and enthusiasm of others, it renews their energy and sparks new energy in others.

Recognize extra effort. A man named Meremoth was mentioned twice by Nehemiah for going above and beyond. First, he repaired a section next to the Fish Gate (Nehemiah 3:4). Then he repaired the section by the high priest's house (verse 21, ISV). Nehemiah recognized Meremoth's extra work and wanted others to notice too.

It's given me great joy to point out the contributions of others and tell them how much they are appreciated. Sometimes it's a conversation. Other times it's a card or a note. But it's become a habit to notice the efforts and attitudes of others, recognize their perseverance, and encourage them to keep going.

It takes practice to live with a spirit of appreciation. You can start practicing today!

JULY 4

What It Means to Magnify God

I will praise the name of God with a song;
I will magnify him with thanksgiving.
PSALM 69:30 (ESV)

Praising God enlarges your perception of him. It makes him bigger in your eyes.

Psalm 69:30 says, *"I will praise the name of God with a song; I will magnify him with thanksgiving"* (ESV). In this verse, *magnify* means "to praise." When you look through a magnifying glass, things look bigger. When you magnify God—when you praise him—he gets bigger in your eyes.

Why is that a big deal? Because when God seems larger in your life, your problems shrink. The opposite is true too. When you focus on your problems instead of God, your problems feel really big while God feels small.

You have to make a choice, because only one thing can be big in your life: your problems or God. When you choose to praise God—to focus on him and magnify him—he seems bigger to you. And the bigger God gets in your life, the less worried you will be about your problems because nothing is too big for God. Your problems become less overwhelming because you remember that God is so much bigger than anything you're experiencing. God can handle it!

Worshiping, praising, and magnifying God are the same thing. When I was pastor at Saddleback Church, we often called our worship team our "magnification team" because it was their job to lead us to magnify God, to make him bigger in all of our eyes.

The Bible says in Psalm 145:3, *"The LORD is great and is to be highly praised; his greatness is beyond understanding"* (GNT). We can't ever know or understand how big and great God really is. It's like an ant trying to understand the internet! We just don't have the brain capacity. If we could completely understand God, then we would be God. But God is God, and we are not.

When we praise and magnify God, we aren't making him bigger. We're just changing our own perspective so that we better understand just how big he is. When that happens, everything else shifts with our new perspective.

Whatever problem has you scared, worried, or fearful right now, the antidote for it is to praise God—to sing about his greatness. The bigger God looks through your eyes, the smaller your problems become.

JULY 5

Why Doesn't God Tell You *Why*?

Surrender yourself to the LORD, *and wait patiently for him.*
PSALM 37:7 (GW)

One reason people struggle with contentment is because we're always looking for explanations for why things happen in our lives. But God doesn't tell us why most things happen, and that can frustrate us.

Sometimes God doesn't tell you why because he's testing you. He wants to see if you will let go of control and learn to be content, whether or not he explains why something happens in your life.

God doesn't owe you an explanation for anything. You're not going to know why most things happen until you get to heaven.

When I was a little kid, the only time our classroom quieted down was during a test. The teacher would say, "No talking! Take your pencils, and fill out your tests." Even the teacher stayed silent.

When God is silent in your life—when you don't hear him, and he feels like he's a million miles away—that is a test!

The teacher is always silent when students take a test—but the teacher is still present. When God is silent in your life, your faith is being tested—but God is still with you.

In that test, will you let go of control, or will you grab on more tightly? Will you learn to be content?

Surrender means leaving the future to God. Proverbs 3:5-6 says, *"Trust in the* LORD *with all your heart, and do not lean on your own understanding. In all your ways acknowledge him, and he will make straight your paths"* (ESV).

What area of your life have you not surrendered to God? Maybe you've surrendered the kitchen and the living room. But what about the bedroom, closet, and garage of your life?

Aren't you tired of fighting against God? Stop fighting and simply surrender. Surrendering to God is the ultimate expression of faith.

The Bible says, *"Surrender yourself to the* LORD, *and wait patiently for him"* (Psalm 37:7, GW).

When you go through pain next week or next month or next year, you don't need God's explanation. You need God's presence. Let go of control, surrender today, and leave the future to him.

JULY 6

Seize the Moment

Jesus said, "No procrastination. No backward looks. You can't put God's kingdom off till tomorrow. Seize the day."

LUKE 9:62 (MSG)

One day, a huge crowd followed Jesus as he left Jericho. A man named Bartimaeus, who was blind, was begging by the roadside. Bartimaeus heard that Jesus was nearby, and he began to shout, *"Jesus, Son of David, have mercy on me!"* (Mark 10:47, NIV).

When Bartimaeus got up that morning, he had no idea that Jesus Christ was going to be passing by him that day. He thought it was just another ordinary day: same place, same situation, same cry for help.

But suddenly Jesus was there. Bartimaeus had no time to prepare or think through his response. It was just an opportunity that dropped into his lap, and he chose to seize the moment. He didn't delay or procrastinate. He was going to do it—*now*.

That's the key to making a fresh start in your life: Whatever you're going to do, do it now. Don't say, "Next year I'm going to make a fresh start" or "Next month I'm going to make some changes" or "Tomorrow I'm going to make that a priority." It's now or never. Seize the moment!

Every day, we have opportunities for a fresh start, but we don't take advantage of them. Why? Because it's often easier to procrastinate.

Procrastination is a strange phenomenon. You think it will make your life easier when it actually does the opposite: It just generates stress.

When you know the right thing to do, today is the time to do it. Don't assume you can wait for tomorrow. Don't think you can put off what God has told you to do today.

The Bible warns us over and over about presuming upon tomorrow. None of us are guaranteed a tomorrow. Jesus said, *"No procrastination. No backward looks. You can't put God's kingdom off till tomorrow. Seize the day"* (Luke 9:62, MSG).

Whatever you're going to do, you'd better do it now. Tomorrow may be too late!

If Jesus is inviting you into a fresh start today, then don't delay. Follow the example of Bartimaeus, and seize the moment.

JULY 7

When You Go to Battle, Trust God to Fight for You

Do not be afraid or discouraged because of this vast army. For the battle is not yours, but God's.

2 CHRONICLES 20:15 (NIV)

Any lifeguard will tell you: You can't save anyone as long as they're trying to save themselves. If you try, that person will just pull you down too. So you have to tread water until they finally give up, and then you can get them back to shore.

It's the same with our relationship with God. When we try to fight through life's troubles on our own, we sink. Instead, God wants us to stop fighting and trust him to do the work.

God taught Israel's army that lesson. Three enemy armies were preparing to battle against them. Israel was far outnumbered. But instead of worrying, King Jehoshaphat led his army to worship God by depending on him to save them.

He prayed, *"We don't know what to do—we are begging for your help"* (2 Chronicles 20:12, CEV).

Then God said to them: *"Do not be afraid or discouraged because of this vast army. For the battle is not yours, but God's"* (2 Chronicles 20:15, NIV).

God wants the same thing from you: He wants you to stop fighting battles and let him fight them for you.

The story in 2 Chronicles continues: *"You will not have to fight this battle. Take up your positions; stand firm and see the deliverance the LORD will give you. . . . Do not be afraid; do not be discouraged. Go out to face them tomorrow, and the LORD will be with you"* (2 Chronicles 20:17, NIV).

Aren't those strange orders? God is telling Israel's army to go to the battlefield, but not fight.

In whatever you are facing today, that's what God is expecting from you too. He's telling you to stand strong, in quiet confidence in him. He's telling you not to be afraid or discouraged.

If you run from your enemies—from your problems—those things never will get better. God wants you to face your enemies, while trusting him to deliver you from them.

Whatever you're fighting today, trust God to win the battle for you.

JULY 8

Where Do You Get the Power to Keep Going?

We get knocked down, but we get up again and keep going.
2 CORINTHIANS 4:9 (TLB)

If you've ever been at a race, then you've heard spectators shout, "Keep going!" to motivate the athletes. That's also great advice when you feel emotionally, mentally, or spiritually exhausted from running the marathon of life: Keep going!

Scripture includes many examples of people who had determination to keep going in the face of opposition, including Jesus and Paul.

Jesus faced constant opposition. Religious and political leaders intimidated him. They tried to stop his ministry by telling him King Herod wanted to kill him.

But Jesus said to them, *"Go tell that fox that I will keep on casting out demons and healing people today and tomorrow; and the third day I will accomplish my purpose. Yes, today, tomorrow, and the next day I must proceed on my way"* (Luke 13:32-33, NLT).

Nothing was going to stop Jesus from accomplishing his purposes—not fear, opposition, or criticism. He was resilient and had the endurance to keep going.

Paul also faced obstacles that threatened to slow him down. In 2 Corinthians 4:8-9, he said, *"We are pressed on every side by troubles, but not crushed and broken. We are perplexed because we don't know why things happen as they do, but we don't give up and quit. We are hunted down, but God never abandons us. We get knocked down, but we get up again and keep going"* (TLB).

Maybe that sounds familiar, because you feel like troubles are coming at you from many directions. You're tired and worn out, and you don't think you'll make it to the finish line.

Where do you get the power to keep going? The same place Jesus and Paul got it: *from God.*

"We can only keep on going, after all, by the power of God, who first saved us and then called us to this holy work" (2 Timothy 1:8-9, MSG).

God doesn't expect you to fulfill your purpose and do his will in your own power. First, he saves you, and then he gives you the power for daily living. He'll give you everything you need to keep going and finish what he called you to do.

JULY 9

How to Fill Up on Gratitude

Be thankful in all circumstances, for this is God's will for you who belong to Christ Jesus.

1 THESSALONIANS 5:18 (NLT)

When you're going through a season of great change and stress, how do you maintain joy?

You do it by developing the habit of thanking God for all that's good, despite all that's bad.

This principle is found in 1 Thessalonians 5:18: *"Be thankful in all circumstances, for this is God's will for you who belong to Christ Jesus"* (NLT). This means we should develop an attitude of gratitude in every situation. It doesn't mean we have to be thankful for everything that happens to us, especially the bad things like cancer or car accidents. We don't have to be thankful for all the evil in the world.

But every time you take a minute to express gratitude to God about anything—your favorite music, nature spot, or Scripture—it helps refill your empty emotional tank so you can move forward in life. Choosing to be thankful is for your own good; it keeps you from getting bitter and helps you make it to the finish line.

Being grateful is easy when your emotional tank is full and life is going great. It's much harder to find something to be thankful for when you're facing a crisis or prolonged chronic stress. But that's when you need to express gratitude the most.

The story of Job is a great example of gratitude during hard times. This wealthy and successful man lost everything in a single day. He didn't know why it all happened to him, and he had every reason to be angry and bitter. Despite this, even in his darkest moment, he fell to the ground and worshiped God, saying, *"May the name of the LORD be praised"* (Job 1:21, NIV).

One of the most practical yet powerful habits you can develop is to make a daily gratitude list. Pause for five minutes each day and ask yourself, "What am I grateful for?" It's a habit that will strengthen your soul and keep you going when you feel like giving up.

Even in our darkest moments, we can follow Job's example and gratefully worship God, knowing that his will for us is to give thanks in all circumstances.

JULY 10

Four Reasons to Stay Strong

We don't look at the troubles we can see now; rather, we fix our gaze on things that cannot be seen.
2 CORINTHIANS 4:18 (NLT)

If you're only thinking about your current difficulties or pain, then it's natural to want to give up.

But if you look at things from an eternal perspective, you'll be able to keep going no matter what happens: *"That is why we never give up. Though our bodies are dying, our spirits are being renewed every day. For our present troubles are small and won't last very long. Yet they produce for us a glory that vastly outweighs them and will last forever! So we don't look at the troubles we can see now; rather, we fix our gaze on things that cannot be seen"* (2 Corinthians 4:16-18, NLT).

According to this passage, here are four reasons why we stay strong emotionally and never give up:

Because *"our spirits are being renewed every day."* Most people wouldn't dream of going a whole week without food. But if you don't open your Bible for a week, that's depriving your soul of essential nourishment it needs! If you want to renew your spirit every day, get into God's Word.

Because *"our present troubles are small and won't last very long."* Problems don't come to stay; they come to pass. Even if we have problems that last our entire lives, they would be minuscule compared to the trillions of years we're going to have in heaven. We know that problems on earth are temporary and that God has long-term plans for us.

Because our problems will *"produce for us a glory that vastly outweighs them and will last forever!"* God is using everything in our lives—even the hard stuff—to build our character for eternity. Romans 8:28 says, *"We know that in all things God works for the good of those who love him, who have been called according to his purpose"* (NIV).

Because we *"fix our gaze on things that cannot be seen."* When we're focused on things that last forever, we're able to finish the race because we have long-term thinking. Our attention is fixed on eternity.

What are you focused on today? Instead of looking at your problems, look at Jesus. And don't give up!

JULY 11

When All Hope Is Lost, Believe God's Promises

While God was testing him, Abraham still trusted in God and his promises, and so he offered up his son Isaac and was ready to slay him on the altar of sacrifice; yes, to slay even Isaac, through whom God had promised to give Abraham a whole nation of descendants!

HEBREWS 11:17-18 (TLB)

Have you ever felt like your hope was dying?

You know hope is dying when you start saying the word *never*: "I'll never get married." "I'll never get that job." "I'll never have children." If that's how you feel today, you're not alone.

When Abraham, one of the Bible's greatest heroes of faith, felt like that, he kept on hoping. Romans 4:18 says, *"Even when there was no reason for hope, Abraham kept hoping—believing that he would become the father of many nations. For God had said to him, 'That's how many descendants you will have!'"* (NLT)

What do you do when hope dies and you're ready to give up? You rely on what God has promised. Where do you turn when everything in you feels like doubting God? You turn to God's Word.

Nothing is more reliable than God's Word! Even when Abraham faced his biggest test, he relied on God's promises. *"While God was testing him, Abraham still trusted in God and his promises, and so he offered up his son Isaac and was ready to slay him on the altar of sacrifice; yes, to slay even Isaac, through whom God had promised to give Abraham a whole nation of descendants!"* (Hebrews 11:17-18, TLB).

After Abraham and Sarah waited many years for a child, God gave them Isaac. And then God told Abraham to sacrifice Isaac. Abraham didn't panic. The Bible shows three ways Abraham responded in faith:

- Abraham believed God could raise his son from the dead (Hebrews 11:19).
- Abraham told his servant, "We'll be back," not "I'll be back" as he and Isaac headed up the hill for the sacrifice (Genesis 22:5).
- When Isaac asked Abraham, "Where is the lamb we will sacrifice?" Abraham answered, "The Lord will provide" (Genesis 22:8).

Abraham knew God would either spare his son or resurrect him. He believed God's promises!

You can show God that you believe in his promises by praying in faith today: "Father, your Word is a gift, and your promises will sustain me all of my life. I believe that you will do for me everything you have said you will do, and so I thank you in advance, even when I don't understand the ways you are working in my life. I'm struggling right now, but I will still trust you!"

When all hope seems lost, put your hope in God. The situation you're facing may be out of your control, but it's not out of God's control. Jesus promised, "*What is impossible with man is possible with God*" (Luke 18:27, NIV).

Put your faith in Jesus; he will never let you down. *"And this hope will not lead to disappointment. For we know how dearly God loves us, because he has given us the Holy Spirit to fill our hearts with his love"* (Romans 5:5, NLT).

What Is Redemptive Suffering?

[God] comforts us in all our troubles so that we can comfort others. When they are troubled, we will be able to give them the same comfort God has given us.

2 CORINTHIANS 1:4 (NLT)

One of the purposes of your life is to serve others. And sometimes God uses your pain to help you serve more effectively. He does this by making you more sensitive to other people's pain.

Pain makes you more empathetic to those who are experiencing the same kind of distress you're in. Rather than focusing on your own pain, you can choose to redirect your focus to helping others who are hurting.

Jesus wants to redeem your suffering. Redemptive suffering is when you use the pain you're going through to help other people. This is what my wife, Kay, and I have tried do with the pain we feel from losing our son through suicide. In the years since Matthew's death, not a week has gone by without someone—a friend or stranger, well-known or unknown, old or young—calling Kay or me and asking for help because they know we've been through it, and we're willing to share God's comfort with them.

The Bible says, *"[God] comforts us in all our troubles so that we can comfort others. When they are troubled, we will be able to give them the same comfort God has given us. For the more we suffer for Christ, the more God will shower us with his comfort through Christ. Even when we are weighed down with troubles, it is for your comfort and salvation! For when we ourselves are comforted, we will certainly comfort you. Then you can patiently endure the same things we suffer"* (2 Corinthians 1:4-6, NLT).

Who is better qualified to minister to a parent grieving the loss of a child than another parent who has experienced such grief? Who is better qualified to help someone with an addiction than someone who has also battled an addiction? Who is better qualified to walk with someone through a cancer diagnosis than someone who has fought their own cancer?

Whatever pain you are suffering right now, God wants to use it to help others if you'll surrender it to him.

JULY 13

You Don't Have to Be Perfect to Be Used by God

Therefore, if anyone cleanses himself from what is dishonorable, he will be a vessel for honorable use, set apart as holy, useful to the master of the house, ready for every good work.

2 TIMOTHY 2:21 (ESV)

If you want to be used by God, you don't have to be a perfect person—but you do need to purify your heart.

The Bible says in 2 Timothy 2:21, *"Therefore, if anyone cleanses himself from what is dishonorable, he will be a vessel for honorable use, set apart as holy, useful to the master of the house, ready for every good work"* (ESV).

God uses all kinds of people—men, women, boys, and girls. He uses shy people, outgoing people, and people of different races, ages, and backgrounds. And he uses plain vessels and ornate vessels.

But there's one thing God will not use: He will not use a dirty vessel. You have to be clean on the inside. No matter who you are or what you've done, you can be made clean.

How do you do that and become pure? Through a simple word: confession. The Bible says in 1 John 1:9, *"If we confess our sins to God, he will keep his promise and do what is right: he will forgive us our sins and purify us from all our wrongdoing"* (GNT).

The word *confess* in Greek is the word *homologeo. Homo* means "same," and *logeo* means "to speak." So *homologeo* essentially means "to speak the same"—in this case, the same as God does about my sin. It means you agree with him: "God, you're right. It wasn't a mistake; it was a sin." It doesn't mean you bargain with God or try to bribe him.

You just admit your sin. Sound too simple? Just admit it, and God will forgive you. It's called grace.

If you want to be used by God, take time this week to ask him, "What's wrong in my life? Please show me." Then, when God gives you an idea, write it down. The first time I did this, my list almost looked as long as a book! And I've done this many times since. Then write 1 John 1:9 over the list and say, "God, I admit these sins to you. These are wrong. I don't want them in my life." Ask God to cleanse your life. God will forgive you!

This is the starting point of being used by God. You must purify your heart.

JULY 14

Let Go of Your Regrets

Forgetting the past and looking forward to what lies ahead, I press on to reach the end of the race.
PHILIPPIANS 3:13-14 (NLT)

The Bible often compares life to a race—a race that's full of distractions that can keep you from running the way God meant for you to run.

To run your race well, you need to remove the distractions. Hebrews 12:1 says, *"Let us run the race that is before us and never give up. We should remove from our lives anything that would get in the way and the sin that so easily holds us back"* (NCV).

Paul says the key to persisting is to simplify your life. That means you get rid of the baggage, remove the diversions, and eliminate the time wasters in your life that keep you from doing your best.

What could distract you from your purpose? A lot of things: trying to be like other people, making wealth your primary goal, keeping bad habits, hanging out with the wrong kind of friends, wasting time on social media. Even some things that are otherwise good can distract you.

But one of the biggest distractions is your past. Your past loads you down and keeps you from running well. When you walk around with guilt, resentment, shame, and bitterness, it's like trying to run a race carrying hundred-pound weights on your shoulders. It's going to slow you down! When you beat yourself up over a bad decision or when you refuse to forgive someone, you get stuck and sidelined.

The apostle Paul had a lot to regret. Before he became a believer in Jesus Christ, he killed Christians for a living. Yet he said, *"Forgetting the past and looking forward to what lies ahead, I press on to reach the end of the race"* (Philippians 3:13-14, NLT).

Paul didn't let himself get stuck in his past. He focused on the finish line, not on how he'd been hurt or had hurt other people.

You need to do that too. To run your race well, you're going to have to conserve your emotional energy for the future instead of spending it all dwelling on the past. Let go of guilt and regret so you can finish strong.

JULY 15

God Is Always Right on Time

The vision will still happen at the appointed time. It hurries toward its goal. It won't be a lie. If it's delayed, wait for it. It will certainly happen. It won't be late.

HABAKKUK 2:3 (GW)

God is never in a hurry, and he's never late. He's always on time. And God's timing is perfect, even when we can't understand it.

Because God is timeless, he has a different view of time. The Bible explains it like this: *"Do not forget this one thing, dear friends: With the Lord a day is like a thousand years, and a thousand years are like a day"* (2 Peter 3:8, NIV).

God's timelessness has big implications for your life. When God created you, he put a dream in your heart. Most people start off with a big vision and a big goal. They have some kind of dream or plan or project for their life.

What vision has God given you? Over the years I've discovered that while everybody tends to start off early in life with a vision, as time goes on, more and more people give up on their dream before it's accomplished. The reason is often because it doesn't happen fast enough.

Maybe your dream has been battered or broken. Or maybe, out of discouragement and disappointment, you have buried your dream. You've given up on it.

God doesn't want you to do that. If God gave you a dream for your life, it *will* happen. It just has to happen on his timetable, not yours.

God says this about your dream: *"The vision will still happen at the appointed time. It hurries toward its goal. It won't be a lie. If it's delayed, wait for it. It will certainly happen. It won't be late"* (Habakkuk 2:3, GW).

When I started Saddleback Church, I was in a hurry to get everything done fast. But God said to me the same thing he will say to you about your dream: "No, it's not all going to happen right now. But slowly, steadily, the vision will be fulfilled."

You will not always understand God's timing, but you don't have to. You only have to remember this powerful truth: God is never early in your life. He is never late in your life. He is always right on time.

How to Get Clean Hands

The righteous will hold to their ways, and those with clean hands will grow stronger.

JOB 17:9 (NIV)

There are many people right now who can relate to how David felt when he wrote, *"I've been out of step with you for a long time. . . . What you're after is truth from the inside out. . . . Soak me in your laundry and I'll come out clean, scrub me and I'll have a snow-white life. . . . God, make a fresh start in me, shape a Genesis week from the chaos of my life"* (Psalm 51:5-7, 10, MSG).

If that describes you, then you need to confess your sin to God.

You can do that right now. All you have to do is pray. But how should you pray? Think about these questions: What do you need to clean up in your life? What do you need to let go of from your past? Simply say those things to God. Evaluate your life and confess anything that keeps you from a right relationship with God. Tell him you were wrong and that you want him to cover your sin with his grace.

Your homework is to make a list. As God shows you what's out of balance in your life, write it down. You may feel some emotion as you do this, but confession has nothing to do with your emotions. It's simply a choice to admit and forsake any known sin in your life and to do the right thing. The only thing standing between you and a clear conscience is your pride.

Job 17:9 says, *"The righteous will hold to their ways, and those with clean hands will grow stronger"* (NIV).

Don't you want to become stronger in the days ahead? If you want to be spiritually strong, even in tough times and on difficult days, then you need to have clean hands.

"Who may ascend the mountain of the LORD? Who may stand in his holy place? The one who has clean hands and a pure heart, who does not trust in an idol or swear by a false god. They will receive blessing from the LORD" (Psalm 24:3-5, NIV).

Focusing on God's Purpose Leaves Little Time for Envy

Let us run with patience the particular race that God has set before us.
HEBREWS 12:1 (TLB)

When you start to get concerned about something God is doing in another person's life and envy starts to build, focus on the plan God has for you. Don't get distracted; instead, center on God's will for *your* life.

God created you with a unique plan for your life, and so he wants you to run the race he has for you. When you focus on God's race, you won't need to worry about the race everybody else is running. You won't be bothered by the crowds that are cheering or jeering in the stands. You're living for an audience of one: God.

In the Bible story about the vineyard workers, some workers grumble because they feel they haven't been paid what they deserve. There's a simple phrase the vineyard owner says to them: *"Take your money and go!"* (Matthew 20:14, GW). He's saying to those who can't get past their envy, "It's time to move on now. Quit having a pity party, and get over it!"

Sometimes we get stuck in the past. Maybe you still envy the person who got to be prom king or queen. But why should you let what someone else got in the past keep you from God's plan for your life right now?

Hebrews 12:1 says, *"Let us run with patience the particular race that God has set before us"* (TLB). The *"particular race"* means your unique race—the race that is only for you. God has a plan that he wants you to pursue, and it's unlike anyone else's. He planned it for you before you were even born, and it includes better things than you could ever dream for yourself. The more you understand your own call from God, the less you'll be worried about what God has called other people to do.

You're released from the tyranny of having to be best all the time. You just have to be the best *you* can be, the person God made *you* to be.

JULY 18

God's Plan for Your Pain

If you are suffering in a manner that pleases God, keep on doing what is right, and trust your lives to the God who created you, for he will never fail you.

1 PETER 4:19 (NLT)

Remember what photography processing was like before everything went digital? When you took a picture, you'd get a negative. Then, in a darkroom, you'd shine a light through the negative onto photographic paper. This turned the negative into a positive, full-color photograph.

That's what God wants to do with the injustices in your life.

We've all experienced injustice. People have mistreated us, passed over us, taken advantage of us. God wants to take all the negatives, shine the light of Jesus through them, and turn them into positives—full-color pictures of the lives we were made to live.

The Bible says, *"If you are suffering in a manner that pleases God, keep on doing what is right, and trust your lives to the God who created you, for he will never fail you"* (1 Peter 4:19, NLT).

When you've been treated unfairly, remember that Jesus is on your side.

Throughout Scripture, God shows special care for people who are treated unfairly. He is a God of justice. He hears your cry, sees your suffering, and knows your hurt. You didn't get what you thought you deserved. But God has a plan for your pain.

When you shine the light of God's love through your circumstances, he can turn your pain into a beautiful picture. He develops your character through it. He makes you stronger. Most importantly, he uses your suffering for his purpose and for your good.

You may never get an explanation for the pain you endure in this life. But you don't need an explanation. You just need to know that God loves you. He has a plan for you. He will settle the score with whoever hurt you.

God never wastes a hurt. So welcome the light of the gospel into your pain, and God will use your hurt—the very real injustice that has happened to you—to create a beautiful picture through your life.

JULY 19

Help Others Get into God's Family

In the same way that you gave me a mission in the world, I give them a mission in the world.

JOHN 17:18 (MSG)

If you are a follower of Jesus Christ, then God has given you a mission in this world. You're not here just to take up space; you're not here just to go after your own personal goals.

You have an assignment from God himself. Once you're in God's family, your life changes. You have a new reason for living. You have a plan and a purpose. Your life isn't about you anymore. It's about God's mission.

God's call on your life fits into his mission for all of history. God created everything in the universe because he wanted a family. He didn't need anything on the earth or in the sky. He created all of it because he knew some people would willingly choose to be part of his family.

The mission that God first gave to Jesus he now gives to the body of Christ—his church. Once you know Jesus, you have to *go*! You must go as far as needed to tell your friends and family about him. But you can't stop there. God has never made anyone he doesn't want saved. He loves everyone—across the entire world.

The Bible says, *"Now the LORD says to me, 'It isn't enough for you to be merely my servant. You must do more than lead back survivors from the tribes of Israel. I have placed you here as a light for other nations; you must take my saving power to everyone on earth'"* (Isaiah 49:6, CEV).

God wants you to live out his mission everywhere: in your family, your community, and the world. His mission for your life is both global and local.

That's God's plan for the world. That's his mission for you. He wants everyone on earth to know him—and he wants to use you to help make that happen.

God's words in Isaiah aren't just for missionaries or pastors. If you're in his family, then he gave his mission to you! When he tells you to go, don't hesitate to obey.

JULY 20

Pain Can Point You toward Your Purpose

God teaches people through suffering and uses distress to open their eyes.

JOB 36:15 (GNT)

Even when you're not aware of it, God is directing your life. Proverbs 16:9 says, *"A person may plan his own journey, but the LORD directs his steps"* (GW).

God likes to direct us through his Word. When we read and study the Bible regularly, that's often all he needs. But many of us don't spend enough time reading God's Word, so another way he'll guide and direct us is through pain.

Job 36:15 says, *"God teaches people through suffering and uses distress to open their eyes"* (GNT).

Have you ever thought about why horse riders put a bit in a horse's mouth? It's not for the horse's comfort. The rider uses discomfort to point the horse in a different direction.

In the same way, pain guides you and often turns you in a new direction.

When King David realized that God used the pain in his life to point him in the direction God wanted him to go, David expressed gratitude for his pain: *"My suffering was good for me, for it taught me to pay attention to your decrees"* (Psalm 119:71, NLT).

C. S. Lewis once said that God whispers to us in our pleasure but shouts to us in our pain. Pain is God's megaphone. It never leaves you where it found you. No matter how bad the pain is or where it came from, God can use it to point you toward your purpose.

Paul said to the believers at Corinth who experienced discomfort and pain, *"Now I am glad . . . , not because it hurt you, but because the pain caused you to repent and change your ways"* (2 Corinthians 7:9, NLT).

You don't have to be glad about experiencing pain. But you can ask God to use it to guide you in the right direction and thank him for all the ways he will provide for you.

Strong Families Help Each Other Grow

Since I . . . have washed your feet, you ought to wash each other's feet. I have given you an example to follow. Do as I have done to you.

JOHN 13:14-15 (NLT)

One mark of a strong family is that you help each other grow. But how do you do that? Here are two methods that help people grow and two that don't.

You *do* help each other grow:

1. **Through example.** Jesus did this in teaching his disciples. John 13:14-15 says, *"Since I . . . have washed your feet, you ought to wash each other's feet. I have given you an example to follow. Do as I have done to you"* (NLT). Your kids don't want to hear a sermon from you. They want to see Jesus reflected in your life.
2. **Through conversations.** If you're not having critical conversations with your kids about real issues, then you're missing opportunities to help them grow. The Bible says in Deuteronomy 6:7, *"You must teach [God's commandments] to your children and talk about them when you are at home or out for a walk; at bedtime and the first thing in the morning"* (TLB).

You *don't* help each other grow:

1. **Through criticism.** Nagging, criticizing, and complaining are totally ineffective in helping a person change. Why? Because when you criticize, you're focusing on what you don't want rather than what you do want.

   Ephesians 6:4 says, *"Don't keep on scolding and nagging your children, making them angry and resentful. Rather, bring them up with the loving discipline the Lord himself approves, with suggestions and godly advice"* (TLB).
2. **Through comparing.** Everybody's unique. That's why comparing never ever works. It's lethal to any relationship! *"Each person should judge his own actions and not compare himself with others. Then he can be proud for what he himself has done"* (Galatians 6:4, NCV).

The Bible is full of instructions and examples about how people should treat each other. God calls us to love one another, encourage one another, and support one another. The most important place to practice treating others this way—and become more like Jesus—is in your family.

JULY 22

Your Family Shields You from the Storm

Two are better off than one. . . . If one of them falls down, the other can help him up. But if someone is alone and falls, it's just too bad, because there is no one to help him.

ECCLESIASTES 4:9-10 (GNT)

Relationships are a raincoat during the storms of life. When someone in your family is going through a rough time, you help each other. You protect each other in the storm because you are committed to each other.

"Two are better off than one. . . . If one of them falls down, the other can help him up. But if someone is alone and falls, it's just too bad, because there is no one to help him" (Ecclesiastes 4:9-10, GNT).

Life brings all kinds of storms when you'll need to protect your loved ones. But one of the most painful storms of all is rejection. When someone you love feels rejected, it's time for you to rally around them. They're going to need you!

Many years ago, my oldest child, Amy, tried out to be a cheerleader. She went to practice after practice for the tryouts. Eventually, her friends got accepted, but she was rejected—and it broke her heart. When she came home, she ran into her room, went into her closet, sat down on the floor, and burst into tears.

Everyone in our family could hear Amy crying. And one by one, all on our own, we ended up walking into her room, sitting down on the floor in the closet with her, and crying with her. We didn't give her any advice; she didn't need advice. We didn't say, "Don't worry. It's not a big deal." It was a big deal! We didn't say, "Don't cry!" That's an insensitive thing to say to somebody who's grieving. Instead, we all sat there for about thirty minutes and just cried with her.

Our family will never forget that incident. Why? Because, at that point, we were being a raincoat for her. We were being a shield and protector. Somebody in our family had been hurt, and we weren't demeaning it. We weren't trying to talk her out of it. We weren't trying to cheer her up. We just wept with her.

Strong families protect each other in the storm and sit with each other until the light can be seen again.

JULY 23

Families Should Be Fun

People ought to enjoy every day of their lives,
no matter how long they live.
ECCLESIASTES 11:8 (NCV)

When my kids were growing up, I determined that what I most wanted them to know about our family was that they were loved and that we had fun together. I created all kinds of things to do just to have fun with my kids.

One of them was called Daddy's Magical Mystery Tour. When the kids were in grade school, I'd wake them up and yell, "Get out of bed! It's time for Daddy's Magical Mystery Tour!" And they'd get excited because that meant they didn't have to go to school and we were about to do something really fun, like driving to a hotel with a pool or making an ice cream run.

People don't remember what you say, but they will remember how you make them feel. My kids don't remember most of what I said in the early years of their lives. But they do remember how Daddy made them feel. They remember that we had a lot of fun.

That's the first common denominator of great families: Awesome families are playful. They enjoy life together! This is the missing ingredient in so many families today, when people are too busy, too negative, too worn-out, and too serious. They don't have time or energy to have fun together.

Yet this is what the Bible tells us to do in Ecclesiastes 11:8: *"People ought to enjoy every day of their lives, no matter how long they live"* (NCV).

Why is it important for you to enjoy every day? Because you're not guaranteed next week or next month or even tomorrow. Whatever living you're going to do, you'd better do it *now*.

If you don't live near your family, then learn to have this kind of fun in your church family. Being part of a small group can give you a great opportunity to find people you can have fun with.

When you have fun with your family, you're showing the world that life with God brings joy and hope. We're not guaranteed tomorrow, but we are guaranteed eternity with him—and that gives us freedom to make the most of every day.

JULY 24

Healthy Relationships Depend on Selfless Behavior

The person who plants selfishness, ignoring the needs of others—ignoring God!—harvests a crop of weeds. All he'll have to show for his life is weeds! But the one who plants in response to God, letting God's Spirit do the growth work in him, harvests a crop of real life, eternal life.

GALATIANS 6:7-8 (MSG)

Selfishness destroys relationships. It is the number one cause of conflict, arguments, divorce, and even war.

James 4:1 says, *"What causes fights and quarrels among you? Don't they come from your desires that battle within you?"* (NIV). Every trouble starts because of self-centeredness.

If selfishness destroys relationships, then it is selflessness that makes them grow. What does selflessness mean? It means less of "me" and more of "you." It means thinking of others more than you think of yourself and putting other people's needs before your own. As Philippians 2:4 says, *"Look out for one another's interests, not just for your own"* (GNT).

Selflessness brings out the best in people. It builds trust in relationships. I've seen it many times: Some of the most unlovable people who are difficult to be around are transformed when someone is kind and selfless toward them. When they're given what they need, not what they deserve, they change in beautiful ways.

The Bible says in Galatians 6:7-8, *"The person who plants selfishness, ignoring the needs of others—ignoring God!—harvests a crop of weeds. All he'll have to show for his life is weeds! But the one who plants in response to God, letting God's Spirit do the growth work in him, harvests a crop of real life, eternal life"* (MSG).

This is the biblical principle of sowing and reaping. What you sow, you're going to reap. When you sow selflessness, you reap God's blessing.

Everything you have is a gift from God, a result of his unselfishness toward you. As you become more like him, you'll learn to think of others and *their* needs—not just your own. And one day, God will reward your selflessness when you get to heaven.

But while you're here on earth, you'll be most fulfilled when you give yourself away. Jesus said, *"Only those who throw away their lives for my sake and for the sake of the Good News will ever know what it means to really live"* (Mark 8:35, TLB).

JULY 25

Strong Marriages Are Good for Everyone

Love sincerely. . . . Hold on to what is good. Be devoted to each other like a loving family. Excel in showing respect for each other.

ROMANS 12:9-10 (GW)

Strong marriages are good for everyone. They benefit the individuals in those relationships and can even help to strengthen whole societies.

Throughout history, marriage has been the fundamental building block of every civilization. When marriages have been strong, nations have been strong. When marriages and families weaken, cultures decline.

God uses marriage to perfect your character. In marriage, you learn to be unselfish and loving. If you get married, no relationship will have a greater impact on your life.

If you're not married, God can *and will* use other people to build your character. Godly, others-focused singles play a critical role in flourishing cultures as well. In fact, sometimes, they play roles that married couples and those with children cannot. Societies need singles to live in strong, fearless relationships with others.

Whether or not you're married, one of the main purposes of life is to grow up and realize it's not all about you. In fact, real happiness comes from giving your life away, being unselfish, serving, and loving. This is called maturity.

Life is a laboratory of learning how to love. It's the most important thing in life because God is love, and he wants you to become like him. He wants to make you more like Jesus Christ by building your character.

If you're married, the number one tool that God uses in your life to build Christlike character is your spouse. Every day you get hundreds of opportunities to think about your spouse instead of yourself.

The Bible says, *"Love sincerely. . . . Hold on to what is good. Be devoted to each other like a loving family. Excel in showing respect for each other"* (Romans 12:9-10, GW).

Do you do that in your marriage? Do you do that with God's family in the church? As you grow in maturity, you'll learn that love serves and gives and doesn't have to have the last word. Love puts the other person first.

Excel in showing respect for each other so that you grow to be more like Christ. It will benefit everyone!

Forgive People Who Oppose You

Be humble when you correct people who oppose you.
. . . They have been trapped by the devil, and he makes
them obey him, but God may help them escape.
2 TIMOTHY 2:25-26 (CEV)

When you face opposition because of your faith, you need to recognize the source of the opposition.

It's not your coworkers. It's not a political party. It's not some other nation or religion. It's not a competitor. The pressure you feel to cave in or be quiet or sit down when you should stand up is not coming from other people. It's really coming from Satan.

In Revelation 12:10 Satan is called the accuser of Christians. His job is to knock you down. There is an unseen spiritual battle going on all around you. The pressure to keep you from doing the right thing is not really coming from other people. It comes from spiritual warfare. Ephesians 6:12 says, *"We are not fighting against human beings but against the wicked spiritual forces in the heavenly world"* (GNT).

Satan knows it's pointless to attack Jesus directly, so instead he attacks those who follow Jesus. He uses the media and music and popular culture and anything he can to ridicule Christians. He's behind the voices saying, "Those Christians are out of date. They don't know what they're talking about. They're bigots."

Here's what the Bible says you should do: *"Stay away from stupid and senseless arguments. These only lead to trouble, and God's servants must not be troublemakers. They must be kind to everyone, and they must be good teachers and very patient. Be humble when you correct people who oppose you. . . . They have been trapped by the devil, and he makes them obey him, but God may help them escape"* (2 Timothy 2:23-26, CEV).

You need to recognize that the source of your opposition is the devil, not the person attacking you—and you're not strong enough to fight Satan's attacks on your own.

Instead of fighting, you need to treat people the way Jesus did. Even on the cross he said, *"Father, forgive them, for they don't know what they're doing"* (Luke 23:34, NLT). The people who attack you don't know what they're doing. So you, too, need to pray, "Father, forgive them." Then you can show love even under attack and have more energy to fight the real enemy.

JULY 27

Change Is for Your Good

As long as the earth remains, there will be planting and harvest, cold and heat, summer and winter, day and night.

GENESIS 8:22 (NLT)

Change is unavoidable. We all know that—but we still often act surprised when things don't stay the same.

When change happens, we can complain and grumble, get mad, and blame other people. We can even try to stop the inevitable change, as if we have any control. But things on earth never stay the same. Every moment of our lives, there is change, for good or for bad.

When God created the earth, this is one of the first things he said: *"As long as the earth remains, there will be planting and harvest, cold and heat, summer and winter, day and night"* (Genesis 8:22, NLT). In his perfect design, God made everything on this planet seasonal. Everything is changing, even when we can't see or feel it. Your family isn't the way it used to be. Your job isn't the same as it used to be. *You* are not the same as you used to be.

But because God designed it and said it was good, we know change is for our benefit. Change keeps us from becoming complacent and keeps us trusting God for the things we cannot understand. When change brings pain into our lives, it makes us depend on him. And change makes spiritual, physical, and emotional growth a natural part of life. Change for the better in your walk with Jesus means you are becoming more like him.

There is no growth without change. There is no change without loss. There is no loss without grief. And there is no grief without pain. A person who wants to grow and be better but not go through the pain of change is like a woman saying, "I want to have a baby, but I don't want to go through the delivery!" It isn't going to happen! To bring new life into the world requires pain. To enjoy a good gift, we sometimes have to experience the painful change required to receive it.

Things change, but remember this: Change will not always be easy, and you might not always understand it. But whatever change God requires from you, you can be sure it's for your good.

JULY 28

Only One Opinion Matters

You are the light of the world—like a city on a hilltop that cannot be hidden.
MATTHEW 5:14 (NLT)

If you're not sure who you truly are, then you can be manipulated and molded by the pressures, problems, and people around you—and that leads to stress!

Our culture is constantly trying to fit you into its mold. When you have a confused and unclear identity and aren't sure who you are, it makes you more vulnerable to the culture's influence. Until you settle in your mind that God loves you unconditionally and that you're a child of God, you'll be prone to stress.

Jesus never had any doubts about his identity. In fact, seventeen times in Scripture he publicly declared who he was. He said things like, *I am the Light of the World. I am the Son of God. I am the Way, the Truth, and the Life. I am the Bread of Life.* Jesus made it clear that he knew exactly who he was.

In John 8:18, Jesus said, *"I testify on my own behalf"* (GNT). He didn't need other people to tell him who he was. He didn't look to others for validation.

When you depend on other people's opinions for validation, you can't be resilient to stress. Because if you don't know who you are, then other people will decide it for you. They'll force you into a mold, and you'll get stressed trying to be someone you're not. You'll end up pretending and wearing a mask. It will wear you out!

Jesus knew he was the Light of the World. But he also said the same thing about you: *"You are the light of the world—like a city on a hilltop that cannot be hidden"* (Matthew 5:14, NLT). Do you realize how special you are? Not because of what other people say but because of what God says. There's nobody in the world exactly like you.

You must accept the truth about you—your strengths and your limitations and weaknesses. God made you with all of those things, and he has given you everything you need to do his will.

When you accept that, you'll be secure in your identity and a lot less stressed.

JULY 29

Do You Need to Fill Up?

If you are tired from carrying heavy burdens, come to me and I will give you rest. Take the yoke I give you. Put it on your shoulders and learn from me. I am gentle and humble, and you will find rest. This yoke is easy to bear, and this burden is light.

MATTHEW 11:28-30 (CEV)

Nothing will change in your life until you get dissatisfied with it. You have to come to the point where you say, "I'm not going to live this way anymore. I've had enough. I'm going to change. I'm going to do something about the way I feel."

Sometimes it seems easiest to put up with everything you're going through, even when you don't like it, simply because it's familiar. Carrying the load of our problems is uncomfortable and maybe even painful—but it's a burden we've carried before.

When you do finally reach the point of desperation because you're fed up with your circumstances and choices and the way they affect you and others, you need to go straight to Jesus.

What does Jesus say when we come to him with an emptiness in our lives—an empty soul and an empty heart? How does he respond when we tell him that we have nothing to give?

He doesn't scold us or judge us. He doesn't bring us down or tell us to figure it out. He does the exact opposite. Jesus said in Matthew 11:28-30, *"If you are tired from carrying heavy burdens, come to me and I will give you rest. Take the yoke I give you. Put it on your shoulders and learn from me. I am gentle and humble, and you will find rest. This yoke is easy to bear, and this burden is light"* (CEV).

As a pastor for over forty years, I've talked to thousands of people, and I've discovered only three things that cause people to change: pain, perspective, and having no other choice. Most people don't change until they feel the heat. There is no breakthrough until you have the breakdown! We all come to a point where there is a breakdown of our pride, our arrogance, and our self-sufficiency. It's the moment when we realize we can't do it on our own—and that we don't have to.

A breakdown is always the door to a breakthrough. Come to Jesus, and let him refill you with the power of the Holy Spirit and the hope of your salvation. He will never turn you away.

JULY 30

Two Ways God Grows Your Faith

Let your roots grow down into him, and let your lives be built on him. Then your faith will grow strong in the truth you were taught, and you will overflow with thankfulness.

COLOSSIANS 2:7 (NLT)

God doesn't want you to have just any faith. He wants you to have a strong and vigorous faith—not a wimpy faith that collapses when things get tough.

The Bible says in Colossians 2:7, *"Let your roots grow down into him, and let your lives be built on him. Then your faith will grow strong in the truth you were taught, and you will overflow with thankfulness"* (NLT).

How does God grow a strong faith like that?

The first way God grows your faith is through his Word. He wants you to know the Bible—to read the Bible, listen to the Bible, study the Bible, memorize the Bible, and talk about the Bible. Why? Because God's Word says, *"Faith comes by hearing, and hearing by the word of God"* (Romans 10:17, NKJV).

If your faith is weak, you're likely not in the Bible very often. But the more you're in God's book, the more it will feed your soul. God's Word is soul food, and spending time in it is the easiest way to grow your faith.

The second way God grows your faith is the hard way—and that's through circumstances that test you. While you may read the Bible only a little bit each day, you have things happening all around you twenty-four hours a day. Your circumstances are what God most often uses to grow your faith and build your character.

Faith is like a muscle. You don't grow muscle without some sort of resistance. The only way you grow a muscle is by stretching it, testing it, and putting weight on it. The same is true with faith. You don't grow faith just by sitting around and saying, "Oh, I want more faith." Faith needs to be tested. So God allows circumstances in your life to build your faith muscle.

Because God cares so much about your faith, you can know that he will always answer this prayer: *"Increase our faith!"* (Luke 17:5, NIV). Make that your prayer as God grows your faith through his Word and through circumstances that test you.

JULY 31

Faithful Friendships Help You Grow

No more lying, then! Each of you must tell the truth to the other believer, because we are all members together in the body of Christ.

EPHESIANS 4:25 (GNT)

Real change requires honest community.

Throughout your life, you'll experience times when you know you need to change—and when you also know that you will never be able to change on your own. At those times, you're going to need people in your life for support—specifically, a small group of people who will be transparent and authentic with you.

It's like in a football game when a player is so big that no opposing player can pull him down on his own. In the same way, some of the challenges in your life have to be team-tackled.

That's when you need a small group—but not just any group of people. Your small group should be made up of a few people you can talk with about your weaknesses and problems—all your hurts, habits, and hang-ups.

That kind of intimacy doesn't happen right away. When you first start a small group, you get together regularly. Then, over time, you begin to trust each other and develop a safe environment. Those people become the friends who can help you change when you can't change on your own.

Ephesians 4:25 says, *"No more lying, then! Each of you must tell the truth to the other believer, because we are all members together in the body of Christ"* (GNT).

When you pretend to be someone you're really not, you waste an enormous amount of energy. You may sincerely want to grow in Christ and to work on your weaknesses. But to do that, you have to be honest with your small group about who you really are. That kind of honesty is essential for spiritual change. If you could change on your own, you would, but you can't—so you don't. You need other people!

One thing that keeps most people from being honest is their desire to look good. Your desire to *look* good often takes precedence over *being* good. And it becomes a hurdle to spiritual growth.

But in a small group of other believers, you're safe just to be yourself. Then you can grow together and make the hard changes you couldn't make on your own.

AUGUST 1

Faith Means Following, Without Knowing Where

It was by faith that Abraham obeyed when God called him to leave home and go to another land that God would give him as his inheritance. He went without knowing where he was going.

HEBREWS 11:8 (NLT)

Sometimes, when God wants to grow your faith, he gives you the Where Test. If you're asking, "Where, Lord?" and feel like God isn't answering, you're probably in the middle of a Where Test.

God wants to see if you'll follow him where he leads—even when you don't understand, don't want to go, or don't know where you're going.

God used the Where Test with Abraham. Hebrews 11:8 says, *"It was by faith that Abraham obeyed when God called him to leave home and go to another land that God would give him as his inheritance. He went without knowing where he was going"* (NLT). Did Abraham want to go? Probably not. He was seventy-five years old; he was settled in his home with his family and household and animals—and there were a lot of them, because Abraham was a wealthy man. That kind of move would have been a massive undertaking.

Would you move if God said, "I'm not going to tell you where you're going, how long it's going to take, where you're going to end up, or what it's going to be like. Just trust me"?

Abraham, by faith, obeyed God. He left home without knowing where he was going. He passed the Where Test.

Maybe you're in the Where Test right now. You know that you should quit your job, but you don't know where you should go. God wants you to sell your house, but he hasn't told you where to move. God is testing your character. He wants you to show and grow your faith as you obey him, whether or not you know where you're going.

Hebrews 11 goes on to say, *"Even when he reached the land God promised him, he lived there by faith. . . . Abraham was confidently looking forward to a city with eternal foundations, a city designed and built by God"* (Hebrews 11:9-10, NLT).

You are called to live your whole life by faith; no matter where God leads you, remember that nowhere on earth is your permanent home. But you can trust God's promises for you. And you can look forward to your eternal home with him.

AUGUST 2

You Need God's Promises, Not Explanations

Even when [Abraham] reached the land God promised him, he lived there by faith—for he was like a foreigner, living in tents.

HEBREWS 11:9 (NLT)

In the Bible, God has made more than seven thousand promises to you—but he doesn't fulfill every one of them instantly. As a follower of Christ, you can expect that God sometimes will test your faith. And one of those tests comes when God's promises are delayed. I call it the When Test.

You know you're facing the When Test when you're asking, "When, Lord? When will you answer my prayer? When will things change in my marriage? When will I get well? When will I graduate? When will I have a baby? When will I get that promotion?"

Abraham faced the When Test: *"Even when he reached the land God promised him, he lived there by faith—for he was like a foreigner, living in tents"* (Hebrews 11:9, NLT). Abraham followed God in faith to a place he didn't know. And once he got there, Abraham and his family were basically nomads for three generations. Even though God had promised to give Israel to Abraham, he was going to do it on his own timetable. But Abraham continued to obey because he was confident in God's promise.

God has all of eternity to fulfill his promises, so some of them will be fulfilled after your earthly life is over. That's why God wants you to build your life on his promises, not his explanations.

Abraham received a big promise from God: God was going to make him into a whole nation! But after Abraham arrived in Israel and was still living like a nomad, I imagine he was constantly asking God, "When, Lord? You gave me this promise. When are you going to fulfill it?"

You may be in a When Test right now. You've been waiting for an answer, and it seems like there's no end in sight. You're asking, "When, Lord? When are you going to take care of this problem? My relationship? My finances? My health? My future?" Faith means that you wait for God's timing, without knowing when.

Are you in a time of waiting? Don't waste the waiting. Show God that you trust him as you cling to his promises. As you do this, God will grow your faith.

AUGUST 3

Impossible? Trust God for the Answer

It was by faith that even Sarah was able to have a child, though she was barren and was too old. She believed that God would keep his promise.

HEBREWS 11:11 (NLT)

When God is growing your character, he sometimes will test you with what seems like an unsolvable problem. I call it the How Test. It's when you ask, "How in the world am I going to solve this one?"

God gave Abraham what seemed like an unsolvable problem. God promised Abraham that he was going to move him to a new country, give him the land in that country, and make him the father of a great nation. He also promised that Abraham's descendants would populate the whole land. He was going to give Abraham, as his heritage, a great nation.

But Abraham was seventy-five years old and childless when God gave him this promise. He moved to Canaan, which would eventually be called Israel, and he kept waiting for his wife to get pregnant. By age ninety-nine, he still didn't have the promised son. It was what you might call an unsolvable problem.

In fact, the Bible says that when God told Abraham and Sarah that they were going to have a baby, they laughed. How in the world were they going to have a baby?

This was their How Test. Hebrews 11:11 says, *"It was by faith that even Sarah was able to have a child, though she was barren and was too old. She believed that God would keep his promise"* (NLT). They named the baby Isaac, which means "laughter."

"And so a whole nation came from this one man who was as good as dead—a nation with so many people that, like the stars in the sky and the sand on the seashore, there is no way to count them" (Hebrews 11:12, NLT). God had the last laugh!

You'll have plenty of times when God tells you to do something that seems impossible. But he doesn't want you to understand everything or know how to do everything. He doesn't even expect you to always know the next step.

Instead, God wants you to believe that *he* knows everything, and he will work things out in his own way and time. Faith is expecting a miracle without knowing *how*. When you show this kind of faith, you become more like Jesus.

AUGUST 4

When You Ask, "How Long, Lord?"

[Moses] kept right on going because he kept his eyes on the one who is invisible.
HEBREWS 11:27 (NLT)

Many people suffer from prolonged pain, whether it's chronic physical, emotional, spiritual, relational, or financial pain. When you're in a season of asking, "How long, Lord?" God may be using the How Long Test to grow your character.

The Bible tells us that Moses had incredible persistence. He endured significant pain, criticism, and conflict. He had every right to say, "How long, Lord?"

Hebrews 11:24-26 says, *"It was by faith that Moses, when he grew up, refused to be called the son of Pharaoh's daughter. He chose to share the oppression of God's people instead of enjoying the fleeting pleasures of sin. He thought it was better to suffer for the sake of Christ than to own the treasures of Egypt, for he was looking ahead to his great reward"* (NLT).

Moses gave up everything that many people spend their lives trying to achieve—fame, fortune, pleasure, possessions, and position—because he had put his faith and identity in God. He trusted in God's promises.

Faith is continuing to persist without knowing how long you'll need to hang on. And sometimes that's very difficult. So how do you continue in faith when you are suffering? How do you develop endurance? How do you handle prolonged pain?

You do what Moses did: You get close to God and stay connected so you can hear from him.

God talked to Moses through a burning bush. But you don't need a burning bush. Why? Because you have the Bible. Everything God wants to say to you is in Scripture. Stop looking for a vision; instead, start looking for a verse in God's Word. Knowing God's revelation, instructions, and promises will give you the ability to pass the How Long Test when you're going through prolonged pain.

Like Moses, keep your focus where it belongs. The Bible says that Moses *"kept right on going because he kept his eyes on the one who is invisible"* (Hebrews 11:27, NLT).

If you keep your eyes on your pain, you won't be able to look up. But if you keep your eyes on your Savior, you're going to walk through difficulty with his grace.

AUGUST 5

Purpose Produces Resilience

You, LORD, give perfect peace to those who keep their purpose firm and put their trust in you.
ISAIAH 26:3 (GNT)

Want to persevere through hard times? You need to know your life's purpose.

When you don't know *why* you do what you do—when you don't know your purpose—you slow down and get discouraged. But when you understand what you were made to do and be, you don't give up easily.

What is your purpose? You were made to glorify God by loving and serving him and others and by growing more like Jesus Christ in every way.

You have to work to keep your purpose firm, especially when you've gone through times of major change. The Bible says in Isaiah 26:3, *"You, LORD, give perfect peace to those who keep their purpose firm and put their trust in you"* (GNT).

Knowing your purpose is key to two very important qualities you need for success: tenacity and resilience. Every successful person—whether they're in law, sports, business, education, government, ministry, volunteer work, or something else—has tenacity and resilience.

Tenacity is the ability to keep going when you feel like giving up. You'll need it often in life, particularly in hard times.

Resilience is a little different. It's the ability to bounce back when you've had a failure or you've been put down by a circumstance or by other people.

Focusing on God's purposes for your life will produce tenacity and resilience. When I find people who give up and don't bounce back, it means they've lost their purpose.

Keep your purpose firm. When everything is changing around you, you have to anchor your life in something that never changes—something eternal. When you anchor your life in God's purpose, you will develop tenacity and resilience.

Psalm 33:11 says that God's *"plans endure forever; his purposes last eternally"* (GNT).

God's goal for you is to endure the tough times with tenacity and resilience. With those qualities, you won't just survive tough times; you'll make it through them changed for the better.

AUGUST 6

It's Time to Take the Plunge

Then Joshua issued instructions to the leaders of Israel to tell the people to get ready to cross the Jordan River.

JOSHUA 1:10 (TLB)

At some point in life, you have to stop talking and take action. After you've thought and prayed about something, the time comes when you take a step of faith.

When the Israelites had wandered in the desert for forty years and were about to pass into the Promised Land, they feared what was waiting for them. But then their moment of truth came: *"Joshua issued instructions to the leaders of Israel to tell the people to get ready to cross the Jordan River"* (Joshua 1:10, TLB).

They had to go for it. They had to take the plunge—literally. To get to the land God had promised them, they had to cross a river.

The Jordan River is not very big. It's only about a hundred feet wide and up to ten feet deep—except in the spring, when snow melts off the mountains and the Jordan becomes a giant, rushing, dangerous river. The Israelites happened to be there during flood season. It must have looked and sounded overwhelming!

There were no bridges or ferries for the thousands of people to use. That means God would have to do a miracle. He had already parted the Red Sea for them to walk through forty years earlier. But this time, he wanted them to walk into the river *before* he would make the waters recede. It was a test. They had to step into the river to show God they were trusting in him for deliverance.

What is your Jordan River? What's the barrier in your life that you think you'll never get around—something that makes you think you can never be used by God or have God's blessing? What's in your way?

Sometimes even when you know something is God's will, you're still going to be scared to death to do it. You're going to be overwhelmed by the obstacles—the fear of failure, the time commitment, the lack of resources—that seem to be in the way.

Do it anyway. Move against your fear. Show courage. Take the plunge!

The first step is always the hardest. But once you take it, the faith will come—and so will God's deliverance.

AUGUST 7

What Are You Feeding Your Mind?

Brothers and sisters, whatever is true, whatever is noble, whatever is right, whatever is pure, whatever is lovely, whatever is admirable—if anything is excellent or praiseworthy—think about such things.

PHILIPPIANS 4:8 (NIV)

You can learn a lot about a person's physical health by looking at their physical diet. Are they eating mostly healthy foods or processed foods? Do the foods they eat give them strength and energy or wear them down?

The same is true spiritually, mentally, and emotionally. You can learn a lot about your spiritual, mental, and emotional health by looking at your mental diet.

Devouring hours of podcasts, news programs, social media, and TV shows is like eating mental junk food. It's not healthy for you. In fact, it's poison. It is wearing down your ability to live a life of purpose.

Proverbs 15:14 says, *"A wise man is hungry for truth, while the mocker feeds on trash"* (TLB).

You have a choice—and every day, you must choose to feed your mind with the best thoughts.

Philippians 4:8 gets specific about the kinds of thoughts that are best for your mental, emotional, and spiritual health: *"Brothers and sisters, whatever is true, whatever is noble, whatever is right, whatever is pure, whatever is lovely, whatever is admirable—if anything is excellent or praiseworthy—think about such things"* (NIV).

Does that list of things describe what you think about most of the time? If we were being honest, we all would answer no. Our minds don't naturally go to these things, because we are human and sinful.

You have to train your mind to think thoughts that are true, noble, right, pure, lovely, admirable, excellent, and praiseworthy. You do that by reading the Bible, meditating on it, and memorizing it. You have to hunger for God's Word.

How you think determines how you live. What you put in your mind is going to affect every area of your life—so you need a steady diet of truth from God's Word.

AUGUST 8

When You Envy, You're in a Battle with God

Friend, I didn't cheat you. I paid you exactly what we agreed on. . . . What business is it of yours if I want to pay them the same that I paid you? Don't I have the right to do what I want with my own money?

MATTHEW 20:13-15 (CEV)

When it looks like God is blessing somebody in a way that he's not blessing you, relax and trust God. Believe that he knows what's best for you, and trust him when life seems unfair.

One of the ways you can tell envy is creeping into your life is by the language you use. If you find yourself using the phrase "It's not fair," you've already fallen into the trap of envy. You say, "It's not fair! Why them? Why not me? I've worked as hard as they do."

In Jesus' parable of the vineyard workers, the workers felt that they were being treated unfairly, not because they weren't paid what they were promised but because other people who worked less were paid the same amount.

Matthew 20:12 says, *"These last workers put in only one easy hour, and you just made them equal to us, who slaved all day under a scorching sun"* (MSG). You can hear the envy: "We worked harder and longer. We're better than them!"

Notice in the next verses the reply of the owner, who represents God: *"Friend, I didn't cheat you. I paid you exactly what we agreed on. . . . What business is it of yours if I want to pay them the same that I paid you? Don't I have the right to do what I want with my own money?"* (Matthew 20:13-15, CEV).

Here's the bottom line: When you're envious, you're in a battle with God. You doubt God's goodness in your life. You resent his decision to bless somebody else. You accuse him of being unfair or playing favorites. You don't believe he has your best interest at heart.

On the contrary, God's extravagant, unconditional, unending love is the same for everyone. God has a good reason for why you don't have what you want. He knows you better than you know yourself, so you can practice praying, "God, I'm going to trust that you have a unique plan for my life and that you know better than me what I need right now."

AUGUST 9

Real Change Requires Faith

Now glory be to God, who by his mighty power at work within us is able to do far more than we would ever dare to ask or even dream of—infinitely beyond our highest prayers, desires, thoughts, or hopes.

EPHESIANS 3:20 (TLB)

Have you ever tried to change something in your life that you didn't believe you actually could change? If you have, you probably weren't successful. That's because real change requires faith. In other words, you have to believe that you can change, with God's help.

God helps you change through two primary ways—by his Spirit living in you and through his Word, the Bible.

Ephesians 3:20 says, *"Now glory be to God, who by his mighty power at work within us is able to do far more than we would ever dare to ask or even dream of—infinitely beyond our highest prayers, desires, thoughts, or hopes"* (TLB).

What is the biggest thing you want to change in your life? No matter how big it is, it's not too big for God.

Maybe you've tried and failed to change on your own. That's because you were never meant to change all by yourself. You change with God's power, which he supplies in response to your faith in him.

Philippians 4:13 is a familiar verse, but the Amplified Bible says it in a way you may not have heard before: *"I can do all things [which He has called me to do] through Him who strengthens and empowers me [to fulfill His purpose—I am self-sufficient in Christ's sufficiency; I am ready for anything . . . through Him who infuses me with inner strength and confident peace.]"*

With the power of Jesus Christ, you can do anything God has called you to do. His power was *infused* in you when you became his follower.

If you want to change, then you need a can-do attitude—not a big ego about what *you* can do but a big faith in what *God* is able to accomplish in and through you. Jesus said in Matthew 9:29, *"According to your faith let it be done to you"* (NIV).

You get to choose how much you change. You get to choose how much God blesses your life. You get to believe in faith that God can help you make the hard changes.

AUGUST 10

You're Secure in God's Hands

I give them eternal life, and they shall never perish. . . .
My Father, who has given them to me, is greater than all;
no one can snatch them out of my Father's hand.
JOHN 10:28-29 (NIV)

When I was growing up, my dad's hands impressed me. From my perspective, they were huge! When he would do carpentry, the hammer looked so small in his hands.

But our heavenly Father's hands hold the whole world! How big are God's hands?

God's hands are big enough to bless you. Jesus laid his hands on people and blessed them. He does the same for you. Isaiah 62:3 says, *"The LORD will hold you in his hand for all to see—a splendid crown in the hand of God"* (NLT).

God's hands are scarred to never forget you. In heaven, the only scars will be in Jesus' nail-scarred hands. The Bible says, *"Can a mother forget the baby at her breast and have no compassion on the child she has borne? Though she may forget, I will not forget you! See, I have engraved you on the palms of my hands"* (Isaiah 49:15-16, NIV).

God's hands are strong enough to keep you eternally secure. John 10:28-29 says, *"I give them eternal life, and they shall never perish. . . . My Father, who has given them to me, is greater than all; no one can snatch them out of my Father's hand"* (NIV).

Once you put your life in God's hands, nobody can snatch you out of them. You may wonder, "Can't you just jump out?" How big do you think God's hands are? You're never going to get to the edge of them. He holds every aspect of your life securely.

When my kids were little, I used to stand in the pool and say, "Trust me. Jump to me." They were always afraid and wondered: "Is he strong enough to catch me? Are his hands slippery? What happens if he doesn't catch me?" But eventually they would get up enough faith to jump, and of course I would catch them. Then they'd want to do it a hundred more times!

Your Father is waiting for you to jump today. He's saying, "You can trust me. I'm working behind the scenes. And I can handle anything you give me."

Don't you want your life to be in God's hands? Trust him today and forever.

AUGUST 11

You Heal from Pain by Helping Others

Since Christ suffered and underwent pain, you must have the same attitude he did; you must be ready to suffer, too. For remember, when your body suffers, sin loses its power.

1 PETER 4:1 (TLB)

When you're in pain, who's the person you're thinking of the most? You!

It's your nature to be self-centered—because you're human. When you're suffering, you want to be comforted. When you're sick, you want to be cared for. When you're sad, you want to be understood. Pain makes you self-centered. But God says, if you're going to learn how to love like he does, try to see other people's pain, even when you're in pain.

Jesus is our greatest example of this. When he was hanging on the cross, he was in enormous physical, emotional, and spiritual pain. He was carrying all the sin of the world! But in his dying moments, he noticed the pain of other people. He prayed, *"Father, forgive them. They don't know what they're doing"* (Luke 23:34, GW). And he said to the guy next to him, *"Today you will be with me in paradise"* (Luke 23:43, GW). He also made sure his mother would be cared for. He wasn't thinking about himself, even when he was in agony.

God's Word says you should have the same attitude as Jesus (Philippians 2:5). That means, when you're in pain, you should look around and see who else is in pain. You should think of others, even as you care for yourself.

But it's not easy to do. So how do you look at the pain of others when you're in pain? The Bible teaches, *"Since Christ suffered and underwent pain, you must have the same attitude he did; you must be ready to suffer, too. For remember, when your body suffers, sin loses its power"* (1 Peter 4:1, TLB).

With God's grace, you can look past your own pain. And when you do, sin loses its power and you become more like Jesus.

This has been true for my family. With God's grace, we've been able to help others who are in pain, even as we carry our own deep hurt. Because of this, God has given us purpose in our pain and allowed us to help many people move forward in healing.

God can use your hurt, too, to help others struggling with their own pain.

AUGUST 12

You've Got the Power of Christ

He rescued us from the power of darkness and brought us safe into the kingdom of his dear Son.

COLOSSIANS 1:13 (GNT)

On the cross, Jesus destroyed Satan's power to control your mind, your life, and your destiny. When Jesus said, *"It is finished"* (John 19:30, NIV), Satan should have said, "I'm finished." His days are numbered!

Jesus has won the victory over death and Satan. But if you don't have the power of Christ in your life, then you are defenseless against the devil. Satan can manipulate your emotions, mess with your mind, and get you addicted to all kinds of stuff. You are powerless without Christ!

Satan has two favorite tools: temptation and condemnation.

With temptation, he minimizes sin: *It's no big deal! Everybody does it! You know what will make you happy more than God does!* Satan doesn't have to speak out loud. He just puts ideas in your mind.

Then, the moment you do that particular sin, Satan reverses strategy with condemnation. Instead of minimizing the sin, he maximizes it: *You did that! Are you kidding me? God will never love you again. It's over. God can never use you. That is so big that you could never ever be forgiven for it.*

First, Satan tempts you. Then, he condemns you. See his strategy? He minimizes sin before you do it and maximizes it afterward.

On the cross, when Jesus said, *"It is finished"* (John 19:30, NIV), he defeated temptation and condemnation. Jesus destroyed temptation's power, giving you the power to resist it: *"He rescued us from the power of darkness and brought us safe into the kingdom of his dear Son"* (Colossians 1:13, GNT).

Jesus' death and resurrection were a fatal blow to Satan.

If you have Jesus Christ in your life, then Satan has zero power over you except in the areas that you choose to give him. When you give in to Satan's temptation, you give him a foothold in your life.

But with God's power in your life, Satan can't harm you. You are *"hidden with Christ in God"* (Colossians 3:3, GNT), and you are protected. You don't have to listen to Satan. You have the power to say no.

AUGUST 13

There's Nothing Right about a Rude Response

Brothers and sisters, if someone in your group does something wrong, you who are spiritual should go to that person and gently help make him right again. But be careful, because you might be tempted to sin, too.

GALATIANS 6:1 (NCV)

There's a good chance everyone in your life is going to disappoint you at some point. Why? Because nobody's perfect!

So how do we respond in love when people disappoint us?

The Bible says in Galatians 6:1, *"Brothers and sisters, if someone in your group does something wrong, you who are spiritual should go to that person and gently help make him right again. But be careful, because you might be tempted to sin, too"* (NCV). The loving response to people who disappoint you is to be gentle, not judgmental.

How do you gently have tough conversations? How do you confront people you love when you see them doing things they shouldn't be doing? The Bible tells us to do it gently and with respect, not harshly or in a rude or mean way.

Here's a little equation to keep in mind: Right + Rude = Wrong.

It doesn't matter if you're right. If you're rude about it, then nobody will care what you have to say. They'll just get defensive! If you want to get through to someone who has disappointed you, then you should respond in a gentle and loving way.

Proverbs 15:4 says, *"Gentle words are a tree of life; a deceitful tongue crushes the spirit"* (NLT). We always have a choice in *how* we speak to somebody—especially with our kids. Hurtful words can wound and scar a child for years. But the Bible tells us that kind words can heal and help. So when your kids mess up, don't get on their case and put them down in the moment. Instead, give them a vision for how things could be! Gently speak words of life and health and hope into them, not harsh words of judgment.

It's the same way in our marriages. How many marriage problems could be avoided if we paused a minute and used words that are gentle and kind, not harsh or vindictive?

We need to learn to cut each other some slack and be kind and gentle in our speech and responses.

AUGUST 14

If You Want to Be Kind, Open Your Eyes

Look out for the good of others.
1 CORINTHIANS 10:24 (NCV)

Kindness always begins with the eyes—the way you observe the world and are sensitive to the needs of others.

The Bible tells the story of the Good Samaritan, who stopped to help a fellow traveler who had been attacked and injured. It says of the Good Samaritan, *"When he saw [the man's condition], his heart was filled with pity"* (Luke 10:33, GNT). Notice that *"he saw."* That is the starting point. If you want to learn to be a kinder person, you need to change the way you look at the world. You've got to become more observant of the needs around you.

Hurry is the death of kindness. To be kind, you have to slow down! When you're always distracted, you don't have time to be kind.

If you were to take a cross-country trip, there are several ways you could get from one side to the other. A plane would get you there fastest, but you wouldn't see much of the country. You could take a train or even a car, and both would give you opportunities to see even more. But if you really wanted to take in as much as possible, you'd walk.

The Bible says, *"Look out for the good of others"* (1 Corinthians 10:24, NCV). The first step toward kindness is to ask God to give you spiritual radar to be on the lookout for people around you who are hurting emotionally, spiritually, and physically.

Maybe you were born with this gift. You automatically sense when people around you are in need. It's not that you're more spiritual than the rest of us. You're just wired that way. If that doesn't describe you, then you're like me: You have spiritual ADHD. It's easy to get distracted. It's easy to be task-focused. It's easy *not* to be sensitive to what's happening around you.

But if you care, you'll be aware. Galatians 6:7-8 says, *"The person who plants selfishness, ignoring the needs of others—ignoring God!—harvests a crop of weeds. All he'll have to show for his life is weeds!"* (MSG). It's not always easy to see the needs of other people. But it's the starting point of kindness.

AUGUST 15

Three Realities of Heaven

Since you have been raised to new life with Christ, set your sights on the realities of heaven, where Christ sits in the place of honor at God's right hand.

COLOSSIANS 3:1 (NLT)

People have many misconceptions about what heaven is like. But we're not going to be little cherubs who wear white robes and float on clouds.

We need a correct view of heaven. The Bible says in Colossians 3:1, *"Since you have been raised to new life with Christ, set your sights on the realities of heaven, where Christ sits in the place of honor at God's right hand"* (NLT).

So what does the Bible say about these *"realities of heaven"*?

Heaven is where God lives and rules. The Bible calls heaven *"the dwelling place of God," "the house of God,"* and *"the city of God."* Heaven is where God lives.

But Jesus also calls heaven *"the Kingdom of God"* or *"the Kingdom of heaven."* So heaven is also where God rules. Psalm 123:1 says, *"LORD, I look up to you, up to heaven, where you rule"* (GNT).

Heaven is a real place. Heaven isn't a state of mind or being. It's a real place. In fact, the Bible says there will be streets, trees, water, and homes in heaven—and even animals! Your physical body will be renewed, and you'll have a *real* place for your *real* body to live: *"There are many rooms in my Father's house. . . . I am going there to prepare a place for each of you"* (John 14:2, CEV).

Heaven is designed for you and me. God didn't design heaven for himself. He designed it for his family, and it's an expression of his love. The Bible says, *"Come, you who are blessed by my Father; take your inheritance, the kingdom prepared for you"* (Matthew 25:34, NIV).

People weren't meant to live on earth forever. We're made for heaven! Hebrews 13:14 says, *"For this world is not our home; we are looking forward to our everlasting home in heaven"* (TLB). Really, this world is not your home; you're just passing through!

"No eye has seen, no ear has heard, and no mind has imagined the things that God has prepared for those who love him" (1 Corinthians 2:9, GW). No matter what you've dreamed up about heaven, the reality will far exceed it!

AUGUST 16

Be Faithful with the Work You've Been Given

Unless you are honest in small matters, you won't be in large ones. If you cheat even a little, you won't be honest with greater responsibilities. And if you are untrustworthy about worldly wealth, who will trust you with the true riches of heaven?

LUKE 16:10-11 (TLB)

If you think you'll be bored in heaven, think again.

You're not going to sit around on a cloud doing nothing. God wired you and knows what interests you. He shaped you with your spiritual gifts, heart, abilities, personality, and experiences. God didn't make you extraordinarily unique just for earth. He's going to use your shape in eternity.

Yes, you will have work in heaven, but here's the difference between work in heaven and work on earth: In heaven, you're guaranteed to enjoy your work. It won't give you heartache or stress. It will be meaningful, enjoyable, and fulfilling all the time. You'll have your dream job forever!

I don't know what your specific roles or responsibilities will be in heaven. But I do know that they will be based on how faithful you are with the roles and responsibilities God has given you on earth. Life is a temporary assignment, and God is watching to see how dependable, faithful, and trustworthy you are with the responsibilities he's given you now.

If you make the most of what you've been given, then God is going to give you more in heaven. You'll make it into heaven because of God's grace, but your rewards and responsibilities once you get there will be based on how faithfully you served God on earth.

The Bible explains: *"Unless you are honest in small matters, you won't be in large ones. If you cheat even a little, you won't be honest with greater responsibilities. And if you are untrustworthy about worldly wealth, who will trust you with the true riches of heaven?"* (Luke 16:10-11, TLB).

God is watching to see how you manage your finances, your time, your relationships, your health, and your opportunities—not because he wants to make you feel guilty but because he wants you to enjoy all the wonderful things heaven has to offer.

When you choose faithfulness in everything God has entrusted to you on earth, then you will be entrusted with much more in heaven.

AUGUST 17

Easy Ways to Love Your Neighbor

If you really keep the royal law found in Scripture,
"Love your neighbor as yourself," you are doing right.
JAMES 2:8 (NIV)

Garages are a wonderful convenience, aren't they? When you come home after a long day at work, you can just drive right in and close the door, ensuring you don't have to see another soul before you reach the comfort of your home.

But that convenience can keep Christians from following one of God's most basic commands: *"If you really keep the royal law found in Scripture, 'Love your neighbor as yourself,' you are doing right"* (James 2:8, NIV).

"Love your neighbor as yourself." It's such a simple command that extends to every person in your life. Yet many people don't even know the neighbors who live next door to them—and you can't love somebody you don't know.

God enjoys watching the people he created have fellowship with each other. In Zechariah 3:10, he said, *"Each of you will invite your neighbor to come and enjoy peace and security, surrounded by your vineyards and fig trees"* (GNT).

You probably don't have a vineyard, but you might have an apartment common area or a backyard patch of grass. You don't need much to create a friendly atmosphere and become acquainted with your neighbors.

Getting to know your neighbors can start with sitting on your front porch and greeting people as they pass by. You never know when a friendly gesture might eventually lead to a conversation about God.

Do you have a yard project? Take your time so you can make more connections with your neighbors. Don't have eggs for the cookies you're baking? Borrow some from a neighbor—and then share the cookies! Go to the dog park, and talk to at least one other person. Move your grill to the front yard for an impromptu bring-your-own-meat party. Do you go on runs or take walks? Ask a neighbor to join you.

Don't let busyness be your excuse not to follow God's command to love your neighbor. Reach out, open up, and share life with your neighbors so they can one day share eternity with you.

AUGUST 18

It's Worth Waiting for God's Miracle

"My thoughts are nothing like your thoughts," says the L*ORD*.
"And my ways are far beyond anything you could imagine."
ISAIAH 55:8 (NLT)

Have you ever faced a big challenge in your life? Something that couldn't be solved without a miracle happening?

If you haven't, you will. And when that time comes, you'll have a choice. You can wait on God's timing and his way. Or you can take matters into your own hands and try to make a miracle happen yourself.

But the truth is, miracles don't come from the places you expect them. And they don't come as a result of your own effort. The source of a miracle is always unexpected.

Take Abraham, for example. God told Abraham he was going to have a son, and that the son would be the father of a great nation. Abraham was nearly ninety years old, and he and his wife had no children. It would take a miracle to make it happen.

But he had trouble believing God's promise, and he didn't wait on God to work a miracle. Instead, he took matters into his own hands and had a child with a woman who wasn't his wife.

But that wasn't God's plan. God's plan had been to work a miracle in Abraham's wife, Sarah. Abraham's solution was inferior to God's.

The same is true for you. Your way of making things happen is always second best—God's way is best.

If you could understand God, you would be God. But you're not! Isaiah 55:8 says, *"'My thoughts are nothing like your thoughts,' says the* L*ORD. 'And my ways are far beyond anything you could imagine'"* (NLT).

Miracles always come in unexpected ways. So there's no need to fret, fear, or try to figure it out.

Trust God and say, "I don't know how God is going to do it, but I know he will." Then simply obey, follow where he leads, and get ready for a miracle.

AUGUST 19

When God Gives You a Second Chance, Seize It

Since we are God's coworkers, we urge you not to let God's kindness be wasted on you.
2 CORINTHIANS 6:1 (GW)

We all make mistakes in life, some big and some small. But sometimes those mistakes lead to missing out on fulfilling God's mission for your life. If that's where you've found yourself, I have good news for you: God is a God of second chances!

When you realize that God is giving you another chance to fulfill your mission, don't waste it. Seize it! That second chance is the perfect time to focus on God's unique calling for your life.

Paul writes in 2 Corinthians 6:1, *"Since we are God's coworkers, we urge you not to let God's kindness be wasted on you"* (GW). God's done so much for you already. He's forgiven your sins. He's given you other second chances.

And he will give you even more opportunities to serve him.

Take a look at Paul. He was killing Christians because he thought they were heretics who were following a dead and disgraced leader.

But then Jesus confronted Paul on the road to Damascus and offered him a second chance, a chance to fulfill his real mission on earth. Paul accepted his assignment and did a 180-degree turn—and he never forgot the second chance God gave him.

Paul said this later in his ministry: *"I don't care about my own life. The most important thing is that I complete my mission, the work that the Lord Jesus gave me—to tell people the Good News about God's grace"* (Acts 20:24, NCV).

Paul was grateful God was using him, and his mission from God became the most important thing to him. Nothing else mattered.

No matter how badly you've messed up—whether it was a big shift away from God's calling or just a gradual drifting—God still hasn't changed your mission. And he's offering you a second chance today.

So go after it. *Get started today.* When God gives you another chance, don't delay—obey.

In offering you a second chance, God is showing you his never-ending grace and love.

AUGUST 20

You Need a Firm Foundation

The mountains may move, and the hills may shake, but my kindness will never depart from you. My promise of peace will never change. . . . I will rebuild your city with precious stones. I will reset your foundations with sapphires. I will rebuild your towers with rubies.

ISAIAH 54:10-12 (GW)

We all need a reset at some point. And God will always be ready to help you do it.

When the nation of Israel was invaded by Babylon, they were exiled and kept captive for seventy years. The Israelites were discouraged, not just because they had lost but because their holy city, Jerusalem, had been destroyed.

In the midst of it all, God did not want them to forget that he was still with them. He loved and cared for them, and he was going to rebuild—or reset—their lives.

God promised, *"The mountains may move, and the hills may shake, but my kindness will never depart from you. My promise of peace will never change. . . . I will rebuild your city with precious stones. I will reset your foundations with sapphires. I will rebuild your towers with rubies"* (Isaiah 54:10-12, GW).

The Israelites may not have had precious jewels in every stone used to rebuild Jerusalem. But God wanted them to understand that he was going to rebuild their city—and their lives—on his peace and kindness.

A foundation of clay and rock might have stood for a few years. But a foundation built on God's promises—the most precious things on earth—would last forever.

When Job was going through hard times, his friend told him to repent, and then, *"Your life will be brighter than sunshine at noon, and life's darkest hours will shine like the dawn. You will live secure and full of hope"* (Job 11:17-18, GNT).

Is it time for you to reset, to make a big change? If so, then you need a strong foundation. And you'll only find that foundation in God, who loves and cares for you.

You can start your reset today by getting rid of the sins and distractions that keep you from focusing on God—or, in other words, by repenting. As he rebuilds your life on his firm foundation, you'll find yourself living in God's kindness and peace. Your life will shine brighter than the sun!

AUGUST 21

God Gives You a Choice

Today I am giving you a choice. You can choose life and success or death and disaster. I am commanding you to be loyal to the LORD, to live the way he has told you, and to obey his laws and teachings. . . . If you obey him, you will live and become successful and powerful.

DEUTERONOMY 30:15-16 (CEV)

A lot of people have a big misunderstanding about God. They know God planned their existence and has a purpose for their lives. But they have the wrong idea that every detail of life is preplanned. They think they have no choice.

In fact, the Bible teaches the exact opposite. Yes, God has a plan and a purpose for you, but it's not automatic. You can miss it. That's because God won't force you to enjoy the plan he has for you. He gives you the choice to accept or reject his salvation, to obey or disobey his directions. He gives you the choice to follow or ignore the purpose for which you were created. Far too many people miss their purpose because of their poor choices. The Bible says repeatedly that God will not force you to do his will.

When Moses led the Hebrews out of Egypt after four hundred years of slavery, he told them about a land of great, bountiful blessing that God had promised them. But before they went into the Promised Land, God, through Moses, said to the people the same thing he says to you: *"Today I am giving you a choice. You can choose life and success or death and disaster. I am commanding you to be loyal to the LORD, to live the way he has told you, and to obey his laws and teachings. . . . If you obey him, you will live and become successful and powerful"* (Deuteronomy 30:15-16, CEV).

God was giving them a choice. God wanted his people to enjoy the bounty of the Promised Land. But he didn't make them accept it. The choice was theirs.

This is a picture of salvation—of coming out of slavery to sin into freedom in Christ. To enjoy life in the Promised Land, the Israelites had to choose to obey God. You, too, have to decide whether you'll accept God's salvation and the good things he's planned for you.

God could have made you a puppet who could only do what he wanted—but he didn't. He gives you the ability to choose. If you choose poorly, that choice is your greatest curse; if you choose wisely, it's your greatest blessing.

Today God gives you a choice between life—choosing salvation and his path—or death. Which path will you choose?

When you choose God's path of life, you can say to him, "Lord, I trust you for my salvation. And I also choose to trust you today for your purpose for my life and your power in me to do everything you have planned for me. I want to go where you tell me to go and do what you tell me to do. I don't know what's around the corner, but I know that you will be with me and that you will help me choose your path at every turn. When I'm tempted to fear or doubt or sin, I want to choose you and your plan instead, because I know it is the only way to truly live. In Jesus' name, amen."

AUGUST 22

Rely on God's Power, Not Your Own

He never grows tired or weary. . . . He strengthens those who are weak and tired. . . . Those who trust in the LORD for help will find their strength renewed.

ISAIAH 40:28-29, 31 (GNT)

The worst times of life can exhaust and drain you. When the roof of your life is falling in, you might look up in despair and say, "What now? What next? I can't handle one more thing."

Paul had similar thoughts: *"We were really crushed and overwhelmed, and feared we would never live through it"* (2 Corinthians 1:8, TLB).

Paul seemed about ready to give up, but see what happened next: *"We felt we were doomed to die and saw how powerless we were to help ourselves; but that was good, for then we put everything into the hands of God, who alone could save us, for he can even raise the dead. And he did help us and saved us from a terrible death; yes, and we expect him to do it again and again"* (2 Corinthians 1:9-10, TLB).

Paul knew that since God can raise the dead, he certainly could help him. And that's true for you too. That same power that raised Jesus is available to you. Jesus' resurrection means no situation is hopeless and no problem is too difficult. If God can raise a dead man, he can resurrect your health or dead marriage. He can infuse new life into your career.

How can you receive that kind of power? You receive it when God fills your life with the Holy Spirit. The Bible says, *"For the Spirit that God has given us does not make us timid; instead, his Spirit fills us with power, love, and self-control"* (2 Timothy 1:7, GNT).

When God's Spirit fills your life, you have true self-control. You are no longer pushed back and forth by circumstances. With Christ as your Master, you can master your situation. You're no longer relying on your own power to hold all the strings of your life together. You're depending on God's power. The Bible promises: *"He never grows tired or weary. . . . He strengthens those who are weak and tired. . . . Those who trust in the LORD for help will find their strength renewed"* (Isaiah 40:28-29, 31, GNT).

God is faithful. No matter what you're facing, he will carry you through it.

AUGUST 23

Prejudice Questions the Beauty of God's Creation

"Love your neighbor as you love yourself." But if you treat people according to their outward appearance, you are guilty of sin.

JAMES 2:8-9 (GNT)

God hates prejudice because it questions his creation.

God made us all different. He thought up race and gender and created us to have different shapes, sizes, and personalities. How boring the world would be if God were not creative!

I love to collect rocks to make borders in my backyard. And I've learned that the secret to a beautiful rock border is to put different colors next to each other. Then you fully put on display the true beauty of those uniquely created rocks.

The same is true of people. God's creative design is fully represented only when we're in community with people who are different from us.

You see, prejudice toward another person is essentially saying, "God, you made a mistake in creating a variety of people. You should've just made everybody like me." It's a blatant expression of pride and arrogance. When you reject what God has created, you reject his perfect plan and design.

"My friends, as believers in our Lord Jesus Christ, the Lord of glory, you must never treat people in different ways according to their outward appearance. . . . You will be doing the right thing if you obey the law of the Kingdom, which is found in the scripture, 'Love your neighbor as you love yourself.' But if you treat people according to their outward appearance, you are guilty of sin" (James 2:1, 8-9, GNT).

We live in a time of more division and partisanship than I have known in my lifetime. When people are intent on tearing each other apart, Christians should stand firm in this truth: We are not meant to be blind to the things that make us unique.

To try not to see the beautiful colors and other differences in creation would be to deny God's character. Our differences reflect God's wonderful creativity.

We all are humans, made in God's image and deeply loved by him. When we see each person we encounter in this way, we can overcome our prejudice with love.

AUGUST 24

Refinement Leads to Your New Assignment

If you keep yourself pure, you will be a special utensil for honorable use. Your life will be clean, and you will be ready for the Master to use you for every good work.

2 TIMOTHY 2:21 (NLT)

I once saw a sign at a gas station that said, "A clean engine has more power." That's true of people too!

When you go through life with a clear conscience, you'll have a lot more power. Nothing drains you faster than guilt, regret, shame, or trying to hide something you feel bad about doing.

As a student of history, I've read about all of the great people of faith who made it through tough times without caving in. There was always refinement before a new assignment. Then they were used in even greater ways because of how they grew and were changed during that tough time.

The first step in keeping your life clean is always personal cleansing. God uses holy, clean people—not perfect people. Anytime you find God using someone, you will see that they've kept their life clean by dealing with their sin and being cleansed by God's forgiveness through Jesus Christ.

The Bible promises, *"If you keep yourself pure, you will be a special utensil for honorable use. Your life will be clean, and you will be ready for the Master to use you for every good work"* (2 Timothy 2:21, NLT).

If you want God to use you, even in hard times, then you start with confession and cleansing. Augustine, the great theologian, said, "The beginning of good works is the confession of bad works."

How do you dump the load of guilt, regret, shame, or fear of being found out? You simply confess by saying, "God, you're right. What I did was wrong." The Bible says in 1 John 1:9, *"If we confess our sins, he is faithful and just and will forgive us our sins and purify us from all unrighteousness"* (NIV).

God doesn't want you walking around in shame and carrying a load of regrets. He wants you to let it go! You'll always struggle to make it through hard times when you're carrying unnecessary junk from the past.

Lighten the load today by confessing your sin to God, and you'll start feeling the pressure lift. You'll be ready for your next assignment!

AUGUST 25

When You're Given the Opportunity, Help Others

All of us must quickly carry out the tasks assigned us by the one who sent me, for there is little time left before the night falls and all work comes to an end.

JOHN 9:4 (TLB)

Every day God gives you opportunities to show kindness to the people around you. As he does, he's watching to see how you'll respond.

Will you choose to be self-centered? Or will you notice the people who need a word of encouragement, a pat on the back, a listening ear, or an errand done for them?

The Bible says, *"Do not withhold good from those who deserve it when it's in your power to help them"* (Proverbs 3:27, NLT).

You won't always have an opportunity to help, so when you do, just do it!

You probably have people in your life you've considered helping. You've thought, "Oh, I'd like to do that for my neighbor" or "I want to do something kind for that person at work." Despite your best intentions, you've done nothing. Why?

Maybe you've made excuses and thought, "I'll do it when things settle down." Guess what? Things never will.

The time to do good in your life is *now*. The Bible says, *"If you wait for perfect conditions, you will never get anything done"* (Ecclesiastes 11:4, TLB).

When God's Spirit gives you an opportunity to do good, it's usually best to do it immediately. In other words, do good now because you're not guaranteed tomorrow.

Jesus said, *"All of us must quickly carry out the tasks assigned us by the one who sent me, for there is little time left before the night falls and all work comes to an end"* (John 9:4, TLB).

God has tasks he wants you to do. Don't wait for perfect conditions to do them. Instead, look every day for the opportunities God gives you to help and encourage others.

What kind act have you been intending to do? You've thought over and over again, "Oh, I'd really like to do this for this person." But you haven't done it yet. It's time to stop delaying.

Just do it.

AUGUST 26

You Don't Have to Understand Why

I will quickly obey your commands.

PSALM 119:32 (NCV)

If there's ever a time in life you need to hurry, it's when God tells you to act—even if you don't understand why.

Psalm 119:32 says, *"I will quickly obey your commands"* (NCV).

You don't need to fully grasp something to benefit from it. I don't understand how airplanes fly in the air, but I fly often. I don't understand how computers work, but I use one all the time.

And you don't have to understand why God tells you to do something in order to benefit from being obedient.

If you're a parent, you've likely told your child to do something, and they responded, "Why should I?" And you may have responded with four little words: "Because I said so."

What you're really saying is, "You're not old enough to understand, but one day you will. I'm telling you to do this for your own good."

If anyone has the authority to say, "Because I said so," it's God, the omnipotent Creator and Ruler of the universe and our heavenly Father.

In the Bible, whenever God gives a command without a specific date on it, he expects immediate action.

It's like when my wife, Kay, used to call the family to dinner at a specific time. When she said, "Come to dinner at 5:30," it meant we needed to be ready to eat at 5:30. But if she said, "Come to dinner," we knew that meant to come immediately.

Like children delaying their obedience, we sometimes pretend we can't hear God, even though he is speaking clearly. Or we read a command in the Bible and convince ourselves he's talking to someone else.

But none of these tricks fool God. These delay tactics are a subtle rebellion that question God's authority and his plan.

Faith is obeying God's command immediately, even when you don't understand or when you see roadblocks ahead. So step forward in faith, knowing God is motivated by his love for you and has your best interest at heart.

The Two Things You Need to Control Your Thoughts

Letting your sinful nature control your mind leads to death. But letting the Spirit control your mind leads to life and peace.

ROMANS 8:6 (NLT)

Have you noticed that your mind doesn't always do what you tell it to do?

Sometimes your thoughts go off in directions that you don't intend. When you need to pray, your thoughts stray.

The Bible says that when this happens, you need to take every thought captive (2 Corinthians 10:5). What does that mean? The Greek word for *captive* here means "to take as prisoner"—in this case, your thoughts. You need to bring them under control.

That's only possible when you use the two weapons every believer has available to them: the Holy Spirit and the Word of God.

First, you need to recognize the power of God's Spirit inside you. Without him, you are defenseless. Romans 8:6 says, *"Letting your sinful nature control your mind leads to death. But letting the Spirit control your mind leads to life and peace"* (NLT).

You need Jesus in your life, because without the Holy Spirit, your sinful nature controls your mind. And that will always lead you in the wrong direction! But when the Spirit controls you, you have the power you need to take every thought captive.

Second, you need the Word of God. Jesus said, *"If you obey my teaching, you are really my disciples; you will know the truth, and the truth will set you free"* (John 8:31-32, GNT).

People like to quote, *"The truth will set you free."* In fact, it's posted on university buildings all over the world. But very few people quote the first part of the verse about obeying Jesus' teaching. People want to detach freedom from God's truth. But God's truth—embodied in his Word and incarnate in Jesus—breaks the chains that keep you bound to sinful thoughts.

As you rely on the Holy Spirit and fill your mind with God's Word, you'll find your thoughts no longer control you. Instead, you'll be able to take them captive and live in the freedom that God offers.

AUGUST 28

God Hears Prayers That Come from Your Heart

Unload all your burden on to him, since he is concerned about you.

1 PETER 5:7 (NJB)

If you've ever prayed, "God, help me. I'm overwhelmed and discouraged. I don't know if I can keep going," you were being honest with God—and it's the kind of prayer God wants to hear from you.

Do you feel under attack, exhausted, rejected, or lonely? Tell God. You have permission to dump everything you're feeling onto the Lord because the Bible says: *"Unload all your burden on to him, since he is concerned about you"* (1 Peter 5:7, NJB).

But sometimes being honest with God feels intimidating. You might even pretend he doesn't already know everything about your life. That's why it's important to remember three facts about God when you pray.

God knows all your emotions. The Bible says, *"The LORD gave us each a mind, and nothing we do can be hidden from him"* (Psalm 33:15, CEV).

When you tell God how you feel, he will never say, "That's a surprise to me." Why? Because he created your mind and everything else. Nothing you say will ever catch him off guard.

God understands your feelings. The Bible says, *"The LORD knows what is in everyone's mind. He understands everything you think"* (1 Chronicles 28:9, NCV).

Most of us don't understand everything we think. Sometimes I'll have an emotion that makes me wonder, "Where did *that* come from?" But because we're made in God's image and he gave us our emotions, he always understands them.

God loves to listen to you. The Bible says, *"I love the LORD, because he hears me. . . . He listens to me every time I call to him"* (Psalm 116:1-2, GNT).

You may get too busy for a conversation with him, but he is never too busy for you. And he doesn't have a short attention span; he won't say, "What were you talking about? Can you say that again?" God is always attentive.

So whenever you're distressed and at the end of your rope, pray honestly and *"cry out in the night, . . . pour out your heart like water in the presence of the Lord"* (Lamentations 2:19, NIV).

AUGUST 29

You Don't Have to Have All the Good Ideas

Wise men and women are always learning, always listening for fresh insights.

PROVERBS 18:15 (MSG)

One of the most important habits that will help you hold on in hard times is to keep learning new things. When you're not learning, you're not growing spiritually. And God always wants you to be growing and becoming more like him.

This is part of what it means to have vision. Vision is seeing how you can use a good idea—even if someone else thought it up. Proverbs 18:15 says, *"Wise men and women are always learning, always listening for fresh insights"* (MSG).

A mark of wisdom is being teachable.

No matter how educated or experienced you are, you can learn from other people by asking good questions. Everybody's ignorant, just on different subjects. That's why the Bible says, *"Iron sharpens iron"* (Proverbs 27:17, ESV). We all still have so much more to learn.

Practically everything you've learned has been by imitation. You learned to walk, talk, and eat, all by imitation. Most of what you know, you learned by watching other people.

That means you don't always need to come up with new ideas and strategies—at your business, in your home, or at school. You just have to keep your eyes open for what's already working. During tough times, strive to have a teachable attitude and take advantage of the wisdom God puts in front of you.

Today, innovation is like an idol in our society. Everybody wants to be an innovator. Everybody wants to be the person who thinks up something new, different, or creative.

Innovation is a good thing. But if something's working already, why reinvent the wheel? Imitation is often more important than innovation.

The apostle Paul said in Philippians 3:17, *"Join in imitating me, and keep your eyes on those who walk according to the example you have in us"* (ESV). Paul often encouraged other people to imitate him because he imitated Christ. He told others, *"Follow me as I follow Christ"* (1 Corinthians 11:1, MEV).

In hard times, look for what's working—what's accomplishing God's purposes, what God is blessing—and imitate it. That's the time to learn from other people of faith!

AUGUST 30

You'll Never Get to the End of God's Love

I give them eternal life, and they shall never perish; no one will snatch them out of my hand.

JOHN 10:28 (NIV)

When I took my kids to the Grand Canyon when they were young, my two boys were especially wiggly. I held on to their hands as we walked up to the edge. They wanted to let go—but there was no way I was letting go of their hands! As their father, I loved them too much to let them go.

After you put your hand in God's hand, there will be times you're going to want to let go. But no matter how your feelings or circumstances change, God is steady, sure, and faithful. When you become a Christian, he promises to keep you saved until heaven.

Jesus said, *"I give them eternal life, and they shall never perish; no one will snatch them out of my hand"* (John 10:28, NIV).

There have been times in my life when I've said, "God, it's not convenient to be a follower of Jesus right now. I'd like to let go for a little bit." God replied, "Well, you might want to let go of me, but I'm not letting go of you. You are in my hand, and no one can snatch you out."

Remember, God's hands are bigger than the universe. You'll never get to the edge of them. And you'll never get to the end of God's love.

Once you are born again, you can't be unborn. Once your name is written in the eternal Book of Life, it's written in indelible ink, the blood of Christ. Once you're saved, you are always saved.

You don't know what your future holds or how many years you've got left. You might lose everything, but you will never lose your salvation. Even when the world seems to have gone mad, you have a loving Father who is working things out for good.

Be confident and rest assured that the one who holds you in his hand will never let you go.

AUGUST 31

God's Correction Is Not Punishment

Let God train you, for he is doing what any loving father does for his children.
HEBREWS 12:7 (TLB)

Do you know the difference between punishment and correction?

Punishment is a penalty for the past, and correction is training for the future. Correction is discipline, not punishment.

When something bad happens, we often think God is punishing us when he's actually just correcting us. How can we know this? Because God doesn't punish his children. Jesus already took all of the punishment for every sin on the cross.

Every sin you've ever committed and will ever commit has already been paid for. So God doesn't punish you for your sins—but he does correct you. His correction is the evidence of his love because he doesn't want you to keep going in the wrong direction.

One way God corrects us is through pain. Hebrews 12:8-10 says, *"If God doesn't discipline you as he does all of his children, it means that you are illegitimate and are not really his children at all. Since we respected our earthly fathers who disciplined us, shouldn't we submit even more to the discipline of the Father of our spirits, and live forever? For our earthly fathers disciplined us for a few years, doing the best they knew how. But God's discipline is always good for us, so that we might share in his holiness"* (NLT).

God doesn't correct those who aren't his children. As a father, I didn't correct other people's kids, but I certainly corrected mine. I did it for their good because I wanted them to know the joy of following God and doing things his way.

If you have chosen to follow him and are his child, God wants the same for you.

Following Jesus means cooperating when God brings any kind of correction into your life—not because he wants to punish you but because he loves you. When God corrects you, he isn't mad at you. He's mad *about* you!

The Bible says, *"Let God train you, for he is doing what any loving father does for his children"* (Hebrews 12:7, TLB).

God's correction is for your good, even when it comes with pain.

SEPTEMBER 1

They'll Know Us by Our Love

Everyone will know that you are my disciples, if you love one another.

JOHN 13:35 (NIV)

The distinguishing mark of a Christian is not a cross, a crucifix, a dove, or a fish on a bumper sticker. The sign of a Christian is love. How many people know you're a Christian because of your loving lifestyle?

We sing about love, talk about love, pray about love, and study love. But do we do it? To develop love as your life principle and make it your greatest aim, you have to take some action as soon as you finish reading this devotional. Love acts!

First, act loving in your current relationships. If you've behaved unlovingly toward someone, it's time to seek reconciliation. Make things right with your kids, your spouse, your boyfriend or girlfriend, your parents, or someone at work or school.

Then, start increasing the number of relationships you have. If the most important aim in life is to love, we need to build as many relationships as possible. Why? Because the world will know about God's love by the way we love each other—and especially by the way Christians love others.

You can't live a loving lifestyle as a hermit. You spell love T-I-M-E. It takes time to love other people. If you love your friends, you've got to spend time with them. If you love your kids, you've got to spend time with them. If you love Jesus, you've got to spend time with him. Love always costs time and energy. But it's always worth it.

Can you imagine what would happen if everyone in the church loved like this—if we all committed ourselves to acting in love and giving our time unselfishly? People would experience a taste of how much God loves them—and it would change the world! It would grow God's Kingdom. It would make God so happy.

People are attracted to Christ more than they are persuaded to him. They're attracted by the love of God shown through the people who claim to follow him. And they won't care what we know until they first know we care.

SEPTEMBER 2

Two Steps toward Knowing God's Will

If you want to know what God wants you to do, ask him, and he will gladly tell you, for he is always ready to give a bountiful supply of wisdom to all who ask him.

JAMES 1:5 (TLB)

If you want to know God's will, start with these two steps:

1. **Admit you need guidance.** Psalm 25:9 says, *"He guides the humble in what is right and teaches them his way"* (NIV). If you've never felt God guiding you, maybe it's because you've never admitted needing his guidance. You go to work assuming you already know what to do without ever praying first. You make financial decisions, vacation plans, or career decisions before stopping to pray about them. If you're single, you might even ask someone out on a date without first asking for God's guidance.

   Stopping to admit you need God's guidance is the first step in knowing God's will for your life.

2. **Ask God in faith for directions.** The Bible says in James 1:5-6, *"If you want to know what God wants you to do, ask him, and he will gladly tell you, for he is always ready to give a bountiful supply of wisdom to all who ask him; he will not resent it. But when you ask him, be sure that you really expect him to tell you, for a doubtful mind will be as unsettled as a wave of the sea that is driven and tossed by the wind"* (TLB).

Notice there are two keys to knowing God's wisdom. First, you've got to ask the right person: God. You don't ask your hairdresser, your mechanic, or a social media influencer. You need to ask the right person!

Then, you ask with the right attitude: expecting God to answer. Have you ever asked God to lead you, but you didn't really expect him to? You must ask, expecting God to answer. God is faithful. What he promises to do, he will do.

God honors faith, and he promises to give you wisdom for the next step of your life.

SEPTEMBER 3

Jesus Protects and Directs You

My purpose is to give life in all its fullness. I am the Good Shepherd. The Good Shepherd lays down his life for the sheep.

JOHN 10:10-11(TLB)

Sheep are essentially defenseless animals, so a shepherd carries a few tools to care for and protect his sheep. He has a rod for guarding and protecting, and he uses a staff with a little crook in it to rescue the sheep.

We are like lost sheep in need of protection and direction—so Jesus came to earth to be our Good Shepherd. He said, *"My purpose is to give life in all its fullness. I am the Good Shepherd. The Good Shepherd lays down his life for the sheep"* (John 10:10-11, TLB).

Just as a shepherd uses the physical tools of the rod and the staff for direction and protection, God wants to direct and protect you. Here are two ways he does that:

If you follow him, Jesus leads you in the right direction. If you visit a major city like Paris without a guide, you'll miss all kinds of important things because you won't know what to look for.

The same is true with your life. You need a guide—a shepherd—to go before you. You need Jesus, the Good Shepherd, who leads from the front and calls you forward. This is different from being a cowboy, who drives cattle from the back. Jesus is not going to push you through life. He gets in front of you and essentially says, "Watch how I do it. Look where I go." John 10:4 says, *"When he has led out all of his sheep, he walks in front of them, and they follow, because they know his voice"* (CEV).

If you bring your hurts to him, Jesus is compassionate. Jesus has compassion on us because he knows we're helpless without him. Matthew 9:36 says, *"When [Jesus] saw the crowds, he had compassion on them, because they were harassed and helpless, like sheep without a shepherd"* (NIV). The sense in the original Greek text is that Jesus hurt deeply for the people in the crowd and wanted to help them.

In the same way, when you bring your pain to Jesus, he doesn't put you down; he lifts you up. He doesn't hassle you; he heals you. He is our Good Shepherd.

Four Strengths in Being Vulnerable

God opposes the proud but gives grace to the humble.
JAMES 4:6 (NLT)

Where you are most vulnerable in life is not a weakness. In fact, it is a strength!

Here's how God can use your vulnerabilities to equip you to fulfill your purpose.

First, being open and honest with other people about your weaknesses is **spiritually empowering** because it opens the door to God's grace. The Bible says, *"God opposes the proud but gives grace to the humble"* (James 4:6, NLT). Grace is the power you need to change.

Vulnerability is also **emotionally healing**. James 5:16 says, *"Admit your faults to one another and pray for each other so that you may be healed"* (TLB). If you want to just be forgiven, then you don't need to confess your sin to anyone other than God. But if you want to be healed, then you've got to share your weaknesses with somebody else.

Next, vulnerability is **relatable**. The Bible says in James 3:2, *"We all stumble in many ways"* (NIV). James even included himself in that statement. When someone admits that they mess up, too, they become more relatable. Nobody wants to be around a narcissist. But when you're vulnerable—when you admit your weaknesses and keep a healthy perspective—you draw people in.

Being vulnerable is also a **requirement for leadership**. If you can't be vulnerable, then you're not a leader. You're just a boss! *"If you are wise and understand God's ways, prove it by living an honorable life, doing good works with the humility that comes from wisdom"* (James 3:13, NLT).

As you gain God's wisdom, you also become humbler. James 4:10 says, *"Humble yourselves before the Lord, and he will lift you up"* (NIV). God honors your humility and vulnerability and uses them to form you into a leader.

The world tells you to keep your guard up and not appear weak. But God says to boast in your weaknesses—because they reveal his power and make you more dependent on him.

Will you let your guard down so that your weaknesses can point others to Jesus Christ?

SEPTEMBER 5

To Bear Fruit, Get Connected

Live in me, and I will live in you. A branch cannot produce any fruit by itself. It has to stay attached to the vine. In the same way, you cannot produce fruit unless you live in me.

JOHN 15:4 (GW)

On the night before his death, Jesus instructed his followers: *"Live in me, and I will live in you. A branch cannot produce any fruit by itself. It has to stay attached to the vine. In the same way, you cannot produce fruit unless you live in me"* (John 15:4, GW).

Jesus says that being spiritually connected is like being attached to a vine. You're not going to have any fruitfulness or productivity in your life if you're out there on your own. You've got to stay connected to Christ and his body, the church.

In plants, a disconnected branch can't bear fruit. It's the same for you. When you're not spiritually connected, you not only start to wither and die, but you also don't have any productivity in your life.

Every spring I grow a bunch of vegetables and fruit. But if I cut off a branch, it won't produce tomatoes or anything else. To produce fruit, it's got to be connected.

What kind of fruit should you produce when you are connected to the body of Christ? *"The fruit of the Spirit is love, joy, peace, forbearance, kindness, goodness, faithfulness, gentleness and self-control"* (Galatians 5:22-23, NIV).

I don't know about you, but I'd like to be more loving. I'd like to be more joyful. I'd like to be more at peace, no matter what happens to the economy. I'd like to be more kind to people who are mean to me. I'd like to be faithful and keep my promises. I'd like to be gentle with people who are not gentle. And I'd like to have more self-control.

That's called the fruit of the Spirit, and it's evidence of being spiritually connected. If you are not seeing yourself grow in all these things, guess what? It means you're not spiritually connected.

God says spiritual connection is essential. I've got to be connected to the body of Christ. You've got to be connected to the body of Christ. We're simply better together.

SEPTEMBER 6

Every Person Is Worthy of Respect

Show proper respect to everyone.
1 PETER 2:17 (NIV)

Respect has become a rare and endangered value over the past few decades.

Yet the Bible makes it clear that stable families—and stable societies—are built around respect. The Bible commands us to honor our parents, respect civil authority, and respect church leaders. Husbands are called to respect wives in 1 Peter; in Ephesians, wives are called to respect husbands. And just to make it clear that God leaves no one out, the Bible also tells us, *"Show proper respect to everyone"* (1 Peter 2:17, NIV).

Everyone, regardless of beliefs or behaviors, is worthy of respect.

Why?

First, God made everyone. Psalm 8:5 says, *"You made them inferior only to yourself; you crowned them with glory and honor"* (GNT). God doesn't make junk. No one is worthless. People make wrong decisions, but they are still valuable to God. Even the most unlovable person in the world is loved by God.

Next, Jesus died for everyone. The Bible says, *"God paid a ransom to save you. . . . He paid for you with the precious lifeblood of Christ"* (1 Peter 1:18-19, TLB). You may not place much value on certain people, but God does. In fact, he says every person you meet is worth dying for.

So when you show respect to people, it shows you know God. And if you know God, then you'll fill your life with love, because God *is* love. The Bible says, *"If a person isn't loving and kind, it shows that he doesn't know God—for God is love"* (1 John 4:8, TLB). Love always treats people with consideration.

When you treat others with respect, you'll be respected too. It's the law of the harvest. You get back whatever you give out; whatever goes around comes around. The Bible says, *"What a person plants, he will harvest"* (Galatians 6:7, MSG).

By learning to love each other, we become *"eager to show respect for one another"* (Romans 12:10, GNT). And in this way, we become more like Jesus.

SEPTEMBER 7

You Need the Support of a Small Group

Then he chose twelve of them to be his apostles, so they could be with him.
MARK 3:14 (CEV)

If I asked you to complete this sentence, "If you want a job done right, . . ." you would probably finish it with this: ". . . do it yourself."

But that's the motto of a perfectionist headed for burnout—because you can't do every job by yourself.

Jesus was human, just like us. And just like us, he was never meant to handle the stress of daily life by himself.

Do you know the first thing Jesus did when he started his ministry? He formed a small group. Mark 3:14 says, *"Then he chose twelve of them to be his apostles, so they could be with him"* (CEV). Jesus gathered this small group because he knew God wanted him to do ministry and walk through his hardest days with friends by his side.

If anybody had a right to say, "If you want a job done right, do it yourself," it was Jesus. He had the power to do anything, yet even *he* knew the power of having a small group for support.

When he went to the garden of Gethsemane, just before the cross, Jesus said to his disciples in Matthew 26:38, *"My soul is overwhelmed with sorrow to the point of death. Stay here and keep watch with me"* (NIV). Even Jesus needed a small group to pray with him when he was in a crisis.

So much of our stress is self-imposed. God hasn't called you to be the general manager of the universe, nor does he expect you to be able to manage your life by yourself. You need his direction and strength *and* the support of a small group.

We often don't accept help from other people because of our insecurity and pride, and so we stay stressed out. But there are people of faith who are willing to help and support us—and people who need our help and support.

Humble yourself and admit you can't do it on your own. God made the church to help you in stressful times. Let your guard down and trust him to provide; he will lead you to the people you need.

SEPTEMBER 8

God's Mercy Frees You to Serve

God has been kind enough to trust us with this work. This is why we never give up.

2 CORINTHIANS 4:1 (CEV)

You were created to make a contribution with your life, not to just exist and live only for yourself. God shaped you to serve him, and it's all because of his mercy.

"God has been kind enough to trust us with this work. This is why we never give up" (2 Corinthians 4:1, CEV).

Some people think *ministry* is a churchy word. It's something only ministers do. But anytime you use the talents, gifts, and abilities God has given you to help somebody else, you're doing ministry. Even your job can be your ministry—whether you're an accountant, teacher, or truck driver!

When you understand that everything God does through you is because of his mercy, you realize two things:

You don't have to prove your worth. Do you ever try to demonstrate your worth through your work? Maybe you think that the more successful you are, the more valuable you are. But your worth has nothing to do with your work. Instead, your worth is found in the fact that God made you, loves you, and sent Jesus to die for you. Understanding God's mercy takes you off the performance track.

You don't have to wallow in your mistakes. We've all made mistakes. We've all sinned. But because of God's mercy, you don't have to dwell on your past. You can repent and turn away from your sin. Your past doesn't have to hold you back from doing the work God has given you to do.

In fact, God has never used a perfect person—because there aren't any, except for Jesus Christ. When you look through the Bible, you'll find all kinds of people God used despite their mistakes: Jacob was a chronic liar. Rahab was a prostitute. Jonah was fearful and reluctant. Martha worried a lot. The Samaritan woman had several failed marriages. Peter was impulsive. Moses, David, and Paul were all guilty of murder. Yet God used each person in incredible ways.

There's nothing that would prevent God from using you. Because of God's great mercy, you can live out his purpose for your life.

SEPTEMBER 9

Why Showing Love at Work Matters

The quality of each person's work will be seen when the Day of Christ exposes it. For on that Day fire will reveal everyone's work; the fire will test it and show its real quality.

1 CORINTHIANS 3:13 (GNT)

God wants to use your job to make you more like Jesus. But learning Christlike qualities such as responsibility, character, and love is never easy. To learn those things, you have to respond to people the way Jesus would—and that can be especially difficult at work.

So why should you make such an effort to become like Jesus in your job, whether you work at home, at an office, or anywhere else?

First, because God is going to evaluate your work one day. The Bible says, *"The quality of each person's work will be seen when the Day of Christ exposes it. For on that Day fire will reveal everyone's work; the fire will test it and show its real quality"* (1 Corinthians 3:13, GNT).

Everything you've done in your career will eventually be seen—because Christ is going to inspect it on the Day of Judgment. It's a day when everyone's work will be tested by fire to show the character and quality of what each person has done.

So much of your work may be done without anyone watching—but God knows. He is watching, and you will give him an account for your work, no matter how menial it seems. You don't have to always get it right. And you certainly don't have to be the best. But you do have to work as if you're doing it for Christ—because you actually are.

Second, you should try to become more like Jesus in your work. Because God is going to give eternal rewards for whatever is done in love, Hebrews 6:10 says, *"God is fair. He won't forget what you've done or the love you've shown for him"* (GW). You need to remember that verse every Monday morning. God is not going to forget how hard you work, how you give your best, and how you show love in his name.

Your work matters to God. One of your purposes in life is to become like Christ. And your job could be one of the most important ways God teaches you to be responsible, to develop character, and to love others. It could be one of the most significant ways he uses you to bring others to him.

SEPTEMBER 10

Look for Ways to Bring People Together

[God] has restored our relationship with him through Christ, and has given us this ministry of restoring relationships. In other words, God was using Christ to restore his relationship with humanity. He didn't hold people's faults against them, and he has given us this message of restored relationships to tell others.

2 CORINTHIANS 5:18-19 (GW)

When you want to repair a relationship, you have to focus on reconciliation, not resolution. There's a big difference! Reconciliation means reestablishing the relationship. It doesn't mean you'll remarry your ex. It just means you're at peace with each other.

Resolution means you resolve every disagreement—but that just isn't going to happen. There are some things you're just never going to agree on because we're all different. But you can disagree without being disagreeable. That's called maturity. That's called wisdom. That's called being like Christ.

We can have unity without uniformity. We can walk hand in hand together without seeing eye to eye. After being married to my wife, Kay, for nearly fifty years, we still don't see eye to eye on a lot of things. But we walk hand in hand and support each other. We are at peace.

There's a lot of conflict out there. The world is filled with wars, division, arguments, prejudice, racism, terrorism, and partisanship. As a result, we have broken relationships, broken economies, broken governments, and broken hearts.

I challenge you as a believer to commit to becoming an agent of reconciliation in a world filled with conflict. Look for ways to bring people together.

The Bible says in 2 Corinthians 5:18-19, *"[God] has restored our relationship with him through Christ, and has given us this ministry of restoring relationships. In other words, God was using Christ to restore his relationship with humanity. He didn't hold people's faults against them, and he has given us this message of restored relationships to tell others"* (GW).

If you are a follower of Jesus Christ, you have a ministry of reconciliation. It's your job to go out in society and say, "God's done everything to put you back in fellowship with him. He's already paid for all your sins. You don't have to be his enemy. Remember: He's not mad at you. He's mad *about* you. Be reconciled to God. Be at peace with God. Then spread that peace to everybody else."

The Real Reason We Argue

Don't look out only for your own interests, but take an interest in others, too. You must have the same attitude that Christ Jesus had.
PHILIPPIANS 2:4-5 (NLT)

Getting into a conflict is easy—but resolving it is challenging. So how do you resolve a conflict? You first have to confess your part of the problem. Then you need to listen for the other person's hurt and perspective.

We think we argue over ideas. But we actually argue over emotion. Anytime there's a conflict, someone's feelings have been hurt. It's not the idea that causes the conflict; it's the emotion behind the idea.

Hurt people hurt people. The more people are hurting, the more they lash out. People who aren't in pain don't inflict pain on others. People who are filled with love are loving toward others. People who are filled with joy are joyful to others. People who are filled with peace are at peace with everybody else. But people who are hurting inside are going to hurt others.

If you want to connect with people, you must start with their needs, hurts, and interests. If you want to be a good salesperson, you don't start with your product. You start with your customer's needs, hurts, and interests. If you want to be a good professor or pastor or anything else, you start with people's needs, hurts, and interests. Philippians 2:4-5 says, *"Don't look out only for your own interests, but take an interest in others, too. You must have the same attitude that Christ Jesus had"* (NLT).

Are you often so busy trying to get people to see your position that you're not listening to theirs? You need to switch your focus from your needs to their needs.

Conflict resolution starts with the way you look at the situation. The word *look* in Philippians 2:4 is the Greek word *skopeō*. The related noun *skopos* is where we get our words "microscope" and "telescope." *Skopeō* means "to fix your eyes on"; in other words, "to focus." The next verse says your attitude should be like Jesus. You are most like Jesus when you're focusing on somebody else's hurts rather than your own.

There's an old proverb that says, "Seek to understand before seeking to be understood." When you're focused on the other person's needs and not your own, you'll be able to get a better understanding of the situation and move forward with resolving your conflict.

SEPTEMBER 12

Gentleness Shows That You Love Jesus

Believers shouldn't curse anyone or be quarrelsome, but they should be gentle and show courtesy to everyone.
TITUS 3:2 (GW)

Your gentleness is a witness to unbelievers. They're watching you all the time to see if you are any different when you're under stress. When you respond to pressure with gentleness, it's an incredible testimony to the world.

The Bible says in Titus 3:2, *"Believers shouldn't curse anyone or be quarrelsome, but they should be gentle and show courtesy to everyone"* (GW).

If you claim to be a follower of Jesus, you are not allowed to speak evil of anyone. You are not allowed to be quarrelsome. Instead, you must be gentle with and show courtesy to everyone. Does that mean even people of a different political party? Yes.

God gave me the gift of evangelism, so I spend a lot of my time speaking with people I totally disagree with. That's because I believe you cannot win your enemies to Christ; you can only win your friends.

People often won't trust Jesus until they trust you. People usually don't ask me if the Bible is credible. They want to see that *I* am credible. Do I live with integrity? Am I gentle? Am I loving? Am I compassionate?

If people like what they see in you, they will listen to what you say.

Here's the thing: If you obey Titus 3:2, you're going to be criticized by other Christians. They're going to say you're compromising. I know this from experience. When I say I have friends who are Muslim, Jewish, or atheists, they say, "How could you do that?" And they accuse me of compromising.

Treating other people with respect does not mean you have to compromise what you believe. I have friends who don't agree with me and friends who don't believe what I believe. Our different beliefs don't keep me from befriending people because there's something more important to focus on: Do they know Jesus?

A great verse to live by is 1 Peter 3:15: *"Always be prepared to give an answer to everyone who asks you to give the reason for the hope that you have. But do this with gentleness and respect"* (NIV).

Goodness and Mercy Will Always Follow You

The LORD *watches over all who love him.*

PSALM 145:20 (NIV)

When you put your trust in Jesus, you never need to fear the future. His goodness and mercy are with you every day.

You're following the Good Shepherd, and he is out in front of you with his rod and staff. And at the back of the flock are a couple of sheepdogs—goodness and mercy—nudging you along, making sure you don't stray away.

God's goodness is watching over you. Did you know a second hasn't passed in your life when God wasn't watching you? God is always paying attention to you because he created you to love you. He knows every detail of your life. Psalm 145:20 says, *"The LORD watches over all who love him"* (NIV).

Not only does he watch over you, but he also protects you. The Bible says, *"God will command his angels to protect you wherever you go"* (Psalm 91:11, CEV).

God's protection doesn't mean that only good things will happen to you. Disappointment and pain will still come your way. But God promises that good will come out of everything that happens to you—whether or not you're able to see in this lifetime how he has worked.

God's mercy and grace are working in you. The Bible says in Isaiah 60:10, *"I will have mercy on you through my grace"* (TLB).

Grace is when God gives you what you don't deserve. Mercy is when God *doesn't* give you what you *do* deserve. For all the ways you've sinned, failed, and made mistakes, you deserve punishment, yet God pardons and forgives you through Christ. That's mercy.

It is God's nature to be merciful. He loves to show his mercy! He doesn't get tired of it. He doesn't get frustrated when you keep coming back for more.

The truth is, God is with you every moment of every day, always offering his goodness and mercy.

Nobody knows what's going to happen next week, much less in the next decade. But when you face the future, remember this: God will fill your life to overflowing, and his goodness and mercy will be with you. There is no need to fear.

SEPTEMBER 14

Seek God, Not His Gifts

The LORD looks down from heaven on all mankind to see if there are any who understand, any who seek God.

PSALM 14:2 (NIV)

When you're praying for healing and restoration, it's okay to want a miracle. But ultimately, it should be God himself you seek. Your prayer should be: "God, I want *you*. I want to know you." Because when you seek God, you get everything else.

God gives many promises in the Bible about those who seek him. Here are a few:

- *"If my people, who are called by my name, will humble themselves and pray and seek my face . . . then I will hear from heaven"* (2 Chronicles 7:14, NIV).
- *"I love those who love me, and those who seek me find me"* (Proverbs 8:17, NIV).
- *"Anyone who comes to him must believe he exists and that he rewards those who earnestly seek him"* (Hebrews 11:6, NIV).
- *"If from there you seek the LORD your God, you will find him if you seek him a merciful God; he will not abandon or destroy you"* (Deuteronomy 4:29, 31, NIV).

Seek God, not just his blessing. Then you'll find joy in knowing God better. Whether or not you get what you think is best for you, you'll be satisfied with what God thinks is best for you. When you're going through a divorce or a miscarriage or a layoff, seek God—even more than you seek deliverance from your pain.

This is not a casual pastime. Don't seek God in your spare moments, after you're done with work or when you're tired of looking at your phone or other device. Make getting to know God the primary focus of your life.

- *"The LORD looks down from heaven on all mankind to see if there are any who understand, any who seek God"* (Psalm 14:2, NIV).

It's rare to find someone who's earnest about seeking God. Most of us want just enough of God to bless us, but not to change us.

You don't become a faithful disciple of Jesus Christ by giving him your left-overs. Seek him first, with all of your heart, and he will keep every promise to deliver and restore you.

SEPTEMBER 15

Get a Good Grip on God's Word

The message of his grace . . . is able to build you up and give you the blessings God has for all his people.

ACTS 20:32 (GNT)

You can't be physically healthy if you don't eat foods that are good for you and nourish your body. In the same way, you can't be spiritually healthy unless you feed on the truth of God's Word.

Would you like to have all the blessings that God has for you? Of course you would!

How do you get those blessings? They're a direct result of spiritual maturity. The Bible says, *"The message of his grace . . . is able to build you up and give you the blessings God has for all his people"* (Acts 20:32, GNT).

God's message of grace in his Word will build you up. When you grow in spiritual maturity, God can give you all the blessings he has for you. There are some gifts you can't give to babies because they aren't mature enough for them yet. In the same way, there are some gifts God wants to give you, but he's waiting for you to grow up.

You can actually use your hand to help you remember how to use the Bible to grow in spiritual maturity. You feed on the Word of God by doing six things: You hear God's Word—that's your pinkie finger. You read it—that's your ring finger. You study it—that's your middle finger. You memorize it—that's your pointer finger. Then you meditate on it—that's your thumb. Your palm represents applying God's Word.

If the only spiritual input you get is hearing the Word of God at church, then you won't have a very strong grip with just your pinkie finger. We forget up to 95 percent of everything we hear within seventy-two hours.

If you hear God's Word and also read and study it every day, then you'll have a better grip on the truth. Satan can't pull it away from you as easily.

When you do all six things, you'll have a firm, strong grip on God's Word. No one will be able to take it away from you! You'll find yourself growing toward spiritual maturity and receiving the blessings that come with it.

SEPTEMBER 16

Cast Yourself on God's Mercy

Cast all your anxiety on him because he cares for you.

1 PETER 5:7 (NIV)

One of the most important things you can do when you experience failure is to cast yourself on God's mercy. We know Peter did this because he wrote two books in the Bible about it.

Peter had a massive failure in his life: denying Jesus three times in one evening. But he didn't waste time suffering in guilt or shame or regret. Instead, Peter cast all his anxiety on God, and his life was filled with hope because of God's mercy.

In 1 Peter 5:7, Peter said, *"Cast all your anxiety on him because he cares for you"* (NIV). In this verse, the Greek word translated as *cast* carries the idea of throwing or tossing.

Imagine you're carrying a really heavy backpack. It's so big you're straining under its weight. But what if you had a horse? You could throw your pack on the back of the horse, and it wouldn't even break a sweat as it carried your burden.

That's what this verse is saying. Take all your fear, insecurity, guilt, and whatever else you're struggling to carry and throw it onto God. Cast yourself on his mercy, and let him carry your load.

But how exactly do you do that? You can pray something like this: "God, I really messed up. I don't deserve your mercy. I've ignored you and made mistakes. But you are kind and forgiving, so I'm throwing myself on your mercy. I need a fresh start!"

This is the antidote to everything Satan says to you. Satan loves to whisper lies in your ear like "You're not good enough. Who do you think you are? Why do you think God could ever use you? Why do you think God would answer your prayers after all the stuff you've done?" Satan doesn't want you focused on God's mercy.

Before Peter's failure, Jesus had reminded him of Satan's schemes. But Jesus also told him that he would pray for him. And he would use Peter's pain to help other people.

These things are true for you too. You'll be tempted, and sometimes you'll fail, but Jesus will always be there for you. And your pain won't be wasted.

When you cast your cares, you lose your despair!

SEPTEMBER 17

It's Time to Admit Your Way Isn't Working

When [Jesus] had finished speaking, he said to Simon, "Put out into deep water, and let down the nets for a catch." Simon answered, "Master, we've worked hard all night and haven't caught anything. But because you say so, I will let down the nets."

LUKE 5:4–5 (NIV)

Simon Peter had been fishing all night but hadn't caught anything. Then Jesus told him to put his nets out just one more time. It must have been difficult to admit failure to Jesus. Simon Peter was a professional fisherman, and he was good at it. It was how he made his living. But sometimes even the professionals fish all night and catch nothing.

Does your life ever feel the same way? Sometimes your best isn't good enough, and sometimes you face situations out of your control. You can't control the economy. You can't control the weather. You can't control a lot of things that affect your life.

What do you do when you keep trying hard in your work, but you just don't have much to show for it?

First, you need to get Jesus in your boat. In other words, let him be the center of your work. Then, once you've asked Jesus to come into your boat, you need to admit your way isn't working so you can let him take over. The Bible calls this confession, and it's not always easy.

Why is it so hard for you to admit your way isn't working? Here are a few reasons:

Pride. You don't want anybody to think you can't handle it. Instead, you want to look like you're in charge and like you've got it all together. You think you can handle everything by yourself, even if it means working long hours at work.

Stubbornness. You're unwilling to change the way you do things. You let yesterday's success become the greatest enemy of tomorrow's success.

Fear. You can't admit you've fished all night and caught nothing. You're afraid people will think less of you. You're afraid to let Jesus into your boat because he might steer it in a direction you don't want to go.

It's time to confess that your way isn't working. It's time to pray, "Lord, I want to have it all together, but I don't! I want to be in charge, but I know I'm not! I want to go my own way, but I know your way is better. And so I want to hand over control to you—because I know you were in control all along. I confess my sin of overwork and trusting in my own abilities instead of you. I don't want to live that way anymore. Please take the wheel, and steer me in whatever direction is your good plan for me."

Let go of your pride, stubbornness, and fear. Be willing to say to Jesus, like Simon Peter did, "Because you say so, I will." Then see how Jesus can take your boat and fill your nets to overflowing.

SEPTEMBER 18

What's Controlling You?

Do not let sin control the way you live; do not give in to sinful desires. . . . Instead, give yourselves completely to God, for you were dead, but now you have new life. So use your whole body as an instrument to do what is right for the glory of God.

ROMANS 6:12-13 (NLT)

Every day you're controlled by something.

You may be controlled by your ego or by the expectations of other people. You may be controlled by fear, guilt, resentment, or bitterness. You may be controlled by a substance or a habit. The bottom line is that you are controlled by something every day.

Freedom comes when you choose what's going to control you. When you choose to let Jesus Christ control your life—when you are mastered by the Master—you can master everything else. If God is not number one in your life, something else is, and it will control you to a negative degree. But when you turn your life completely over to God, he always moves you in the right direction.

Romans 6:12-13 says, *"Do not let sin control the way you live; do not give in to sinful desires. . . . Instead, give yourselves completely to God, for you were dead, but now you have new life. So use your whole body as an instrument to do what is right for the glory of God"* (NLT).

Giving God control is a choice. Here are some steps to help you do this:

- Admit that you've been trying to play God.
- Admit that you can't change on your own.
- Humbly ask God to help you change.
- Be honest with someone else about the things that need to change in your life.
- Give Jesus Christ total ownership of your life.

Do you want to change? Are you willing to follow these steps? You say, "I'm so tired of trying and failing." Stop trying. Instead, start trusting. God gives you the option to either depend on him or depend on yourself. The result is either freedom or frustration.

Why not give it all to Christ? What do you have to lose?

SEPTEMBER 19

God's Remedy for Feeling Worn Down

Don't you know? Haven't you heard? The L*ORD* *is the everlasting God; he created all the world. He never grows tired or weary.*

ISAIAH 40:28 (GNT)

The bigger the changes that happen in your life, the more time you need to spend with God.

That time with God is called a quiet time. You read the Bible, talk to God in prayer, and remain quiet so you can listen to what God wants to say to you.

When you're stressed out, time alone with God is the great stabilizer. It's also the greatest reenergizer when you're worn out. With the many changes that happen in our lives, it's no wonder that chronic stress has drained us.

Are you feeling fatigued? That's natural. It's what stress does to our bodies. No matter how much sleep we get at night, we're often still tired when we wake up or start to drag a few hours into the day. If you feel like you're just getting by, you are not alone.

When you feel overwhelmed, exhausted, stressed out, and like you're barely hanging on, then you need to remember Isaiah 40:28: *"Don't you know? Haven't you heard? The* L*ORD* *is the everlasting God; he created all the world. He never grows tired or weary"* (GNT).

God created the entire universe in six days—and he only rested on the seventh day to model a Sabbath for us. He never gets tired! He is never overwhelmed or worn out. He never gets stressed. He can handle anything—including all the things you can't.

If you spend more time with God, who never grows tired or weary, then you're going to have more energy. Spending time with God is not a burden or a drudgery or a drain—it's the opposite! He gives strength to those who are weary. He gives peace and rest.

If you're stressed, don't seek a quick fix. Don't look for a shortcut. Don't fight changes that you can't possibly control. Instead, spend time with God every day.

SEPTEMBER 20

Play the Truth of God's Word

We take captive every thought to make it obedient to Christ.

2 CORINTHIANS 10:5 (NIV)

I have good news for you: Your brain stores everything. But it's also bad news: Your brain stores *everything*. And what your brain stores becomes the soundtrack of your life.

Day after day, you're confronted with truth and with lies—and your brain takes in both. While you have all kinds of good things stored in your brain, there's a lot of garbage too. And you probably base a lot of your decisions on that garbage.

Maybe when you were a child, adults said you weren't good enough or you'd never amount to anything. Those were lies—but you believed them. And you might still be believing those lies. As you go throughout each day, those lies are still there, quietly playing in the background of your thoughts.

So what do you do? You need to change the soundtrack that's playing in your mind. Instead of playing lies, you need to play the truth of God's Word.

Second Corinthians 10:5 says, *"We take captive every thought to make it obedient to Christ"* (NIV). And Romans 12:2 says it this way: *"Let God transform you into a new person by changing the way you think"* (NLT). How do you change the way you think? You play a soundtrack of truth.

First, ask God to heal your memories. Tell God, "I need you to heal these memories of rejection, sin, resentment, guilt, and abuse. They hurt. Please heal me."

Next, fill your mind with God's Word. The more truth you put in your mind, the more lies you push out. Instead of spending all your time watching television and listening to music, fill your mind with God's Word.

God's Word says you're lovable (John 3:16), capable (2 Peter 1:3), valuable (Luke 12:7), forgivable (Psalm 103:12), and usable (Ephesians 4:12).

Let those messages become the soundtrack of your life, and God will transform your mind.

SEPTEMBER 21

For Meaningful Conversations, Plan and Pray

Intelligent people think before they speak;
what they say is then more persuasive.
PROVERBS 16:23 (GNT)

Do you want to have a meaningful conversation with someone? Then you need to plan and pray. You need to say to God, "Teach me *what* to say, teach me *when* to say it, and teach me *how* to say it."

Even Jesus did this.

Jesus said in John 12:49, *"I have not spoken on my own. Instead, the Father who sent me told me what I should say and how I should say it"* (GW). Jesus didn't speak on his own power. He talked to his Father, who told him what he should say, when he should say it, and how he should say it.

God will do the same for you. If he hasn't, it's because you haven't asked! You haven't tapped into God's wisdom and power. You haven't taken advantage of your right as God's child to ask him for what you *think* you need and trust him to provide what he *knows* you need.

You would never walk into an important meeting unprepared. In the same way, before you have a critical conversation with your child, spouse, boss, or neighbor, you need to plan and pray. It's the only way you're going to get anywhere in your conversations.

The Bible says, *"Intelligent people think before they speak; what they say is then more persuasive"* (Proverbs 16:23, GNT). In other words, if you want to be persuasive, put your mind in gear before you put your mouth in motion. Plan what you're going to say.

Planning your conversations gives you the space to think through the circumstances and context with a clear head. It gives you perspective. Then you can enter a conversation with grace.

Colossians 4:6 says, *"Everything you say should be kind and well thought out"* (GW).

If you'll just practice that one verse, then you will learn to communicate more like Jesus. The only way to ensure your words are kind and well thought out is to plan ahead and pray.

Great Listeners Ask Great Questions

A person's thoughts are like water in a deep well,
but someone with insight can draw them out.
PROVERBS 20:5 (GNT)

One of the clearest signs of a great listener is when someone knows how to ask open-ended questions.

To really engage someone in conversation, don't ask questions that require only a yes or no answer. Instead, ask open-ended questions that allow people to really share their heart.

For example, instead of asking, "Did you enjoy the concert?" you could say, "What was your favorite part of the concert?" It may seem like a subtle change, but it makes all the difference in how someone opens up to you.

Proverbs 20:5 says, *"A person's thoughts are like water in a deep well, but someone with insight can draw them out"* (GNT). If you really want to go deeper in your relationships and better understand your family and friends, then you need to put thought into how you word your questions.

Here's one phrase that will make you a master listener: "Tell me more." You can use it over and over again as you interact with all kinds of people throughout your life.

When people open up to you, don't let them stop after two or three sentences. Instead, when they finish talking, say, "Tell me more." Then, just when they think you're done listening, say again, "Tell me more." Every time you ask for more, you go deeper in relationship—you draw deeper from the well—and allow them to express more of themselves.

You might tell someone that you really care about what they have to say. But the best way to *show* them is to ask for more. It tells them you're interested. It proves you're paying attention. And attention is love! Asking open-ended questions shows people you're willing to give them your time, your focus, and your love so they can be heard and feel understood.

God made you for relationship. When you learn to listen to others share what's on their heart, your relationships will be transformed!

Leave a Legacy of Hospitality

Let us think about each other and help each other to show love and do good deeds.
HEBREWS 10:24 (NCV)

In a strong family, kids are taught that God made them and shaped them for a mission. Strong families model dedication, service, generosity, and prayer. The average family doesn't do those things. *Awesome* families do.

I am the person I am today, first of all, because of my parents. They instilled in me the value of caring about other people. They embodied Hebrews 10:24: *"Let us think about each other and help each other to show love and do good deeds"* (NCV).

My parents didn't have much money, but they had the gifts of hospitality and generosity. They loved to give to others, even though they didn't have much. We lived out in the country, and my dad would plant an acre garden with all kinds of vegetables. There was no way our family could eat all that food, but he did it just so he could give it away—because he didn't have any extra money to give. We always planted more so we could give more away.

Our home was constantly filled with visitors. One day my dad added up how many meals my mom had cooked for guests in our home in one year. It was over a thousand meals! I grew up learning a "give your life away" attitude. My parents taught me that life's not about ourselves; it's about helping other people.

That's what awesome families do: They teach each other how to show love and do good deeds—to minister and to serve.

A good example of this in the Bible is Cornelius's family in the book of Acts: *"He and all his family were devout and God-fearing; he gave generously to those in need and prayed to God regularly"* (Acts 10:2, NIV). What a great legacy! Wouldn't you like to have people writing that about you and your family one day?

Whether or not you have children, God wants you to leave a legacy like that. You'll find people younger in age or younger in the faith all around you. As you model hospitality and service for them, you'll help them discover God's mission for their lives.

SEPTEMBER 24

You Can't Change It, but God Can Use It

You intended to harm me, but God intended it all for good. He brought me to this position so I could save the lives of many people.

GENESIS 50:20 (NLT)

Remember the story of Joseph?

His brothers were jealous because he was the favorite son, so they sold Joseph into slavery. He was taken to Egypt, and for the next thirteen years of his life, everything went wrong. He was sold into slavery, falsely accused of rape, and thrown in jail for a crime he didn't commit.

But God put Joseph exactly where he wanted him to be. He knew Joseph would be raised up to become the second most powerful leader in Egypt, the most powerful nation in the world at that time. And because of that, Joseph was able to save Egypt and Israel from famine.

Besides saving two nations from starvation, he also saved his family—the ones who sold him into slavery. When his brothers appeared before him, Joseph could've confronted them and punished them for what they had done to him.

Instead, he treated them with grace, not bitterness. He was able to do that because he saw God's greater perspective and purpose. He knew God could use even the biggest hurt in his life for good. Joseph said to his brothers, *"You intended to harm me, but God intended it all for good. He brought me to this position so I could save the lives of many people"* (Genesis 50:20, NLT). God took the terrible sin of Joseph's brothers and used it to eventually save many people.

There will always be people in your life who have bad intentions, who will resent you, criticize you, and hurt you. There might even be times when you are the innocent victim of someone else's sin. You may not understand it—but you don't have to! You can trust that God sees, he cares, and he will have justice. Like Joseph, maybe you can't change your circumstances. And maybe you're wondering what God is doing and how you're going to make it through.

God can use everything, good or bad, to accomplish his purposes. His good plan to grow your character and make you more like Jesus will not be changed by other people. What others intend for bad, he will use for good.

When You Can't Forgive, You Only Hurt Yourself

If you do not forgive others, then your Father will not forgive the wrongs you have done.

MATTHEW 6:15 (GNT)

Have you ever expected God's forgiveness for the bad things you've done while, at the same time, wanting someone else to be punished rather than forgiven?

That kind of unwillingness to forgive reveals bitterness and resentment in your life, and it will just make you miserable. You'll end up only hurting yourself.

Jesus was clear about how forgiveness works. He said, *"If you do not forgive others, then your Father will not forgive the wrongs you have done"* (Matthew 6:15, GNT).

Forgiveness involves your past, present, and future:

- God has forgiven you multiple times in the past.
- Lack of forgiveness will make you miserable today.
- You will need God's forgiveness in the future.

After Jonah warned Israel's enemy, the Ninevites, about God's judgment, they repented, so God forgave them and didn't punish them. This made Jonah bitter.

But remember how Jonah originally turned away from God and then cried out to him from the belly of the fish? He wanted God's forgiveness for his own sin of disobeying. Yet he didn't want God to forgive the Ninevites.

In his bitterness, Jonah prayed, *"I knew that you are a loving and merciful God, always patient, always kind, and always ready to change your mind and not punish. Now then, LORD, let me die. I am better off dead than alive"* (Jonah 4:2-3, GNT).

Jonah's resentment only hurt him. The Ninevites were enjoying God's grace while Jonah was wallowing in self-pity. Jonah did not experience the joy and freedom that come with receiving and showing grace until he accepted God's plan.

Are you holding on to resentment and unforgiveness like Jonah? It's critical that you forgive anyone from your past who has hurt you and forgive anyone who wrongs you today. The Bible says, *"If we confess our sins, he is faithful and just and will forgive us our sins and purify us from all unrighteousness"* (1 John 1:9, NIV).

God has forgiven you for your past sins, and he has promised to forgive you in the future. Those who have been shown such extravagant grace must be willing to extend it to others.

SEPTEMBER 26

Three Ways to Thank God in Advance

I will sacrifice to you with songs of thanksgiving.
I will keep my vow. Victory belongs to the LORD!
JONAH 2:9 (GW)

Whenever you feel hopeless, it seems counterproductive to express gratitude. Why would you feel grateful when you've hit rock bottom?

Jonah understood why. When he was in the belly of a big fish, before God rescued him, he showed us how to thank God in advance for answering our prayers: *"I will sacrifice to you with songs of thanksgiving. I will keep my vow. Victory belongs to the LORD!"* (Jonah 2:9, GW).

What's the difference between thanking God *before* and thanking God *after*? If you wait to thank God until after he answers your prayer, then that's gratitude. But if you thank God in advance, before he answers your prayer, that's faith. We always want to thank God when he answers our prayers, but we show faith in God if we also thank him beforehand.

How do you thank God in advance? Jonah shows us three ways:

Jonah thanked God by praising him. The Bible tells us how to do this: *"Through Jesus, therefore, let us continually offer to God a sacrifice of praise—the fruit of lips that confess his name"* (Hebrews 13:15, NIV).

Jonah thanked God by returning to his mission. Jonah knew he'd messed up. We've all been there! But that doesn't stop God's purpose for us. Jonah's life mission remained the same. Your life mission remains the same, too, even when you mess up.

Jonah thanked God by trusting him for success. Proverbs 3:5-6 says, *"Trust in the LORD with all your heart; do not depend on your own understanding. Seek his will in all you do, and he will show you which path to take"* (NLT).

Jonah ran away from God. But he had faith that God hadn't abandoned him, even though Jonah disobeyed him. Jonah showed his faith in God's grace as he thanked God in advance—while he was still in the belly of the fish.

You can trust that God will never abandon you either, even if you disobey his will. That's why you can thank him, even before your prayers are answered.

SEPTEMBER 27

Warning Others Is an Act of Love

Jonah obeyed the LORD and went to Nineveh. The city was so big that it took three days just to walk through it. After walking for a day, Jonah warned the people, "Forty days from now, Nineveh will be destroyed!"

JONAH 3:3-4 (CEV)

When God sent Jonah to Nineveh, Jonah's mission was to warn the people about the severe consequences for their disobedience. God wanted them to know that his judgment was near but that they still had a chance to repent and obey him.

God wanted to give the people of Nineveh a second chance.

But he ended up needing to give Jonah a second chance too! Instead of heading straight to Nineveh, Jonah ran in the opposite direction and ended up sitting in a big fish. God rescued him, and Jonah took advantage of his second chance. He decided to obey God.

The Bible says, *"Jonah obeyed the LORD and went to Nineveh. The city was so big that it took three days just to walk through it. After walking for a day, Jonah warned the people, 'Forty days from now, Nineveh will be destroyed!'"* (Jonah 3:3-4, CEV).

Look again at what the Bible says Jonah did: He *"warned the people."* A warning is cautionary advice about a danger, trap, or problem. When we're not listening to his warning, God sometimes brings people into our lives to warn us. In fact, more than a hundred verses in the New Testament tell us to warn others. It's one of our responsibilities as followers of Jesus.

In Acts 20:31, Paul wrote, *"Remember that for three years I never stopped warning each of you night and day with tears"* (NIV). Notice that Paul said he was so desperate for the Ephesians to heed his warning that it brought him to tears. Why? Because he loved them!

God gives all believers the ministry of warning others. When you warn someone, it shows you love God and you love that person. If you knew a bridge was out and you saw someone driving toward it at 50 miles per hour, then warning them would be the loving thing to do.

In the same way, if you love the people in your life, then you will warn them of the consequences of their unwise actions or decisions—because a godly warning is an act of love.

SEPTEMBER 28

New Day, New Opportunity to Fulfill Your Mission

The Lord . . . is being patient for your sake. He does not want anyone to be destroyed, but wants everyone to repent.

2 PETER 3:9 (NLT)

One common mistake we make is turning people from the Bible into superheroes. But there are no superheroes—in Scripture or anywhere else.

In the Bible and in the world today, God uses only imperfect, broken people. Spend some time reading the Bible, and you'll soon realize that if you're willing to be used by God, then he will use you, no matter what you've done in the past. Nothing you've done or experienced will make God give up on his mission for your life.

Jonah is a great example of this. He was an ordinary guy who didn't even want to do what God told him to do. In fact, when God first gave him his assignment, Jonah ran away from it. But God gave him another chance, and Jonah eventually did what he'd been called to do—but with a bad attitude.

God had sent Jonah to call the people of Nineveh to repentance. Other Old Testament prophets made pleading, passionate speeches—but not Jonah. He went to the people with a simple, seven-word sermon: *"In forty days Nineveh will be destroyed!"* (Jonah 3:4, GNT). He was basically telling the people, "You guys are going to die. Bye."

But God still used Jonah, despite his bad attitude. In fact, Jonah's simple message led to one of the largest spiritual revivals in history. A huge city turned to God. That's really a bigger miracle than getting Jonah out of the belly of a big fish!

God used this imperfect, reluctant prophet to lead an incredible revival. God was patient with Jonah and never gave up on him. God won't give up on you either. The Bible says, *"The Lord . . . is being patient for your sake. He does not want anyone to be destroyed, but wants everyone to repent"* (2 Peter 3:9, NLT).

If you wake up tomorrow morning, it means God is giving you one more day—another opportunity—to fulfill your mission.

Expect God to use you, and he will!

SEPTEMBER 29

Any Believer Can Pray for Healing

Confess your sins to each other and pray for each other so that you may be healed.

JAMES 5:16 (NIV)

Does someone in your life need healing? Do *you* need healing? You can pray for healing, starting today! Just follow these steps:

First, make sure your heart is clean from sin. Holding on to unconfessed sin will always hinder your prayers for healing. The Bible says in James 5:16, *"Confess your sins to each other and pray for each other so that you may be healed"* (NIV). You're never going to be sinless, but you can *sin less*. God wants you to approach him with confidence. And you do that by making sure there is nothing between you and God that needs to be set right through confession.

Second, be specific when you ask for healing. Too many people are afraid to put God in a box, so they just say, "Lord, be with this sick person, show them your love, and help them to know you're with them." But how are you going to recognize God's provision when you don't ask him for anything specific? Name the thing you are asking God for—not because he needs to know the details but because he wants you to see how he works in those details.

Finally, ask in faith. James 1:6 says, *"But when you pray, you must believe and not doubt at all. Whoever doubts is like a wave in the sea that is driven and blown about by the wind"* (GNT). Pray with expectation, trusting God will answer your prayers in his time and his way. The person you're praying for may never be healed in this life. But you can still pray for healing—without doubt and in faith—because you know God never stops working out his purposes. He hears you, and he cares about the person you're praying for or about the sickness that may be burdening you.

Get your heart right with God. Confess your sin. Ask him for the specific thing you want him to do for you and others. Then expect God to work.

Delayed Obedience Is Disobedience

Without delay I hurry to obey your commands.
PSALM 119:60 (GNT)

The Bible is full of instructions for life. They're sometimes called decrees of God, precepts of God, and commands of God. Whatever you call them, God expects you to obey his commands right away, and he expects you to obey them fully.

Imagine if a parent tells a child to do something and the child says, "I'll think about it." Wouldn't there be consequences?

But people do that to God all the time. God says he wants you to do something, and you say, "I'll think about it."

But you don't have that kind of authority. It's no different from a child telling a parent, "I'll think about it."

When the Creator of the universe tells you to do something, he expects you to do it—*now*. Every parent knows *delayed obedience is disobedience.*

God also wants you to obey his commands fully. You can't pick and choose, making one list of instructions you'll follow and another list you won't. Partial obedience is disobedience.

The Bible says, *"Without delay I hurry to obey your commands"* (Psalm 119:60, GNT).

We often think of *hurry* as a negative word; it reminds us of the stress and pressures of today's world. But hurry is good when it comes to obeying God. It means you don't pause to question God's instructions before you obey them. You obey first—and seek understanding later. In fact, you won't fully understand many of God's commands until you've first obeyed them. In many cases, it's your obedience that unlocks your understanding.

That's what happened with the disciples. When Jesus called them to follow him, they had no idea what was in store for them—but they obeyed without hesitation. Here's what happened when Jesus called Simon and Andrew: *"Jesus said to them, 'Come follow me.' . . . So Simon and Andrew immediately left their nets and followed him"* (Mark 1:17-18, NCV).

What about you? What has God told you to do that you haven't started doing yet? What are you waiting for? God has your best interests at heart. So go ahead and do what he's told you to do.

OCTOBER 1

Spiritual Growth Requires Change

The fruit of the Spirit is love, joy, peace, patience, kindness, goodness, faithfulness, gentleness, self-control.

GALATIANS 5:22-23 (ESV)

God's purpose in every change in your life is to make you more like Jesus.

The promise of Romans 8:28 is wonderful: *"We know that God causes everything to work together for the good of those who love God and are called according to his purpose for them"* (NLT). But it doesn't make sense until you read the next verse: *"For God knew his people in advance, and he chose them to become like his Son"* (Romans 8:29, NLT).

God doesn't just want you in his family. He also wants you to develop the family characteristics of a child of God. He wants you to grow spiritually. And your model for maturity is Jesus Christ.

So what is Jesus like? The best picture of Jesus' character is the fruit of the Spirit in Galatians 5:22-23: *"The fruit of the Spirit is love, joy, peace, patience, kindness, goodness, faithfulness, gentleness, self-control"* (ESV).

God produces that kind of fruit in you by putting you in situations full of the exact opposite circumstances, where you get a chance to learn and practice these character qualities.

You don't learn kindness when you're around the nicest people; you don't learn contentment when you have everything you want. So when God teaches you how to love, he doesn't put you around people who are easy to love; he puts you around unlovable people.

Anybody can be happy when everything's going their way. But God teaches you true joy in the middle of suffering and grief and heartbreak.

It's easy to be peaceful when there is no struggle in your life. When God teaches you peace, he'll allow chaos and conflict in your life to teach you the peace that passes understanding.

How does God teach you patience? By placing you in a long line at the DMV or in a waiting room at a delayed doctor appointment. Anytime you have to wait, God is teaching you patience to make you more like Jesus.

Change is not always easy, but the big *and* small ways you're growing in spiritual maturity will make it worth it.

It's Time to Start Doubting Your Doubts

The world's sin is unbelief in me.

JOHN 16:9 (TLB)

At the root of every sin rests at least a momentary doubt about God.

Jesus said, *"The world's sin is unbelief in me"* (John 16:9, TLB). When you don't believe Jesus is who he says he is or will do what he says he'll do, that's the root of all sin.

There are emotions you can look for that can help you know when you're doubting God.

When you become fearful or anxious, it reveals your unbelief in God's promises. The Bible offers more than seven thousand promises. Your fear shows your unwillingness to claim those promises that God gives to everyone who follows him.

When you become impatient, it reveals your doubt in God's perfect timing. God has a plan for your life, but he's never going to be in a hurry. When you forget that, it becomes easier to take matters into your own hands instead of waiting on God.

When you become resentful or bitter, it reveals your doubt in God's wisdom. God is wise, good, and loving. But when things don't turn out like you expect, you think he messed up, and you don't believe he can bring good out of bad.

When you dwell on guilty feelings, it reveals your unbelief in God's forgiveness. How long should a follower of Jesus feel guilty? About one second. That's how long it takes to confess a sin. If you're carrying around guilt, it means you can't forgive yourself because you don't believe God has forgiven you.

When you feel inadequate, it reveals your doubt in God's power. God has said, *"My power works best in weakness"* (2 Corinthians 12:9, NLT). But when you don't believe that truth, it shows you think power should come only from yourself, which will always leave you disappointed.

Do you want to turn around those feelings of fear, impatience, resentment, guilt, and inadequacy? Then you need to start doubting your doubts and believing God's Word. Trust that God keeps his promises, has perfect timing, is wise, forgives you, and works powerfully through you.

OCTOBER 3

Why You Need Community for a Reset

A person standing alone can be attacked and defeated, but two can stand back-to-back and conquer. Three are even better, for a triple-braided cord is not easily broken.
ECCLESIASTES 4:12 (NLT)

If you need God to do a reset in your life, you just have to ask him. Then you need to find people to support your reset.

On your own, you can't succeed at something as big as a life change. If you could, you would—but you can't, so you won't. That's because God has wired us to find healing when other people get involved in our lives.

The Bible says in Ecclesiastes 4:10 and 12, *"If one person falls, the other can reach out and help. But someone who falls alone is in real trouble. . . . A person standing alone can be attacked and defeated, but two can stand back-to-back and conquer. Three are even better, for a triple-braided cord is not easily broken"* (NLT).

In other words, when you have the support of another person, you won't be easily defeated. And a whole group of supporters is even better!

Anytime you make a change in your life, you're going to make mistakes. You're not perfect—none of us are. In your desire to live with purpose and become the person God wants you to be, you're going to fall. You need loving people in your life to help you get back up.

Community is God's antidote to discouragement. Your small group or group of Christian friends can help you keep the right perspective. They can see what you can't see. They can remind you of God's truth.

Romans 12:5 says, *"We are many parts of one body, and we all belong to each other"* (NLT). In the family of God, you belong to me, and I belong to you. The people in your church and Christian community are your brothers and sisters. You're going to need their encouragement as God does a reset in your life.

If you haven't found them already, find your people. It will take courage and vulnerability, and if you feel those people are in short supply right now, then ask God for help. He will give you everything you need for a reset that makes you more like him.

OCTOBER 4

Got Worries? Remember What God Has Done

With God everything is possible.
MATTHEW 19:26 (NLT)

When you're facing tough times, worry is a natural human response. But instead of worrying, God wants you to worship. One way you can worship God is by believing who he is and what he can do.

In the book of 2 Chronicles, King Jehoshaphat and the people of Judah found themselves in a tough spot. Three enemy nations were on their way to make war against them.

Though he was afraid, the king's first response was to gather his people before the Lord. He stood before the whole nation and prayed aloud. His prayer is a great model to show you how to seek God when you feel stressed out and overwhelmed.

First, when you pray during a stressful time, remind yourself of who God is. Focus on his strength, character, and power. God can handle anything, including whatever you're facing right now. Jesus said, *"With God everything is possible"* (Matthew 19:26, NLT).

King Jehoshaphat reminded himself of this truth as he prayed, *"Are you not the God who is in heaven? You rule over all the kingdoms of the nations. Power and might are in your hand, and no one can withstand you"* (2 Chronicles 20:6, NIV).

The king's enemies were coming against him. But he chose to take his eyes off the problem and instead put his eyes on God's strength and power. He reminded himself of who God was.

After you remember who God is, remind yourself of what he has done. Remember when God has helped other people and when he has helped you. Recalling those things will give you confidence that God will handle whatever you are facing.

When King Jehoshaphat prayed, *"Did you not drive out the inhabitants of this land before your people Israel?"* (2 Chronicles 20:7, NIV), he was remembering when Moses led the Israelites out of Egypt to the Promised Land.

Remembering that God had helped Israel in the past gave King Jehoshaphat confidence that God would do it again.

What are you anxious about today? Instead of worrying, spend some time in prayer, remembering who God is and what he has done. Believe he can handle whatever you're facing.

OCTOBER 5

How to Show Faith and Gratitude in Your Battle

At the moment they began to sing and to praise, the Lord caused the armies of Ammon, Moab, and Mount Seir to begin fighting among themselves, and they destroyed each other!
2 CHRONICLES 20:22 (TLB)

When the people of Judah and their king, Jehoshaphat, were outnumbered by three enemy nations, the king chose not to worry. Instead, King Jehoshaphat led his people to worship God. One way they worshiped was by thanking God for the victory in advance.

It was almost time for the battle to begin, and Israel was on one side of the valley, their enemies on the other. You'd expect Judah's troops to begin arming themselves and lining up to march into the fight. But here's what happened instead: *"Then [the king] chose men to be singers to the LORD, to praise him because he is holy and wonderful. As they marched in front of the army, they said, 'Thank the LORD, because his love continues forever'"* (2 Chronicles 20:21, NCV).

Yes, you're reading that correctly. Instead of choosing warriors to lead the troops into battle, the king assembled a choir. Can you imagine what those men thought as they walked, singing and unarmed, onto the battlefield? Can you imagine what their enemies thought? Despite the odd strategy, the men obeyed. The choir marched in front of the army, declaring God's unending love and thanking him in advance for delivering them.

That's how God wants you to approach your battles too. He wants you to thank him in advance for solving your problems. Don't forget that when you thank God afterward, you're showing gratitude, which is important. But if you thank him in advance, you're also showing faith.

In the next verse, we see the effect of this unorthodox battle plan: *"And at the moment they began to sing and to praise, the Lord caused the armies of Ammon, Moab, and Mount Seir to begin fighting among themselves, and they destroyed each other!"* (2 Chronicles 20:22, TLB). God's people didn't even have to pick up a weapon.

That's what God wants for you too. He wants you to lay down your weapons—all the ways you've been trying to solve your problems on your own—and trust him as you face your enemy. Then thank him for deliverance and watch in gratitude as God fights on your behalf.

OCTOBER 6

How to Spot Your Blind Spots

Why do you look at the speck of sawdust in your brother's eye and pay no attention to the plank in your own eye?
MATTHEW 7:3 (NIV)

What sin do you tend to see most clearly and readily in others? What does that tell you about the sin that might be in your own life?

Before you judge someone else, remember that you have blind spots—attitudes or weaknesses in your life that you don't see, even though they cause conflict with others.

When you feel the urge to judge someone for their blind spots, choose to uncover and deal with your own instead. Jesus said it like this: *"Why do you look at the speck of sawdust in your brother's eye and pay no attention to the plank in your own eye? How can you say to your brother, 'Let me take the speck out of your eye,' when all the time there is a plank in your own eye? You hypocrite, first take the plank out of your own eye, and then you will see clearly to remove the speck from your brother's eye"* (Matthew 7:3-5, NIV).

He's saying, "Why are you so concerned about the sin in someone's else's life when you haven't dealt with your own sin? Take care of your blind spots so that you will be able to see clearly to help others."

We tend to judge in others what we dislike in ourselves. If you're lazy and wish you weren't, then you tend to judge others for their laziness. If you're prideful or greedy, then you'll spot that quickly in someone else.

But the Bible says in 1 Corinthians 11:31, *"If we judged ourselves in the right way, God would not judge us"* (NCV). Think about what that verse is saying: When we seriously examine our lives and evaluate our own weaknesses, faults, and failures, then God doesn't have to judge us.

God is for you, not against you. He already knows your blind spots, and he wants to help you address them so that you can mature in your faith.

OCTOBER 7

In a Storm, You Need "I Am"

When they saw him walking on the lake, they thought he was a ghost. They cried out, because they all saw him and were terrified. Immediately he spoke to them and said, "Take courage! It is I. Don't be afraid."

MARK 6:49-50 (NIV)

If you're going through a storm right now, you need to remember this: It's only in the storms of life that you learn what Jesus is really like. You see that he's not a mere man. He's not just a nice teacher or an ethical leader. He is God, the Creator of the universe.

In Mark 6, Jesus noticed that the disciples were in distress. They were in the middle of a lake, where the wind and waves were pounding their boat and keeping them from making any progress. And so Jesus walked out to them on the water. *"When they saw him walking on the lake, they thought he was a ghost. They cried out, because they all saw him and were terrified. Immediately he spoke to them and said, 'Take courage! It is I. Don't be afraid'"* (Mark 6:49-50, NIV).

The disciples still had some nagging doubts, like maybe Jesus was just a nice prophet who could do some miracles. But by walking on water, Jesus revealed he was far more than just a man. He showed them he was God.

He also gave them a challenge: *"Don't be afraid."* And he reassured them: *"It is I."*

In Greek, the language this part of the Bible was originally written in, the phrase *"It is I"* is actually two words: *egō eimi*, which simply means "I Am." Why is that important? The name of God is "I AM"—not "I was" or "I will be" or "I hope to be." When Jesus says, "I am," he is saying that you don't need to be afraid. You don't have to sweat it. He is God—and that is enough.

In a storm, you don't need a job—you need Jesus. You don't need a plan—you need a person. You don't need a system—you need a Savior. You don't need a new goal—you need God.

When you're going through a storm, remember that God is not distant, apathetic, or uninvolved. He is "I AM." He is in the storm with you, and he will get you through it.

OCTOBER 8

Can You See Where God Is Already Working?

Keep your eyes open for G*OD, watch for his works; be alert for signs of his presence.*

PSALM 105:4 (MSG)

During tough times, you need to be more aware and alert than ever to what God is doing. Why? Because God wants to teach you important lessons and help you grow in the middle of adversity.

Psalm 105:4 says, *"Keep your eyes open for* G*OD, watch for his works; be alert for signs of his presence"* (MSG).

Are you looking for God in the middle of your struggles? Are you looking for him in all the stuff that's going on in your life? You need to keep your eyes open. Look for all the ways God is working. Be alert to how he is showing you his presence.

There is one word for keeping your eyes open and being alert. It's *vision*. Most people have a wrong understanding of what it means to have vision.

Vision is one of the most misunderstood terms in leadership books and seminars. People often talk about it as if being a visionary means you can somehow predict the future. That's not what it means to be a person of vision.

What is vision? Vision is seeing God at work in your present situation and moving on it. It's making the most of what's happening right now. Vision is not predicting the future. Vision is seeing God at work and then deciding that you're going to join him in it. You keep your eyes open. You see God working. And then you take advantage of the situation. You see the wave, and you decide to catch it!

You need to stop praying for God to bless what you're doing. Instead, you need to ask him to help you see and do what he is blessing!

Every morning, say to God, "I know you're going to do a lot of really cool things in the world today. Would you give me the privilege of getting in on what you're doing? Help me to see it. And then give me the courage to step up and be a part of it."

When you're going through hard times, God still wants to use you for his purposes. Just keep your eyes open!

OCTOBER 9

It's Time to Face the Truth

If we claim to be without sin, we deceive ourselves and the truth is not in us.

1 JOHN 1:8 (NIV)

Sin always involves self-deception. At the moment you're sinning, you're deceiving yourself because you think that what you're doing will produce better results than what God already told you to do.

To stop defeating yourself, you must stop deceiving yourself. You need to take an honest look at your life, face the truth, and deal with the issues. What in your life are you pretending isn't a problem or you're not addicted to? What are you saying "It's no big deal" about?

It doesn't matter whether you're relying on narcotics or running up your credit card, whether you're watching pornography or reading a trashy novel—you're using it all to try to escape your pain and sin. But you're not going to get healing until you first acknowledge the root of your problem.

You don't have to hit rock bottom before you change. You don't have to go the way of destruction. You can admit the root of the issue and then deal with it.

When asked, "What's the biggest problem you encounter?" church counselors will say over and over, "People wait too long before they ask for help. Then it's almost impossible to turn around." Most people are in denial about the problem, wait until it's too late, and then go through unnecessary pain. The Bible says, *"If we claim to be without sin, we deceive ourselves and the truth is not in us"* (1 John 1:8, NIV).

What are the hard questions you need to be asking about the sin in your life? What are the warning signs you've been ignoring?

If you want healing, you need to acknowledge the root of your problem and face the truth about *yourself*. This is never the easy choice, but it's always the right one.

Jesus understands what you're going through. The Bible says, *"He faced all of the same testings we do, yet he did not sin. So let us come boldly to the throne of our gracious God. There we will receive his mercy, and we will find grace to help us when we need it most"* (Hebrews 4:15-16, NLT).

God is for you and is working in you. With his power, you can overcome anything.

OCTOBER 10

Faithful People Don't Give Up

That is why we never give up. Though our bodies are dying, our spirits are being renewed every day. For our present troubles are small and won't last very long. Yet they produce for us a glory that vastly outweighs them and will last forever!

2 CORINTHIANS 4:16-17 (NLT)

You're never a failure until you quit, and it's always too soon to quit. Why? Because God uses tough times to test your persistence. While he is using your pain for his good purpose, he is watching to see if you will remain faithful to him.

One difference between faithful and unfaithful people is that unfaithful people give up at the first sign of difficulty. Faithful people keep on keeping on.

Faithful people are determined. Faithful people are diligent. Faithful people are persistent. Faithful people don't know how to quit! You know how a little acorn becomes an oak tree? An oak tree is just an acorn that refused to give up.

Saddleback Church existed for fifteen years and had already grown to more than ten thousand people by the time we built our first building. In our first fifteen years, we used seventy-nine different facilities. There's not a lot of glory in setting up and taking down a church for ten thousand people every week. It's just hard work.

Do you know how many times I felt like giving up? Every Monday morning! God used those tough times to test our persistence.

If you're going through tough times, then this verse is for you: *"That is why we never give up. Though our bodies are dying, our spirits are being renewed every day. For our present troubles are small and won't last very long. Yet they produce for us a glory that vastly outweighs them and will last forever!"* (2 Corinthians 4:16-17, NLT).

God is more interested in what you're becoming than what's happening to you. He often allows trials, troubles, tribulations, and problems in your life to teach you diligence, determination, and character. As you trust God and keep your focus on eternity, he will renew you and give you energy to keep going. Galatians 6:9 says, *"Let us not become weary in doing good, for at the proper time we will reap a harvest if we do not give up"* (NIV).

The problems you're going through right now are a test of your faithfulness. Will you continue to serve God, even when life gets tough?

OCTOBER 11

For Everyone Who Needs a Second Chance

Forget the former things; do not dwell on the past. See, I am doing a new thing! Now it springs up; do you not perceive it? I am making a way in the wilderness and streams in the wasteland.

ISAIAH 43:18-19 (NIV)

God is the God of second chances—and hundredth and thousandth chances!

The Bible is full of people who got a second chance. Abraham pretended his wife was his sister because he didn't have faith that God would protect him. Moses murdered someone. Samson gave in to his overpowering feelings of rage and lust. Rahab worked as a prostitute. David committed adultery and then had the woman's husband put to death. And yet every one of these people are in God's "Hall of Faith" in Hebrews 11.

God loves to give second chances. If you had to be perfect to receive God's grace, no one would stand a chance!

One of Job's friends offered this advice on recovering from losses in life and returning to God's original plan: *"Put your heart right, Job. Reach out to God. Put away evil and wrong from your home. Then face the world again, firm and courageous. Then all your troubles will fade from your memory, like floods that are past and remembered no more. Your life will be brighter than sunshine at noon, and life's darkest hours will shine like the dawn. You will live secure and full of hope; God will protect you and give you rest"* (Job 11:13-18, GNT).

What an amazing promise! When you repent, God always offers another chance—and it's filled with courage, hope, protection, and rest.

If you want to move forward into God's awesome dream for your life, then you're going to have to shut the door on the past. You're going to have to give up your grief, your guilt, and your grudges so that you can move forward in faith.

"Forget the former things; do not dwell on the past. See, I am doing a new thing! Now it springs up; do you not perceive it? I am making a way in the wilderness and streams in the wasteland" (Isaiah 43:18-19, NIV).

Trust God today for your second chance. You'll learn that even the darkest days of your past can shine like the dawn. And in the wasteland of your pain, streams will spring up.

OCTOBER 12

Love Lets It Go

A person's wisdom yields patience; it is to one's glory to overlook an offense.
PROVERBS 19:11 (NIV)

Some people always want their own way. They've got a right way and a wrong way to do something, and your way is always wrong. When you don't meet their standards, they let you know about it, and it seems you can't ever please them.

So how do you respond in love to demanding people?

The Bible says patience comes from perspective: *"A person's wisdom yields patience; it is to one's glory to overlook an offense"* (Proverbs 19:11, NIV). The more you understand a person's background, battles, and burdens, the more patient you'll be with them.

We often look at people and think, "Look how far they have to go." But we don't stop and say, "I wonder how far they've come?"

Maybe they were raised in a family where they had no model of kindness or courtesy. Maybe they grew up in a dysfunctional home, and it's a miracle they've made it this far.

What burdens are they carrying? Illness? Family issues? Lost job? There are all kinds of burdens people carry that you and I don't know about.

Proverbs 19:11 tells us to overlook offenses. Are you offended by offenses? Are you so touchy and irritable that you're offended by anybody who looks at you funny or forgets to say something or doesn't see you? Love lets it go.

Luke 6:31 says, *"Do to others as you would have them do to you"* (NIV). Love is understanding, not demanding. It's what you would want others to do to you when you're having a bad day, aren't feeling well, or are carrying heavy burdens.

Does that mean you're just supposed to let people run over you? Do you act like a doormat, cave in, and let them say whatever they want?

No. Here's the key: Be tender without surrender. Jesus never caved in to manipulators—the demanding and legalistic religious leaders and Pharisees. They had all kinds of demands that they themselves couldn't keep. But Jesus did not let demanding people push him into a corner.

He was tender without surrender. That's love in action.

OCTOBER 13

The Right Motivation Matters

Our message is not about ourselves. It is about Jesus Christ as the Lord. We are your servants for his sake.

2 CORINTHIANS 4:5 (GW)

The more you lead a self-focused life, the more prone you are to discouragement.

When you forget that life is not about you, you often get prideful or fearful or bitter. Those feelings will always lead to discouragement because they keep you focused on yourself.

The Bible says in 2 Corinthians 4:5, *"Our message is not about ourselves. It is about Jesus Christ as the Lord. We are your servants for his sake"* (GW).

It's not about you! God put you on this earth, and he has a message he wants to declare to the world through you. It's your life message. But your life message is not about you. It's about Jesus Christ.

I chose those four words—"It's not about you"—to start my book *The Purpose Driven Life*, because that's the most countercultural message you could give in today's world. Nearly everything in society—songs, video games, TV shows, news stories, and advertisements—says to think about yourself first.

Sometimes I wish I hadn't put that sentence in the book, because I had no idea that for the rest of my life, I would be constantly tested on that phrase. I have to repeat it to myself twenty times a day! When someone praises me, criticizes me, misjudges me, or disagrees with me, I have to remind myself, "It's not about me." Why? Because when I focus on me, I get discouraged.

Instead, as Paul said in today's verse, we are servants for Jesus' sake. That means we are motivated to serve others because of what Jesus has done for us.

God is always more interested in *why* you're doing what you're doing than he is in *what* you're actually doing. He cares about the motivations of your heart. *Why* you're doing something always determines how long you're going to do it. If you're motivated by selfish ambition, that will never be good enough. You'll eventually get discouraged and quit.

But when you're motivated to do something because of how it advances the gospel and glorifies Jesus, you will have the encouragement you need to see it through.

OCTOBER 14

What Moves God to Answer Prayer?

LORD, you have heard the desire of the humble; you will strengthen their hearts. You will listen carefully.

PSALM 10:17 (CSB)

God always responds to humility. It's the attitude that moves him to answer your prayers.

The Bible says, *"LORD, you have heard the desire of the humble; you will strengthen their hearts. You will listen carefully"* (Psalm 10:17, CSB).

In the Old Testament, Daniel had the attitude of humility. Even though he faced enormous pressure to conform to cultural expectations, he threw himself on the grace of God. Instead of depending on his own strength, he prayed, *"We have sinned and done wrong."* But he didn't stop there: *"We have been wicked and have rebelled; we have turned away from your commands and laws. We have not listened to your servants. . . . Lord, you are righteous, but this day we are covered with shame"* (Daniel 9:5-7, NIV).

Daniel knew that he and the other Israelites didn't deserve God's blessing, so he humbly confessed his sin, acknowledged his weakness, and asked God for mercy: *"Lord, in keeping with all your righteous acts, turn away your anger and your wrath from Jerusalem. . . . Hear the prayers and petitions of your servant. . . . Look with favor on your desolate sanctuary"* (Daniel 9:16-17, NIV).

How did God respond to Daniel's humble prayer? With grace communicated by a messenger from the Lord: *"Daniel, you are very precious to God, so listen carefully to what I have to say to you. . . . Since the first day you began to pray for understanding and to humble yourself before your God, your request has been heard in heaven. I have come in answer to your prayer"* (Daniel 10:11-12, NLT).

When you humbly confess your sin to God, you're surrendering your will to his and acknowledging your weakness. That's the kind of prayer God honors because he promised: *"I will bless those who have humble and contrite hearts"* (Isaiah 66:2, NLT).

Many people hesitate to admit their weaknesses and sins because they think they're going to get punished. But God already knows about all your sins! He just wants you to confess them. When you show humility, he'll respond with grace.

Anytime you pray, "God, I need you. I can't do this on my own," he hears you and strengthens you.

OCTOBER 15

God Gives the Bitter Ingredients Purpose

We know that God causes everything to work together for the good of those who love God and are called according to his purpose for them.

ROMANS 8:28 (NLT)

Most people don't know that I am a "master" cake builder (my family, at least, thinks I am).

Years ago, I decided to learn how to bake cakes. I figured that if I wanted to eat them, I ought to know how to make them. One of my favorite creations was one of the more difficult cakes to make: a German chocolate cake made from scratch for my wife's birthday.

Making cakes has made me appreciate that the individual ingredients for a cake don't taste good on their own. Some of them are quite bitter. If you eat flour by itself, it doesn't taste good. If you eat baking powder or raw egg or oil by itself, you'll be grossed out. Even the vanilla by itself doesn't taste good—none of the ingredients do! But if you mix them all together and put them in the oven, it's delicious.

One of the greatest promises of the Bible is in Romans 8:28: *"We know that God causes everything to work together for the good of those who love God and are called according to his purpose for them"* (NLT).

Notice that verse does not say *everything* is good. A quick look at the news headlines proves that it isn't. And the passage doesn't say this promise is for everyone—just for those who love God.

The way God works all things together for good is kind of like baking a cake.

In your life and in the world, there will be elements that are bitter and unpleasant. You might think, "That doesn't taste good. I don't like that change in my life. I don't like what's happening in the world today."

When you're in a season of rapid and relentless change, and some of the elements don't taste good, determine that you will not become bitter by seeing only the negative in your circumstances. Because even when you can't see it, you can trust that God takes it all—the good and the bitter—and uses it for his good plan.

You can't see it now, but you will taste its sweetness in heaven one day.

OCTOBER 16

No More Mixed Motives

I am not trying to do what I want, but only what he who sent me wants.

JOHN 5:30 (GNT)

What motivates you to get up in the morning? To go to work? To study hard? To serve and give and love others? To keep going when life gets stressful?

If you don't want to be fighting stress all the time, you need to know your deepest motivation.

Why is that? Because mixed motivations will leave you feeling like you're being pulled in different directions. Jesus said, *"No one can serve two masters"* (Luke 16:13, NLT).

Even God can't please everybody. When somebody's praying for it to rain, someone else is praying for it to be sunny. As a pastor for forty-two years, I knew that I was always disappointing somebody, because people often have different expectations. I can't please everyone, and neither can you.

The Bible says the fear of man is a trap. It will capture your heart and mind and cause you to stumble. That's why Jesus said in John 5:30, *"I am not trying to do what I want, but only what he who sent me wants"* (GNT). Jesus knew who he was trying to please.

If you're not trying to please God, then in all likelihood, you're trying to please a bunch of people. It's a lot easier and less stressful to decide you're going to please God—because whatever you do that pleases God will always be the right thing. This is why Jesus was so stress resistant. He was only trying to please one person.

Whose approval are you depending on for your happiness? Who are you still trying to please? For some, it's a parent who never showed approval or encouragement. For others, it may be a boss who's impossible to please, no matter how hard you try.

But you are not a victim. You are as free as you choose to be. Nobody can pressure you into meeting their expectations without your permission.

When living for God is your deepest motivation, you won't be controlled by the fear of rejection. Instead, you'll be motivated by love and free to be the person God made you to be.

OCTOBER 17

Jesus Wants to Share Your Load

Take my yoke upon you and learn from me, for I am gentle and humble in heart, and you will find rest for your souls. For my yoke is easy and my burden is light.

MATTHEW 11:29-30 (NIV)

Are you feeling overloaded? You may be trying to control things too much. We do it all the time, sometimes without realizing it. Even when we don't try to, we act subconsciously as if it all depends on us. We have to hold everything together and make it all happen.

The greater your need to control things, the more overloaded and empty you're going to feel. You have to learn to give up control!

When you come to Jesus because you're running on empty, this is the next step of obedience: *"Take my yoke upon you and learn from me, for I am gentle and humble in heart, and you will find rest for your souls. For my yoke is easy and my burden is light"* (Matthew 11:29-30, NIV).

A yoke is not the middle of an egg (that's a *yolk*) but the wooden frame that you put over two animals so they can pull a piece of farm equipment together. When you already feel like you're carrying a heavy load, taking on Jesus' yoke may sound like more of a burden. Why would you want to take on a different yoke and keep pulling?

The purpose of a yoke is to lighten the load, not to make a heavier load. Sharing a yoke means sharing the load you're carrying. When two animals team up together, it makes the load lighter, not heavier.

When you're not yoked to Jesus, you can easily move at a pace that's too fast and go off into a ditch. But if you're yoked to him, then there's no way he's going to let you outpace yourself, and he's not going to let you end up in a ditch.

Galatians 5:25 says, *"Since we live by the Spirit, let us keep in step with the Spirit"* (NIV).

You keep in step with God's Spirit by being yoked to Jesus—partnering with him and letting him set the pace. Jesus was never in a hurry, and you won't be either when you're connected to him.

OCTOBER 18

Being Content Is a Learning Process

Isn't everything you have *and everything you* are *sheer gifts from God? So what's the point of all this comparing and competing? You already have all you need.*

1 CORINTHIANS 4:7-8 (MSG)

Instead of focusing so much on what we don't have and what doesn't happen, we can be grateful for what we do have. This doesn't come naturally to me, and it probably doesn't for you either. It wasn't even easy for the apostle Paul, who said, *"I have learned to be content"* (Philippians 4:11, NIV). Being content requires a learning process.

The Bible says in 1 Corinthians 4:7-8, *"Isn't everything you* have *and everything you* are *sheer gifts from God? So what's the point of all this comparing and competing? You already have all you need"* (MSG).

Envy is based on the myth that you need more to be happy. Envy always looks at others and asks, "Why them? Why did they deserve it? I deserve what they have." And if you find yourself using the phrase "It's not fair," you've already fallen into the trap of envy. But gratitude says, "Why me? Why did God give me this? I'm blessed because I don't deserve what I have." It totally flips our perspective.

Although we all struggle with envy, it's hard to admit because it's such an ugly emotion. When you're envious of others, you really want them to fail to make you feel better that they don't have more than you. That's pretty crazy, isn't it? If we could only learn to be grateful for what we have, we could begin to get rid of these feelings of envy.

It's important to understand that envy is not the same as having a desire or a dream or a goal. It's good to have those. Envy is not the same as looking forward to something or hoping that something can happen in your life or even wondering if you should have some *thing*. Envy is instead resenting somebody who already has what you desire or has reached a goal you have yet to obtain. And sometimes envy is fed by imagination. You often imagine things that aren't true about others and think everything is wonderful behind your neighbors' closed doors. But their reality usually looks much different.

The truth about envy is that you can't be happy until you get that desire or goal. Envy happens when you aren't grateful for what you do have.

Yet the Bible tells us that we already have more than we need and far more than we deserve. Every good thing in our lives is a gift from God, and it is up to him to decide when and how he blesses us. It's up to us to choose to be grateful and make the most of what we've been given.

You can choose gratitude every day by saying to God, "I know you have given me everything, and everything you have given me is good. I have all I need to do what you want me to do and more than enough to be generous with others. I choose to be grateful for what you've given me but most of all that you have given me yourself. I choose to share in the joy of others you have blessed and to be joyful in my salvation. I choose to be content in the knowledge that you are with me, you take care of me, and you are always working in me to make me more like Jesus."

As Ecclesiastes 6:9 says, *"It is better to be satisfied with what you have than to be always wanting something else"* (Ecclesiastes 6:9, GNT).

How God's Greatness Removes Fear

[Jesus] got up and rebuked the winds and the waves, and it was completely calm. The men were amazed and asked, "What kind of man is this? Even the winds and the waves obey him!"

MATTHEW 8:26-27 (NIV)

Anytime you're in a situation you have no control over, switch your focus to the greatness of God. When you're focused on God's greatness, you're actually worshiping—and worship is one of the greatest defenses to help you withstand the potentially devastating winds of life.

During stormy days—when your health is declining, your spouse is unfaithful, or your friends are distant—you have a choice. Are you going to worry? Or are you going to worship?

The New Testament gives a beautiful example of this. Jesus was in a boat with his disciples on the Sea of Galilee. The Sea of Galilee was—and still is—a huge lake, making it easy for storms to come up suddenly. And that's exactly what happened.

Matthew 8:24-25 says, *"Suddenly a furious storm came up on the lake, so that the waves swept over the boat. But Jesus was sleeping. The disciples went and woke him, saying, 'Lord, save us! We're going to drown!'"* (NIV). The ship was tossing and turning, but Jesus kept on sleeping. He was at peace—but the disciples panicked.

Jesus said to them, *"'You of little faith, why are you so afraid?' Then he got up and rebuked the winds and the waves, and it was completely calm. The men were amazed and asked, 'What kind of man is this? Even the winds and the waves obey him!'"* (Matthew 8:26-27, NIV).

The experience left the disciples in awe of Jesus. They had forgotten for a moment who Jesus was. But seeing him display his power over nature turned their focus away from their fear and onto God's greatness. In other words, the experience made them worship.

Worship is one way to set your sail so that the winds of life drive you toward Jesus. Stormy winds can push you off course and threaten to drown you. Instead, let winds of pain, trauma, and stress drive you to focus on God and set your sail toward him.

What are you afraid of in this season of your life? Whatever it is, with Jesus aboard, your boat is unsinkable. He has power over nature—and over everything else.

OCTOBER 20

When Work Gets Overwhelming

I think you ought to know, dear brothers, about the hard time we went through in Asia. We were really crushed and overwhelmed, and feared we would never live through it. We . . . saw how powerless we were to help ourselves; but that was good, for then we put everything into the hands of God, who alone could save us, for he can even raise the dead.

2 CORINTHIANS 1:8-9 (TLB)

Everyone experiences problems at work. But sometimes those problems keep growing to the point that they become overwhelming, and you feel like they're about to swallow you up.

What do you do then? You do what Paul did when he was overwhelmed.

Remember, Paul was an apostle of Jesus Christ, and he traveled throughout the world to share the Good News. He said in 2 Corinthians 1:8-9, *"I think you ought to know, dear brothers, about the hard time we went through in Asia. We were really crushed and overwhelmed, and feared we would never live through it. We . . . saw how powerless we were to help ourselves; but that was good, for then we put everything into the hands of God, who alone could save us, for he can even raise the dead"* (TLB).

When you're experiencing an overwhelming problem at work, you need to do three things.

First, turn the problem over to God through prayer. You can say, like Paul, "God, I'm overwhelmed. I feel helpless. I'm confused. I feel like I'm not going to make it through." Cry out to God, and surrender the problem to him.

Second, make sure you're in a small group. In the 2 Corinthians passage, the word *we* is used six times. When Paul was going through an overwhelming circumstance in his job, he was not alone. Like Paul, you need fellow believers you can count on. Specifically, you need a small group of friends who will study the Bible with you, pray for you regularly, and encourage you when work gets tough.

Third, remember that God uses people at work to teach you how to love. The Bible says in 1 Corinthians 16:14, *"Do all your work in love"* (GNT). One simple—but not necessarily easy—way to learn to love at work is by treating your coworkers how you want to be treated.

At work—and in every area of your life—as you learn to get along with other people, you're actually learning how to love. And that's what life is all about.

OCTOBER 21

The Key to a Balanced Life: Jesus

Seek first God's kingdom and what God wants.
Then all your other needs will be met as well.

MATTHEW 6:33 (NCV)

If you want to live a truly balanced life, look to only one person in all of history as your model: Jesus. If you put him at the center of your life, your life will be more balanced.

Think of your life like a wheel. The center of the wheel is a hub. All of the spokes of your life (which represent your relationships, your family, your career, your goals, and so on) come from that hub. We all build our lives around some sort of focal point. The question is, what will be your hub? Will it be your family? Will it be your career? Will it be money?

Or will it be Jesus?

How do you know what you're building your life around? Take a look at whatever you think about the most. That's what is driving you.

The center of your life is critical to developing a balanced life. A solid center leads to a solid life. A weak, flimsy center leads to a weak life. When I hear people tell me their lives are coming unglued, it usually means one thing: They have a faulty center. Something other than God has taken priority in their lives.

Not only does the hub create stability, but it also controls and influences everything else about your life. Whatever you put at the center of your life will be your source of power. The power of a wheel always emanates from the center outward—never the other way around.

Make Jesus the hub of your life, and he'll provide the stability, control, and power you need. The Bible says, *"Seek first God's kingdom and what God wants. Then all your other needs will be met as well"* (Matthew 6:33, NCV).

When you choose to put Jesus at the center, all the other areas of your life—from your family to your career to your goals—will find balance in him. He will direct your life, influence it, empower it, and give it stability.

OCTOBER 22

It's Good to Be Only Human

Only someone too stupid to find his way home
would wear himself out with work.
ECCLESIASTES 10:15 (GNT)

You're not God. You don't have all the answers. You can't do everything. If you're struggling to find balance in your life, admitting those things can transform everything.

The Bible says, *"Only someone too stupid to find his way home would wear himself out with work"* (Ecclesiastes 10:15, GNT).

It's foolish to wear yourself out with work. Do you realize that when you overwork, you're playing God? Overwork is a way of saying that it all depends on you, that everything will crash down if you don't keep the world spinning.

That's just not true! You're not the general manager of the universe. The universe will not fall apart if you take time to rest and to balance your life. God has it under control.

Often overwork comes from trying to please everyone. But you can't make everyone happy. Even God can't please everyone! When someone is praying for their team to win, someone else is hoping the opposing team comes out on top. It's absurd to try doing what even God can't do.

When you live for others' expectations, you pile "shoulds" on your shoulders. You may think, "I should work more hours," "I should be as active as all the other parents," or "I should volunteer for this project." But no one is forcing you to do those things. You choose to take on the extra work or not to take it on. And you choose the consequences that come with your decision.

When you deny your humanity and try to do it all, you're robbing God of his glory. The Bible declares in 2 Corinthians 4:7: *"We have this treasure in jars of clay to show that this all-surpassing power is from God and not from us"* (NIV).

Paul reminds us that we're human beings. We're feeble and fragile. Jars of clay break easily. If you drop them, they shatter. Clay pots have to be handled with care. If not, they'll be destroyed.

But the good news is that our feebleness allows God's power and glory to shine through. Your humanity isn't something to hide. Instead, you can celebrate the power of God working through your limitations.

So admit it: You're human. Thank God for that!

OCTOBER 23

The Right Question to Ask during Hard Times

That is why we never give up. . . . For our present troubles are small and won't last very long. Yet they produce for us a glory that vastly outweighs them and will last forever!

2 CORINTHIANS 4:16-17 (NLT)

When life becomes really challenging, most people will eventually ask, "Why me?" But this is the wrong question. Instead, try asking, "God, what's your purpose in this?"

The Bible says in 1 Peter 1:6-7, *"There is wonderful joy ahead, even though you must endure many trials for a little while. These trials will show that your faith is genuine. It is being tested as fire tests and purifies gold—though your faith is far more precious than mere gold"* (NLT).

Nothing comes into your life accidentally. God does not cause evil. But he can bring good from every single thing, even from evil. Trials reveal your character, maturity, security, values, and faith.

One of the major figures in the Bible is the apostle Paul. He devoted his entire life to serving God. But in many ways, Paul's life was worse than you can imagine. He was stoned, shipwrecked, beaten, left for dead, imprisoned, whipped, and robbed.

But he was never bitter. Instead of asking, "Why me?" he looked for and trusted God's purpose. He learned to trust God in his problems, even when he didn't understand.

What is the secret to his persistence? *"That is why we never give up. . . . For our present troubles are small and won't last very long. Yet they produce for us a glory that vastly outweighs them and will last forever!"* (2 Corinthians 4:16-17, NLT). You can hold on to hope because God has a purpose and even a reward that exceeds your pain.

When Jesus died on the cross, his followers thought it was a senseless tragedy, a total mistake. But what they couldn't see was God still on his throne, carrying out a bigger purpose. After Jesus' resurrection, he appeared to the disciples and said, *"Peace be with you! As the Father has sent me, I am sending you"* (John 20:21, NIV).

Just moments before, they could see no reason for their pain. But here was Jesus, telling them that God was giving them a new assignment that was part of a grand plan.

God's purpose for your life is always greater than your problems. Trust him. He loves to turn crucifixions into resurrections. He specializes in hopeless situations.

OCTOBER 24

Do You Want to Feel God's Presence?

The righteous will praise you indeed;
they will live in your presence.
PSALM 140:13 (GNT)

Praising God helps you sense his presence.

I said *sense* because God is always present with you, whether or not you feel it. There's never been one second of your life when God was not with you and paying attention to you. But you don't always feel it. Sometimes it even feels like he's a million miles away! You may *know* he's with you, but you don't *feel* it.

What should you do when you want to feel God's presence but can't? Get together with some other people in God's family and praise God with your whole heart. Praise makes God's presence real to you.

You need to praise God with your whole heart, even when you don't feel like praising him at all. Why? Because it's easier to act your way into a feeling than feel your way into an action. If you wait for a certain feeling to come before you do something, then that feeling often will never come. Feelings always follow actions.

This is true in every area of your life. If you don't feel close to your spouse or someone else significant in your life, then you need to start acting in a more loving way. That's what makes the feelings return.

When you don't feel like praising God, that's exactly the time you *need* to praise him. If the only time you ever pray is when you feel like it, then the devil will make sure you never feel like it. If the only time you praise God is when you feel like it, then the devil makes sure you never feel like it.

Immature people live by their feelings. When you're mature, you do what's right, whether you feel like it or not.

Psalm 140:13 says, *"The righteous will praise you indeed; they will live in your presence"* (GNT).

You're in God's presence all the time. But when you *live* in his presence, as Psalm 140:13 says, you sense it and recognize it.

If you want to feel God's presence in your life, then just praise him more. Praise and presence go together!

OCTOBER 25

What to Do When You Start to Worry

Be still before the LORD and wait patiently for him;
do not fret when people succeed in their ways.
PSALM 37:7 (NIV)

You may not hear the word *fret* much anymore. It's an old-fashioned word that just means "worry." When you fret, you get stressed out, anxious, and impatient. You worry because things are either happening too fast and you can't handle the change or because things are going too slow and you want God to speed things up.

We don't usually mind waiting if we can gripe about it. But when you choose to wait patiently on God instead of fretting, it is actually a statement of faith. You're making a declaration about God's character. When you wait patiently, you're saying that you trust God and have faith in him. You're humbly admitting that you're dependent on him.

The Bible says in Psalm 37:7, *"Be still before the LORD and wait patiently for him; do not fret when people succeed in their ways"* (NIV).

One of the biggest reasons we get stressed out is because we're constantly comparing ourselves to others. Instead of focusing on God's love and what he's done for us, we look at other people, focusing on what they have that we don't.

Comparing yourself to others isn't a wise choice because you're one of a kind. God has a plan for your life that's different from his plan for anyone else. If you're wishing you had another person's plan, then you're going to miss the plan for *your* life! Comparing leads to fretting. When you compare, you start worrying.

But worry is totally worthless. Any second you spend worrying is wasted because worry can't accomplish anything. Worry can't change the past. It can't control the future. It's only going to make you miserable today. It's like sitting in a rocking chair, going back and forth, back and forth. You don't make any progress, and you use a lot of energy.

Philippians 4:6 says, *"Don't fret or worry. Instead of worrying, pray. Let petitions and praises shape your worries into prayers"* (MSG).

Worry will never change anything, but prayer can change things. So don't fret about it. Just pray!

OCTOBER 26

What's Your Emergency Plan for Temptation?

Run from all these evil things.
1 TIMOTHY 6:11 (NLT)

Do you have an emergency plan for getting away when you're tempted? Do you have preventative strategies to help you stay away from your biggest temptations? If you don't have those things, you need them now!

The Bible is clear about what that emergency plan is: You run. When you find yourself tempted, you need a panic button, an escape route.

First Timothy 6:11 says, *"Run from all these evil things"* (NLT).

The Bible says you need to move quickly out of any situation that causes you temptation. Never argue with a temptation. You'll always lose. Emotions will take over, and emotions aren't always logical.

No matter the temptation, you have to get away. It could be a temptation to cheat in business. It could be a sexual temptation. But your response should be the same: Get out.

But even better than running from temptation is to prevent temptation in the first place. Another way to say that is this: If you don't want to get stung, stay away from the bees.

Years ago when I was a youth minister, I'd tell kids, "Don't decide in the back seat of a car that you're going to be sexually pure and save yourself for marriage. Hormones will kick in, and you'll be overwhelmed." You must make a preventative strategy in advance and not put yourself in the tempting situation.

The same principles apply throughout life.

If you know you get short-tempered with your children when you're tired, develop a preventative strategy. Set an earlier bedtime for your kids or schedule some quiet time for everyone during the part of the day that's most difficult for you.

Don't wait until you're faced with a morally questionable deal to decide that your business will be above reproach. Build accountability into your business plan to help prevent you from being tempted in the moment.

Take time today to develop preventative strategies for temptation. And when those don't work out, have your emergency plan: Don't resist temptation—run from it. That's the simplest and surest way out.

OCTOBER 27

Changing Starts with Choosing

Be careful how you think; your life is shaped by your thoughts.
PROVERBS 4:23 (GNT)

Are you looking for a fresh start? I don't mean moving to a new town. I'm talking about a reset in any area of your life that is stuck. You will go through many resets in your life. That's because God didn't just create you; he also wants to transform you into who he's always intended for you to become.

To reset and experience transformation, you first need to work on your mindset—how you see yourself, how you see others, how you see your problems, and, most importantly, how you see God.

If you don't change your mindset, a change in your location won't help much. Why? Because you could go to the ends of the earth, but you will still take *you* with you wherever you go.

For example, let's say you're stressed, so you go to a beach for relaxation. But you just end up taking the stress with you because it's in your body. If you don't deal with the mental stress first, then it's going to continue to cause trouble in all other areas.

Life change begins in your mind because your thoughts direct your life. Proverbs 4:23 says, *"Be careful how you think; your life is shaped by your thoughts"* (GNT).

Every action and reaction, everything you feel and do, starts as a thought. It all begins in your mind! If you don't think it, it doesn't happen.

You can use this truth for good or for bad: Good thoughts lead to good habits and good choices; bad thoughts lead to unhealthy habits and behaviors.

The truth is, we don't realize how often we sabotage our own success by the way we think and talk to ourselves. The Bible says, *"For as he thinks in his heart, so is he"* (Proverbs 23:7, NKJV).

Your relationship problem doesn't start with the relationship; it starts in your brain. This is true for money, sex, habits, food, work, or anything else. You cannot reset any area of your life without first changing how you think.

Changing starts with choosing. You can decide what you think about. It's time to make choices that reflect the kind of person God wants you to be.

OCTOBER 28

God Turns Messes into Masterpieces

Create in me a clean heart, O God. Renew a loyal spirit within me.

PSALM 51:10 (NLT)

One day God told the prophet Jeremiah to go to a potter's house and watch the potter make clay pots.

Jeremiah watched the potter mold the clay, and he noticed something: *"Whenever the pot the potter was working on turned out badly, as sometimes happens when you are working with clay, the potter would simply start over and use the same clay to make another pot"* (Jeremiah 18:4, MSG).

As Jeremiah watched the potter, God gave him a message for Israel: *"In the same way that this potter works his clay, I work on you"* (Jeremiah 18:6, MSG).

You may have really made a mess of your life. Perhaps your "pot" is scarred from poor decisions you made or things that were done to you. As a result, your life has not turned out as you intended.

But you are the clay. You're not the potter! God is the potter, and he doesn't discard clay that's been misshapen. He doesn't waste the pain that you've been through.

God won't throw out your personality or the essence of who he created you to be. Instead, he takes every part of you—the good, the bad, and the messy. He puts it all in his gentle, strong hands. And then he starts to reshape your life. He applies pressure at just the right places to mold you and make you into a beautiful, priceless piece of art.

That's what happens when you surrender yourself completely to God and to the work of his loving hands.

God specializes in fresh starts. You can have a new beginning today, simply by praying King David's prayer in Psalm 51:10: *"Create in me a clean heart, O God. Renew a loyal spirit within me"* (NLT).

It's never too late to start over. Bring whatever chaos you have going on in your life to God, the Great Potter. Trust him to do a new work in you.

OCTOBER 29

How to Handle Our Differences

Welcome with open arms fellow believers who don't see things the way you do.
ROMANS 14:1 (MSG)

When God says he wants his followers to be united, it doesn't mean he wants us all to be alike. If he had wanted that, he would have created us all the same!

For unity's sake, we must never let differences in the church divide us. We should appreciate those differences while staying focused on what matters most: learning to love each other as Christ has loved us and fulfilling God's purposes for each of us in his church.

But how can you be unified with people who irritate you to no end?

The Bible gives clear instructions: *"Welcome with open arms fellow believers who don't see things the way you do. And don't jump all over them every time they do or say something you don't agree with—even when it seems that they are strong on opinions but weak in the faith department. Remember, they have their own history to deal with. Treat them gently"* (Romans 14:1, MSG).

When you don't see eye to eye with a fellow church member—or with anyone—be quick to listen and slow to anger. Why? Not everyone who bugs you realizes what they're doing. Oftentimes they're responding to their own hidden pain, and they don't even know that they're causing conflict with those around them. If you knew how much someone had already overcome in life, then you'd probably be rejoicing with them instead of criticizing them for where they are now.

When you have conflict with someone whose background is unknown to you, don't dismiss them or judge them for behavior you don't understand. Stop thinking, "What is wrong with this person?" Instead ask, "What happened to them that could be influencing their behavior?"

People who hurt other people have likely experienced trauma or crisis themselves.

The people you think deserve your kindness the least are those who need extra doses of love the most. To achieve unity in the church, offer empathy and compassion instead of judgement.

Affirming someone's worth and the story God is writing through their life doesn't just change that one person's life. It can transform a whole community!

OCTOBER 30

Love Helps Us Face the Truth

Love should always make us tell the truth. Then we will grow in every way and be more like Christ.
EPHESIANS 4:15 (CEV)

When you believe a lie, you can't make the changes you really need—which leads to self-defeat.

Maybe you're believing a lie about what will make you happy, about what God is really like, or about what real success looks like. You may be believing a lie about yourself, or about your past or present circumstances.

The Bible says in 1 John 1:8, *"If we claim we have no sin, we are only fooling ourselves and not living in the truth"* (NLT). This is the first step to change: You have to admit that there is a problem and that the problem is in you. When you blame others or refuse to accept the truth, you're just fooling yourself—and establishing dangerous habits.

Personal change requires you not only to learn the truth about yourself but also to face it and take the steps necessary to move forward.

In fact, learning to face the truth about yourself is the most loving thing you can do for yourself, for others, and for God. Ephesians 4:15 says, *"Love should always make us tell the truth. Then we will grow in every way and be more like Christ"* (CEV).

Do you want to grow? Do you want to change? Do you want a new life? Do you want a fresh start in some area of your life?

Look again to Ephesians 4:15: *"Love should always make us tell the truth."* If you love yourself, if you love God, if you love other people, then you need to face the truth about yourself.

So then the question becomes this: What is the best source for finding truth? Consult your owner's manual—your Bible. The only way you can learn your purpose in life is to know your Creator and read the Bible.

To overcome your weaknesses—whether they come from circumstances, your genes, your parents, or your choices—you need to face the truth about yourself.

And that truth is found in God's Word.

OCTOBER 31

Love Drives Out Fear

Those who make a practice of sin are straight from the Devil, the pioneer in the practice of sin. The Son of God entered the scene to abolish the Devil's ways.

1 JOHN 3:8 (MSG)

Jesus defeated death, and that means he also defeated Satan. In fact, that's why he came to earth. The Bible says, *"The Son of God entered the scene to abolish the Devil's ways"* (1 John 3:8, MSG).

What is the devil's work? He messes with your mind. He fills it with worry, guilt, resentment, anger, fear, and confusion. He whispers in your ear that you're worthless, helpless, hopeless, and aimless.

Satan uses these thoughts and emotions to keep you enslaved.

The biggest tool Satan uses to mess with your life is fear. The Bible clearly says that fear doesn't come from God: *"There is no fear in love. But perfect love drives out fear"* (1 John 4:18, NIV). The Bible also says, *"God is love"* (1 John 4:16, NIV). So when you're afraid, that's not from God—because there is no fear in love, and God is love.

As a pastor, I've learned the number one thing most people fear is death. Satan will use that fear to manipulate you.

But Jesus defeated death; he destroyed the Devil's work. And so, when you as a Christian grieve a death, you grieve with *hope*.

You grieve because you miss those you've lost. You grieve, but you know that if they believed in Jesus, you will see them again in heaven. They are waiting there, where we all were designed to be in the first place.

In Hebrews 2:14-15, the Bible says, *"Since all of these sons and daughters have flesh and blood, Jesus took on flesh and blood to be like them. He did this so that by dying he would destroy the one who had power over death (that is, the devil). In this way he would free those who were slaves all their lives because they were afraid of dying"* (GW).

So whenever you feel fear creeping into your heart—whether it's the fear of death or another fear—remember that fear isn't from God. Then ask God to drive out that fear with his perfect love.

NOVEMBER 1

The One Habit That Keeps You Going

Through thick and thin, keep your hearts at attention, in adoration before Christ.

1 PETER 3:15 (MSG)

Developing a habit of gratitude is key to holding on during hard days. When you're going through a tough time, you need to lean into thanksgiving to God. The Bible says in 1 Peter 3:15, *"Through thick and thin, keep your hearts at attention, in adoration before Christ"* (MSG).

What's adoration? It's praise and thanksgiving. Adoration is praising God for who he is and thanking God for what he has done. Keeping adoration as the focus of your heart when you're going through tough times will keep you going.

In fact, both thanksgiving and praise are antidotes to discouragement. That's because you can't be grateful and discouraged at the same time. Gratitude destroys the temptation to look at your situation as out of God's control. It reminds you that no matter what you're going through, God's purposes for your life never change. Gratitude is a mark of spiritual and emotional health.

It's also true that if you don't stay grateful, you'll become cynical. Why? Because there will always be problems in this world that are going to hurt you. But gratitude gives you perspective and helps you remember what you can be thankful for even when you're going through problems.

Maybe it's difficult to be grateful right now because you have a lot of unmet needs in your life. God cares about those needs, and he's ready to help. He just wants you to ask him!

As you seek God's help to meet those needs, it's important that you ask with a grateful heart. How do you do that? You acknowledge what God has already done for you. You thank him for always being good to you. You say to him, "God, you've helped me in the past. I know you're going to help me in the future. I need you to help me right now."

Philippians 4:6 says, *"In all your prayers ask God for what you need, always asking him with a thankful heart"* (GNT).

Petition and gratitude should always go together. Thanking God for his grace in the past will give you confidence in his grace and provision for you now, in your tough time, and in the future.

NOVEMBER 2

To Change Your Life, Change Your Thoughts

Happy are those who . . . find joy in obeying the Law of the LORD, and they study it day and night. They are like trees that grow beside a stream, that bear fruit at the right time, and whose leaves do not dry up. They succeed in everything they do.

PSALM 1:1-3 (GNT)

If you want to change your life, then start by changing the way you think.

Changing your thoughts is the key to a fresh start in any area—a hobby, career, relationship, marriage, or parenting. Ephesians 4:23 says, *"Be renewed in the spirit of your minds"* (ESV).

Having a renewed mind means you have fresh thoughts and fresh attitudes. It means you take your wrong attitudes and thoughts and surrender them, letting *"God transform you inwardly by a complete change of your mind"* (Romans 12:2, GNT).

You renew your mind by doing two things:

First, listen to God's Word more than the world. The Bible says, *"Happy are those who . . . find joy in obeying the Law of the LORD, and they study it day and night. They are like trees that grow beside a stream, that bear fruit at the right time, and whose leaves do not dry up. They succeed in everything they do"* (Psalm 1:1-3, GNT). Would you like those characteristics to be true in your life? If so, then meditate on God's Word every day.

Second, think about what you think about. Instead of automatically accepting every thought you have, challenge your thoughts. When you have a thought, ask yourself: "Do I *want* to think about this? Is this true? Is this helpful? How does it make me feel—and do I want to feel that way?"

The Bible tells us to *"take every thought captive and make it obey Christ"* (2 Corinthians 10:5, GNT). All your feelings start with a thought. What you think about is your choice, and you don't have to believe every thought you have. When you confront a thought you know isn't true, you can replace it with God's truth. The only way to know the truth is to read God's Word.

Start changing your thoughts today. It will give you a fresh start, and it will change your life!

NOVEMBER 3

Be Aware of Satan's Predictable Patterns

When I forgive whatever needs to be forgiven, I do so with Christ's authority for your benefit, so that Satan will not outsmart us. For we are familiar with his evil schemes.

2 CORINTHIANS 2:10-11 (NLT)

You can't defeat temptation if you don't understand how it works.

Satan doesn't have any new ideas. He's used the same temptations over and over since humans were created.

The tactics he used on Adam and Eve are the same ones he's using today. God had clearly told Adam and Eve they could eat from any tree in the Garden except the tree of the knowledge of good and evil. But when Satan tempted Eve, he basically said, "Did God *really* say to not eat this?" And then he said, "Go ahead and try it. You're not going to die if you eat this! You're going to be a god yourself."

Satan uses that same pattern in your life every day. First, it starts with a wrong desire inside you, like envy, lust, or impatience. Or it starts with a right desire, like for food or sex or love, but it's paired with the temptation to fulfill it in the wrong way at the wrong time. Satan can take any desire and make it destructive.

Then he causes you to doubt God's Word and whispers, "Did God *really* say that?" He takes the seed of your doubt and grows it into a lie he knows you are vulnerable to accepting. Behind every sin is a lie you choose to believe. Remember, Satan is crafty. He knows where in your life you are most likely to fall, and he focuses on turning your doubt into full-blown deception.

When you believe Satan's lie, you're saying, "I know what will make me happy more than God does." You legitimize your wrong desire. You convince yourself it's not that bad. And then you fall into disobedience. The Bible says, *"When I forgive whatever needs to be forgiven, I do so with Christ's authority for your benefit, so that Satan will not outsmart us. For we are familiar with his evil schemes"* (2 Corinthians 2:10-11, NLT).

God doesn't want you to be ignorant of how Satan works because when you understand Satan's tactics, you can see him coming with his schemes. The key to resisting temptation is knowing how to respond to Satan's predictable patterns.

NOVEMBER 4

Serve Jesus by Serving Others

Then the righteous will answer him, "Lord, when did we see you hungry and feed you, or thirsty and give you something to drink? When did we see you a stranger and invite you in, or needing clothes and clothe you? When did we see you sick or in prison and go to visit you?" The King will reply, "Truly I tell you, whatever you did for one of the least of these brothers and sisters of mine, you did for me."

MATTHEW 25:37-40 (NIV)

Just before Jesus died on the cross, he said, *"I am thirsty"* (John 19:28, NIV). That moment shows his humanity, that Jesus was God living among us as a man.

The Bible says that the Roman soldiers soaked a sponge in a jar full of wine vinegar and lifted it to Jesus' lips. The sour wine was meant to relieve his thirst. Wouldn't you like to have been there to be able to give water to Jesus for his thirst? In fact, you'd probably have considered it a privilege and blessing to serve him in that moment.

But that moment is long past, and you can't help Jesus in that way. On the other hand, you can help those around you on behalf of Jesus. People everywhere are spiritually thirsty, searching for purpose and significance. They want to know what to do with their lives and if their lives have any meaning.

People need to know that Jesus can quench their thirst, that he is what they are looking for when they hop from one thing to another. They need to know that he meets them in their depression, discouragement, and despair.

Jesus says that when you serve others, you're serving him. So when you want to do something for Jesus, look for people around you who are in need. Jesus said, *"Truly I tell you, whatever you did for one of the least of these brothers and sisters of mine, you did for me"* (Matthew 25:40, NIV).

Whenever you give a drink to someone who is thirsty, you are giving it to Jesus. The same is true when you lead those who are spiritually thirsty to Jesus. Love in action is when you meet the needs of other people in their thirst—physical, emotional, or spiritual—out of love for Christ, who endured thirst on the cross for you. The only way you can serve God is by serving people and helping others in his name.

Who are the people around you who appear to be spiritually thirsty? Ask God to show you who they are and the best way to lead them to Jesus.

NOVEMBER 5

Forgive and Forget?

Wait passionately for GOD, don't leave the path. He'll give you your place in the sun while you watch the wicked lose it.

PSALM 37:34 (MSG)

You've heard this phrase over and over: "Forgive and forget." There's only one problem with it: You can't do it. It's impossible!

You really can't forget a hurt in your life. In fact, you can't even try to forget it. Because when you try not to think about it, you actually focus on the very thing you want to forget.

And the truth is that God doesn't want you to forget. Instead, he wants you to trust him and see how he can bring good out of the hurt. That's more important than forgetting. When you see God bring good out of a bad situation, you can thank him for that good work. You can't thank God for things you forget.

Romans 8:28 says, *"And we know that in all things God works for the good of those who love him, who have been called according to his purpose"* (NIV).

It doesn't say that all things are good—because all things are not good. Disease is not good. A broken relationship is not good. War is not good. Abuse is not good.

There are a lot of things in life that are evil. Not everything that happens in this world is God's will.

But God says he will work good out of the bad things in life if you will trust him. You can go to him and say, "God, I give you all the pieces of my life."

He will take your pieces and instead give you peace in your heart. This peace will come when you realize you can forgive, even without understanding the hurt in your life, because you know God will use that pain for good.

You don't have to forget the wrong thing someone did to you. You couldn't do it even if you tried! But God says there's no need to forget it. You just have to forgive and then see how God will bring good out of the hurt.

NOVEMBER 6

Don't Settle for False Fixes

All who worship worthless idols turn from
the God who offers them mercy.
JONAH 2:8 (CEV)

When we're in trouble, we're often tempted to find a quick fix—or at least something that will relieve our stress.

People's families may be falling apart. Their finances may be falling apart. Their careers may be falling apart. Their health may be falling apart. With their backs against the wall, they try everything imaginable to solve the problem—everything, that is, except asking God for help.

We need to reject any attempts at a false fix and instead turn to God.

Jonah had time to think about this when he was stuck in the belly of a big fish. Here's what he prayed: *"All who worship worthless idols turn from the God who offers them mercy"* (Jonah 2:8, CEV).

Today few people carve idols. But we still have them. Some idolize their cars. Others idolize their homes or their clothes. Sometimes people idolize fortune, pleasure, or fame. Anything we place above God is an idol.

The only solution for our problems is God's grace. Anytime we turn to something else, we're turning to an idol.

Years ago, my family was on vacation, and because I like learning about rocks and minerals, we went into a store that sold collectible rocks. There was a whole section of quartz crystals that could supposedly solve a variety of problems. The labels claimed the different crystals would provide contentment or confidence, create a protective shield, or even give you psychic intuition.

But I knew they wouldn't help me with any of those things. In fact, the crystals and the promises about them reminded me of Romans 1:25: *"They exchanged the truth about God for a lie, and worshiped and served created things rather than the Creator"* (NIV).

When you choose to believe that something other than God will solve your problems, you're placing your trust in an inanimate object. You're serving a created thing rather than the Creator himself.

When Jonah was at the bottom of the ocean in a big fish, he didn't turn to an idol. He trusted God to help—and God came through.

God will do the same for you.

Resilient People Know How to Be Still

Very early in the morning, while it was still dark, Jesus got up, left the house and went off to a solitary place, where he prayed.

MARK 1:35 (NIV)

The key to resisting stress is the very thing some Christians do the least: spending time alone with God. But this spiritual practice is essential to building a resilient spirit and managing chronic stress.

Prayer is a great stress reliever. It's a decompression chamber, where you can release the stress of keeping up appearances and living up to others' expectations. It's how you unload your burdens and admit you can't carry them alone. It's where you're reminded that God is ready and willing to help you with every stressful thing you experience in life.

How do you develop a habit of spending time alone with God? Through practice and repetition. It's not a habit unless you do it over and over again, regularly and consistently.

Jesus developed spiritual habits. The Bible says in Luke 22:39 that it was Jesus' habit to leave Jerusalem and go to the Mount of Olives to pray. And Mark 1:35 says, *"Very early in the morning, while it was still dark, Jesus got up, left the house and went off to a solitary place, where he prayed"* (NIV).

No matter how busy he was, Jesus knew he needed time alone with God to pray. Do you have time like that in your life? Do you ever slow down and get quiet before God so you can reflect and be renewed? If you want to be a resilient person, develop the habit of spending time with God.

While word spread about Jesus and huge crowds of people were coming to hear him speak, Jesus made time alone with God a habit. The Bible says, *"Jesus often slipped away to be alone so he could pray"* (Luke 5:16, NCV). If Jesus felt the need to frequently leave the crowd and get alone with God, then think about how much more we must need that.

Because noise often causes stress, consider starting your morning with God instead of with your phone, TV, or social media. Be still, be quiet, and be open to the work God wants to do in you. Make a habit of meditating on his Word and being in his presence.

NOVEMBER 8

God Loves to Hear You Sing

Let us come before him with thanksgiving
and sing joyful songs of praise.
PSALM 95:2 (GNT)

Not all humans have the same love languages. We like to be loved in different ways because we're all different.

Did you know that God has love languages too? God is happy when we express our love to him in certain ways.

One of the ways God likes for us to show our love and gratitude to him is by singing to him. And the Bible tells us that God sings too! He sings love songs and joyful songs about *you*. Zephaniah 3:17 says, *"The LORD your God is living among you. He is a mighty savior. He will take delight in you with gladness. With his love, he will calm all your fears. He will rejoice over you with joyful songs"* (NLT).

You've never heard God sing over you. But one day in heaven, you're going to hear God sing about you—and it's going to be the most beautiful, joyful sound you've ever heard.

There are several places where God tells us to express our thanks to him through singing. Psalm 147:7 says, *"Sing out your thanks to him; sing praises to our God"* (TLB). Psalm 95:2 says, *"Let us come before him with thanksgiving and sing joyful songs of praise"* (GNT).

Worshiping God through singing is one of the main reasons for coming together to worship. The Bible says in Colossians 3:16, *"Sing psalms, hymns, and sacred songs; sing to God with thanksgiving in your hearts"* (GNT).

You may not like singing, or you may think you don't sing very well. You may even say, "I just don't sing," for whatever reason.

But God loves your voice and he wants to hear it because he gave it to you! You need to learn to accept yourself the way God does. God enjoys hearing you sing praise to him, no matter how it sounds.

Don't wait until you go to church to sing. Sing to God all the time, anywhere, with thanksgiving and joy in your heart because of who he is and what he has done for you.

"All day long we praise our God" (Psalm 44:8, GW).

NOVEMBER 9

Communion Leads to Gratitude

Is not the cup of thanksgiving for which we give thanks a participation in the blood of Christ? And is not the bread that we break a participation in the body of Christ?
1 CORINTHIANS 10:16 (NIV)

When we take Communion, we are reminded of what Jesus did for us on the cross.

It's not an empty ritual that Christians do just because they have to. Instead, God wants us to practice Communion to help us remember. Why do we need to remember? So we can be grateful. You can only be grateful for those things that you remember.

Jesus used the bread and the wine as a memory tool to help us practice gratitude for what he did for us on the cross.

The Bible says in 1 Corinthians 11:23-25, *"On the night he was betrayed, the Lord Jesus took bread and spoke a prayer of thanksgiving. He broke the bread and said, 'This is my body, which is given for you. Do this to remember me.' When supper was over, he did the same with the cup. He said, 'This cup is the new promise made with my blood. Every time you drink from it, do it to remember me'"* (GW).

Another word for Communion is the *Eucharist.* This comes from a Greek word that means "thanksgiving." Communion is a reflection of thanksgiving. It's one of God's favorite ways that we give thanks to him! We can show thanks to God in many ways—through songs of thanksgiving, through thanksgiving offerings, and through the thanksgiving cup.

"Is not the cup of thanksgiving for which we give thanks a participation in the blood of Christ? And is not the bread that we break a participation in the body of Christ?" (1 Corinthians 10:16, NIV).

When we drink from a Communion cup and eat the bread, we are not just going through the motions of Christian living. We're not just containing our gratitude to an event at church. We are saying to God, "Father, thank you for sending your Son to live a perfect life and die for our sins so that we can be forgiven."

As we remind ourselves of the high price Jesus paid to save us, the only reasonable response is deep gratitude—the kind that spills over into every area of life.

NOVEMBER 10

Your Guide to Facing Giants

Though the wicked hide along the way to kill me,
I will quietly keep my mind upon your promises.
PSALM 119:95 (TLB)

You're probably familiar with the story of David and Goliath. It's full of remarkable details. First, David—who was just a boy at the time—chose to face a giant in battle. But it's even more noteworthy that David faced Goliath with such confidence and optimism.

You may never do battle against a literal Goliath, but everyone eventually faces some kind of giant. Maybe you're up against a medical, financial, or relational Goliath. How can you face that giant with God-given confidence and optimism like David did?

The Psalms give insight into four habits that gave David confidence. If you develop these same habits, you'll be able to face the biggest giants, trusting God will see you through.

Tune in to God every morning. Before David talked with anyone else in the morning, he talked with God: *"In the morning, LORD, you hear my voice; in the morning I lay my requests before you and wait expectantly"* (Psalm 5:3, NIV).

Think on God's promises throughout the day. David faced constant pressures, but he wasn't overwhelmed because he kept his mind on God's Word. He said, *"Though the wicked hide along the way to kill me, I will quietly keep my mind upon your promises"* (Psalm 119:95, TLB).

Trust in God's deliverance even when things look bad. David said, *"O my soul, don't be discouraged. Don't be upset. Expect God to act! For I know that I shall again have plenty of reason to praise him for all that he will do"* (Psalm 42:11, TLB). David knew that God had helped him in the past, and he had a positive expectation that God would help him again in the future.

Talk with other believers. David didn't face his life's giants on his own. He had emotional and spiritual support. He said, *"I'm a friend and companion . . . of those committed to living by your rules"* (Psalm 119:63, MSG).

Is there a giant in your life today? Face it with a confidence and optimism that can only come from trusting God.

NOVEMBER 11

Don't Repeat the Hurt. Let It Go!

Whenever you pray, forgive anything you have against anyone. Then your Father in heaven will forgive your failures.
MARK 11:25 (GW)

When people hurt us, we have two natural tendencies: to remember and to retaliate.

But 1 Corinthians 13:5 tells us the opposite: *"Love does not count up wrongs that have been done"* (NCV).

So how should you respond to the people who have hurt you? How do you handle the wounds and hurts stockpiled in your memory?

Don't repeat them, delete them. Let the hurts go. Forgive, and get on with your life.

When we get hurt, we tend to repeat that hurt in three ways: emotionally in our minds, relationally as a weapon, and practically by telling other people.

First, we repeat it by going over and over it in our minds. But resentment is self-destructive. It only perpetuates the pain. It never heals or solves anything. Whatever you think about most is what you move toward. If all you think about is past hurts, then you'll move toward the past. But if you focus on potential, then you'll move toward potential.

Second, we repeat our hurt in relationships. We use hurt as a wedge and a weapon. We say things like, "Remember when you did that?" Proverbs 17:9 says, *"Love forgets mistakes; nagging about them parts the best of friends"* (TLB). Nagging also parts marriages and every other relationship you have.

Third, we repeat our hurt by gossiping about it. We tell everybody except God and the person with whom we have the problem. Did you know God hates gossip? He hates it as much as he hates pride—because that's what gossip is. Gossip is pure and simple ego, or trying to make ourselves look and feel better. Every time you share gossip, you're being prideful, and God hates pride and gossip.

Love keeps no record of wrongs. Love doesn't repeat a wound so that it turns into resentment, gossip, or pride.

Mark 11:25 says, *"Whenever you pray, forgive anything you have against anyone. Then your Father in heaven will forgive your failures"* (GW). This verse in the Amplified Bible says to *"let it go."*

That's how love responds.

NOVEMBER 12

Faith Thanks God Ahead of Time

Abraham never doubted. He believed God, for his faith and trust grew ever stronger, and he praised God for this blessing even before it happened. He was completely sure that God was well able to do anything he promised.

ROMANS 4:20-21 (TLB)

Faith means joyfully expecting God to deliver you, even if it's not the way you planned.

That's what Abraham did. When he faced an impossible situation—having a child at age one hundred—Abraham thanked God before the Lord acted.

The Bible says, *"Abraham never doubted. He believed God, for his faith and trust grew ever stronger, and he praised God for this blessing even before it happened. He was completely sure that God was well able to do anything he promised"* (Romans 4:20-21, TLB).

When you thank God *after* he works, that's gratitude. When you thank him *before* he works, that's faith. Being *"completely sure"* about something that seemed impossible to everyone else shows the incredible faith that Abraham had.

Even Jesus thanked God in advance! He prayed in faith before raising Lazarus from the dead: *"Father, thank you for hearing me"* (John 11:41, TLB).

God doesn't always deliver you in ways you expect. In fact, there are three different ways God may deliver you:

- **Circumstantial:** God changes the circumstances.
- **Personal:** God changes *you*. He gives you a bigger perspective, grows your character, or changes your attitude.
- **Ultimate:** Sometimes God only delivers you in heaven, where there will be no more tears and no more pain.

God hasn't promised to take away all your pain. He hasn't promised you won't have any delays or dead ends. Instead, God has promised that one day you'll be in heaven, with no more pain or suffering. Until then, he'll give you all the strength you need to make it through this life. He's promised to walk with you through every painful and seemingly impossible circumstance.

Paul wrote in Romans 5:2, *"We boast in the hope of the glory of God"* (NIV). You show God you trust him when you thank him for his deliverance, even though you know it might not happen until you get to heaven. This is faith, the *"confidence in what we hope for and assurance about what we do not see"* (Hebrews 11:1, NIV).

Try Writing Down Your Prayers

The Lord gave me this answer: "Write down clearly on tablets what I reveal to you, so that it can be read at a glance."
HABAKKUK 2:2 (GNT)

If you want to hear God speak, do this: Withdraw to a quiet place, wait patiently and expectantly, and ask God to give you a picture of what he wants to say to you. Then write down God's responses to your questions.

In the book of Habakkuk, the Lord commands the author to *"write down clearly on tablets what I reveal to you, so that it can be read at a glance"* (Habakkuk 2:2, GNT).

That's how we got the book of Habakkuk. In chapter 1, Habakkuk wrote down what he said to God. And in chapter 2, he wrote down what God said back to him.

That's also how we got the book of Psalms; many of those psalms came directly from David's quiet times. David meditated on the first five books of the Bible, the Torah, and then he wrote down his thoughts—they're called psalms. In many of the psalms, he starts with what he's feeling and then ends up writing down what God says.

If your prayer life is stuck in a rut, and you tend to pray the same things over and over—"God, be with this person" or "Bless this food to the nourishment of our bodies"—then try this: Start writing down your prayers.

"What? You mean I don't have to say them?" Nope. Writing them down is a prayer. God can hear it in your thoughts. Just write them down.

Is it okay to write out a prayer and then read it? Of course it is. When you're writing it, you're praying. When you're reading it, you're praying.

This is the spiritual habit of journaling, and it's one that all Christians would benefit from.

A journal is not a diary. A diary is about the things you do. A journal is about the lessons you learned—the mistakes you made and what God taught you.

Start your spiritual journal today. It will help you to hear and to remember what God is telling you.

Problems Force Us to Depend on God

Don't be bewildered or surprised when you go through the fiery trials ahead, for this is no strange, unusual thing that is going to happen to you.

1 PETER 4:12 (TLB)

Jesus warned us that we'd have problems in life. No one is immune from pain or insulated from suffering, and no one gets to skate through life problem-free.

But the apostle Peter assured us that problems are normal. He said, *"Don't be bewildered or surprised when you go through the fiery trials ahead, for this is no strange, unusual thing that is going to happen to you"* (1 Peter 4:12, TLB). God uses these problems to draw you closer to himself. The Bible says, *"The LORD is close to the brokenhearted; he rescues those whose spirits are crushed"* (Psalm 34:18, NLT).

Your most profound and intimate experiences of worship likely will be in your darkest days: when your heart is broken, when you feel abandoned, when you're out of options, when the pain is great—and when you turn to God alone. It is during suffering that we learn to pray our most authentic, heartfelt, honest-to-God prayers. When in pain, we don't have the energy for superficial prayers.

Joni Eareckson Tada said, "When life is rosier, we may slide by with knowing *about* Him. With imitating Him and quoting Him and speaking of Him. But only in the fellowship of suffering will we *know* Jesus." We learn things about God in suffering that we can't learn any other way.

God could have kept Joseph out of jail, kept Daniel out of the lion's den, kept Jeremiah from being tossed into a slimy pit, kept Paul from being shipwrecked three times, and kept the three young Hebrew men from being thrown into the blazing furnace, but he didn't. He let those problems happen, and each of those people was drawn closer to God as a result.

Problems force us to look to God and depend on him instead of ourselves. Paul testified to this benefit: *"We felt we were doomed to die and saw how powerless we were to help ourselves; but that was good, for then we put everything into the hands of God, who alone could save us"* (2 Corinthians 1:9, TLB). You'll never know that God is all you need until God is all you've got.

NOVEMBER 15

The Uncomfortable Path to a Miracle

Then the LORD spoke his word to Elijah, "Go to Zarephath in Sidon and live there. I have commanded a widow there to take care of you." So Elijah went to Zarephath.

1 KINGS 17:8-10 (NCV)

Sometimes you're scared to death and vulnerable. You don't know where you're going, how long it's going to take, or what's going to happen when you get there. So what do you do?

You remember that the path to a miracle often goes through uncomfortable territory. The Bible gives an illustration in 1 Kings 17:8-10: *"Then the LORD spoke his word to Elijah, 'Go to Zarephath in Sidon and live there. I have commanded a widow there to take care of you.' So Elijah went to Zarephath"* (NCV).

God's instructions meant Elijah had to walk over a hundred miles through dangerous territory. He had just angered King Ahab by prophesying a lengthy drought—and everyone Elijah met would know who he was.

When Elijah finally made it to Zarephath, he met a poor widow who was going to feed him. But the town still was full of pagan people who wouldn't hesitate to kill him. How could the widow defend or protect him?

Elijah didn't say, "God, there are three things wrong with this plan: You're sending me in the wrong direction, to the wrong location, and to the wrong protection." Elijah just obeyed.

God's path to a miracle often takes you through uncomfortable territory so you'll learn to depend on him. It was true for God's people throughout the Bible:

- When Moses led the Israelites out of slavery and toward the Promised Land, they had to go through the Red Sea first.
- Before David could slay Goliath, he had to walk onto the battlefield.
- To win the victory, God told Jehoshaphat to put the choir before the army.

Miracles never happen in your comfort zone. When everything's settled in your life, you don't need a miracle. You only need a miracle when you're at a low point.

Do things feel uncomfortable—financially, emotionally, or physically? Maybe you're nervous, unsettled, or insecure. Congratulations. You're on the path to a miracle!

Now follow the example of Elijah: Obey God so you can see his miracle at the end of the road.

The Many Facets of Mercy

The wisdom from above is first of all pure. It is also peace loving, gentle at all times, and willing to yield to others. It is full of mercy.

JAMES 3:17 (NLT)

Mercy will transform your relationships. If you want to be an agent of mercy, here are seven facets of mercy to understand:

1. **Mercy means being patient with people's quirks.** *"The wisdom from above is first of all pure. It is also peace loving, gentle at all times, and willing to yield to others. It is full of mercy"* (James 3:17, NLT). The wiser you become, the more patient and merciful you become.

2. **Mercy means helping anyone around you who is hurting.** *"Whenever you possibly can, do good to those who need it"* (Proverbs 3:27, GNT). You cannot love your neighbor as yourself without being merciful.

3. **Mercy means giving people a second chance.** *"Stop being bitter and angry and mad at others. . . . Instead, be kind and merciful, and forgive others, just as God forgave you because of Christ"* (Ephesians 4:31-32, CEV). When somebody hurts you, you might want to get even, but God's way is different.

4. **Mercy means doing good to those who hurt you.** *"Love your enemies, do good to them, and lend to them without expecting to get anything back. . . . Be merciful, just as your Father is merciful"* (Luke 6:35-36, NIV). Mercy gives people what they need, not what they deserve—because that's what God does with us.

5. **Mercy means being kind to those who offend you.** *"Show mercy to those who have doubts. Save others by snatching them from the fire of hell. Show mercy to others, even though you are afraid that you might be stained by their sinful lives"* (Jude 1:22-23, GW). You've got to be more interested in winning people to Christ than in winning the argument.

6. **Mercy means building bridges of love to the unpopular.** *"'I want you to show mercy, not offer sacrifices.' For I have come to call not those who think they are righteous, but those who know they are sinners"* (Matthew 9:13, NLT). Mercy intentionally builds friendships with people who aren't accepted.

7. **Mercy means valuing relationships over rules.** *"Love fulfills the requirements of God's law"* (Romans 13:10, NLT). Put people before policies. Put their needs before procedures. Put relationships before regulations.

Choose love over law. Ask for help to do this by praying, "God, I want to be full of mercy, because you are full of mercy. You've shown me how to do that in your Word, but I can't do it on my own. I need the Holy Spirit to remind me every moment of the day of how Jesus treated people so that I can try to treat others the same way. Please help me to look at every decision and consider how I could choose mercy and love and grace instead of serving myself. Help me to choose your way instead of my own so that others can see your mercy through me. In Jesus' name, amen."

NOVEMBER 17

Choose to Hope Again

Why am I so sad? Why am I so troubled? I will put my hope in God, and once again I will praise him, my savior and my God.
PSALM 42:5 (GNT)

The world is and always has been searching for hope. Even a popular business magazine once had a cover headline that said, "Searching for Hope." But as Christians, we're not searching anymore; we've found our hope in Jesus!

Even though we know where hope comes from, we're still going to get discouraged in this life. We live in a broken world, and we're going to keep sinning. Sometimes it's easy to feel like we've lost hope.

Psalm 42:5 says, *"Why am I so sad? Why am I so troubled? I will put my hope in God, and once again I will praise him, my savior and my God"* (GNT).

Notice two words in that verse: *hope* and *praise*. Those two ideas go together. If you want to be a hopeful person, then you've got to praise God. That's what builds hope in your life.

When you praise God, here's what God offers you: *"To all who mourn in Israel, he will give a crown of beauty for ashes, a joyous blessing instead of mourning, festive praise instead of despair"* (Isaiah 61:3, NLT).

Mourning is how you express grief over losing something. Many of us have lost a lot in recent years. Maybe you've lost friends or family, your job, your confidence, your security, your money, or your dream.

In Isaiah 61:3, God gives you a choice. Do you want beauty or ashes? Joy or sadness? Praise or despair?

Of course, you want beauty. You want to be joyful. You want to be able to praise.

And you can have those things! Even when you are discouraged and in mourning, you can choose to praise God. You can choose to worship him, even in your pain. The choice to praise God will restore your hope because it will remind you of what is true and why you can hope again.

NOVEMBER 18

You're Free to Be You

For we are God's masterpiece. He has created us anew in Christ Jesus, so we can do the good things he planned for us long ago.

EPHESIANS 2:10 (NLT)

God didn't create you to be somebody else. When you get to heaven, he's not going to ask you why you weren't more like your sister, your father, or your neighbor. God made you one of a kind, and he wants you to be real.

He wants you to be *you.*

The Bible says, *"For we are God's masterpiece. He has created us anew in Christ Jesus, so we can do the good things he planned for us long ago"* (Ephesians 2:10, NLT).

God wants you to be who he created you to be so you can do the work he planned for you to do.

The problem is, many people try to be someone they're not. They live for the approval of others. Or they think God would love them more if they acted differently. But God's love isn't based on how you act. He loves you, no matter what you do.

When you're afraid of being real, of being yourself, it keeps you from living out your purpose. Being afraid people won't like you if they find out who you really are will make you live an insecure life. But the Bible says, *"The Spirit we received does not make us slaves again to fear; it makes us children of God"* (Romans 8:15, NCV).

The antidote to insecurity is God's Spirit at work in you. When you live as a child of God, despite your mistakes and weaknesses, you're free to be who God made you to be.

Did you know your imperfections are actually a good thing? People don't grow from strengths. They grow from weaknesses. Showing only your strengths to the world won't make others feel close to you; it may even make them feel jealous or distant. But when you admit your imperfections—when you're real with others—people draw closer to you.

Are you ready to be real? It's your choice: You can be stuck and enslaved by fear. Or you can be the real you and enjoy the good things God planned for you long ago.

NOVEMBER 19

Another Chance to Start Over

A man who refuses to admit his mistakes can never be successful. But if he confesses and forsakes them, he gets another chance.

PROVERBS 28:13 (TLB)

I have a confession to make: I really don't like golf. But my brother loved golf, and when he was alive, I loved to play golf with him because it gave us a chance to be together.

As we played, I learned there's one thing I actually like about golf: the mulligan. In an informal game of golf, a mulligan is a do-over. If you make a poor shot, a mulligan lets you try again without counting that poor shot on your scorecard.

As followers of Jesus, we ought to live in the mulligans of God, the grace of God. God forgives us over and over and over. He gives us a chance to try it again, to give it our best shot—to not have our mistakes count against us.

You might say, "Well, that's not fair." Of course it's not fair. It's grace; it's mercy.

The Bible is full of mulligan verses, verses about God's grace and mercy. One is Proverbs 28:13: *"A man who refuses to admit his mistakes can never be successful. But if he confesses and forsakes them, he gets another chance"* (TLB). In other words, he gets a mulligan. That's the amazing grace of God. If you refuse to admit your mistakes, you'll never be successful—but if you confess and forsake your wrongs, you get another chance.

Another mulligan is found in Lamentations 3:22-23: *"The faithful love of the LORD never ends! His mercies never cease. Great is his faithfulness; his mercies begin afresh each morning"* (NLT). God's never going to stop loving you—because his love is based on who he is, not on what you do. Every new day is another chance from God.

You need to start looking at each new day as a mulligan day—another chance from God. Every morning God is giving you another chance—a new opportunity.

When you wake up tomorrow, remember: *"For God's gifts and his call can never be withdrawn; he will never go back on his promises"* (Romans 11:29, TLB). No sin you've committed will change God's call or God's gifts in your life. God's mercies are new every morning.

NOVEMBER 20

More Mercy, More Like Jesus

Love is . . . never haughty or selfish or rude. Love does not demand its own way. It is not irritable or touchy. It does not hold grudges.

1 CORINTHIANS 13:4-5 (TLB)

One of the best ways to show love to your family is to choose mercy. Mercy is love in action. So when you overlook irritations and choose to be kind to your family—even when they don't deserve it—you're being merciful.

Another important way you can show mercy in your home is by letting go of past hurts.

Do you keep a mental record every time someone in your family does something wrong?

Are you quick to remind someone of how they have hurt you? The Bible says that real love doesn't store up hurts and offenses to be used later for revenge. When you hold on to a hurt like that, you are not being loving.

The Bible says, *"Love is . . . never haughty or selfish or rude. Love does not demand its own way. It is not irritable or touchy. It does not hold grudges"* (1 Corinthians 13:4-5, TLB).

Notice how *"rude"* and *"does not hold grudges"* are in the same verse. That's the reason people are rude: They're reacting to a past hurt they've been holding on to and then taking it out on others. When they react to a past hurt, they can't relate well to people in the present.

Leviticus 19:18 says, *"Do not take revenge on others or continue to hate them, but love your neighbors as you love yourself"* (GNT).

Are past grudges holding your relationships hostage today? Don't hold resentment over your spouse's or children's heads. And don't tell other people about your grudges, either. That's gossip! Instead, just let it go.

Sometimes it's hardest to show mercy to the people who are closest to you. But when you can let it go and be merciful, you are learning to be more like Jesus.

Your choice to show mercy also creates ripple effects that go beyond your family. Choosing love and mercy demonstrates to others that following Jesus brings peace to your relationships. Letting it go shows the world the kind of love that heals and restores.

NOVEMBER 21

Why Should Christians Be Grateful?

Give thanks to the LORD for his unfailing love.
PSALM 107:8 (NIV)

There are many reasons to be thankful to God—not just at Thanksgiving but all the time. Here are some reasons why, as Christians, we need to be the most grateful people of all.

We can be grateful because God gave us life. Psalm 139:13-14 says, *"You made all the delicate, inner parts of my body and knit me together in my mother's womb. Thank you for making me so wonderfully complex!"* (NLT). You wouldn't even be alive if it weren't for God. That's a good place to start being grateful!

We can be grateful that we're *still* alive. God created you, and he has brought you this far. Every day is a gift! The Bible says in Ecclesiastes 11:8, *"Be grateful for every year you live"* (GNT).

We can be grateful that God saved us. Psalm 13:5 says, *"My heart is happy because you saved me"* (NCV).

We can be grateful because God is good. The Bible says, *"I will give you thanks because you are good"* (Psalm 54:6, GNT).

We can be grateful that God answers our prayers. *"I give thanks to you, because you have answered me"* (Psalm 118:21, GW).

We can be grateful that God guides us. Psalm 16:7 says, *"I praise the LORD, because he guides me"* (GNT).

We can be grateful that God forgives us. The Bible says in Psalm 118:1, *"Tell the LORD how thankful you are, because he is kind and always merciful"* (CEV).

We can be grateful that God will never stop loving us. Psalm 107:8 says, *"Give thanks to the LORD for his unfailing love"* (NIV).

I want to give you some homework for Thanksgiving Day if you gather with friends and family. The verses above are your starter list to help with discussion and acknowledgment of some of the most important reasons you have to be thankful. When you all are gathered, go around the room and have everyone read one of the verses and say why they are specifically thankful for that attribute of God.

You'll find your thanksgiving overflowing!

NOVEMBER 22

Eight Ways God Blesses Gratitude

Be strong in your faith, just as you were taught. And be grateful.

COLOSSIANS 2:7 (CEV)

When God wants to help you do the right thing, he always attaches a benefit to doing it. That's true for gratitude. When you have a gratitude mindset, it yields great blessings! Here are eight ways gratitude benefits you:

Gratitude improves your brain and your physical health. Ask your doctor, and they'll probably tell you that gratitude is the healthiest human emotion.

Gratitude creates happiness. If you want to be happy, practice gratitude by remembering all that God has done for you. The happiest people are those who are the most grateful.

Gratitude helps you sleep. Practicing gratitude reminds you of how God takes care of you and provides for your needs. Trusting in God's provision will help you replace worry with rest.

Gratitude is the antidote to toxic emotions. It helps defeat feelings of worry, anger, and fear.

Gratitude improves relationships. When you express gratitude to others more often, you will have a lot less conflict in your relationships.

Gratitude opens the door to opportunities. When you express gratitude to people, you make friends and have access to more opportunities than you would have had otherwise.

Gratitude is the evidence of spiritual maturity. Colossians 2:7 says, *"Plant your roots in Christ and let him be the foundation for your life. Be strong in your faith, just as you were taught. And be grateful"* (CEV). The more spiritually mature you are, the more grateful you'll be.

Gratitude brings blessing because it pleases God. The Bible says God loves *"a sacrifice of thanksgiving"* (Psalm 116:17, NLT).

It's easy to make Thanksgiving Day about a lot of things besides being thankful. We spend a full day preparing the meal. We spend several hours watching football and talking and hanging out. We spare a minute or two to thank God in prayer—anything longer would make the food go cold!

It's important to create practices of gratitude on Thanksgiving, but God doesn't want you to be thankful just one day a year. He wants you to develop a spirit of thankfulness throughout the year so that you can experience his blessings every day.

The *Real* First Thanksgiving

Celebrate the Harvest Festival, to honor the LORD *your God, by bringing him a freewill offering in proportion to the blessing he has given you.*
DEUTERONOMY 16:10 (GNT)

The gathering most Americans think of as the first Thanksgiving happened four hundred years ago.

But three thousand years before that, God told the nation of Israel to establish a thanksgiving festival called the Feast of Weeks or Harvest Festival. They were to celebrate God's goodness and express their gratitude by bringing him a special, annual thanksgiving offering.

Deuteronomy 16:10-11 says, *"Celebrate the Harvest Festival, to honor the* LORD *your God, by bringing him a freewill offering in proportion to the blessing he has given you. . . . Do this at the one place of worship"* (GNT).

On this original Thanksgiving Day, the Israelites were to bring a gift of thanksgiving to the place where they worshiped. This thanksgiving offering has been practiced by God's people for thousands of years and is mentioned often in Scripture.

God said in Psalm 50:23, *"Those people honor me who bring me offerings to show thanks. And I, God, will save those who do that"* (NCV). The Bible tells us many times that our offering should be the first part of our income—not the leftovers—so that God is first in our finances.

Anytime you give an offering to God, it represents three kinds of gratitude: past, present, and future. Your offering represents gratitude for God's blessing in the past, God's blessing today, and faith in God's continued blessing in the future. God always honors faith with his blessing.

In the Bible, there are more promises attached to faithful giving and generosity than any other subject. Why? Because God wants his children to be like him. And he is a generous God! Jesus said in Luke 6:38, *"If you give, you will get! Your gift will return to you in full and overflowing measure, pressed down, shaken together to make room for more, and running over. Whatever measure you use to give—large or small—will be used to measure what is given back to you"* (TLB).

If you've trusted Jesus to forgive your sin and save your soul, then you can trust God to take care of you. Your thanksgiving offering shows God that you trust him for all things and at all times.

NOVEMBER 24

The Key to Lasting Love

Love never gives up, never loses faith, is always hopeful, and endures through every circumstance.

1 CORINTHIANS 13:7 (NLT)

Lasting love is persistent. It is determined. It is diligent. It is resolute. It endures the worst and doesn't give up on a relationship. It's stubborn!

The purpose of a relationship is not just to make you happy but also to make you holy. Relationships—whether with a spouse or a child or even a close friend—teach you to think of others more than you think of yourself. As you persevere with them through difficult times, you will learn certain things that you would never learn any other way.

When my wife and I got married, we discovered that we were complete opposites. We started arguing on our wedding night, and from there, it just got worse. We loved each other, but we did not get along.

But we had made a vow, and we decided divorce was not an option. We said, "We're going to make this thing work if it kills us"—and it nearly did! We got counseling, even though we were broke. We sacrificed so that we could honor our commitment to each other. We grew up. We struggled for the first two years of our marriage, but we became better through it.

Maybe you need to hear this today: Don't give up. Keep on. Persevere. Be stubborn. Don't let go of God's gift of lasting love just because you have to work for it. It will always be worth the fight.

Learning to love is the single greatest lesson in life. It is why God put you on this planet. But it's not always easy—and it's just plain hard to love some people.

There really isn't a "secret" to lasting love. The key, however, is to let God's love flow through you.

Philippians 2:5 says, *"You must have the same attitude that Christ Jesus had"* (NLT). Human love wears out. But having Jesus' love in you lets you offer lasting love to others.

Open your life to him—and then let him love others through you.

NOVEMBER 25

Do You Need More Balance? Start Praising God

I bless the holy name of God with all my heart. Yes, I will bless the Lord and not forget the glorious things he does for me. He forgives all my sins. He heals me. He ransoms me from hell. He surrounds me with loving-kindness and tender mercies. He fills my life with good things!

PSALM 103:1-5 (TLB)

When overwhelming problems come, we tend to overlook all the good in our lives and only see the bad things.

But focusing on the problem leaves you imbalanced. For example, if you have a conflict in an important relationship, it can affect the way you look at everything else in life. It's difficult to see blessings when you're focused on problems. Praising God helps you remember his blessings. It rebalances you! Praising, worshiping, and thanking God remind you that not everything in your life is bad.

In Psalm 105, the psalmist described some really tough times that God's people had gone through. But the author also made a list of all the things they could thank and praise God for: *"I bless the holy name of God with all my heart. Yes, I will bless the Lord and not forget the glorious things he does for me. He forgives all my sins. He heals me. He ransoms me from hell. He surrounds me with loving-kindness and tender mercies. He fills my life with good things!"* (Psalm 103:1-5, TLB).

Focusing on a problem tends to overemphasize it so much that you neglect all the good in your life. But your life is never all good or all bad.

Because we live on a broken planet, there will never be a time in your life when everything is good. So no matter how good things are in your life, there will always be something you need to be working on. But there's never a time in your life when everything is bad either. Even on the worst days, there are things you can thank God for. When you're imbalanced, you forget your identity in Christ and can become insecure. Praise brings your system back into balance.

When you praise God, you remember how he has blessed you and you remember who you are. Praise balances your life between the negative and the positive *and* between what other people say you are and who you really are.

NOVEMBER 26

How to Show Gratitude in Hard Times

God will strengthen you with his own great power so that you will not give up when troubles come, but you will be patient. And you will joyfully give thanks to the Father.
COLOSSIANS 1:11-12 (NCV)

Showing gratitude can be especially challenging during hard times. That's because you have to look past your circumstances and your pain to God's unchanging truth and goodness.

You can always find something in your own life to be grateful for, even in tough times. But there are also three truths about God we can all be grateful for, whatever our circumstances. We can be grateful because . . .

God will give us the strength to get through them. Colossians 1:11-12 says, *"God will strengthen you with his own great power so that you will not give up when troubles come, but you will be patient. And you will joyfully give thanks to the Father"* (NCV).

Bad times cannot change God's plan. When you're anchored in God's eternal purposes, your anchor holds no matter how bad the storm gets. Bad times cannot change God's purposes for your life—no matter what has happened to you or how you've messed up.

"Do you see what we've got? An unshakable kingdom! And do you see how thankful we must be? Not only thankful, but brimming with worship, deeply reverent before God" (Hebrews 12:28, MSG).

God is changing our lives. God is growing and changing you step by step, one day at a time. It's not an instant change, but it is consistent. And what God started in your life, he will finish. He's going to take you to eternity!

The Bible says in 2 Corinthians 3:18, *"All of us who have had that veil removed can see and reflect the glory of the Lord"* (NLT).

What healthy habits does God want you to develop so that you can become more like him? While you're working on those habits, God is working on you. When you're open to God's work in your life, he will move you from one degree of maturity to the next.

Nothing will stop God's work in your life. Be patient with yourself as God moves you to maturity, and look for ways to praise him and be grateful.

NOVEMBER 27

How Gratitude Can Change Your Life

In everything you do, stay away from complaining and arguing.
PHILIPPIANS 2:14 (TLB)

If you want to move from an overwhelmed life to an overflowing life, start being grateful, and stop complaining.

Choosing gratitude is something you can start the moment you wake up. Before you get out of bed, make a list of things you're grateful for. For example, "God, I'm grateful for air; I'm grateful for this bed; I'm grateful I'm not in danger." Even if you can't think of anything to be grateful for, the simple act of *trying* to be grateful will change your brain chemistry by producing feel-good chemicals that make you feel peaceful and happy.

The Bible says, *"In everything you do, stay away from complaining and arguing"* (Philippians 2:14, TLB).

When you complain about something, how does that help you? If you complain about the weather, does it change the weather? If you complain about the way you look, does it change the way you look? If you complain about your spouse, children, or job, do they change?

Complaining is a total waste of time. It's stewing without doing. Complaining will never make you feel better. Instead, God wants your life to *"overflow with joy and thanksgiving for all he has done"* (Colossians 2:7, TLB).

Sometimes people say to me, "Pastor Rick, I just want to know God's will. What does God want me to do in my relationship? What does he want me to do in my career? What does he want me to do in school?"

Why would God teach you step two when you haven't done step one? If you want to know God's will, God wants you to do step one—always be thankful—and then you can move on to step two. *"Always be thankful, for this is God's will for you who belong to Christ Jesus"* (1 Thessalonians 5:18, TLB).

If you want to live an overflowing life rather than an overwhelmed life, take the first step: stop complaining, and start being grateful.

Forgive Because God Forgave You

Be kind and compassionate to one another, forgiving each other, just as in Christ God forgave you.

EPHESIANS 4:32 (NIV)

Life is hard—we all know that by now!

You will, unfortunately, be hurt in this life. And many of those hurts will be intentional—the direct result of what people do to you or say about you. In fact, anytime you read the word *forgiveness*, it may instantly call to mind certain heartaches from your past. The memories still feel fresh when you've been hurt very deeply.

When someone hurts you, it's often hard to consider forgiving them. Sometimes it's easier to hold on to the hurt and keep score. You think it will make you feel better or make the other person feel worse. But in the end, it just makes you unhappy—while the other person goes on with their life.

Forgiveness gives you the peace you need to move forward with purpose. But there's an even more important reason you need to forgive.

You forgive others because God forgave you.

The Bible says in Ephesians 4:32, *"Be kind and compassionate to one another, forgiving each other, just as in Christ God forgave you"* (NIV).

Thinking about how much God has forgiven you will help you be more forgiving of those who have hurt you.

The opposite is also true. If you don't believe and accept in faith that you've been forgiven by God, then you'll likely have a hard time forgiving others. If that's the case, consider whether you truly believe God has forgiven you. Talk to God about any doubts you have.

Think of it like this: God has completely wiped your slate clean of sin because of what Jesus Christ did on the cross. All of the things you deserve to be punished for have been cleared away because God has forgiven you. As you accept this truth, you'll find it increasingly tough to hold a grudge against someone else.

Ask God for faith to accept that Jesus did everything needed to make you right with God. And remember: No matter what anyone does to you, you'll never have to forgive another person more than God has already forgiven you.

NOVEMBER 29

Your Pain Can Make You More like Christ

Even though Jesus was God's Son, he learned obedience from the things he suffered.
HEBREWS 5:8 (NLT)

Every pain in your life is an opportunity to grow in character. How do you learn to love when you feel unloved? How do you learn joy in the middle of grief? How do you learn peace when everything's in chaos? How do you learn patience when you're not feeling patient?

You learn those qualities, with God's grace, when you're going through pain. You have to decide if you're going to let the pain be a stepping stone to maturity or a stumbling block to spiritual growth.

Once you decide to follow Jesus, God's number one purpose in your life is to make you more like Christ. If you're a part of God's family, then he wants you to grow up! He helps you do that by taking you through everything Jesus went through. There were times when Jesus was lonely, frustrated, misunderstood, criticized, and in pain.

But the Bible says, *"Even though Jesus was God's Son, he learned obedience from the things he suffered. In this way, God qualified him as a perfect High Priest, and he became the source of eternal salvation for all those who obey him"* (Hebrews 5:8-9, NLT).

If Jesus was made perfect through suffering, then you are matured the same way.

There are some things you learn only through pain. In that sense, pain becomes a gift if you let it draw you closer to God in worship, closer to others in fellowship, and deeper in discipleship.

When Paul wrote to the Corinthian church, he recognized the many ways they grew through their pain. He said in 2 Corinthians 7:11, *"Isn't it wonderful all the ways in which this distress has goaded you closer to God? You're more alive, more concerned, more sensitive, more reverent, more human, more passionate, more responsible"* (MSG).

Those seven qualities of Christlikeness are developed in you, too, when you ask God to use your pain to build your character. If you'll do that, the pain won't leave you where it found you—it will transform you!

NOVEMBER 30

What Makes You Vulnerable to Temptation?

Above all else, guard your heart, for everything you do flows from it.
PROVERBS 4:23 (NIV)

If you want to be able to fight the persistent temptations in life, then you need to know what makes you vulnerable to Satan's efforts.

Ephesians 4:27 says, *"Do not give the devil a foothold"* (NIV). A foothold is a secure position that can be used to advance something or make it progress. So when the Bible says not to give the devil a foothold, it means this: Don't give Satan a place in your life to start leveraging your weaknesses and messing you up.

There's one common foothold that makes you particularly vulnerable to temptation. What is that foothold? It's any negative emotion. Anytime you dwell on a negative emotion, you've just given Satan a foothold in your life, and you're going to be vulnerable to temptation. That's why the Bible says in Proverbs 4:23, *"Above all else, guard your heart, for everything you do flows from it"* (NIV).

You might think that if you want to defeat temptation, you need to focus on your behavior. Instead, God wants you to focus on your thoughts and the feelings that grow out of those thoughts. In other words, as Proverbs 4:23 says, he wants you to focus on your heart.

That's how Satan hooks you—not with your behavior but with your thoughts. He plays with your emotions every day of your life. He hooks your feelings. He is a master manipulator of your moods. Satan stirs your emotions by influencing your thoughts and causing you to doubt God's Word.

Once he's got you emotionally involved—once your heart is involved—you're hooked. Satan knows your negative emotions will lead you to sin.

Satan knows which negative emotions are most tempting for you, and he will work them for your destruction. If those emotions have so much power, shouldn't you know what they are too?

The only way you'll be able to fight any persistent temptation in your life is by identifying the emotions that make you vulnerable. Then, refocus your mind on God's Word so that you can replace those negative emotions with God's love.

DECEMBER 1

You Don't Need to Know Everything

Without faith it is impossible to please God, because anyone who comes to him must believe that he exists and that he rewards those who earnestly seek him.

HEBREWS 11:6 (NIV)

Going through hard times is inevitable for all of us. Have you ever been in the middle of a trial and thought, "Why couldn't God have given me a heads-up about this? That sure would have helped!"

God doesn't explain his plan to us in advance for two reasons: First, we likely wouldn't understand it. Our brains aren't big enough to understand all of God's ways. God is God, and we are not.

The second reason is that God wants us to trust him. The Bible tells us over and over that the only way to please God is not through ritual or rules or religion but through *faith*. Hebrews 11:6 says, *"Without faith it is impossible to please God, because anyone who comes to him must believe that he exists and that he rewards those who earnestly seek him"* (NIV).

The major characters in the Bible—Moses, Joseph, Esther, the prophets, Ruth, Peter, Paul, John, Mary, and more—all of them probably wanted God to give them a heads-up as they experienced trials, temptations, persecution, suffering, unmet expectations, and circumstances that seemed out of control. Their faith was tested in incredible ways.

Like us, all they could do when they didn't understand was trust. They had to trust that God knew better than they did, could see more than they could see, and was working out a good plan.

That's what you're going to have to do in those moments when you don't understand why the plan isn't going the way you want. When the business starts to fail, when your kid walks away from God, when your investments aren't doing well, when your health takes an unexpected turn—that is God testing your faith. That's your time to step up and show him what you believe!

When life doesn't make sense, keep on trusting in God's plan. Trust his wisdom, his timing, his promises, and his love.

DECEMBER 2

Why Hope in God?

What a gift life is to those who stay the course! You've heard, of course, of Job's staying power, and you know how God brought it all together for him at the end. That's because God cares, cares right down to the last detail.

JAMES 5:11 (MSG)

The big question everyone asks when they go through a long, dark valley is this: "When will things get back to normal?"

But things don't always go back to the way they were. Sometimes it gets harder before it gets better. Sometimes we end up with a new normal.

Instead of asking when things will get back to normal, you need to ask, "What will I do if life *doesn't* get back to normal?" The answer is simple: Don't put your hope in circumstances, the economy, or other people to make things right again. Instead, put your hope in God.

Why hope in God? Because he holds the future. Because he's already written the end of the story. Because he works out the details of our lives, so we don't have to worry if things will be okay.

The story of Job demonstrates this. Imagine being Job when everything was taken from him, including his health, everything he owned, and even his family. He didn't know the future. He had no idea God would restore things in the end—but he still trusted God.

"What a gift life is to those who stay the course! You've heard, of course, of Job's staying power, and you know how God brought it all together for him at the end. That's because God cares, cares right down to the last detail" (James 5:11, MSG).

God worked through the details of Job's life because he cared about him. God will do the same for you, no matter what you've been through so far in life. As you trust God to handle the details, he'll show you the next step to take. He'll bring it all together in the rest of your story.

Your story is part of God's greater story. He planned it all for his good purposes, and he is always working to bring it to its fulfillment—in his time, in his ways, and for his glory.

No matter what you're going through right now, God promises to make it all right in the end. That's a reason to hope and to faithfully trust him.

DECEMBER 3

God Is Aware, and He Cares

As a father has compassion on his children, so the
LORD has compassion on those who fear him.
PSALM 103:13 (NIV)

God is a caring, loving, compassionate Father. He loves you more than you could ever comprehend.

God *is* love, and he made you so he could love you. He is loving toward you in everything he does; his compassion is one of his most outstanding qualities.

The Bible says in Psalm 103:13, *"As a father has compassion on his children, so the LORD has compassion on those who fear him"* (NIV). He cares about everything in your life—compassionately.

Most of Jesus' disciples were professional fishermen. One day while out on the water with them, Jesus got tired and went to sleep inside the boat. When a storm came, it shouldn't have bothered the disciples. As fishermen, they were used to storms. But this must have been a big one because they got scared. The ship rocked and rolled; water came into the boat. They were frantic and woke up Jesus to ask him one of the most important questions in life: "Lord, don't you care?"

You and I ask God that question all the time and in a thousand ways: "God, did you see my doctor's report? Don't you care?" "Do you see what a mess my marriage is in? Don't you care?" "Do you see how my kids are struggling in school? Don't you care?" "You know how fear grips my mind. Don't you care?"

The answer is this: Yes, God cares. He cares more than you know. He wants to help more than you want help. He knows what will help you more than you know what will help you. He is aware, and he cares.

The Bible says, *"Cast all your anxiety on him because he cares for you"* (1 Peter 5:7, NIV).

If you knew and felt how much your heavenly Father constantly and compassionately cares, you couldn't help but love him back.

Take the first step toward inner peace today, and *"cast all your anxiety"* on your compassionate heavenly Father.

DECEMBER 4

God Wants Whatever You've Got

"Where shall we buy bread for these people to eat?" He asked this only to test him, for he already had in mind what he was going to do.

JOHN 6:5-6 (NIV)

Do you remember the story of Jesus feeding five thousand people with only five loaves of bread and two fish? Out of that many people, I think it's amazing that only one person brought a lunch. I'm thinking a lot of people probably hid picnic baskets under their robes because they didn't want to share with anybody else.

But one little boy offered the bread and fish he had packed for his lunch. He gave Jesus what little he had, and God used it not just to feed thousands of people but also to show them how much he cares and how powerful he is.

God always starts with what you have. You may not have much time. Your finances may not be worth much. You may not think you have much talent.

But you can give God everything in your life. Give him your heart. Give him your reputation. Give him your past, present, and future. It may not be much, but you can give him your five loaves and two fish.

In John 6:5-6 Jesus asked, *"'Where shall we buy bread for these people to eat?' He asked this only to test him, for he already had in mind what he was going to do"* (NIV).

Jesus wasn't worried about how to feed five thousand people. He already had in mind what he was going to do. He saw the need long before the disciples did—and he had a plan.

You need to understand this truth today: God always has the answer before you even know the problem. God is not worried about your unsolvable problem. It's not too late in the day for Jesus. He saw your problem long before you did. He knew it was coming, and he already had a plan for it. God knows the solution to your problem before you even recognize it's a problem.

So why are you worrying? Just admit you have an unsolvable problem, and then give God everything you have. Watch him take your loaves and fish and turn them into a feast.

DECEMBER 5

Humility Starts Here

"God opposes everyone who is proud, but he blesses all who are humble with undeserved grace." Surrender to God!

JAMES 4:6-7 (CEV)

It takes courage to be humble. Why? Because humans do not naturally lean toward humility. You have to constantly choose to be humble.

One of the most important ways to practice courageous humility is to surrender your plans to God. But this is what we usually do instead: We make our plans without even consulting God. Then we pray and ask God to bless our plans, which we didn't ask him to be a part of in the first place. Then we get angry with him when our plans don't happen.

Scenarios like that show our pride—and God hates pride. James 4:6-7 says, *"'God opposes everyone who is proud, but he blesses all who are humble with undeserved grace.' Surrender to God!"* (CEV).

I can think of a lot of people I wouldn't want to have as an opponent. I would not want to compete in the swimming pool against Michael Phelps or on a basketball court opposed by LeBron James.

But I *really* don't want to be opposed by God, because there's no way I'm going to win that battle. Yet the Bible says that when I am prideful, God is not just irritated at me. It says he's in opposition to me. Anytime I'm full of pride, I'm an enemy of God. That's how serious it is.

So what does it mean to surrender yourself and your plans to God?

Romans 6:13 says, *"Give yourselves to God, as those who have been brought from death to life, and surrender your whole being to him to be used for righteous purposes"* (GNT).

Surrendering means praying something like this: "God, I'm going with your plans for my life, not my own. I know you're not going to reveal your plan to me all at once, so I'm going to take it one step at a time. And I'm going to trust you to provide for me every step of the way."

Gather your courage and pray that prayer of humility today—and every day. Then you'll see how God starts blessing you with his grace as you live out his plans for your life.

DECEMBER 6

What Are You Waiting on God to Do?

Three different times I begged the Lord to take it away. Each time he said, "My grace is all you need. My power works best in weakness." So now I am glad to boast about my weaknesses, so that the power of Christ can work through me. . . . For when I am weak, then I am strong.

2 CORINTHIANS 12:8-10 (NLT)

God has used the most physically painful thing in my life to shape me and make me depend on him.

I was born with a brain disorder that, among other things, makes public speaking painful. Essentially, my brain runs extremely hot and fast, and it causes all kinds of problems in my body. For more than fifty years, I've asked God every day to heal it. And he has said to me every time, *"My grace is all you need."*

Though God has chosen not to remove one of the things I've prayed about the most, like Job, I say, *"Though he slay me, yet will I hope in him"* (Job 13:15, NIV).

Even the apostle Paul did not get answers to all of his prayers. In fact, he had what he called a *"thorn in the flesh"*—a lifelong problem that caused great pain in his life. The Bible says in 2 Corinthians 12:8-10, *"Three different times I begged the Lord to take it away. Each time he said, 'My grace is all you need. My power works best in weakness.' So now I am glad to boast about my weaknesses, so that the power of Christ can work through me. . . . For when I am weak, then I am strong"* (NLT).

If God never says yes to another one of my prayers, I still owe him the rest of my life, and you do too. He has a better plan, a bigger perspective, and a greater purpose.

What have you been praying about that hasn't happened? Maybe you want to be married, move somewhere else, or get that promotion at work. Maybe you've asked God to give you something or take away something, like a chronic illness. Maybe you've gone through something that makes you feel like it's the end of your story.

This chapter will pass, but your story is not over. Whatever you've been waiting on, you can trust that God is working for your good. Even when he doesn't take away your pain, God will give you his grace and power to walk through it.

DECEMBER 7

Three Things to Pray in Your Pain

"Abba, Father," he cried out, "everything is possible for you. Please take this cup of suffering away from me. Yet I want your will to be done, not mine."
MARK 14:36 (NLT)

The night before he went to the cross, Jesus prayed in the garden of Gethsemane. He knew that the next day he was going to face torture and death on the cross. He didn't want to go through that pain any more than you or I would have wanted to.

"He went on a little further and fell to the ground. He prayed that, if it were possible, the awful hour awaiting him might pass him by" (Mark 14:35, NLT).

Jesus wanted to know if there was any other way that God could accomplish his will for the salvation of the world. So he prayed and asked his Father to make a way for him. In doing that, Jesus showed you that it's okay to tell God that you don't want to go through your suffering.

Mark 14:36 says, *"'Abba, Father,' he cried out, 'everything is possible for you. Please take this cup of suffering away from me. Yet I want your will to be done, not mine'"* (NLT).

In this prayer, Jesus models the three things you should pray when you're in pain:

Affirm God's power. Tell God, "Father, you have power over everything! I know you will take care of this situation. I know you could keep me out of this suffering. I know you could take away the pain instantly."

Ask with passion. Then say to God, "Lord, please give me what I ask. Take away this suffering and pain. You see my hurt. I know you care and you are with me. And I know you will answer my prayer. Please don't let this pain be my burden any longer."

Accept God's plan. Finally, tell him, "God, I don't want to go through this suffering. But what I want most is your plan, your purpose, and your perspective. Please do your will in my life, even if it means I have to bear this pain. I know you will be with me and help me and make me more like you."

This is not an easy prayer, especially when you're in pain. But it will always be the prayer God honors and answers.

DECEMBER 8

What's on the Other Side of Your Troubles?

Our light and momentary troubles are achieving for us an eternal glory that far outweighs them all. So we fix our eyes not on what is seen, but on what is unseen, since what is seen is temporary, but what is unseen is eternal.

2 CORINTHIANS 4:17-18 (NIV)

When a crisis hits, you have to do the smart things necessary to get through it. You listen to God's Word and godly advice, you make good choices, and you keep moving forward while remembering that this will pass. It's not going to last forever!

The Bible says in 1 Peter 4:12, *"Dear friends, don't be bewildered or surprised when you go through the fiery trials ahead, for this is no strange, unusual thing that is going to happen to you"* (TLB).

In this world, there will be trials and testing. Since sin entered the world, nothing works perfectly. Everything on this planet is broken—the weather, the economy, your body, and even your best plans. Isaiah 24 says, *"The land suffers for the sins of its people. . . . The people have twisted the laws of God and broken his everlasting commands. . . . The earth has broken down in utter collapse"* (verses 4-5, 19, TLB). On earth, everything is lost, abandoned, and confused. Even nature is groaning.

Naturally, you may wonder why God allowed sin and evil to enter the world. It's because God wanted us to have a choice. And we often choose evil; we're selfish and self-centered and cause problems in society and in our environment.

This earth is not heaven. That's why Jesus taught us to pray the Lord's Prayer—*"your will be done, on earth as it is in heaven"* (Matthew 6:10, NIV). Heaven is perfect, with no sorrow, sickness, sadness, or stress, but we shouldn't expect heaven on earth. One day we'll get there, but we're not there yet. You will get through whatever trial you're experiencing. As you look at it from the other side, you'll marvel at all that God did through your trouble.

You will face more challenges and endure more adversity. But you can always hope in this truth: *"Our light and momentary troubles are achieving for us an eternal glory that far outweighs them all. So we fix our eyes not on what is seen, but on what is unseen, since what is seen is temporary, but what is unseen is eternal"* (2 Corinthians 4:17-18, NIV).

DECEMBER 9

Surrender Your Defense to God

You prepare a table before me in the presence of my enemies.

PSALM 23:5 (NIV)

King David knew what it meant to be attacked emotionally, verbally, and physically. As a young man, he was anointed by the prophet Samuel to be the next king of Israel, but Saul was still king.

Even though David served him loyally, Saul felt jealous of the future king and decided to kill him. David hid in caves while lies were being told about him across the kingdom.

Yet David never said a bad word against King Saul. He never retaliated—because God was preparing David to be a king who followed God's heart.

David said of God, *"You prepare a table before me in the presence of my enemies"* (Psalm 23:5, NIV).

David didn't have to use up all his energy defending himself, because he trusted God to be his defender.

It takes a lot of faith and humility to trust God and rest when you're under attack and misunderstood, and when rumors are spreading about you. When that happens, everything in you wants to rise up and do something about it. But when people attack you, trust God to be your defender—let God handle them.

God wants to defend you and fellowship with you: *"You'll welcome us with open arms when we run for cover to you. Let the party last all night! Stand guard over our celebration"* (Psalm 5:11, MSG).

Both Psalm 23 and Psalm 5 paint the picture of a banquet, or a party, at an unlikely time—not only during good times but also when you're under attack.

Are you in the heat of a battle? God knows. Maybe you're fighting for your job, health, sanity, or dignity. While the battle rages, he wants to throw a banquet on a battlefield to encourage you. That encouragement is available today when you surrender your worry, pain, and control to Jesus and rest in his promises to you.

If you're a child of God, your heavenly Father is proud of you. Critics may slander, ignore, ridicule, or spite you, but they can't stop God's blessing on your life. As the Bible says, *"He brought me to his banquet hall and raised the banner of love over me"* (Song of Solomon 2:4, GNT).

DECEMBER 10

The Good Shepherd Directs and Protects

All of us, like sheep, have strayed away. We have left God's paths to follow our own.
ISAIAH 53:6 (NLT)

God sees everyone as valuable and worth seeking, finding, and saving. The Bible says, *"[God] desires all people to be saved and to come to the knowledge of the truth"* (1 Timothy 2:4, ESV).

But so many people are spiritually lost. This means they're following their own plan for their lives rather than God's plan. Spiritually lost people lose two things: direction and protection.

You can see this in the story of the lost sheep in Luke 15:3-6. It's about a shepherd who leaves ninety-nine saved sheep to go out and search for the one lost sheep. He doesn't say, "I've got ninety-nine saved sheep, so forget the lost one!" No, they all matter to him. And when he finds the lost sheep, *"he joyfully puts it on his shoulders"* (Luke 15:5, NIV) and goes home to celebrate.

Like sheep, people who are spiritually lost lose their **direction**. In fact, all humans are this way. You don't intend to get lost. You just think, "That grass looks greener." And soon you follow your own way and lose your direction. The Bible says, *"All of us, like sheep, have strayed away. We have left God's paths to follow our own"* (Isaiah 53:6, NLT).

Another thing spiritually lost people lose is God's **protection**. Like sheep who wander away from their shepherd, you, too, are vulnerable when you don't have a shepherd to protect you from the wolves of life. That's why you need to follow Jesus, the Good Shepherd, so you're not alone and defenseless.

The Bible also says, *"My people are wandering like lost sheep; they are attacked because they have no shepherd"* (Zechariah 10:2, NLT).

But when you place yourself under the Good Shepherd's care, you get direction and protection. This doesn't mean you will be free from trouble—it means God will work *"all things together for the good of those who love Him"* (Romans 8:28, BSB).

Maybe you or someone you know is lacking God's direction and protection today. Remember: Jesus is the Good Shepherd who sees everyone as extremely valuable and *"desires all people to be saved."*

DECEMBER 11

No Matter What You've Done, God Will Take You Back

With deep love I will take you back.
ISAIAH 54:7 (GNT)

This Christmas season, do you need a little refreshment in your life? Are you feeling a little dried up? Do you need some revival?

Come back to God.

You may say, "Rick, you don't know what I've done." I don't need to know, because it doesn't matter who you are or what you've done. God still wants you to come back to him.

You may say, "Isn't God going to scold me? I've been away from him for months, years, even decades." Here's what God says he will do if you come back to him: *"With deep love I will take you back"* (Isaiah 54:7, GNT).

Remember: God isn't mad at you. God is mad *about* you! God the Father created you, Jesus the Son died for you, and God's Spirit wants to live in you. Christmas is proof of God's love for you.

Many people can't feel God's love because they're listening to the wrong voices. If you listen to what other people say about you or what you tell yourself, it will get you down. Stop believing everything you tell yourself. It's not all true! You lie to yourself more than you lie to anybody else. You're not the best judge of you because your feelings lie all the time. (This is true for all of us!)

You have to decide who you're going to believe. Are you going to build your life on what everybody else thinks about you? Are you going to listen to what the critics say about you on social media? Are you going to listen to your own feelings?

Or are you going to listen to what God says about you, which is the truth?

Acts 3:19 says, *"Now it's time to change your ways! Turn to face God so he can wipe away your sins [and] pour out showers of blessing to refresh you"* (MSG).

You're deeply flawed, but you are deeply loved, and you are infinitely valuable. You may have come to the end of yourself and feel like you don't have anywhere to turn. But there is always Someone to turn to.

DECEMBER 12

How to Fight Destructive Thoughts

Those who are dominated by the sinful nature think about sinful things, but those who are controlled by the Holy Spirit think about things that please the Spirit.

ROMANS 8:5 (NLT)

Freeing your mind from destructive thoughts will never be easy. Three forces battle in your mind against good intentions—and none of them give up ground easily. You have to fight to free your mind!

What are the enemies—the forces—that battle in your mind?

The first is your old nature. Romans 8:5 says, *"Those who are dominated by the sinful nature think about sinful things, but those who are controlled by the Holy Spirit think about things that please the Spirit"* (NLT). You have a new nature, but your old nature—who you were before you became a Christian—still influences you.

The second thing working against you is Satan. Though Satan can't force you to *do* anything, he continually plants negative thoughts in your mind. But you can fight against those thoughts by resisting the devil. The Bible says, *"Place yourselves under God's authority. Resist the devil, and he will run away from you"* (James 4:7, GW).

The third enemy of your mind is the world's value system. The Bible says, *"For everything in the world—the lust of the flesh, the lust of the eyes, and the pride of life—comes not from the Father but from the world"* (1 John 2:16, NIV).

The Bible tells us how to fight this mental battle: *"The weapons we fight with are not the weapons of the world. On the contrary, they have divine power to demolish strongholds. We demolish arguments and every pretension that sets itself up against the knowledge of God, and we take captive every thought to make it obedient to Christ"* (2 Corinthians 10:4-5, NIV).

"Take captive" means to bring your thoughts under control. Don't let your thoughts go anywhere they want. Instead, bring them into submission to the truth of God's Word.

God gives you the power you need to overcome your thoughts. When they start going in the wrong direction, change direction!

DECEMBER 13

Weakness Can Be a Good Thing

You bless all who depend on you for their strength.

PSALM 84:5 (CEV)

Are you tired all the time? Feel like you're running on fumes?

The reason why is simple: You're human.

Your strength is limited. But God's strength is unlimited. Your strength is finite. But God's strength is infinite. Your strength is exhaustible. But God's strength is inexhaustible. He never gets tired or runs out of energy.

Psalm 84:5 says, *"You bless all who depend on you for their strength"* (CEV). Do you want God's blessing on your life? Then depend on God for your strength.

One of the most well-known Christians of the nineteenth century, Hudson Taylor, was a missionary to China. He was a spiritual giant and a brilliant man, but in his old age he lost his health and became quite weak. He sent a letter to a friend and said, "I am so weak I cannot write; I cannot read my Bible; I cannot even pray. I can only lie still in God's arms like a little child, and trust."

At some point in your life you may be too weak to work, pray, read the Bible, or go to a Bible study. What do you do in those moments? You rest in the strength of the Lord, in his arms like a little child—and you trust.

Weakness can be a good thing if it causes you to depend on God. In 2 Corinthians 12:8-10, Paul said this: *"Three different times I begged the Lord to take it away. Each time he said, 'My grace is all you need. My power works best in weakness.' So now I am glad to boast about my weaknesses, so that the power of Christ can work through me. That's why I take pleasure in my weaknesses, and in the insults, hardships, persecutions, and troubles that I suffer for Christ. For when I am weak, then I am strong"* (NLT).

That's the paradox of depending on God: The weaker you get, the more you depend on him. And the more you depend on God, the stronger you get.

DECEMBER 14

When Opposed, Choose Worship over Worry

If you suffer for doing what is right, God will reward you for it. So don't worry or be afraid of their threats. Instead, you must worship Christ as Lord of your life. And if someone asks about your hope as a believer, always be ready to explain it.

1 PETER 3:14-15 (NLT)

Christianity is not for weaklings or the faint of heart. It takes courageous men and women to follow Jesus.

What is it costing you to follow Christ? Unlike many believers around the world, you may not live in an area where you face violent oppression. But you likely deal with silent repression every single day as most cultures are becoming more and more secularized and anti-Christian.

No matter where you're from, when you're faced with opposition because of your faith, it's natural to feel afraid. So how do you get rid of the fear of opposition? How do you get rid of the fear of disapproval? How do you get rid of the fear of being rejected?

You need to be filled with God's love. The Bible says, *"There is no fear in love, but perfect love casts out fear"* (1 John 4:18, ESV). When you face opposition, choose to focus on the love God has for you. People who rest in the assurance of God's love don't fear rejection or disapproval.

The Bible says in 1 Peter 3:14-15, *"If you suffer for doing what is right, God will reward you for it. So don't worry or be afraid of their threats. Instead, you must worship Christ as Lord of your life. And if someone asks about your hope as a believer, always be ready to explain it"* (NLT).

When you feel pressured to be quiet about your faith, you have a choice: You can worry, or you can worship. That means either you panic or you pray; you focus on the problem, pressure, and persecution, or you focus on God.

When you're opposed because of your faith, you're going to feel pressure. But choose to turn away from the pressure you feel and put your focus on God. In other words, choose to worship—because focusing on God is essentially worship.

Next time you face opposition for your faith, decide to worship instead of worry.

DECEMBER 15

The Good News of God's Love

There is only one God, and Christ Jesus is the only one who can bring us to God. Jesus was truly human, and he gave himself to rescue all of us.

1 TIMOTHY 2:5 (CEV)

Christmas is all about good news. But it's not the good news of special gifts. It's not the good news of a big meal. It's not even the good news of spending time with friends and family.

Christmas is about the Good News of God's love.

The Bible says that every person is lost without God. Without God, you're directionless. Your potential eternal impact upon the world is unrealized. You're without real joy. Your eternity in heaven isn't secure.

But the good news about Christmas is that God sent Jesus to seek and save the lost. The Bible says, *"There is only one God, and Christ Jesus is the only one who can bring us to God. Jesus was truly human, and he gave himself to rescue all of us"* (1 Timothy 2:5, CEV).

If you've ever spent time in church, you've probably heard the word *salvation* many times. But you may not know what the Bible means when it uses that word. Salvation is like a diamond—you can look at it from many angles. Here are just a few:

- **Jesus came to rescue you.** You can't solve all your problems on your own. You might try to change over and over again, but you don't have the power you need to transform your life. Jesus came to give you that power.
- **Jesus came to recover you.** You long to reclaim parts of your life that have been lost—your strength, confidence, reputation, innocence, and relationship with God. But only Jesus can recover those things.
- **Jesus came to reconnect you.** Many people think that God will scold them if they come back to him. But God isn't mad at you. He's mad *about* you. Jesus came to give you harmony with him again.

Too many people celebrate Christmas without accepting Jesus' free gift of salvation. The gift goes unwrapped year after year after year. Don't make that same mistake in your life! You were made by God and for God. Until you understand that, life will never make sense.

This Christmas, open up the most important gift you've ever been given: a new relationship with God through Jesus.

DECEMBER 16

Don't Just Hope You'll Go to Heaven

And this is the testimony: God has given us eternal life, and this life is in his Son. Whoever has the Son has life; whoever does not have the Son of God does not have life.

1 JOHN 5:11-12 (NIV)

If you went to a shopping center today and asked people if they were going to heaven or hell, you'd likely hear many of them say, "I *hope* I'll go to heaven."

But hope just isn't good enough. I pray that's not your answer. Your eternal destiny is too important not to know for sure.

You're not guaranteed another minute on this planet, much less another hour. The most recent statistics show that mortality rates in the world remain at 100 percent! Death is inevitable—so it's foolish not to be prepared. Don't put off the most important choice you'll ever make.

The Bible says in 1 John 5:11-12, *"And this is the testimony: God has given us eternal life, and this life is in his Son. Whoever has the Son has life; whoever does not have the Son of God does not have life"* (NIV).

That's about as clear as you can get. If you have Jesus, you have life. If you don't have Jesus, you do not have life. You have a choice.

You won't go to heaven because of someone else's faith. You'll never go to hell because of someone else's choice. It's *your* choice! You get to decide where you'll spend eternity.

This is why we celebrate Christmas and Easter. If Jesus hadn't come at Christmas—and then if he hadn't died and come back to life on Easter—our situation would be hopeless. Nothing you do would matter. You wouldn't have this choice.

The Bible says, *"You were dead because of your sins and because your sinful nature was not yet cut away. Then God made you alive with Christ, for he forgave all our sins. He canceled the record of the charges against us and took it away by nailing it to the cross"* (Colossians 2:13-14, NLT).

The cross is the answer to your deepest problem: your separation from God. Make the choice today to be reconciled to God through Jesus and to secure your eternity in heaven.

Open Your Whole Heart to Jesus

Listen! I am standing and knocking at your door. If you hear my voice and open the door, I will come in and we will eat together.
REVELATION 3:20 (CEV)

Have you ever considered what the innkeeper must have thought that first Christmas when he realized he hadn't made room for the Son of God? Here's how I think his testimony might have been written: "It was the busiest season I had ever seen as an innkeeper, courtesy of Caesar Augustus and his census. My inn was booked solid for a month, and that income set me up for life.

"But then *that* couple showed up. How was I to know who they were? They looked no different than a dozen other families that I'd already turned away. So I just said, 'Sorry, we're booked. We have no vacancies. There is no room for you.'

"I thought I would at least do them a favor and allow them to sleep with the animals in the stable behind the inn. Now I'll forever be known as the man who said, 'Sorry, no room.' I'm the one who put the Savior of the world out back with the animals. That's my legacy: I didn't make room for Jesus.

"I missed Jesus because I was too busy to realize what God was doing right in front of me. It was an inconvenient time for Jesus to show up, so I just pushed him off in a corner. But now that I think about it, it seems that there's always some distraction, inconvenience, or preoccupation to use as an excuse not to make room for Jesus.

"If I could do it all over, I would have given him the whole inn. I missed the knock on my door. But for you, there's still time to receive him. There's still time to look at your life, to consider whether your rooms are filled with what matters most or if they're just cluttered. You still have time to reserve a place for the most important guest of all."

When Jesus knocks, you can give him the welcome and the reception that he deserves. In fact, he's knocking right now: He is saying, *"If you hear my voice and open the door, I will come in and we will eat together"* (Revelation 3:20, CEV).

Can you hear him? Are you paying attention? Will you open the door?

DECEMBER 18

Three Barriers to Hearing God's Voice

Get rid of all the filth and evil in your lives, and humbly accept the word God has planted in your hearts, for it has the power to save your souls.

JAMES 1:21 (NLT)

What do God's voice and cell phones have in common? For both, you need to be positioned correctly to hear them clearly!

In a huge, sturdy building, your cell coverage may be spotty. In a wilderness area, you'll likely have no service at all. You need to be in the right position to have a clear, reliable signal.

The same is true with your relationship with God. If you want to hear God's voice clearly and consistently, you must be positioned correctly.

When you're in the wrong position to hear God, your mind is closed—you want to do what you want, not what he wants. In the wrong position, your heart is hardened—you're unwilling to listen.

Here are three barriers that keep your heart and mind closed to God's message:

1. **Pride.** If you think you don't need God in your life and you want to handle things yourself, you're probably not listening for God to speak. Pride keeps you from being open to the possibility that God might want to say something to you.

2. **Fear.** Many people can't hear God because they're afraid to hear him speak. You might think hearing God's voice or sensing his leading makes you some kind of religious fanatic. Or maybe you're afraid of the changes you'd need to make in your life if you listened to God's leading.

3. **Bitterness.** When you hold on to hurt, resentment, or a grudge, you're not able to hear God—because your heart is hardened. A hard heart grows cold and makes you defensive, even to God's love.

James 1:21 says, *"Get rid of all the filth and evil in your lives, and humbly accept the word God has planted in your hearts, for it has the power to save your souls"* (NLT).

It's time to get rid of the bitterness, fear, and pride that keep you from hearing God's voice and living out his purpose for your life. Then you'll be able to hear God with an open heart and mind and humbly accept what he's saying to you.

DECEMBER 19

You Have to Want to Hear from God

You will search again for the LORD your God. And if you search for him with all your heart and soul, you will find him.
DEUTERONOMY 4:29 (NLT)

You're not going to hear God unless you really, really want to.

God doesn't tell you his dream for your life if you want to debate it. God doesn't tell you his vision for your life if you want to discuss it. God doesn't tell you what he put you on earth to do just so you can say, "Let me think about it."

No! It's got to be a necessity. You have to say, "I've got to know why I'm here. I've got to know what you want me to do with my life. I've got to hear your voice. I've got to have your vision."

King David wrote in the book of Psalms, *"My God, I want to do what you want"* (Psalm 40:8, NCV), and Psalm 119:20 tells us, *"What I want most of all and at all times is to honor your laws"* (CEV).

David was passionate in his declaration that what he wanted most of all was to honor God. Being obedient and following God were not options for him. They were *the only things David wanted to do*. He used phrases for seeking God like "I long for it," "I crave it," "I hunger for it," and "I'm like a deer panting for water."

When you get that desperate, you're going to hear from God.

A lot of people talk to God but never hear from God. For them, prayer is a monologue. But you can't have a relationship through a monologue. What if I had married my wife and talked to her, but she never talked to me? That's not a relationship. You've got to have a conversation.

Just as important as talking to God in prayer is listening to God and letting him talk to you. How does that happen? First, you've got to want it more than anything else.

Deuteronomy 4:29 says, *"You will search again for the LORD your God. And if you search for him with all your heart and soul, you will find him"* (NLT). It's guaranteed!

DECEMBER 20

Your Time Is in God's Hands

I trust in you, LORD; I say, "You are my God."
My times are in your hands.
PSALM 31:14-15 (NIV)

When things don't happen on your timetable, you're going to be tempted to doubt and question God and his timing. You may start to feel afraid of the future and stressed that things are not happening like you planned.

But the more you trust God, the less afraid you will be. Why? Because the opposite of fear is faith. When you fill your life with faith, there is no more room for fear.

In Mark 5:36, Jesus said, *"Don't be afraid. Just trust me"* (TLB).

This message is so big throughout the Bible that the phrase "fear not" is repeated over and over in both the Old and New Testaments. God wants us to get the message that we don't have to be afraid because we can trust his timing.

Trusting God is the number one stress reliever in your life. The more you trust God, the more your stress is going to decrease. You can demonstrate your trust in God by asking him for something in prayer. When you do, don't try to set a time limit or deadline on his answer. Leave the timing up to God. Show him that you want his will to be done in your life more than your own will.

To help your faith grow deeper, you need to pray a prayer like Psalm 31:14-15: *"I trust in you, LORD; I say, 'You are my God.' My times are in your hands"* (NIV).

Why not memorize those verses? When you get up every morning, read Psalm 31 as a prayer and tell God, "I trust you, Lord. You're my God. My times are in your hands."

You probably have more to do today than you have time to get it all done. So you ask God to help you sort everything out so that you can do what matters most and not worry about the rest. You say to him, "I surrender my schedule. I surrender my calendar. I surrender my agenda. My times are in your hands, and so I'm not going to fear. I'm going to trust you."

That is how your faith grows. That's how faith replaces fear!

DECEMBER 21

Let Go of Your Need to Get Even

Never avenge yourselves. Leave that to God,
for he has said that he will repay those who deserve it.
ROMANS 12:19 (TLB)

The heart of real forgiveness is relinquishing your right to get even. The Bible says in Romans 12:19, *"Never avenge yourselves. Leave that to God, for he has said that he will repay those who deserve it"* (TLB).

You say, "If I give up my right to get even with somebody who's hurt me, that's unfair." You're right, it is! But whoever said forgiveness is fair? Was it fair for Jesus Christ to forgive everything we've ever done wrong and let us go free? No. We don't want God to be *fair* to us, though. We want God to be *gracious* to us. We all want justice for everybody else and forgiveness for ourselves.

We know life isn't fair—and neither is forgiveness. It's called grace, and God has shown it to you. One day, God will have the last word, right the wrong, and settle the score. Leave the justice part to him. You just focus on forgiveness so there can be peace in your heart and you can get on with your life.

If you don't do this, you will fall into the trap of bitterness. Resentment and bitterness are worthless emotions. Doctors tell us they are the unhealthiest emotions. They will eat you alive like cancer. All your resentment and bitterness toward people who hurt you won't change the past, and it certainly won't change the future. All it can do is mess up today.

When you hold on to resentment, you allow people from your past to continue to hurt you today. That's not smart! The people in your past are past. They cannot continue hurting you unless you choose to hold on to the hurt. Instead, let go of your need to get even or make things fair. Leave it up to God.

Hebrews 12:15 says, *"Look after each other so that none of you fails to receive the grace of God. Watch out that no poisonous root of bitterness grows up to trouble you, corrupting many"* (NLT).

DECEMBER 22

Confronting for the Right Reasons

Why worry about a speck in your friend's eye when you have a log in your own? . . . First get rid of the log in your own eye; then you will see well enough to deal with the speck in your friend's eye.

MATTHEW 7:3, 5 (NLT)

Learning how to love like Jesus is a process. You start off with simple, easy ways of loving. As you mature, you learn to navigate more complex situations with love. Eventually, you'll learn how to face relationship issues that scare you—and you'll learn how to do that with love.

One of those scary, complex relationship challenges is learning how to confront someone about issues in your relationship that are keeping you from being closer. That kind of confrontation feels scary to almost everyone, but there's one thing you can do from the get-go that will make all the difference: Check your motivation.

Checking your motivation allows you to determine whether you're confronting someone for the right reason. What is the right reason? The right reason is when you're doing it for the other person's benefit and not your own. What's the wrong reason? If you want to say something because you need to vent or unload, then you're not confronting someone in love.

We all tend to criticize other people for the weaknesses we hate in ourselves. If you tend to be prideful, you can pick out ego in a second. If you tend to be lazy, you notice other lazy people. In other words, if you know your weaknesses and you don't like them in yourself, then you *really* don't like them in somebody else.

That's why Jesus says, *"Why worry about a speck in your friend's eye when you have a log in your own? . . . First get rid of the log in your own eye; then you will see well enough to deal with the speck in your friend's eye"* (Matthew 7:3, 5, NLT).

You don't have to be perfect to speak the truth in love. You just have to make sure that you're not guilty of that exact same sin. So before you confront anybody in the spirit of love, make sure you're not also doing the thing you're criticizing.

Start a confrontation with the correct motivation. What is the right motive? To help, not to hurt. Do everything in love!

DECEMBER 23

Give the Gift of Your Time

We must show love through actions that are sincere, not through empty words.

1 JOHN 3:18 (GW)

Have you finished your Christmas shopping?

Your friends and family may have given you their Christmas wish lists, full of things they would love to receive. Maybe they asked for the newest tech gadget or toy or tickets to a special event.

But what people really want is not something they can hold or wear or play with. What they really want is your time.

Time is your most precious commodity because your time is your life. You only have a certain amount of it. God has already decided the number of days you are going to live—and you're not going to get any more.

When you give someone your time, you are giving that person a portion of your life that you will never get back. That's why it is a priceless gift!

Relationships should always take priority in our lives. But many relationships are starved for time. Even people who live in the same home pass each other like ships in the night, with a goodbye kiss here and there. Relationships die when time together dries up.

Many things can rob a relationship of the time it needs to thrive. Work can rob a relationship. Activity can rob a relationship. Hobbies can rob a relationship. Even too much ministry can rob a relationship.

If you're wondering how you can have more time for the people you love, then it's really quite simple: Start by turning off the TV and setting down your phone! Those two simple changes will help you make time for others a priority.

God has only given you a certain amount of time on this earth. But he has also given you enough time to do the things that really matter. You have to decide what those things are. Then you have to make time for them.

Christmas is one of the busiest times of the year. Time probably feels in short supply. But all you really need to do is put the most important things—like people—at the top of your list.

As you go about your Christmas shopping and all the other activities of the season, remember what matters most. This Christmas, give the gift of your time.

DECEMBER 24

This Christmas, Receive the Best Gift Ever Given

By entering through faith into what God has always wanted to do for us—set us right with him, make us fit for him—we have it all together with God because of our Master Jesus.

ROMANS 5:1 (MSG)

If you gave me a Christmas gift and I never opened it, then you would be disappointed. And it would be a worthless gift, too, because I wouldn't receive the benefit of a gift I never opened.

Jesus Christ is God's Christmas gift to us. Yet some of us have gone Christmas after Christmas and never opened the best gift of all: God's gift of salvation. Why even celebrate Christmas if you're not going to open the biggest gift? It doesn't make sense to never unwrap the gift of your past forgiven, a purpose for living, and a home in heaven.

God has made a way for you this Christmas to be right with him, and all you have to do is receive his gift of salvation. The Bible says, *"By entering through faith into what God has always wanted to do for us—set us right with him, make us fit for him—we have it all together with God because of our Master Jesus"* (Romans 5:1, MSG).

Below is a prayer I prayed years ago when I took a step of faith and accepted Jesus. It's a simple prayer. If these words express the desire in your heart, then you can pray them right now. When you do, this will be your best Christmas ever!

"Dear God, I don't understand it all, but I thank you that you love me. Thank you for being with me. Thank you that you are for me, that you didn't send Jesus to condemn me but to save me.

"Today I want to receive the Christmas gift of your Son. I confess that I have sinned and ask you to forgive me. Please save me from my past, my regrets, my mistakes, my sins, my habits, my hurts, and my hang-ups. Save me from myself!

"I commit to following you the rest of my life and ask for the grace, strength, and wisdom I need to be obedient and faithful to you.

"Thank you that I have peace with you and peace in my heart. Help me to tell everyone I know about the peace they can have with you too. In Jesus' name I pray, amen."

DECEMBER 25

Christmas Still Brings Good News

I bring you good news that will cause great joy for all the people.

LUKE 2:10 (NIV)

No matter what is going on in the world or in your life, you can still spend this Christmas rejoicing. The good news of great joy proclaimed by the angel more than two thousand years ago is *still* good news and a source of everlasting joy.

The angel said, *"I bring you good news that will cause great joy for all the people. Today in the town of David a Savior has been born to you; he is the Messiah, the Lord. This will be a sign to you: You will find a baby wrapped in cloths and lying in a manger"* (Luke 2:10-12, NIV).

You can celebrate this Christmas with great joy because of three reasons:

God loves you. God sent Jesus on a mission of love. In fact, the Bible says God *is* love. God created the entire universe just so he could create the human race, just so he could create *you*, just so he could love *you*.

God's love isn't based on what you do. His love is based on who he is. The Bible says, *"Glory to God in the highest heaven, and on earth peace to those on whom his favor rests"* (Luke 2:14, NIV).

God is with you. The Bible says Jesus is Immanuel (Matthew 1:23). He truly was *"God with us"*—and he is still with us today. You may not feel his presence, but that doesn't make it any less true. You may have been abandoned in life, but God will never abandon you.

Knowing God is near means you don't have to worry or be anxious about what's coming next. God, not your circumstances, is in control. When he is near, there is no need to fear.

God is for you. He's on your side. He wants you to succeed. In fact, Jesus said, *"God sent his Son into the world not to judge the world, but to save the world through him"* (John 3:17, NLT). Many people are afraid of God because of their guilt. But Jesus didn't come to condemn the world. He came to save it.

That's good news! That's a reason to celebrate this Christmas.

DECEMBER 26

How to Get the Help You Need for Today

When you go through deep waters and great trouble, I will be with you. When you go through rivers of difficulty, you will not drown! When you walk through the fire of oppression, you will not be burned up—the flames will not consume you. For I am the Lord your God.

ISAIAH 43:2-3 (TLB)

When you became a Christian, did you expect life to be perfect?

If you did, I bet you found out pretty quickly that Christians face all kinds of trials—including relational, financial, physical, and mental. Some people expect life to be heaven on earth. But this is not heaven!

On earth, God's will is seldom done. Everything on this planet is broken. The weather, the economy, our bodies, and our relationships don't always work right. Because of sin, bad things happen.

But we can trust God's promises to support us: *"When you go through deep waters and great trouble, I will be with you. When you go through rivers of difficulty, you will not drown! When you walk through the fire of oppression, you will not be burned up—the flames will not consume you. For I am the Lord your God"* (Isaiah 43:2-3, TLB).

When you go through deep waters and rivers of difficulty, God doesn't promise that you won't get wet, but God *does* promise that you won't drown. When you go through the fire, it's going to get hot. But God promises that you won't burn up. You're going to make it through.

Philippians 4:13 says, *"I can do all things [which He has called me to do] through Him who strengthens and empowers me [to fulfill His purpose—I am self-sufficient in Christ's sufficiency; I am ready for anything and equal to anything through Him who infuses me with inner strength and confident peace]"* (AMP).

That doesn't mean that you can do anything because of who *you* are. It means that you can have confidence in whatever trouble life brings because you face it with the power of Christ in you.

You may not feel very strong right now. But the strength you need will come when you need it. The Bible doesn't say to ask God for your weekly or monthly bread. It says to pray, "God, give me my *daily* bread. I need just enough strength for today."

God will support you in your trouble. He always gives you the strength you need for today.

DECEMBER 27

How to Examine Your Life

Let each person examine his own work, and then he can take pride in himself alone, and not compare himself with someone else.
GALATIANS 6:4 (CSB)

God formed you intentionally and uniquely, but sometimes you may find yourself not knowing how to move forward. Maybe, when you think about the future, you feel more confusion and less joy.

If this describes you, it might be because you've forgotten the advice the Bible gives in Galatians 6:4: *"Let each person examine his own work, and then he can take pride in himself alone, and not compare himself with someone else"* (CSB).

The Bible gives two-part guidance here. First, you should examine your own work—look at your past and learn from it. Next, you should not compare yourself with someone else. Don't let your eyes wander to how God has worked in other people. Concentrate on what he's done in and through you. When you compare yourself to other people, you become either discouraged or prideful. Either attitude robs you of your joy.

God has a better way for you to discover his next steps for you. He wants you to take a close look at your past to help you move into your future. That's right—God doesn't want you to waste your past. *God wants to use it.*

But sometimes it can be hard to know how to look back effectively over your life. Here's one easy exercise: Sit down with a piece of paper. Separate it with a line for each period of your life (five-year periods or decades work well).

Now it's time to examine your own work by creating a life inventory and answering these two questions for each time period of your life: *What were you good at doing? What did you enjoy doing?*

Now go back and look for patterns. If you were good at something when you were younger, you probably still are. Maybe there's something you enjoyed a few years ago that you have forgotten about. After you've identified patterns in your life, ask God what he wants you to do with this information—victories to celebrate or work he might have for you in the future.

Don't get caught in a comparison trap. Instead, take an honest look at your own past. And then step forward with confidence into your future.

DECEMBER 28

You Can't Out-Give God

Give, and you will receive. Your gift will return to you in full—pressed down, shaken together to make room for more, running over, and poured into your lap. The amount you give will determine the amount you get back.

LUKE 6:38 (NLT)

When you give from a heart motivated by love for Jesus, your goal isn't to get a blessing. But the truth is that God *will* bless you.

Sometimes it seems like God is saying, "Let's see who can out-give the other. You give to me and to other people, and I'll give to you—and we'll see who wins."

God always wins! He says over and over in Scripture that you will end up with more if you learn to be generous. Sometimes those blessings will be material. But sometimes they'll be the spiritual blessings that come from a generous heart.

Jesus said, *"Give, and you will receive. Your gift will return to you in full—pressed down, shaken together to make room for more, running over, and poured into your lap. The amount you give will determine the amount you get back"* (Luke 6:38, NLT).

Imagine you're going to a market to buy grain. You bring a burlap sack and pay to have the whole sack filled. As the shop owner is pouring grain, you press it into your sack. Then you gently shake the sack so the grain settles down even more. You want to fit the maximum amount of grain in your sack.

Jesus is saying that God's blessings are the same. When you give generously, he'll give so generously to you that you'll have to make room for more. He gives in full measure—and then some—when you learn to be generous like him. The way you give to others is the way God will give to you. He wants you to be generous because he wants you to be like him. You can't become more like Christ without learning to give generously.

This is one of the most important decisions you will make: Is your life going to be about giving away what God has blessed you with? Will it be marked by a joyous desire to grab hold of God's promises as you let go of the things of this earth?

"The amount you give will determine the amount you get back." You determine how much God blesses your life.

DECEMBER 29

This Is Not the End of the Story

We often suffer, but we are never crushed. Even when we don't know what to do, we never give up. In times of trouble, God is with us, and when we are knocked down, we get up again. . . . We know that God raised the Lord Jesus to life. And just as God raised Jesus, he will also raise us to life. Then he will bring us into his presence together.

2 CORINTHIANS 4:8-9, 14 (CEV)

When the future is uncertain and you're afraid, it might feel like your story is coming to an end.

But the Bible says, *"We often suffer, but we are never crushed. Even when we don't know what to do, we never give up. In times of trouble, God is with us, and when we are knocked down, we get up again. . . . We know that God raised the Lord Jesus to life. And just as God raised Jesus, he will also raise us to life. Then he will bring us into his presence together"* (2 Corinthians 4:8-9, 14, CEV).

When life seems uncertain, remember this truth: You can't lose! You'll win in the end, no matter what happens. Even if you lose your life, you're going straight into the presence of God if you believe in Jesus Christ as Savior.

And when you arrive in heaven, your story is just beginning.

Have you ever watched a drama series where every episode ends in a cliff-hanger and leaves you thinking the hero might not survive? The tension can feel enormous.

But when all the episodes from all the seasons have already been released, you don't feel as tense because you know the hero survives for another six seasons. You know each episode is not the end of the story. The hero will make it out of a tight spot and go on to the next season.

That's how your life is. Even when you're in a difficult circumstance, you know that the tough spot isn't the end of your story. You can live with hope in the middle of a crisis when you have an eternal perspective.

One day, when you meet Jesus in heaven, all your pain, sickness, sorrow, sadness, stress, and grief will end. Here's what you have to look forward to in heaven: *"He will wipe every tear from their eyes. There will be no more death or mourning or crying or pain, for the old order of things has passed away"* (Revelation 21:4, NIV).

This life is not the end of the story. We don't know what the future holds, but we do know who holds the future.

How to Praise God When You're Stuck

About midnight Paul and Silas were praying and singing hymns to God, and the other prisoners were listening to them. Suddenly there was such a violent earthquake that the foundations of the prison were shaken. At once all the prison doors flew open, and everyone's chains came loose.

ACTS 16:25-26 (NIV)

Have you ever gotten to the end of the year, when everyone else is excited about new things to come, and all you can do is look back and think about how it feels like nothing changed at all in a year? If that's happened to you, then you know what it feels like to be stuck.

If you feel imprisoned by a fear, addiction, or situation that's out of your control, there's never been a better time for you to thank God and praise him in advance. Praising God breaks chains in your life. It also opens doors for opportunities you can't seem to bust through.

In Acts 16, Paul and Silas were thrown in prison because the city officials didn't like that they talked about Jesus. At midnight they decided to have a praise and worship session. They didn't wait for their release to praise God; they did it while they were in chains! *"About midnight Paul and Silas were praying and singing hymns to God, and the other prisoners were listening to them. Suddenly there was such a violent earthquake that the foundations of the prison were shaken. At once all the prison doors flew open, and everyone's chains came loose"* (Acts 16:25-26, NIV).

What a miracle! This miracle also serves as a metaphor for what God does when you praise him while feeling stuck. He breaks the chains that seem to be holding you back. He changes the way you think and helps you see how he is still working for good in your life.

Notice how the other prisoners listened to Paul and Silas praise God. Your praise is always a witness to nonbelievers. We think people are impressed by our prosperity, but instead they're impressed by how we handle adversity. It's not how successful you are that makes people want to come to Christ—it's how you handle problems.

No matter what you're facing, decide that you're going to praise God. As you develop a habit of praise, you'll see how God will change your life—starting with the way you think.

DECEMBER 31

Leaning on the Promises of God

For the Lord, *the God of heaven, who took me from my father's house and my native land, solemnly promised to give this land to my descendants. He will send his angel ahead of you, and he will see to it that you find a wife there for my son.*

GENESIS 24:7 (NLT)

Many people start the calendar year off with a goal. They resolve to lose weight, to spend more time with their kids, to read more, to achieve something specific at work, or to complete some other noble (or not so noble) goal.

But not every goal is a godly one. Godly goals are attached to God's promises in his Word. His promises give us the courage and faith to move forward when it's much more natural to be scared or worried.

In Genesis 24, Abraham gave his servant Eliezer a very tough goal: find a wife for his son Isaac. At first Eliezer let fear get the best of him. He asked Abraham, "What do I do if I find a wife for Isaac, but she won't come with me?"

Abraham then reminded his servant of God's promise: *"For the* Lord, *the God of heaven, who took me from my father's house and my native land, solemnly promised to give this land to my descendants. He will send his angel ahead of you, and he will see to it that you find a wife there for my son"* (Genesis 24:7, NLT). After Abraham reminded Eliezer of the Lord's promise, his fear vanished. The same thing happens with us. It's scary to put everything we have into a big goal. No one wants to fail.

But the Bible urges us not to look to our own strength to reach our goals. In fact, if we can accomplish our goals in our own power, we're not pursuing godly goals in the first place. Over and over in Scripture, God promises to give us his strength. Isaiah 40:31 says, *"But those who trust in the* Lord *for help will find their strength renewed. They will rise on wings like eagles; they will run and not get weary; they will walk and not grow weak"* (GNT).

All throughout Scripture, God promises to help us as we set goals to get healthy, become better parents, eliminate our debt, and pray more throughout the next year. But unless we know those promises and claim those promises, we'll worry needlessly about achieving those goals.

The truth is, you don't have to have big faith to accomplish huge goals. You just need a little faith—in a big God! Your God is the God of the universe. He can do anything.

Are you ready to trust God for the unbelievable? Then say to him today, "God, I believe you are doing big things in the world, and I want you to use me to do great things for your Kingdom. Help me to be faithful to study your Word so I can know your promises and build my plans and goals and dreams on what you have said is true. Give me your wisdom to know the right way to go and the courage to go that way, even when I'm scared. As I look for all the amazing ways you are working, help me to remember that the greatest work I could do may be in quietly and faithfully serving and loving others in your name. I pray for bold belief this coming year as I trust in your plan, your purpose for me, and your love. In Jesus' name, amen."

Acknowledgment

I want to express my heartfelt appreciation to Jon Walker, a valued member of my editorial team for more than two decades. His commitment and collaboration have been integral to the development of hundreds of resources, contributing immeasurably to the creation of spiritual growth tools that God has used to transform millions of lives around the world!

Notes

FEBRUARY 2

God takes your sins and puts them: Corrie ten Boom, *Tramp for the Lord* (Washington, PA: CLC Publications, 1974), 55.

MARCH 23

In January 1956, five American missionaries: For more on their story, see Elisabeth Elliot, *Through Gates of Splendor* (Carol Stream, IL: Tyndale, 1996).

MARCH 26

"He is no fool who gives": Justin Taylor, "They Were No Fools: The Martyrdom of Jim Elliot and Four Other Missionaries," The Gospel Coalition, January 8, 2016, https://www.thegospelcoalition.org/blogs/justin-taylor/they-were-no-fools-60-years-ago-today-the-martyrdom-of-jim-elliot-and-four-other-missionaries/.

MARCH 28

It was a common word in ancient Greek society: "Tetelestai—Paid in Full," Precept Austin, updated November 7, 2022, https://www.preceptaustin.org/tetelestai-paid_in_full.

MAY 20

"I can't say as ever I was lost": John Bakeless, *Daniel Boone: Master of the Wilderness* (Lanham, MD: Stackpole Books, 1939), chapter 20.

JUNE 1

It produces brain chemicals: Sarah Moore, "The Science of Gratitude," News Medical, last updated April 7, 2023, https://www.news-medical.net/health/The-Science-of-Gratitude.aspx.

JUNE 9

"Expect great things from God": As quoted in Tom Houston, "Cooperation and Unity in Evangelisation," September 14, 2007, ALCOE III Compendium Documents, Lausanne Movement, https://lausanne.org/content/alcoe-iii-compendium.

JUNE 11

"Living one day at a time": See "Serenity Prayer," Celebrate Recovery, https://www.celebraterecovery.com/resources/serenity-prayer.

JUNE 20

the phrase "next to him" or "next to them" twenty-one times: Nehemiah 3, NIV.

JULY 20

God whispers to us in our pleasure: C. S. Lewis, *The Problem of Pain* (New York: HarperCollins, 2001), 88–89.

AUGUST 24

"The beginning of good works": "Homilies on the Gospel of St. John," *Augustine of Hippo: Selected Writings*, trans. Mary T. Clark (New York: Paulist Press, 1984), 291.

NOVEMBER 14

"When life is rosier": Joni Eareckson Tada, *31 Days toward Intimacy with God* (Colorado Springs, CO: Multnomah Books, 2005), 9.

NOVEMBER 17

Even a popular business magazine: *Bloomberg Businessweek*, November 15, 2021.

DECEMBER 13

"I am so weak I cannot write": L. B. Cowman, *Streams in the Desert* (Grand Rapids, MI: Zondervan, 2006), May 10.

Scripture Credits

Scripture quotations marked AMP are taken from the Amplified® Bible (AMP), copyright © 2015 by The Lockman Foundation. Used by permission. www.lockman.org. Scripture quotations marked BSB are taken from The Holy Bible, Berean Study Bible, BSB. Copyright © 2016, 2018 by Bible Hub. Used by permission. All rights reserved worldwide. Scripture quotations marked CEB are taken from the Common English Bible, copyright 2011. Used by permission. All rights reserved. Scripture quotations marked CEV are taken from the Contemporary English Version, copyright © 1991, 1992, 1995 by American Bible Society. Used by permission. Scripture quotations marked CSB are taken from the Christian Standard Bible,® copyright © 2017 by Holman Bible Publishers. Used by permission. Christian Standard Bible® and CSB® are federally registered trademarks of Holman Bible Publishers. Scripture quotations marked ERV are taken from the *Holy Bible*, Easy-to-Read Version, copyright © 2013, 2016 by Bible League International. Used by permission. All rights reserved. Scripture quotations marked ESV are from The ESV® Bible (The Holy Bible, English Standard Version®), copyright © 2001 by Crossway, a publishing ministry of Good News Publishers. Used by permission. All rights reserved. Scripture quotations marked GNT are taken from the Good News Translation in Today's English Version, Second Edition, copyright © 1992 by American Bible Society. Used by permission. Scripture quotations marked GW are taken from *GOD'S WORD*®. Copyright © 1995, 2003, 2013, 2014, 2019, 2020 by God's Word to the Nations Mission Society. Used by permission. Scripture quotations marked ICB are taken from the International Children's Bible®. Copyright © 1986, 1988, 1999 by Thomas Nelson. Used by permission. All rights reserved. Scripture quotations marked ISV are taken from the Holy Bible: International Standard Version.® Copyright © 2003 by The ISV Foundation. Used by permission of Davidson Press, Inc. ALL RIGHTS RESERVED INTERNATIONALLY. Scripture quotations marked KJV are taken from the *Holy Bible*, King James Version. Scripture quotations marked MEV are from the Modern English Version. Copyright © 2014 by Military Bible Association. Used by permission. All rights reserved. Scripture quotations marked MSG are taken from *The Message*, copyright © 1993, 2002, 2018 by Eugene H. Peterson. Used by permission of NavPress. All rights reserved. Represented by Tyndale House Publishers. Scripture quotations marked NCV are taken from the New Century Version.® Copyright © 2005 by Thomas Nelson, Inc. Used by permission. All rights reserved. Scripture quotations marked NIV are taken from the Holy Bible, *New International Version,*® *NIV.*® Copyright © 1973, 1978, 1984, 2011 by Biblica, Inc.® Used by permission. All rights reserved worldwide. Scripture quotations marked NJB are taken from *The New Jerusalem Bible*, copyright © 1985 by Darton, Longman & Todd, Ltd., and Doubleday & Co., Inc. Scripture quotations marked NKJV are taken from the New King James Version,® copyright © 1982 by Thomas Nelson. Used by permission. All rights reserved. Scripture quotations marked NLT are taken from the *Holy Bible*, New Living Translation, copyright © 1996, 2004, 2015 by Tyndale House Foundation. Used by permission of Tyndale House Publishers, Carol Stream, Illinois 60188. All rights reserved. Scripture quotations marked NLV are taken from the Holy Bible, New Life Version. Copyright © 1969–2003 by Christian Literature International, P. O. Box 777, Canby, OR 97013. Used by permission. Scripture quotations marked TLB are taken from *The Living Bible*, copyright © 1971 by Tyndale House Foundation. Used by permission of Tyndale House Publishers, Carol Stream, Illinois 60188. All rights reserved. Scripture quotations marked TLV are taken from the Holy Scriptures, Tree of Life Version,* copyright © 2014, 2016 by the Tree of Life Bible Society. Used by permission of the Tree of Life Bible Society.

About the Author

Rick Warren was named in a *Time* magazine cover article as the most influential spiritual leader in America and one of the 100 most influential people in the world.

Tens of millions of copies of Warren's books have been published in 200 languages. His best-known books, *The Purpose Driven Life* and *The Purpose Driven Church*, were named three times in national surveys of pastors (by Gallup, Barna, and Lifeway) as the two most helpful books in print.

Rick Warren and his wife, Kay, founded Saddleback Church, the Purpose Driven Network, the PEACE Plan, and Hope for Mental Health. Warren is also the cofounder of Celebrate Recovery. He has delivered speeches in 165 countries and at the United Nations, US Congress, numerous parliaments, the World Economic Forum, TED, and the Aspen Institute and lectured at Oxford, Cambridge, Harvard, and other universities.

Warren is executive director of Finishing the Task coalition, a global movement of denominations, organizations, churches, and individuals working together on the Great Commission goals, which include ensuring that everyone everywhere has access to a Bible, a believer, a local body of Christ, and breakthrough prayer.